WHITE COUNTY ARKANSAS

BIOGRAPHICAL AND HISTORICAL MEMOIRS

Goodspeed

Heritage Books
2025

HERITAGE BOOKS

AN IMPRINT OF HERITAGE BOOKS, INC.

Books, CDs, and more—Worldwide

For our listing of thousands of titles see our website
at
www.HeritageBooks.com

A Facsimile Reprint
Published 2025 by
HERITAGE BOOKS, INC.
Publishing Division
5810 Ruatan Street
Berwyn Heights, MD 20740

Previouly published:
Mountain Press
Signal Mountain, Tennessee
2005

International Standard Book Number
Paperbound: 978-0-7884-9880-0

WHITE COUNTY.

White County—Location and Description—Boundary Lines—Topography and Geology—Water Supply—Drainage—Streams—Timber—Soil—Resources—Lumber Interests—Census Enumeration—Taxable Property—Live Stock Industry—Real and Personal Property—Railroad Facilities—Population—Era of Settlement—County Organization—Seat of Justice and Public Buildings—County Officers—Politics—Court Affairs—Roll of Attorneys—Civil War History—Towns and Villages—Schools—Churches—Biographical.

O the pleasant days of old, which so often people praise!
True, they wanted all the luxuries that grace our modern days;
Bare floors were strewed with rushes, the walls let in the cold;
O how they must have shivered in those pleasant days of old.—*Brown.*

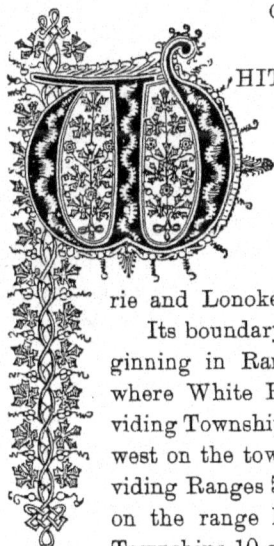

HITE COUNTY is located in the northeast part of Central Arkansas, and is bounded north by Cleburne, Independence and Jackson Counties, east by Woodruff, south by Prairie and Lonoke, and west by Faulkner.

Its boundary lines are as follows: Beginning in Range 3 west, at the point where White River crosses the line dividing Townships 9 and 10 north; thence west on the township line to the line dividing Ranges 5 and 6 west; thence north on the range line to the line dividing Townships 10 and 11 north; thence west on the township line to the line dividing Ranges 7 and 8 west; thence south on the range line to Little Red River; thence up said river, in a westerly direction, following its meanders, to the middle of Range 8 west; thence south on section lines to the line dividing Townships 8 and 9 north; thence west on the township line to the line dividing Ranges 10 and 11 west; thence south on the range line to Cypress Creek in Township 5 north; thence down Cypress Creek following its meanders to the line dividing Ranges 5 and 6 west; thence north on the range line to the line dividing Townships 5 and 6 north; thence east on the township line to White River; thence up White River following its meanders to the last crossing of the line dividing Townships 7 and 8 north; thence west on the township line to the southwest corner of Section 35, Township 8 north, Range 4 west; thence north on section lines until White River is again intersected; thence up the river following its meanders to the place of beginning; containing an area of 1,015 square miles, or 650,000 acres. Of this about 12,000 acres belong to the United States, 27,000 to the State, 81,000 to the St. Louis, Iron Mountain & Southern Railway Company, and the balance to individuals. Only about 10 per cent of the land is improved. Prices range from $5 to $25 per acre for improved, and from $1 to $10 for unimproved property.

The face of the county is somewhat rolling,

HISTORY OF ARKANSAS.

with three-fifths hilly and two-fifths level. The course of the streams show that the general trend is toward the southeast; White River, forming the eastern boundary line, is navigable for large vessels to points above. All the other streams of the county empty into this river. Little Red River enters from the northwest, and flows in an easterly and southeasterly direction through these limits and empties into White River near the line dividing Townships 6 and 7 north. It so divides the county as to leave about one-third of its area to the northeast and two-thirds to the southwest. Glaize Creek makes its appearance from the north, in Range 5 west, and flows thence in a direction east of south, emptying into White River a short distance above the mouth of Red River. Bayou Des Arc rises in the county's western part and, flowing southeasterly, finds an outlet in Cypress Creek at the southern boundary near the line between Ranges 6 and 7 west. Cypress Creek, which forms most of the southern boundary, runs in a general eastern direction and empties into White River at a point southeast of the county. These, the principal streams in this territory, together with their several tributaries, supply the entire drainage of the immediate region. Little Red River is navigable at all seasons of the year as far as West Point, and in high water it has been ascended to a point opposite Searcy. The United States has recently completed a dredge and two other boats at Judsonia, making necessary preparations to dredge and enlarge the river that it may be navigable at all seasons up to Judsonia.

There are numerous springs throughout the county, from which flows the purest of water. The most noted possessing mineral properties are the White Sulphur, Chalybeate and Alum Springs, at Searcy; the Armstrong Spring, nine miles west, and Griffin's Spring, four miles south. Well water of the best quality can be obtained at nearly all points at a moderate depth. The supply of water for family use is had from wells, springs and cisterns. Of timber, many varieties are common here, such as white, black, red, post, Spanish and overcup oak, black walnut, hickory, ash, cedar, pine, pecan, cypress and sweet and black gum.

Valuable white oak grows abundantly in nearly all parts of the county.

The most conspicuous geological feature of the county is the escarpment of sandstone along the bluffs of Little Red River, known as the "Bee Rock." The sandstone forming the cliffs in the foreground of this landscape is part of the conglomerate and millstone grit formation that intervenes between the overlying coal measures proper, and the underlying subcarboniferous limestone. The pebbly sandstones and millstone grit, which occur along the escarpments of Little Red River, attaining a thickness of from 150 to 200 feet, impart wild and romantic scenery for many miles along the banks of the stream. The dip of these sandstones at the old Patterson Mill is one and one-half to two degrees to the south, or a little west of south. In digging wells in the vicinity of Searcy, a blackish gray, indurated, argillo-siliceous shale is encountered, containing small scales of disseminated mica. This material is brittle and crumbles, by exposure, to a clay. Similar shales are struck, usually ten feet below the surface, under the red land situated west of Searcy. The first ten feet passed through, generally consists of soil, subsoil and gravel overlaying the shales. The red soil of these level farming lands is quite productive, yielding good crops of cotton, corn, wheat and the finest oats in ordinary seasons: 800 to 1,500 pounds of cotton in the seed to the acre, 20 to 25 bushels of wheat, and 40 to 60 bushels of oats, when there are seasonable rains.* This description of land covers a large proportion of the area of the county. The bottom lands along the streams are largely alluvial and exceedingly productive. The soil of that portion not previously mentioned, is composed of vegetable mold, sand and clay, and with proper cultivation all the lands of the county, excepting some thin soil on the ridges, yield abundantly.

There are some mineral deposits, such as iron, manganese, lead and coal here, but they have not yet been developed in paying quantities. It is thought, however, that a few of these ores may be found to exist to that extent which will warrant their mining.

* Quotations from State Geological Report.

WHITE COUNTY.

Among the resources of the county, lumbering constitutes a considerable industry, there being many saw and shingle mills throughout its territory. Manufacturing has also been commenced; there is a wagon factory at Searcy, and a fruit-canning factory, and a factory for the manufacture of fruit boxes and crates at Judsonia.

Agriculture is here, as elsewhere, the leading occupation, but both horticulture and the raising of live stock are beginning to receive attention. The agricultural products are cotton, corn, wheat, oats, rye, peas, grass, potatoes, turnips, sorghum, etc. "Cotton is King," and is raised largely to the exclusion of other crops. Farming might, perhaps, be carried on more scientifically, as the lands have been cropped from year to year, some of them for half a century, without a proper rotation, with but very little fertilizing matter being returned to the soil. Clover and the tame grasses succeed well, and are most profitable for refertilizing the lands.

In 1880 there were 2,319 farms in White County, 83,679 acres of improved lands, and the value of all farm products for the year 1879 amounted to $925,392. The cereal and vegetable productions were as follows: Indian corn, 444,893 bushels; oats, 95,359 bushels; rye, 399 bushels; wheat, 17,220 bushels; hay, 295 tons; cotton, 11,821 bales; Irish potatoes, 14,876 bushels; sweet potatoes, 23,098 bushels; tobacco, 28,184 pounds. These actual statistics taken from the reports of the United States census show conclusively what the soil is best adapted for.

In the cultivation of sweet potatoes and tobacco the county then ranked as third in the State, in Irish potatoes fifth, and in cotton fourteenth. The number of head of live stock, as given by the same census report, was: Horses 3,048; mules and asses 1,860; neat cattle 15,944; sheep 5,388; hogs 29,936. The abstract for taxable property for 1888 shows the following: Horses 4,157; mules and asses 2,052; neat cattle 19,839; sheep 3,678; hogs 23,330. Of the first four grades of animals there was a large increase from 1880 to 1888, a probable decrease being noticed in the other two. Perhaps the decrease in sheep is real, while that

in hogs is only apparent, for the reason that the abstract of taxable property shows the number on hand when the property was assessed and does not include those slaughtered and sold during the year, as is the case with the census report.

Live stock is receiving considerable attention of late, and the county is well adapted to its growth. Improved breeds are being introduced to a great extent. Horses, mules, cattle and hogs succeed best, and sheep do tolerably well. The stock business is steadily increasing and will be one of the most profitable industries of this locality in the near future.

The county's horticultural resources (especially the raising of small fruits) are being developed to a considerable extent along the line of the St. Louis, Iron Mountain & Southern Railway. Peaches, plums, strawberries, raspberries and blackberries are already quite extensively raised and shipped from Bradford, Russell, Judsonia and Beebe. These fruits are all grown to perfection; apples and pears, however, do not succeed as well. Grapes are also grown and used to some extent in the manufacture of domestic wine. The increasing demand for fruits will make this variety a leading industry here.

It is very evident that owing to natural resources, mildness of climate, the trifling cost of fuel, and the small amount of feed and care required to winter live stock, a farmer can live much cheaper and with greater pecuniary profit hereabouts, than in the cold settlements of the north and northwest. The industrious poor man desiring to emigrate to a new country, where may be had a home of his own, will do well to investigate the many advantages offered by this and contiguous portions of Arkansas, before venturing with his all into cold and forbidding regions of less favored localities. Let a farmer practice the same economy and industry here that usually prevail in Indiana, Illinois and other Northern States and he will find it comparatively easy to gain a competency within a few years.

In 1880, the real estate of White County was assessed for taxation at $1,850,394 and the personal property at $744,821, making a total of

HISTORY OF ARKANSAS.

$2,595,215, on which the total amount of taxes charged for all purposes was $32,633. In taxable wealth it then ranked as fourth in the State. In 1888, the real-estate assessment was $2,440,883, and personal property $1,252,715, aggregating $3,693,598. The total amount of taxes charged thereon for all purposes was $56,407.88. These figures bear evidence that from 1880 to 1888 the taxable wealth of the county increased a little over 42 per cent—a most encouraging showing.

The St. Louis, Iron Mountain & Southern Railroad enters White County about five miles west of its northeast corner, and runs thence through the limits in a southwesterly direction, its length here being about thirty-nine miles. It was completed in 1872. Soon after the Searcy & West Point Railroad was constructed, running from West Point to Searcy, and crossing the St. Louis, Iron Mountain & Southern at Kensett. The cars on this road are drawn between Searcy and Kensett by an engine, and between Kensett and West Point by horses. Its length is ten and a half miles. The Memphis branch of the St. Louis, Iron Mountain & Southern Railroad connects Memphis with the main line at Bald Knob in the county's northeast part, its length being about ten miles, thus making the combined length of railroads within the county sixty-one miles or more. These roads, together with White River as a navigable outlet, afford excellent transportation facilities.

The population of White County, according to the United States census reports, has been as follows at the various decades mentioned: 1840, 920; 1850, 2,619; 1860, 8,316; 1870, 10,347; 1880, 17,794. Immigration to the county since 1880 has been so large that at the present its population must considerably exceed 20,000. The colored population was, in 1860, 1,435; in 1870, 1,200; in 1880, 2,032, at about which figure it still remains.

The Royal Colony, consisting of several families from Tennessee, was founded by James Walker and Martin Jones at the head of Bull Creek, in the northwest part of what is now White County. Lower down on Bull Creek were the settlements of Fielding and Frederick Price. Lewis Vongrolman founded a German settlement on Big Creek and Little Red River with John Magness, Philip Hilger, James King, the Wishes, Yinglings and others. Philip Hilger established and kept the "Hilger's Ferry" across Little Red River, on the old military road leading from Cape Girardeau to Little Rock. Farther north, near the Independence County line, was the Pate Settlement, founded by Lovic Pate. Alfred Arnold, John Akin and John Wright founded the settlement on Little Red River below where West Point is situated. Near the present town of Judsonia was a settlement founded by William Cook and Henry R. Vanmeter. Reuben Stephens settled in the Pate Settlement on the creek that now bears his name. Samuel Guthrie and John Dunaway also settled in that neighborhood.

The list just given includes the names of some of the most prominent pioneer settlers, all of whom according to the best information now obtainable, located in their respective places during the decade of the 20's. Others soon followed, and by the date of the organization of the county, 1836, all parts of the territory composing it were more or less sparsely settled. By reference to the population previously stated it will be seen that the settlement, until since the close of the Civil War, continued slow and gradual. Since 1880 there has been a large influx from the northern and eastern States. Most of the early settlers came from Tennessee and other southern States. The early county officers and all mentioned elsewhere in connection with the organization of the county were, of course, pioneer settlers. The names of those likewise prominent in county affairs will be found in subsequent pages of this volume.

White County was organized in accordance with the provisions of an act of the legislature of Arkansas Territory, approved October 23, 1835. The first sessions of court were held at the house of David Crise, on the place now known as the McCreary farm, three and a half miles east of Searcy. The organization of the county was completed early in 1836.

The place where the courts were first held, and the site of Searcy became competing points for

WHITE COUNTY.

the location of the permanent seat of justice. The commissioners who located the seat of justice were John Arnold, Jesse Terry, Byram Stacy, David Crise and Reuben Stephens. A majority of them were in favor of locating it at Searcy, where it has ever since remained. Soon after the site was selected, a log-cabin court house was erected at a point about 100 yards southwest of the present court house, and the first term of the circuit court was held therein in November, 1838. The next court house was a two-story frame, erected on the site of the present one. A short time before the Civil War this was moved away preparatory to erecting a new one. It now stands two blocks south of the public square and is known as the Chambliss House. The war coming on, the proceedings for the erection of the new court house were stopped, and until the present one was erected, the courts were held in the Masonic Hall at the southeast corner of the public square. In 1868 the county court appropriated $25,000 for the erection of a new court house, and for that amount the contract was let to Wyatt Sanford of Searcy, who erected the present court house in 1869–70. It is a large and substantial two-story building, the first story containing cross halls, a large fire-proof vault and county offices, being constructed of stone, and the second, containing the court room, of brick. Above the center of the building is a handsome tower containing a "town clock."

The first county jail was made of hewed logs, ten inches square, and was two stories high. The first story or "dungeon" was entered by means of a trap door from above. It stood on the same lot on which the present jail stands. The second jail, built on the same lot, was a one-story brick building containing four iron cells and cost $1,800. Becoming unsafe it was removed. The present jail and jailer's residence, standing about 100 yards northwest of the court house, was erected in 1882–83 by James E. Winsett at a cost of about $3,800. It is a two-story brick building containing three iron cells, a dungeon, and jailer's residence. The county owns a "poor farm" on which the paupers are supported. It consists of 120 acres, with ample buildings, and is located one and a half miles east of Searcy.

The following official directory contains names of the county's public servants with date of term of service annexed from date of organization to the present:

Judges: Samuel Guthrie, 1836–42; William Cook, 1842–44; Samuel Guthrie, 1844–46; M. Sanders, 1846–50; P. H. McDaniel, 1850–52; J. F. Batts, 1852–54; John Hutches, 1854–56; L. S. Poe, 1856–58; William Hicks, 1858–60; R. M. Exum, 1860–61; John Hutches, 1861–62; M. Sanders, 1862–64; John Hutches, 1864–66; M. Sanders, 1866–72; A. M. Foster, 1874–78; L. M. Jones, 1878–82; F. P. Laws, 1882–84; R. H. Goad, 1884–88; N. H. West, present incumbent, elected in 1888.

Clerks: P. W. Roberts, 1836–38; J. W. Bond, 1838–44; E. Guthrie, 1844–46; J. W. Bond, 1846–48; Samuel Morgan, 1848–52; R. S. Bell, 1852–56; Dandridge McRae, 1856–62; J. W. Bradley, 1862–68; J. A. Cole, 1868–72; A. P. Sanders, 1872–80; J. J. Bell, 1880–84; L. C. Canfield, 1884–88; C. S. George, present incumbent, elected in 1888. From 1872 to 1874, Allen Mitchel was circuit clerk, and from 1880 to 1882, T. C. Jones was county clerk, and from 1882 to 1884, J. R. Jobe was county clerk, and from 1884 to 1886, R. H. McCullough was circuit clerk. J. J. Bell is the present circuit clerk.

Sheriffs: P. Crease, 1836–38; William Cook, 1838–40; Milton Sanders, 1840–44; T. J. Lindsey, 1844–46; J. G. Robbins, 1846–50; J. M. Bowden, 1850–52; J. G. Robbins, 1852–54; R. M. Exum, 1854–60; J. W. Bradley, 1860–62; B. B. Bradley, 1862–64; W. C. Petty, 1864–66; J. G. Robbins, 1866–67; W. C. Petty, 1867–72; N. B. Petty, 1872–78; B. C. Black, 1878–84; J. H. Ford, 1884–88; R. W. Carnes, present incumbent, elected in 1888.

Treasurers: Michael Owens, 1836–38; John Arnold, 1838–42; James Bird, 1842–44; T. R. Vanmeter, 1844–46; J. Belew, 1846–48; J. M. Johnson, 1848–50; E. Neaville, 1850–52; W. T. Gilliam, 1852–54; W. B. Isbell, 1854–56; John Critz, 1856–60; S. B. Barnett, 1860–68; R. J.

HISTORY OF ARKANSAS.

Rogers, 1868–72; W. A. B. Jones, 1872–74; M. B. Pearson, 1874–80; D. L. Fulbright, 1880–84; J. M. Smith, 1884–88; J. G. Walker, present incumbent, elected in 1888.

Coroners: M. H. Blue, 1836–40; Hiram O'Neale, 1840–42; Samuel Beeler, 1842–44; D. Dobbins, 1844–46; E. K. Milligan, 1850–52; G. W. Davis, 1852–56; Alex Cullum, 1856–58; T. T. Britt, 1858–60; W. G. Sanders, 1860–72; T. L. Miller, 1872–74; Z. T. Haley, 1874–82; J. P. Baldock, 1882–84; J. H. Claiborne, 1884–86; J. M. Carter, 1886–88; Frank Blevins, present incumbent, elected in 1888.

Surveyors: S. Arnold, 1836–52; I. M. Moore, 1852–54; Thomas Moss, 1854–56; W. B. Holland, 1856–60; Thomas Moss, 1860–64; W. B. Holland, 1864–66; Thomas Moss, 1866–68; J. O. Hurt, 1868–72; Pres. Steele, 1872–74; J. P. Steele, 1874–76; Thomas Moss, 1876–80; B. S. Wise, present incumbent, elected in 1880, and served continuously since.

Assessors:* T. W. Leggett, 1868–70; I. S. Chrisman, 1870–72; J. H. Black, 1872–74; D. L. Fulbright, 1874–76; B. B. Bradley, 1876–84; J. J. Deener, 1884–88; G. W. Dobbins, present incumbent, elected in 1888.

Delegates in Constitutional Conventions: 1836, W. Cummins, A. Fowler and J. McLean, for Pulaski, White and Saline Counties; 1861, held March 4 to 21, and May 6 to June 3, J. N. Cypert; 1864, held January 4 to 23, not represented; 1868, J. N. Cypert and Thomas Owen; 1874, J. N. Cypert and J. W. House.

The first State senator for White County was R. C. Byrd, and the first representative in the house was Martin Jones.

The number of votes cast at the late elections for several candidates, as stated below, will show the political aspect of the county. At the September election 1888, for Governor, James P. Eagle, Democrat, 1,608; C. N. Norwood, combined opposition, 1,949. November election in 1888, for president, Cleveland, Democrat, 1,948; Harrison, Republican, 550; Streeter, Union Labor, 249; Fiske, Prohibition, 45.

*This office was not established until 1868.

The various courts held in the county are county, probate, circuit and chancery. The regular sessions of these bodies are held as follows: County court, commencing on the first Monday of January, April, July and October; probate, on the second Monday of the same months; circuit, on the third Monday of January and July; chancery, on the second Monday of June and December. The chancery court was made a separate court by an act of the General Assembly approved March 15, 1887, and was attached to the First chancery district, composed of Lonoke, Pulaski, Faulkner and White Counties. Prior to that time the circuit court had jurisdiction of all chancery business.

The legal bar (local) of White County is composed of the following-named attorneys: W. R. Coody, J. N. Cypert, D. McRae, B. Isbell, John B. Holland, S. Brundidge, Jr., J. F. Rives, Sr., J. F. Rives, Jr., E. Cypert, John M. Battle, John T. Hicks, J. D. DeBois, C. D. James and J. E. Russ.

Upon the approach of the Civil War a strong Union sentiment prevailed in White County, and when the Hon. J. N. Cypert was elected representative in the State convention held in March, 1861, he was instructed to, and did, vote against the secession of the State from the Federal Union. Afterward, when the "dogs of war" were let loose, and President Lincoln called upon the State for its quota of the first 75,000 troops for the Union army, the sentiment materially changed, and the people concluded to cast their lot in general with the Southern project of establishing a separate Confederacy. To this end companies of soldiers began to be organized, and in 1861, five companies first commanded, respectively, by Capts. F. M. Chrisman, John C. McCauley, Henry Blakemore, J. N. Cypert and J. A. Pemberton, and in 1862 three companies first commanded, respectively, by James McCauley, B. C. Black and Boothe Jones, were enlisted and organized within the county for the Confederate army. All were infantry companies except that of Capt. Chrisman, which was cavalry. Capt. James McCauley's company was mounted infantry. Some individuals joined commands outside of the county. No troops

WHITE COUNTY.

were organized within this territory for the Federal army, but a very few persons who refused to yield their Union sentiments left the county and enlisted as their principles dictated.

In 1862, when a division of the Federal army was moving from Batesville to Helena, an escort of its forage train, numbering about 500 men, was suddenly attacked at Whitney's Lane, five miles east of Searcy, by about 150 Confederates under Capt. Johnson. The latter made a bold and sudden attack and then retired, losing only about five men, while the Federals lost from fifty to 100. This was the only fight worthy of mention within the county. The county was overrun by scouting and foraging parties of both armies, and much provision was thus taken from the citizens. Three or four men were killed in the county during the war by scouts.

White County contains within its territory a number of towns of prominent local importance, besides those whose size has given them substantial reputation in the outside world. Of these Beebe is a flourishing place situated on the St. Louis, Iron Mountain & Southern Railroad, about sixteen miles southwest of Searcy. It began to build in the spring of 1872 (upon the completion of the railroad), but did not improve much until 1880, when it had reached a population of 428, and since then it has more than doubled in population. It has ten general, four grocery, three drug, two hardware, one furniture, two millinery and one notion store; also the White County Bank, two hotels, several boarding houses, two meat markets, two blacksmith and wagon shops, one saw and grist mill combined, two cotton-gins, two livery stables, railroad depot, postoffice, one photograph gallery, a fruit evaporator, five church edifices for the white and two for the colored people, a public school-house, five physicians, a dentist, two weekly newspapers, etc., etc. The Beebe Argus, published by W. B. Barnum, is an eight-column folio, Democratic in politics, and has for its motto: "A school-house on every hilltop and not a saloon in the valley." The Arkansas Hub is a seven-column folio, published by Sam J. Crabtree, and is independent in politics. Both of these

papers are ably edited and are well sustained, proving important factors in the influence of the community. Beebe is the center of one of the best fruit growing regions on the line of the St. Louis, Iron Mountain & Southern Railway, and ships a vast amount of fruit, especially small fruits, berries, tomatoes and the like, to the city markets. It is incorporated and has a full line of corporate officers. It also has lodges of the Masonic and Odd Fellow fraternities. It is thirty-three miles from Little Rock.

Bradford is a shipping station on the St. Louis, Iron Mountain & Southern Railroad, near the northern boundary of the county. It contains four general, one drug and one millinery store, one grist and one saw mill, a public school-house, two blacksmith shops, two physicians and a lodge each of Masons, Knights of Honor and Triple Alliance. The school-house is used for religious meetings. The population is about 100.

Bald Knob is situated in the northeastern part of White County, on the St. Louis, Iron Mountain & Southern Railroad at the junction of the Memphis branch. It contains three general, one hardware and grocery, one grocery, one drug and grocery and a millinery store, a grist-mill and a saw-mill, school-house, etc., etc.

Garner and Higginson are shipping stations on the St. Louis, Iron Mountain & Southern Railroad, the former about ten miles south of Searcy, and the latter five miles southeast.

Judsonia, formerly Prospect Bluff, is located on the west side of the St. Louis, Iron Mountain & Southern Railroad, and on the north bank of Little Red River. It is a comparatively old town. About the year 1870 a colony from the East settled there, and secured the change of the name of the town from Prospect Bluff to that of Judsonia. The place now contains four general, one dry goods, three grocery, one hardware, one hardware and furniture, one harness, one millinery and two drug stores; also a music store, meat market, two blacksmith shops, a wagon shop, a fruit and vegetable canning factory, fruit-box factory, two saw-mills, a grist-mill and cotton-gin, a grist-mill and wool-carding mill, a tanyard, two hotels, a restau-

HISTORY OF ARKANSAS.

rant, a bakery, two livery stables, two church edifices for the white and two for the colored people; also a public school-house for the white and another for the colored people, three physicians, a lodge each of several secret and benevolent societies, a newspaper, the Judsonia Weekly Advance, etc., etc. The Advance is a six-column folio published by Berton W. Briggs, and has for its motto, "Overcome prejudice. Let free thought and free speech be encouraged." The Judsonia University is also located at this place. [See Schools.]

The White County Agricultural and Industrial Fair Association was organized at Judsonia in 1883, and grounds fitted up where exhibitions are held in the fall of the year.

The first fair was held in October, 1883. That of the past fall was a successful one. The present officers are Capt. D. L. McLeod, president; James L. Moore, vice-president; Charles D. James, secretary, and J. S. Kelley, treasurer. Messrs. D. L. McLeod, J. D. DeBois, J. S. Eastland, S. N. Ladd, Willis Meadows, James L. Moore, E. C. Kinney and J. S. Kelley are directors.

Judsonia's location in the midst of a wonderful fruit-growing community gives it prominent intercourse with the outside world. In 1889 immense shipments of fruit were made from this point, and in 1888 some 96,000 packages found their way to different sections. This will be the head of navigation on Little Red River when the Government shall have finished its work of improvement, for which appropriation was made.

Judsonia, like Beebe, is located in the center of a great fruit-growing region, is surrounded with many small fruit farms, and ships immense quantities of fruits, berries, tomatoes, etc., to the city markets. The town is incorporated and has a mayor and other corporate officers. It had a population of 267 in 1880, and now boasts of about 600, besides a dense population on the small fruit farms adjoining and surrounding it.

Kensett is situated on the St. Louis, Iron Mountain & Southern Railroad, at the crossing of the Searcy & West Point Railroad, four and a half miles east of Searcy. It contains the railroad depot, a general store, postoffice, hotel, a grocery,

blacksmith shop, a church edifice and a few dwelling houses.

Russell is a station on the St. Louis, Iron Mountain & Southern Railroad, between Bradford and Bald Knob. It contains two general stores, a drug and a millinery store, a saw-mill, grist-mill, cotton-gin, railroad depot, postoffice, etc.

There are some other small villages in the county containing a postoffice, general store, etc.

Searcy, the county seat, is situated in the geographical center of the county, at the western terminus of the Searcy & West Point Railroad. Its origin has been given in connection with the organization of the county. It was established in 1836, and a Mr. Howerton opened the first hotel in a double log-house south of what is now Spring Park. Moses Blew opened the first store, and was soon joined in the mercantile business by John W. Bond. At the beginning of the Civil War the place contained about six business places facing the public square. Its business was almost wholly destroyed during the war period, but revived soon thereafter. It now contains thirteen general, four grocery, three drug, two hardware, one furniture, one undertaking, one harness and saddle, two millinery stores, two meat markets, two restaurants, a bakery, two hotels and several boarding-houses, two grist and planing mills and cotton-gins combined, a wagon factory, two livery stables, six church edifices—three for the white and three for the colored people—a lodge each of Masons, Odd Fellows and Knights and Ladies of Honor, a Woman's Christian Temperance Union, Woman's Aid and Woman's Missionary Society, seven physicians, a dentist, three tailors, jewelers, etc. In addition to the interests mentioned, there are the Searcy Male and Female College, the Galloway Female College and three public schools—two for white and one for the colored people. One of the public school-houses, used by the former, was built for a male and the other for a female academy. Two weekly newspapers are also published here, the Arkansas Beacon and the White County Wheel. The former is a five-column quarto, published by Holland & Jobe. It is now in its eleventh volume, and is Democratic in politics. The

WHITE COUNTY.

latter is also a five-column quarto, published by R. A. Dowdy. It is in its second volume, and is published in the interest of the labor movement. These journals faithfully represent the interests of this section.

Spring Park, at Searcy, inclosing several acres, is located near the center of the city. It contains three never-failing mineral springs—White Sulphur, Chalybeate and Alum. The former of these have the most health-giving qualities, aiding digestion and curing constipation. This park contains bath-houses, is shaded by natural forest trees and is a very pleasant retreat for all persons. The town of Searcy is laid out "square with the world," its streets running east and west and north and south. It is beautifully located and is substantially built up, both in its churches, colleges, residences and business houses—the latter being mostly of brick. The healthfulness of location of the place is all that could be desired. The city is an educational center, and, especially a summer health resort, as many health and pleasure-seekers spend their summer months here. Its population is estimated at from 1,500 to 2,000. The residences are generally owned by the occupants, and there are very few renters, probably less than in any town of its size in the State. The town is incorporated and has a full complement of corporate officers.

West Point is situated on an eminence on the south side of Little Red River, at the eastern terminus of the Searcy & West Point Railroad. It was laid out in 1850 by J. M. West, hence its name, West Point, it being the point to which the river was navigable at all seasons of the year. At the beginning of the Civil War it had attained a population of 350 and did an immense amount of business, being the distributing point for a large scope of country to the westward. During the war period it lost nearly all its business, but afterward revived and flourished until the Iron Mountain Railroad was completed through the county. Then it again lost its prosperity, and in 1880 its population had run down to 123. Its population is now about 150. It contains three general stores, a drug store, a grist-mill and cotton-gin, a black-smith and wood shop, a church edifice, a public school-house and the railroad depot. It is supplied with a daily mail.

The advancement made in the cause of education in White County, under the free school system, is best shown by the following statistics as given in the report of the State superintendent of public instruction for the year ending June 30, 1888:

Scholastic population: White, males 3,384, females 3,173, total 6,557; colored, males 410, females 404, total 814. Number of pupils taught in the public schools: White, males 2,159, females 1,971, total 4,150; colored, males 295, females 283, total 578. Number of school districts, 101; districts reporting enrollment, 76; number of districts voting tax, 44. Number of teachers employed: Males 86, females 41, total 127. Average monthly salaries paid teachers: First grade, males $50, females $40; second grade, males $45, females $35; third grade, males $30, females $27.50. Amount expended for the support of the public schools: For teachers' salaries, $20,500.79; for building and repairing, $3,275; for treasurers' commissions, $565.60; total $24,341.39.

Assuming these statistics to be correct, only 63 per cent of the white and 71 per cent of the colored scholastic population were taught in the public schools. It must be noticed, however, that out of the 101 school districts, twenty-five failed to report the enrollment in the schools, which if ascertained and added to those that made reports, would largely increase the per cent of scholastic population attending. The fact that the school law does not compel full statistical reports to be made, is a strong argument in favor of its revision. Education for the masses is growing in popularity.

On July 23, 1888, a normal institute was opened at Searcy by Prof. T. S. Cox, conductor. This institute was in all respects a grand success. Its beginning noted the presence of thirty-four teachers, though seventy-one were in attendance at the close. A strong effort had been put forth by the county examiner, Mr. B. P. Baker, to secure a large attendance, and his energies in the work was the cause of bringing out nearly all the pro-

HISTORY OF ARKANSAS.

gressive teachers of the county, and many others friendly to education. Great interest was manifested, and much good work accomplished.

The Searcy Male and Female College is a chartered institution for the higher education of young men and women. The building is located within a campus of five acres, on a beautiful site in Searcy, convenient to the public square, and yet sufficiently removed to avoid the noise and bustle of business. It was organized in 1883, by Prof. W. H. Tharp (who conceived the idea of starting a reputable educational institution), and it at once become recognized as a school of a high order. Gen. D. McRae is president and Col. V. H. Henderson is secretary and treasurer of the board of trustees, and W. H. Tharp is president of the faculty. The members of the faculty are selected from colleges and universities of national reputation and most of them have supplemented their college or university course by thorough normal training, and hence in their teaching are prepared to use the most approved methods. Following the Preparatory Department is the Collegiate Department, divided into these Schools: Ancient Languages, Modern Languages, History, Natural Sciences, Mathematics, Philosophy and Belles-Lettres, Engineering, Elocution, Biblical History, Pianoforte, Vocal Culture, Harmony, Theory and Art.

A Normal Class is also taught, and the college cadets are organized into a company under the immediate supervision of the instructor in military tactics, Lieut. Albert J. Dabney (U. S. Naval Academy) commanding company.

The buildings consist of college hall, president's office and mathematics, a two-story boarding hall, music and art department, primary department, president's residence and cooking department, all separate, the dining-hall being under college hall. The history of the founding of this institution is most interesting. Prof. Tharp was aided in his work of starting the school by Prof. Conger of Ouachita College, Arkadelphia, the latter serving eighteen months as one of the principals. Subsequently Prof. Tharp was left in entire charge. Upon starting thirty-seven pupils were enrolled. A noticeable growth attended the worthy efforts of the founder and last year 204 pupils were in attendance. The capacity of the college has been doubled and still more room is needed. Its graduates have included persons of ability and influence, who have attained to prominence in their varied walks. The collegiate course is being strengthened and improved yearly, and every effort is being made to make this the leading educational institution of the State.

Galloway Female College was organized in the spring of 1888, under supervision of the several Conferences of the Methodist Episcopal Church, South, in the State of Arkansas. The citizens of Searcy secured its location by subscribing $25,000 toward its erection. The college building stands between a half and three-fourths of a mile southeast of the court house, on an eminence in a beautiful native forest, consisting of eighteen acres. It was erected in 1888–89, and consists of the main building and an east, west and north wing, with the kitchen department on the east side of the north wing, and its entire length from east to west is about 200 feet. Above the southern or front entrance is a tower eighty feet high. The building, the walls of which are constructed of brick on a rock foundation, has four stories above the basement, and contains a chapel 48x60 feet in size and twenty feet in height, five recitation rooms, a dining-room forty-eight feet square and twelve feet high, two double parlors, four reception halls, sixty-four bed-rooms, three bath-rooms, eleven halls and a kitchen with four rooms, storeroom and pantry. In the basement is the furnace room with two engines. The building in general is heated with steam, the rooms are all supplied with fire-places, and it is lighted with gas. The corner, or memorial stone, sets in the south wall, east of the main entrance, and has on its face the following inscription:

Galloway Female College.
C. B. Galloway, Bishop.

Building Committee.
P. A. Robertson,   G. B. Greer,
B. P. Baker,   A. W. Yarnell,
J. E. Skillern.

Elliott & Elliott,   A. B. Melton,
Builders,   Architect.

WHITE COUNTY.

Near the building is a superior bored well, ninety-three feet deep, with sixty feet of water in it. The grounds cost $2,000, and the building about $32,000. The building is well supplied with piazzas, and is exceedingly well ventilated. R. W. Erwin is president of the college. The first session opened in September, 1889. Too much can not be said in favor of the location of this college, on account of the healthfulness of Searcy, the morality of its people, and many other advantages.

Judsonia University is a Baptist school located at Judsonia. It was founded by the colony that came from the East and located about the year 1870. The school-house is a large frame structure. The faculty is composed of five teachers. It is a good school and has the advantages of being in a quiet, moral town, removed from the vices and temptations of large cities.

The several religious denominations of White County are the Methodist Episcopal, Methodist Episcopal, South, Baptist, Presbyterian, Cumberland Presbyterian and Christian.

Of the Methodist Episcopal Church, South, there are the following: Searcy Station, Rev. J. M. Talkington, pastor, with a membership of 210; Searcy Circuit, consisting of six appointments, Rev. E. M. Baker, pastor, membership 386; El Paso Circuit, consisting of four appointments, Rev. H. F. Harvey, pastor, membership about 250; Lebanon Circuit, consisting of seven appointments, Rev. W. A. Pendergrass, pastor, membership 356; Bradford Circuit, consisting of seven appointments, Rev. C. H. Cary, pastor, membership 164; Beebe and West Point, C. H. Gregory, pastor, membership 225; Red River Circuit, only three appointments in this county, Rev. James A. Brown, pastor, membership about 150; and Kentucky Valley Circuit, with six appointments, Rev. M. B. Corrigan, pastor, membership 359; thus making an aggregate of 2,100 members. The Sunday-schools of this denomination have also a large membership. These organizations all belong to Searcy District of the White River Conference, of which Rev. George M. Hill is the presiding elder.

Of the Methodist Episcopal Church there is Beebe Station, Rev. R. R. Fletcher, pastor, membership 44; Judsonia Station, Rev. George H. Feese, pastor, membership 118; and Bald Knob Circuit, consisting of four appointments in White County and one in Jackson, Rev. F. M. Hughes, pastor. These comprise all the organizations of this denomination within White County, and all belong to the Little Rock District of the Arkansas Conference.

The Baptist Church organizations, pastors and memberships within the county, are as follows: Beebe, Isom P. Langley, 134; Bethlehem, W. H. Hodges, 27; Cane Creek, W. J. Kirkland, 20; Centre Hill, J. D. Doyle, 141; Elon, same pastor, 55; El Paso, same pastor, 206; Garner, L. F. Taylor, 12; Hepsibah, W. H. Hodges, 32; Higginson, R. J. Coleman, 13; Judsonia, B. F. Bartles, 116; Kensett, J. M. Davis, 38; Kentucky Valley, J. A. Chamblee, 39; Liberty, J. M. Davis, 112; Plateau, John Stephens, 26; Rose Bud, M. T. Webb, 78; Searcy, 137; Shiloh, W. J. Kirkland, 76; South Antioch, J. A. Chamblee, 57; Wake Forest, W. J. Kirkland, 13; West Point, J. M. Davis, 54. All of these belong to the Caroline Baptist Association, from the last published proceedings of which the above information has mostly been taken. Since then some changes may have been made in pastors, and the memberships may have increased. The aggregate membership as above given is 1,386.

There are two Presbyterian Church organizations within the county, one at Searcy, Rev. Richard B. Willis, pastor, with a membership of 53, and one near Centre Hill, Rev. W. S. Willbanks, pastor, and a membership of 14.

Below is the list of Cumberland Presbyterian Church organizations in White County, together with names of pastors and membership of each annexed: Beebe, Finis Wylie, 60; Stony Point, J. A. Pemberton, 40; Antioch, same pastor, 86; Pleasant Grove, same pastor, 40; Gum Spring, Finis Wylie, 60; New Hope, J. C. Forbus, 40; Good Springs, Rev. Barlow, 60; aggregating a closely estimated membership of 386.

Of the Christian Church there are Beebe, Clear Water, Garner and Bald Knob. The first has a

HISTORY OF ARKANSAS.

membership of 70, and the others have a fair membership. Elder J. B. Marshall is pastor of the Beebe organization, and Elder Brown of Clear Water and Garner.

There are also a number of church organizations among the colored people, at Searcy, Beebe, Judsonia and other places. Sunday-schools are taught with much success in connection with most of the churches, and all in all much is accomplished in the cause of Christianity.

Saloons for the selling of intoxicating drinks are not allowed in the county.

The people are generally moral and law-abiding, and cheerfully extend the hand of welcome to all honest and industrious newcomers.

H. K. Adams, merchant at El Paso, Ark., and one of the leading citizens of that city, was born in Rockingham County, N. C., January 29, 1846, being the son of Samuel and Francis (Reid) Adams. Samuel Adams was a farmer by occupation, and a native of Virginia, but most of his life was passed in North Carolina. He was married in that State (where he had a fine farm), and died there in 1870, at the age of sixty-three years. He was magistrate for a number of years, and an energetic, enterprising citizen, and in whatever place he resided that locality might well consider itself the better for his citizenship. His wife died in 1854. She was a sister of Ex-Gov. Reid, of North Carolina, and her mother was a lady of national fame, who had near relatives on the supreme bench of Florida. H. K. Adams is the fifth in a family of eight children, five of whom are now living: Fanny B. (wife of J. W. Thompson, teacher in the Edinburgh High School, in Cleburne County, Ark.), Henrietta (wife of W. P. Watson, a farmer of Monroe County, Ark.), Reuben (a teacher in Prattsville) and Frank R. (a printer, married, and residing in Texas.) Those deceased are: Samuel F. (who lost his life at the hands of raiders, in 1865), David R. (died in college at Madison, N. C., aged eighteen) and Annie E. (who died in infancy.) H. K. Adams was reared on a farm, receiving a good common-school education at the district schools, and at the age of twenty-one launched his bark and began life for himself. He had nothing with which to cope with the world but a stout heart and his wit, and though it was rather discouraging, he never lost heart, and as a natural result was successful. He began first as a clerk in a country store at Boyd's Mill, N. C. A year later he enlisted in Company E, Forty-fifth North Carolina Regiment, and served until the surrender, in May, 1865, participating in the battle of the Wilderness and numerous other skirmishes, but through his entire career was never wounded. At the battle of Spottsylvania he was taken prisoner and held at Point Lookout and Elmira, in all about six months. He was again captured on the retreat from Petersburg, a few days before the surrender of Gen. Lee, and carried to Point Lookout, and remained in prison six weeks after the close of the war. After this Mr. Adams returned to his native State and engaged in farming until 1869, then coming to Arkansas (St. Francis County) where he resided two years. His next move was to El Paso, and after tilling the soil some two years he was engaged as clerk for W. H. Grisard, a prosperous merchant, for several years. For two years he was with C. P. Warren, and at the end of that time (1884) formed a partnership with J. T. Phelps and J. C. Harkrider, under the firm name of Adams, Phelps & Co. A short time later Mr. Phelps sold his interest to the other gentleman, the firm name becoming Adams & Harkrider. Mr. Adams eventually purchased the entire stock, and after a time formed a partnership with B. A. Neal, whose interest he bought, and then Mr. J. T. Booth purchased an interest, and since that time the firm has been known as Adams & Booth. They are doing a splendid business, and carry a well-assorted stock of general merchandise. Being wide-awake merchants and eminently responsible they command the respect of the entire community. Mr. Adams was united in marriage June 7, 1874, to Miss Florence Harkrider, a native of Alabama and a daughter of W. H. Harkrider, a farmer and mechanic of White County. Their union has been blessed with ten children, six of them now living: Martha F. (born in April, 1875), William S. (born

WHITE COUNTY.

in July, 1876, died in August, 1883), Hugh K., Jr. (born in March, 1878, and died in September, 1879), David C. (born in November, 1879), Dean (born in May, 1881, died in August, 1883), Eva E. (born in November, 1882), Horace E. (born in July, 1884), Sarah Florence (born in November, 1885, died in July, 1886), Myrtle I. (born in January, 1887), and Grace (born in February, 1889). Mr. Adams is giving his children all the advantages of good schools, and is determined that they shall have every opportunity for an education, regardless of expense. Himself and wife are members of the El Paso Methodist Episcopal Church, and Mr. Adams is at present a member of the school board and a notary public. He has served his township as bailiff for a number of years. In addition to his mercantile business he owns a small farm, which is carefully cultivated and yields excellent crops. In his political views he is a Democrat, but not an enthusiast.

James H. Adkins, a man of good repute and thoroughly respected in his community, is a Tennesseean by birth and is the son of Elcaney N. and Elizabeth (Hughes) Adkins. The mother of the subject of this sketch was a daughter of Harden and Sarah Hughes, of Tennessee. Mr. Adkins followed farming in Tennessee, and in 1845 immigrated to White County, Ark., and died shortly after his removal to this county, leaving three children: James H., William and Visey. James H. was born in 1844, and enlisted in the cavalry service when eighteen years old, in the Confederate army, and saw some hard fighting from the time of his enlistment, in 1864, until peace was declared. After the war he returned to this county and bought eighty acres of land and commenced to farm for himself. He now owns 140 acres, with over one-half of it in a good state of cultivation, and he vouches that his farm will produce almost everything. Mr. Adkins was married, in 1866, to Frances E. Woodle, a daughter of Turner and Catharine (Matthews) Woodle. Mrs. Adkins died September 3, 1867, leaving one daughter, Sceproney B. Mr. Adkins took unto himself a second wife (their marriage being solemnized in 1876), Mary F. Cullum, a daughter of Matthew and Mar-

garet C. (Childers) Cullum, natives of Tennessee. Mr. and Mrs. Adkins are the parents of eight children: Dora A., Martha A. (deceased), William O. (deceased), Henry B., James S., Cynthia L. (deceased), Robert C. and Ella A. Himself and wife are members of the Methodist Episcopal Church, South. Mr. Adkins is an A. F. & A. M., belonging to the Mount Pisgah lodge No. 242. He takes a prominent part and is deeply interested in all work beneficial to the community.

Hon. John M. Allen, well and favorably known in this vicinity as a prosperous farmer, and, indeed, throughout this portion of the State, was born in Tennessee, in 1839, being one of two children born to the marriage of Thomas J. and Anna E. (Black) Allen, the father a native of Tennessee, born about 1812, and a son of Daniel Allen, who was a descendant of the famous Ethan Allen. Thomas J. was reared and married in his native State, the latter event taking place about 1834, and there he reared the following family of children: William, John, Neal S., Richard J., Allie, Mary and Hall B., who is deceased. Mr. Allen was a farmer throughout life, and is now living in Arkansas with his son John, and is about eighty years of age. He is a member of the Agricultural Wheel, and he and his wife, who died in 1872, were members of the Baptist Church. John M. Allen received excellent educational advantages in Tennessee, and completed his education in Pulaski College, after which he (in 1856) started out to fight the battle of life for himself and engaged in farming, and this occupation has received his attention up to the present time. In 1859 he married Emma Sparkman, a daughter of William Sparkman, of Tennessee, but in 1877 he was called upon to mourn the death of his wife, she having borne him a family of five children: William (who is married and resides in Beebe), Lizzie (Mrs. Hubbard, residing in Dogwood Township), Arch, Claude and Eugene. Later Mr. Allen wedded Mrs. Hannah (Walker) Seawell, and by her has three children: Adella, Eula and Lonnie. In 1860 Mr. Allen moved with his family to Butler, Mo., and from there, in 1861, enlisted in Company B, Col. Lowe's regiment, as captain, and was

HISTORY OF ARKANSAS.

shortly promoted to the rank of major. After the battle of Belmont his company was disorganized and his regiment transferred to the Army of the Tennessee and was in nearly all the principal battles of the war from that time until the close. He returned to Missouri after peace was declared and engaged in farming and the mercantile business, but becoming dissatisfied with his location he came to White County, Ark., in 1880, and a year later purchased the farm of 320 acres now belonging to him in Dogwood Township. He has 150 acres under cultivation, but, as his home is in Beebe, he only goes to his farm to attend to the gathering of his crops. He has always been found ready to assist worthy enterprises, and for years past has given much of his attention to politics, and is a member of the Farmers' and Laborers' Union of America, and is the present representative of that party in the State legislature from White County, Ark. He belongs to the State executive committee and is a Mason, holding a demit from Faithful Lodge No. 304. He and wife are members of the Baptist Church. Through his grandmother he is a distant relative of Chief Justice Hale.

Thomas Smith Anderson, a prosperous merchant and cotton dealer, of El Paso, Ark., was born in Madison County, Tenn., August 2, 1832, and is a son of Samuel Lindsay Anderson, who is of Scotch-Irish descent and was born in the "Palmetto State." His ancestors, as well as his wife's (Eliza Braden), came to this country while it was still subject to the British crown and fought in the Revolutionary War. The paternal grandparents were married in Newberry District, S. C., and removed to Tennessee between 1800 and 1812, their son, Samuel L., being born in 1800, and died May 22, 1884, his wife dying in Tennessee in 1847. A great uncle, Joshua Anderson, was under the jurisdiction of Gen. Jackson during the War of 1812, and took part in the battle of New Orleans. In 1858 our subject came to Arkansas and located in Pulaski County (now Faulkner), where, in company with his brother, James A. Anderson, he purchased 420 acres of land, and at the time of his brother's death, in June, 1885, had cleared about 100 acres. In July, 1861, Thomas S. Anderson

enlisted in Company B, Tenth Arkansas Infantry, Confederate States army, and served as second sergeant until the fall of 1862, when he was promoted to brevet second lieutenant, remaining such until the summer of 1865. He was at the battle of Shiloh in charge of the commissary department of his regiment. He was captured at Port Hudson, La., and was a prisoner of war for twenty-one months, being confined at Johnson's Island, Lake Erie, Point Lookout (Md.), and then transferred to Fort Delaware, about forty miles from Philadelphia. He was exchanged at Richmond, Va., and started to rejoin his command at Marshall, Tex., but in his attempt to regain his regiment he was compelled to endure many hardships, and, owing to exposure, he contracted rheumatism, but finally managed to reach Shreveport, that garrison being under command of Gen. Kirby Smith, and with him surrendered. He arrived at home the middle of June, and again, in company with his brother, who had also been in the Confederate army, took up farming. On May 12, 1868, he was united in marriage to Miss Margaret Ann Laws, of Haywood County, Tenn., origin, and a daughter of J. P. and Minerva (Leathers) Laws, who were born in North Carolina. In 1878 Mr. Anderson purchased a stock of general merchandise and opened a store at El Paso, where he has successfully conducted business ever since, and, in connection with this, keeps a line of such furniture as is demanded in his community. He is also an extensive dealer in cotton, and his annual sales for this commodity amount to $10,000 to $12,000. Mr. Anderson votes with the Democratic party, and while a resident of Faulkner County, and since the war, he has served as justice of the peace. He is a Mason, having been initiated into that society in 1859; was secretary of El Paso Lodge for several years, but has been demitted to Velonia Lodge, being its Master one year. He and wife are members of the Methodist Episcopal Church, South.

Moses E. Andrews has been actively and successfully engaged in farming in White County since twenty-one years of age. He was born in Lincoln County, Tenn., in 1844, to the union of Samuel and Marion (Adking) Andrews, natives of

WHITE COUNTY.

Virginia and Tennessee, respectively. They were married in Lincoln County, Tenn., and there remained until 1851, when they removed to Arkansas, and located in White County, near the place upon which the village of Judsonia is now located. This was then in the woods, but Mr. Andrews cleared up a good farm and made a home. He was a prominent Democrat, and served as justice of the peace for several years, and died May 20, 1867, at the age of fifty-six. Mrs. Andrews died in 1864, leaving a family of seven children, two of whom only are living: Moses E. (our subject) and Joseph D. (who is a farmer of White County.) Moses E. Andrews was married in 1873 to Elizabeth Eaton, a daughter of E. S. Eaton, an old settler of White County. She was born in 1851. They are the parents of two children: Benjamin W. and Rosella. Mrs. Andrews is a member of the Missionary Baptist Church. Mr. Andrews is a prominent Democrat and a leading citizen.

Moses Morgan Aunsspaugh, farmer and stock raiser of Little Red, Ark., is one of the much respected and esteemed residents of Denmark Township, where he has made his home for many years. He is the son of Benjamin and Ruhama (Hartley) Aunsspaugh, the former of German descent and a native of Pennsylvania. George Aunsspaugh, the great-grandfather of the subject of this sketch, came from Germany at an early day, located in Pennsylvania, and served in the Colonial army from that State in the capacity of drum-major in Gen. Washington's immediate command. The great-grandfather Hartley was a native born Englishman, came to America before the Revolution, settled in Pennsylvania, and served as a private soldier. Grandfather Aunsspaugh was a soldier in the War of 1812, and arrived in New Orleans the day after the battle, having served with the Ohio State troops. Benjamin Aunsspaugh came to Arkansas in 1833, in company with John Hartley and his family, and located in Jefferson County, of that State, all having traveled from Zanesville, Ohio, on a keel-boat, leaving that point in the early part of the fall of 1833, and arriving in the above county in December of the same year. Benjamin married Miss Ruhama

Hartley in Jefferson County, Ark., and the following children were born to this union: Jobe (born 1834), Moses Morgan (born 1835), John (born 1837), George (born 1839) and Amoa (born 1840). The mother of these children died in the last of June, 1845, in White County, Ark., whither Benjamin Aunsspaugh had moved with his family in October of the previous year, and here the father also died in 1876. In this county Jobe, Moses and John grew to manhood. Moses Morgan Aunsspaugh was born on the keel-boat, upon which his father and the Hartley family journeyed from Ohio, on April 12, 1835. He attended school about three weeks and had got as far as "baker" in his spelling book when his school days suddenly terminated. He learned the blacksmith trade with his father and followed this occupation for a number of years. On January 17, 1858, he was wedded to Miss Sarah Winford, a native of Tennessee, and the daughter of Samuel and Martha (Morris) Winford, who came to Arkansas in 1844, settled in Poinsett County, where the father died the same year. The Winford family consisted of these children: Margaret (married Thomas Anderson and became the mother of eight children; she died in 1859), Jane (married Dave Ellster, and has one child) and Sarah. To Mr. and Mrs. Aunsspaugh were born three children: Martha Ann Ruhama (born November 4, 1858), Samuel Benjamin Franklin (born August 31, 1862) and George Washington (born April 25, 1872). Martha Ann Ruhama married Albert M. Bryant on August 4, 1874, and became the mother of four children: John Thomas, Lindsay E., Oliver and Mary Ella. Samuel B. F. married Miss Martha Porter on March 4, 1879, and became the father of three children. He, his wife and all his children are deceased. Benjamin Aunsspaugh bought eighty acres of land in White County, improved it, and in 1846 moved to Searcy, where he carried on his trade as blacksmith. He and his son Moses ironed the first wagon sent out of White County to California in 1849. In 1851 he returned to the neighborhood of his old home, and there bought 160 acres of land, subsequently adding to this until he at one time owned 320 acres. At the time of his death he owned 240

16   **WHITE COUNTY, ARKANSAS - BIOGRAPHICAL AND HISTORICAL MEMOIRS**

****

HISTORY OF ARKANSAS.

acres, with thirty acres under cultivation, and in connection with tilling the soil he also carried on the blacksmith trade up to that time. Benjamin Aunsspaugh was married the second time in 1853 to Mrs. Jane McDonald, a native of Alabama, and these children were the result: William (born 1854), twins (born 1855), James and an infant who died unnamed and another infant died unnamed. James W. married Mrs. Jennie Copeland, who bore him three children, two living. He resides on a farm in White County. Moses M. Aunsspaugh made his first purchase of land in 1858, paying 50 cents an acre for eighty acres. In 1862, much against his will, he was conscripted by the Confederates, and served three years in that army, participating in the battle of Helena, but did not fire a gun. He served his company in the capacity of cook, and returned home in 1864. He sold his first purchase of land in 1860, and in 1861 purchased 160 acres near Searcy, which was partly improved. He then cleared twelve acres, erected a log-house 16x16 feet and lived there for eight years, two and a half years of which time he rendered Union service in the Confederate army. In 1869 he sold his farm and moved to his present property, where he has since made his home. He first purchased 170 acres, but afterward added to this eighty acres, and soon had fifteen acres under cultivation, and resided in a log-house for six years. In 1875 he erected his present comfortable house, and there he has since resided. The same year he noticed a peculiar looking stone on his place, picked it up, called the attention of an experienced geologist to it, and it was pronounced gold quartz. Mr. and Mrs. Aunsspaugh are members of the Cumberland Presbyterian Church, and their daughter Martha D. and her husband are members of the United Baptist Church. Mr. Aunsspaugh is a member of the Agricultural Wheel No. 176.

William C. Barclay, postmaster and merchant of Russell, Ark., of Jackson County, Ala., nativity, and whose birth occurred January 28, 1858, is the son of James C. and Melinda (Wright) Barclay, natives of Alabama. James C. Barclay is still a citizen of Alabama, and follows farming for a livelihood. The wife of James C. died in November, 1864, having borne him eight children: Anna, Penelope, Tommie, John P., James P., William L., Jane and Sarah, all living. Mr. Barclay again married, choosing for his second wife Miss Ransom of Jackson County, Ala., and the result of this marriage is one child, Wiley F. Barclay, born in 1868. In February, 1875, Mr. Barclay was married the third time to Miss Galbreath of De Kalb County, Ala., and to them has been given one child. The grandparents of William C. came direct from Ireland to Alabama. Our subject was reared in Jackson County. His advantages for learning were limited in his youth by reason of the Civil War and its attendant and subsequent hardships. But by constant study and close observation, he is well informed on the important events of the day. Mr. Barclay began for himself in July, 1870, as a farm hand, then as a salesman in a general merchant mill in Alabama. In 1877 he moved to Arkansas, settling in White County, and engaging in farming followed it for two years. At the expiration of the two years he accepted a position as salesman in Russell, but soon after accepting this he was appointed railroad and express agent of that city, which office he filled for one year. Mr. Barclay then started a general merchandise business, in this meeting with flattering success. He carries a good stock, which is valued at $2,500 to $3,000, and by his courteous manner and upright dealing has obtained a liberal patronage from the surrounding community. Mr. Barclay was united in matrimony, December 23, 1880, to Miss Fannie N. Watson, a daughter of Hiram B. and Henrietta (Bankston) Watson, of Columbus County, Ga. By this marriage two children have been born: Fred B. (born August, 1881, now deceased), and Frank Carlton (born November 28, 1884). Mr. Barclay received the appointment of postmaster at Russell in 1881, holding that position until 1885, when he was re-elected, and is still filling the office, discharging the duties that devolve upon him in a manner that is entirely satisfactory to all and commendatory to one in that responsible position. He is president of the school board, and takes an active part

WHITE COUNTY.

in all educational interests; contributes liberally to the relief of the poor, and is a thorough worker in all public enterprises. He is a Democrat in his political views and a Methodist in religious belief, though not a member of the church. Mr. Barclay is a Master Mason in good standing, also belongs to the Triple Alliance, a mutual benefit association.

John M. Bartlett is the son of George Bartlett, who was born in Kentucky in 1811, being married in Illinois, about 1830, to Mahala Gowens. She was brought up among the Indians and had Indian blood in her veins, her mother being a half Cherokee. Mr. Bartlett after his marriage settled in Illinois, where he remained three years. He then moved to Kentucky and remained there until his death, which occurred in May, 1864, his wife also dying within a few days. They were the parents of six children: Martha J., William, Thomas J., John M., Dudley and Elizabeth P. Thomas and Dudley are deceased. John M. Bartlett was born in Fulton County, Ky., in 1843. At the outbreak of the war, inspired by patriotism, he enlisted, May 1861, in the Fifth Tennessee Infantry and participated in the battle of Shiloh and in a number of skirmishes. After his term of service had expired he returned home before the close of the war and engaged in farming, and married, in 1864, Miss Josephine Baldridge, a daughter of one of the early pioneers of Kentucky. Following his union Mr. Bartlett immigrated to Arkansas, and settled in Van Buren County and three years later, came to White County, where he has since made his home. He has a fine farm of 120 acres, seventy-five of which are under cultivation. Mrs. Bartlett was a Free Will Baptist, and died in 1883, leaving four children: George (deceased), Jennie, Ida and Josephine. Mr. Bartlett was married the second time to Mrs. Sutton, a widow. By his second marriage he has one boy: Edgar. Mr. Bartlett is a member of the Christian Church, and is a member and the vice-president of the County Wheel. His influence in the affairs of this community has been of decided good.

Judge J. J. Bell, the present efficient clerk of the circuit court and recorder of White County, is a native of Arkansas and a son of Robert S. and Louisa (Jacobs) Bell, natives of Kentucky and Vermont, respectively. Robert S. Bell was born in 1805, and when a young man moved to Arkansas and located in Monroe County, being one of the early settlers of that locality. In 1850 he became settled in White County, where he was engaged in his work as a Presbyterian minister, also serving as county clerk for four years. While in Monroe County he served as county clerk, and besides occupied the office of county judge for several years. He remained in White County ten years, but subsequently removed to the Chickasaw Nation, going there as a missionary and a teacher to that tribe. In their midst he remained until his death, which occurred in 1880. He was a son of James Bell, of Irish descent, who was a missionary Baptist minister, and died in White County. Louisa Jacobs was a daughter of Joseph Jacobs, of Vermont, who came to Monroe County at an early day, being one of the early settlers, and where he died. Mrs. Bell died in 1848, after which Mr. Bell married Arvilla A. Waterman, who is still living. By his first marriage he was the father of six children, our subject being the only one living. By his second marriage there are two children: Robert S., Jr. (who is a resident of the Indian nation), and Albert G. J. J. Bell first saw the light of day in Monroe County December 11, 1841, but accompanied his parents to White County when nine years of age. When sixteen years old he commenced farming for himself, at which he was occupied until the breaking out of the war, when he enlisted in the Eighth Arkansas Infantry, serving as second lieutenant of Company K, and participating in the battles of Murfreesboro, Chickamauga, Missionary Ridge, Atlanta, and a number of others. He was captured at Jonesboro, Ga., September 1, 1864, and was held twenty-one days when he was exchanged and rejoined his regiment. At the battle of Murfreesboro he was wounded by a gunshot in the forehead, and at the battle of Nashville he was again slightly wounded in the head. After the war he went to Tyler, Tex., then to Ouachita County, Ark., and in 1870 returned to White County, when he again

HISTORY OF ARKANSAS.

turned his attention to farming.   In 1880 Mr. Bell was elected clerk of the circuit court, which office he held for four years.   In 1887 he was elected to fill the unexpired term in the office of county judge, and in 1888 was again elected clerk of the circuit court.   His official duties have been discharged in a manner above reproach, and to the satisfaction of all and his own credit.   Mr. Bell was married May 22, 1865, to Miss Sarah A. Banks, who was born in Alabama August, 1846.   She came to White County with her parents when a child.   Mr. and Mrs. Bell became the parents of eleven children, eight of whom are still living; William H., George H., Franklin, Charles E., Joseph T., Richard L., Sarah A., and Katie.   Mr. Bell is a member of the Agricultural Wheel and is a strong Democrat.   He and his wife are also associated with the Cumberland Presbyterian Church.

John W. Benton has been worthily identified with White County's affairs for a long period. His parents, William and Malinda E. (Wilson), were natives of Virginia and Georgia, respectively. The former was born in 1803, and was a son of John Wilson, who moved from Virginia to Georgia when the father of our subject was a boy.   William Wilson married in 1824, and was engaged in the milling business all of his life.   He became the father of eight children: Willis R., James W., Catharine, William M., Lucinda, John W., Steven and Martha.   Mr. Benton died in 1887, and his wife in 1843.   John W. Benton's birth occurred in Georgia in 1839, he spending his early life in the mill of his father.   In 1858 he was married to Rachel Burket, a daughter of William and Rachel (Hughs) Burket, in White County, Ark., whither he had moved some two years before.   Mr. and Mrs. Benton are the parents of thirteen children: Linda E. (who married David Volenteer), Francis B. (who married Frances Nipper), John Steven (married to Katie Coffey), James W. (married to Emma Horton), William M. (who married Etta Scruggs), Willis R. (married Jennie Copper), Jessie A., David H., Fannie S., Elneo L., Charley W., Mamie L. and Henry V.   Mr. Benton enlisted during the war (in 1863) in Capt. Thompson's company, and took part in the Missouri raid, being captured at Van Buren and taken to Little Rock. Mr. Benton has a fine farm of 160 acres, with over half of it cleared.   Himself and wife are members of the Presbyterian Church, Mr. Benton being one of the elders.   He is a Democrat in politics, and an esteemed citizen.

T. B. Bobbitt, M. D., is one of the most worthy men engaged in the practice of medicine in White County, and is much esteemed and respected by all his medical brethren.   He was born in Gibson County, Tenn., November 8, 1849, and while assisting his father on the farm, he attended school at every opportunity, and by applying himself closely to his books he, at the age of twenty years, had a much better education than the average farmer's boy.   Not being satisfied with the education thus acquired, he entered the high school at Gibson, Tenn., and formed while there a desire to enter the medical profession.   In 1872 he entered the Nashville Medical College, graduated in the class of 1873 and the following year engaged in selling drugs.   He next farmed one year and in 1876 began the practice of medicine in Madison County, Tenn., continuing there until 1879, when he settled in White County, at Antioch Church, and in 1886 came to Beebe.   Since his residence here he has practiced his profession, kept a drug store and has farmed, and in all these enterprises has been successful, being now the owner of 500 acres of good farming land, lying in several different farms, and has 200 acres under cultivation.   In 1873 he was united in marriage to Miss Eddie James, a daughter of Edward James, a native of Tennessee.   They have four children: Nora (born March 1, 1875), Pinkie (born in 1879), Lawson (born in 1881) and Edgar (born in 1886). The Doctor is a member of the A. F. & A. M. and was a member of the K. of L.   He and his wife and eldest daughter are members of the Cumberland Presbyterian Church.   His parents, T. J. and Elizabeth (Wallace) Bobbitt, were born in South Carolina and Tennessee, respectively, and the former at the age of seven years was taken to Tennessee by his father, James Bobbitt, who had previously been an influential planter of South Carolina.   They were married in Gibson County,

WHITE COUNTY.

Tenn., in 1835, and reared the following family: William H. (a lawyer of Humboldt, Tenn.), Caroline (wife of W. F. Lawson, at present mayor of Eureka Springs, Ark.), James (a carriage and wagon maker of Joplin, Mo.), Mattie (who died at the age of twenty at Eureka Springs, Ark.), Ellen (wife of H. M. Brimm, a druggist at Eureka Springs), Mollie (wife of William Boyd, an editor of Seneca, Mo.) and Lena (who died in infancy). Both parents are living in retirement at Eureka Springs and are members of the Cumberland Presbyterian Church, the former a Mason and a member of the Union Labor party. J. N. Wallace, the maternal grandfather of our subject, was a soldier in the War of 1812, was a farmer and one of the pioneers of Tennessee.

Robert I. Boggs, a leading planter and stock raiser of White County owes his nativity to the State of Mississippi, and was born in June, 1843, being the son of John W. Boggs, of South Carolina. The former was born in 1815 and received his education in Yorktown, S. C., immigrating to Mississippi in 1840, where he married Catherine J. Smith in 1841. Mrs. Boggs was a daughter of John and Martha Smith, and a devout member of the Methodist Church. Her death occurred in 1889. Mr. and Mrs. Boggs were the parents of fifteen children: Mandy, Joseph W. (deceased), Robert I., James P., Newton J. (deceased), John (deceased), Martha (deceased), Lucy and Sarah (died at the ages of twenty-five and twenty-three, respectively), Franklin L. George P., Charley W., Margaret M., Addie E. and Harrison B. Mr. Boggs was a Democrat, and a man who manifested a great interest in all church and educational matters. He helped to organize the first church at Mount Pisgah, Mount Pleasant and Oak Grove, and has acted as class-leader in the Methodist Episcopal Church for fifty years. He is a member of the Wheel and also the Grange, and is enjoying good health, though passed his seventy-fourth year. Robert I. received his education in the county schools of White County near Searcy, and there married November 12, 1867, Miss Eliza J. Whisenant, of Mississippi, and a daughter of Nicholson and Nancy Whisenant, natives of South Carolina. To the union of Mr. and Mrs. Boggs six children have been born: Ida M., James M., Edward, Robert C., Annie J. and John W. Ida and Edward are deceased; the rest reside at home. Mr. Boggs owns about 150 acres of good land, sixty in cultivation, and well stocked with all that is requisite to successfully operate a farm of that size. He is a member of the Wheel, in which he has held the office of president and vice-president, discharging in a highly commendable manner the duties of that office. He served in the late war on the Confederate side and entered in October, 1862, returning home in 1863, but again enlisted, remaining only a short time. In 1864 he enlisted again under Gen. Dobbins, his first hard fight being at DeVall's Bluff. He was wounded in the Big Blue Fight by a ball which struck him in the left cheek, but did not prove serious. Mr. Boggs received an honorable discharge and at once returned home, engaging in farming, which has been his occupation ever since, and proving very successful. He is a member of twenty years' standing in the Methodist Episcopal Church, and his wife has held a membership in the Cumberland Presbyterian Church for twenty-three years.

M. Love Booth, retired farmer and merchant, was born in Middle Tennessee, Bedford County, in 1819, but owing to his father's early removal to Haywood County, he was reared there. The parents, James and Mary (Lofton) Booth, were both Virginians, and after residing in Tennessee for many years they removed to White County, Ark., and died at the home of their son in 1861. He was a member of the Baptist Church, a Mason, a lifelong Democrat, and was for years sheriff of Bedford County. After his wife's death, which occurred in 1851, he married again and came to Arkansas. M. Love Booth is the third of their six children, four now living: John (deceased, who was a farmer in Tennessee), William (a farmer of West Tennessee), Samira (deceased), M. Love, Susan (the wife of Henry Bacon, of Mississippi) and Louisa (who is the wife of a Tennessee farmer). Our subject has been familiar with farm work from his earliest boyhood, but his early advantages for acquiring an education were not so good. At the

HISTORY OF ARKANSAS.

age of twenty he was a farm hand, later a trader and stock breeder, and after his marriage to Miss Elizabeth Budrell he became an overseer, and successfully followed that occupation for forty years. He then gave up that work and built a livery stable in Brownsville, his establishment there being the largest of the kind in the State. In 1858 he came to Arkansas and purchased 320 acres of land near El Paso, seventy acres of which he cleared the first year. He was signally successful until the war broke out, when all his personal property was lost. He did not espouse either cause, and was not molested during those turbulent times. When he came to El Paso there were only two farms open here, but now the greater part of the land is in a high state of cultivation. After the war he, with Thomas Warren, built a large mill, which was destroyed by fire, when he returned to his farm, which he again began to till. He became the possessor of 1,000 acres, and has cleared over 300 acres, and since giving each of his children a farm he still holds 310 acres. His wife died October 1, 1887, and since that time he has made his home with his children, and is at present living with J. T. Phelps, his son-in-law, in El Paso, where he has an interest in the store of M. L. Phelps & Co. Mr. Booth was the first man to build a store in El Paso after the war, and is now managing a livery stable in that place, and, although he has attained the age of seventy years, he is an excellent business manager and is very active. Although quiet in his habits of life, he has always been interested in the public affairs of the county, and has done his full share in making the county what it is. He joined the Masons while in Tennessee, and he as well as his children are members of the Baptist Church. His children's names are here given: Nancy (is the wife of Monroe Oakley, a prosperous farmer of White County), Rebecca (is the wife of John C. Harkness, a farmer of El Paso), Elizabeth L. (is the wife of Thomas K. Noland, a farmer of the county), Narcissus (is the wife of John Russ, a farmer and president of the State Wheel), Martha A. (is the wife of J. T. Phelps, a merchant of El Paso), Mosella B. (deceased) and three infants, deceased.

Gilliam Harper Booth, known to the citizens of White County as one of its wide-awake, energetic, ever-pushing men, is of Tennessee nativity, and a son of William A. and Delia Jane (Leathers) Booth, who claim Virginia and North Carolina, respectively, as the land of their birth. William A., the father of our subject, was born in 1811, and when a young man came with his parents to Mississippi, and later on removed to Fayette County, Tenn., and thence to Haywood County. He was married in Fayette County. In 1856, after the election of James Buchanan to the presidency of the United States, they removed to Arkansas. He was an emphatic Democrat, casting his vote with that party, and a member of the Methodist Episcopal Church, South. William A. Booth was a son of Harper Booth, a Revolutionary War veteran, who served in that memorable conflict, and who died in 1859 at an extreme old age. The grandfather was a Virginian by birth, and a descendant of the Harper family from whom Harper's Ferry derives its name. Delia Jane Leathers was born in 1817, and was taken to Tennessee by her mother when a child of seven years. Mr. and Mrs. Booth were the parents of twelve children, four of whom are still living: Isabella J. (the wife of Dr. W. P. Lawton), Martha Ann (the wife of Capt. Rayburn, deceased), Gilliam H. (our subject) and Charles L. Gilliam H. Booth received his education at the public schools of West Point and at Judsonia University. His birth occurred August 26, 1850, in Haywood County, Tenn. He has been actively engaged in teaching school, clerking and farming, and owns a fine farm of 356 acres, with 150 under cultivation. In religion he is a member of the Methodist Episcopal Church, South, and a Prohibitionist, but, being a radical free trader, inclines toward the Democratic party, voting that ticket. In the community in which he lives he is regarded as a highly respected citizen.

William F. Bradley is a traveling salesman for a Lynchburg (Va.) tobacco firm, and is a gentleman who enjoys the respect and esteem of the people of White County. He was born in Caldwell County, N. C., June 6, 1847, and is a son of Jackson and Martha (Ferguson) Bradley, who were

WHITE COUNTY.

born, reared and married in that State, the latter event taking place in 1841. Mrs. Bradley was born in 1825, was of Scotch descent, her grandfather having emigrated from Scotland to North Carolina before it became a State, and took part in the Revolutionary War, being in sympathy with the cause of the Americans. Jackson Bradley was born in 1818, and was of Welsh descent, his ancestors having come to America long before the Revolution. After his marriage he was engaged in farming in his native state until 1855, and after residing successively in Mississippi, Georgia, and Missouri, he came to Arkansas in 1861, and to White County in 1875. He resided on a farm two miles east of Beebe till his death in March, 1887, his wife preceding him to the grave by ten years. Both worshiped in the Missionary Baptist Church. William F. Bradley was the third in a family of seventeen children, the following of whom are living: Madelia (Mrs. Thomas), Amelia (Mrs. Mosier), Susan (Mrs. Bailey), Burton and William F. The latter received his education in the various States in which his father lived, and after attaining his twenty-first year, he worked as a farm hand for two years, then attended school at Butlerville, Lonoke County, for ten months. After teaching one term of school he engaged as a clerk at Beebe, at the end of six years engaging in the same business in partnership with J. T. Coradine, under the firm name of Bradley & Coradine. At the end of two years they took a Mr. Burton into the business, the firm then becoming Bradley, Coradine & Co., continuing such one year. Mr. Bradley then sold his interest, and became associated with Richard S. Bradley under the firm name of W. F. & R. S. Bradley, general merchants; but a few months later they made an assignment, losing all their goods. After this misfortune Mr. Bradley began working as a salesman, then secured a position as traveling salesman for Charles G. Peper & Co. of St. Louis, but at the end of a few months was compelled to give up this position on account of poor health. After recovering he worked for some time as a railroad clerk, then resumed clerking, continuing until May 1, 1889, when he accepted his present position with J. W. West & Co., tobacco manufacturers of Lynchburg, Va. He is nicely situated in the town of Beebe, and has a pleasant and comfortable home, and socially is a member of Beebe Lodge No. 145, of the A. F. & A. M. He has belonged to the city board of aldermen, and he and wife, who was a Miss Emma S. Dement, and whom he married November 4, 1874, are members of the Missionary Baptist Church. They have a charming young daughter, Maud E., who was born October 26, 1876, and is attending the schools of Beebe. Mrs. Bradley is a native of De Soto County, Miss., and is a daughter of James T. and Ellen (Binge) Dement, the former of Alabama, and the latter of Tennessee. Mr. Dement was a farmer, and in 1872 came with his family to White County, dying there a year later, at the age of forty-five years. His wife survives him, and lives with Mrs. McIntosh in Beebe. The following are her children: Betty J. (born in 1857, the wife of Dr. McIntosh, the leading physician of Beebe), Emma S. (Mrs. Bradley, born June 24, 1859), Ella (born 1861, wife of A. M. Burton, a prosperous merchant of Beebe), Jennie (wife of Maxwell Welty, a railroad agent at Beebe), and James T. (who was born in February, 1874, and is attending the high school at Beebe).

William Sackville Brewer. Ever since his connection with the agricultural affairs of White County, Ark., Mr. Brewer has displayed those sterling characteristics—industry, perseverance and integrity, that have resulted in awarding him a representative place in matters pertaining to this community. The paternal ancestors came to America prior to the Revolutionary War and settled in Virginia, the grandfather, Barrett Brewer, an Englishman, participating in that struggle. He married Malinda Pollard, and by her became the father of four children: Martha (Mrs. Sanders), Sarah (who first married a Mr. Harder, and afterward a Mr. Scott), Benjamin and John Pollard (the father of our biographical subject). The maternal ancestors were also English, and came to America while it was still subject to the crown. The maternal grandmother was a Sackville, belonging to the distinguished English family of that

HISTORY OF ARKANSAS.

name. John Pollard Brewer was married to Susan Jefferson Townsend September 1, 1833, and to them the following children were born: William Sackville (born June 10, 1834), Martha M. (born July 18, 1836), James M. (born July 3, 1838), Pollard J. (born October 24, 1840), Sarah W. (born March 5, 1843), Andrew T. (born November 19, 1845), Benjamin A. (born May 19, 1848), John B. (born January 22, 1851), Mary E. (born September 19, 1853) and Karilla W. (born July 2, 1855). The father and mother of these children were born October 15, 1812, and March 14, 1817, respectively, the latter being of German descent, and a daughter of Andrew Criswell and Elizabeth (Barnett) Townsend. The father was one of the early settlers of Alabama, and represented Pike County in the State legislature. William Sackville Brewer was born in Pike County, Ala., and was educated in the subscription schools and reared on a farm. At the age of nineteen years he left home and united his fortunes with those of Miss Eliza H. Clayton, their union taking place October 10, 1852. She was born in Fayette County, Ga., June 6, 1834, and is a daughter of Richard and Jane (Carter) Clayton, the paternal ancestors being emigrants from Ireland to America prior to the Revolution. Mr. and Mrs. Brewer have a family of ten children: Susan E. (born September 6, 1853, became the wife of W. J. Turner in 1872, and died in 1883, leaving two children), Howell C. (born December 8, 1855, and died September 3, 1863), John William (born January 8, 1858), Ara Anna (born March 30, 1860, and died September 12, 1864), James R. (born September 18, 1862), Lela Lewis (born January 8, 1865, married D. A. King in 1882 and became the mother of two children), Henry W. (born September 1, 1867, and died June 8, 1871), Minnie Lee (born August 4, 1870), Robert B. (born March 23, 1872) and Richard J. (born December 24, 1874). Mr. Brewer has been a resident of Arkansas since 1873, and for two years farmed on rented land near Searcy. He continued to farm rented land until 1878, when he bought the farm of 129 acres where he now lives, of which about thirty-five acres are under cultivation. The buildings on the place were badly dilapidated, but Mr. Brewer now has all the buildings in excellent repair and his farm otherwise well improved. Mr. Brewer and his wife are professors of religion, and he at one time belonged to the Masonic fraternity, and is now a member of the Agricultural Wheel.

Charles Brown, M. D., was a native of Virginia, and was born May 3, 1783. He was the son of Bernard and Elizabeth (Dancy) Brown. He received his early education in Virginia, and later attended the Jefferson Medical College at Philadelphia, from which he graduated about 1807, subsequently settling in Charlotteville, Albemarle County, Va., and commenced the practice of medicine. Mr. Brown was married April 1, 1813, to Mary Brown, a daughter of Bezakel and Mary (Thompson) Brown, originally of Virginia, who was born April 24, 1790. They were the parents of the following children: Bernard O. (deceased), Elvira (deceased), Elizabeth D. (now Mrs. Jones, of Virginia), Bezaleel T. (deceased), Charles T., Algerion R. and Ezra M. Mr. Brown held the office of high sheriff of his county for two terms. His death occurred in 1879, at the age of ninety-six years; at the time of his death he was still a strong man with a wonderful memory. Algerion R. Brown was born in Albemarle County, Va., March 5, 1831. He attended the University of Virginia and in 1850 left it and studied medicine with his father a short time, and in 1852 went to Marshall County, Mississippi, where he engaged in the mercantile business until the war broke out. Mr. Brown was married January 26, 1855, to Mary F. Williams, a daughter of Alexander and Martha (Delote) Williams, of North Carolina nativity. Mrs. Brown was a native of Tennessee. Mr. Brown enlisted in 1861 for three years or during the war, in Company F, of the Thirty-fourth Mississippi Infantry in the Army of Tennessee. During the first twelve months he was first lieutenant, afterward was on staff of "general inspector," and after the battle of Lookout Mountain he went back to his regiment and was placed in command of three companies for some time and was then promoted to captain of the engineer department of staff duty, filling this position till the time of surrender. He

WHITE COUNTY.

participated in the battles of Shiloh, Murfreesboro, Chickamauga, Lookout Mountain, Missionary Ridge, and nearly all of the principal battles during the terrible conflict. Mr. Brown removed from Mississippi to Tennessee in 1881, remaining there four years, then moved to White County, Ark., settling in Cane Township on eighty acres of land, where he now has about thirty acres under cultivation. Mr. and Mrs. Brown have a family of five children and one deceased: Martha E. (deceased), Mary W., Susan W., Charles E., Samuel H., Walter L. Himself and wife are members of the Methodist Episcopal Church, South. Mr. Brown has served as delegate to the district and annual conferences, and is one of the stewards of the church. He is an energetic and well-educated man, and a fine talker, and takes an interest in all school and religious work. He was one of the committee from Mississippi to the New Orleans fair in 1883.

Dr. R. L. Browning, physician and surgeon, Judsonia, Ark. Prominent among the comparatively young men of White County, whose career thus far has been both honorable and successful, is the subject of the present sketch. His father, R. C. Browning was a native of Kentucky, and while attending school in Indiana, met and married the mother of the Doctor, her maiden name being Miss Eliza Frady. She was born in North Carolina, but was reared in Indiana. After their marriage the parents settled in Kentucky, and here the father followed teaching until 1849, when he moved to Sac County, Iowa, where he followed agricultural pursuits for a means of livelihood. He took an active part in politics, was county treasurer of Sac County one term, and in the fall of 1870 moved to Judsonia, where he continued tilling the soil. In 1877 he engaged in merchandising and still continues in that business. He and wife reside in Judsonia. Their family consisted of the following children: J. H. (married and living in Judsonia), W. C. (married and residing in Kirksville, Mo., engaged in merchandising), R. L., Maggie (now Mrs. Marsh, of Judsonia), Viola (now Mrs. Drake, of Judsonia). Dr. R. L. Browning was born in Sac County, Iowa, in 1859, assisted his father on the farm, and received

his education in the Judsonia University, one of the best schools of the county. He commenced reading medicine in Judsonia in 1877, and in 1878-79 took a course of lectures at the Cincinnati Eclectic Medical Institute, Cincinnati, Ohio, graduating in the class of 1882. He then came back and commenced the practice of medicine, where he was reared, and continued the same until the summer of 1882, having met with success and built up a big practice. He was married in Judsonia, Ark., on November 27, 1882, to Miss Emily B. Ellis, a native of New York, and the daughter of John Ellis, of English origin. Mr. Ellis came to this country, settled in New York, was civil engineer, and also engaged in horticulture. He came to Judsonia, Ark., in 1882, and died the same year in San Francisco, Cal., the mother dying in New York in 1872. To the union of Mr. and Mrs. Browning were born two children (only one now living): Harry R. (who was born in 1887), and Carroll Ellis (who died in 1884, at the age of eight months and twelve days). Dr. Browning is not very enthusiastic in regard to politics, but his vote is cast with the Republican party. Socially he is a member of Judsonia Lodge No. 45, I. O. O. F., at Judsonia, and has been Noble Grand of the order. He belongs to the Missionary Baptist Church and Mrs. Browning to the Episcopal Church. The Doctor is secretary of the Building Association, also of the board of Judsonia University, and is one of the first men of the county. He has been unusually successful in his practice and has won the confidence and esteem of all.

Prof. Augustine W. Bumpass, a prominent citizen and teacher of White County, is a native of Madison County, West Tenn., where he was born, near Jackson, on January 22, 1851. He is the eldest son of Dr. E. L. and Lucinda E. (Young) Bumpass. His father was a native of Giles County, Tenn., where he was born April 15, 1816, being reared in Lauderdale County, Ala., and there educated both in literature and medicine. Graduating at the Louisville Medical College, in the class of 1841-42, with the highest honors, he was for many years a prominent physician in Alabama, but removed to Madison County, Tenn., in the latter part

HISTORY OF ARKANSAS.

of 1850, where he resided until 1856, at which time he removed to Arkansas and settled in Prairie (now Lonoke) County. Here, in a wild and unsettled country, he purchased land and opened up a farm, which he conducted in connection with his practice until his death, December 3, 1883. He was a man of generous and humane impulses, a warm-hearted and devoted Christian, and a member of the Christian Church. He was a Master Mason and a member of the I. O. O. F., standing high in both of those societies. An old line Whig until the dissolution of that party, he then affiliated with the Democratic party until his death. The mother of our subject, Lucinda E. (Young) Bumpass, was a native of Alabama, where she was reared, educated and married. She was the daughter of Elder James Young, a prominent minister of the Christian Church in Alabama. He died in 1852. Mrs. Bumpass died on December 5, 1881, aged fifty-nine years, eight months and nine days. Dr. Gabriel Bumpass, grandfather of Augustine W., was a native of North Carolina and died in Lauderdale County, Ala., in 1875, aged one hundred and seventeen years. He was the oldest physician in America, if not in the world, having practiced medicine for more than eighty years. He was a remarkable man in many respects, and as physician, farmer or merchant, was very successful. Our subject's parents were married in Lauderdale County, Ala., on May 18, 1845. To their marriage seven children were born, five sons and two daughters, five of whom are living, as follows: Mary E. (at Pine Bluff, Ark.), Augustine W. (near Searcy, in White County, Ark.), Samuel J. (at Lonoke, (Ark.), Edward K. and Ross H. (at Pine Bluff, Ark.). The two last named are mechanics and buggy and carriage manufacturers; Samuel J. is a farmer, stock-raiser and trader. Romelia C., the eldest, a daughter, and Robert W., the fourth child, are dead. A. W. Bumpass was reared in Tennessee to the age of five years, and from that time in Arkansas, where he was educated, obtaining a good academic instruction and preparing himself for the profession of law. However, he began teaching early in life and has paid but little attention to the law, except in the lower courts.

Commencing for himself at the age of eighteen as a teacher in the public schools of his State, he has been occupied in teaching more or less for twenty years, gaining an enviable reputation in many counties where he has been engaged in the public and private schools and academies. He is a politician of some note, and represented his county (Lonoke) in the legislature, in 1879 and 1880, taking always an active interest in the campaigns of his party, Democratic. He was married in Lonoke County, Ark., on April 25, 1875, to Miss Virginia C. Kirk, a native of Marshall County, Miss., born April 11, 1856, a daughter of Richard L. and Virginia (Hayes) Kirk. Her father is dead, but her mother is a resident of White County, at the home of her daughter. Prof. Bumpass and wife have five children, four sons and one daughter: Edward W., Herbert R., Robert H., Prentice and Mary Moyner. The Professor is a member of the Christian Church and takes an active interest in church and Sunday-school matters. He has been Sunday-school superintendent for many years, was notary public from 1885 until 1889 in White County, and is a highly educated, intelligent gentleman, having the respect and confidence of those with whom he comes in contact. Generous to a fault, he aids all worthy enterprises to the extent of his time and means.

Patrick Burns was the second settler in White County, and for this reason, if for no other, deserves prominent mention in the present volume. Now the oldest resident of the county, he came here in 1844 and located some land, having to make the journey from Springfield on foot and passing about fifteen days en route. His arrival was in September and he remained in the wilderness country until the following February, when he returned on foot to Sangamon County, Ill., going thence to Ohio in the same manner. After about one year's stay in the Buckeye State he again came to White County and was engaged in farming until 1863. Going to Missouri he worked there at farm labor also, and in 1865 settled permanently on the farm where he now lives. His career since that time has been one of which he need not feel ashamed. Mr. Burns was born in

WHITE COUNTY.

Washington, D. C., in 1814, being a son of Thomas and Katie (Larner) Burns, of Irish descent. Thomas Burns was a laborer, and after marriage settled in Washington, where he died from the cholera, in 1833. His wife had preceded him a few years. Patrick was reared up to ten years of age in Washington, and then passed his time on a farm in Virginia, attending the subscription schools of that State. He went to Ohio in 1835, but one year later removed to Morgan County, Ill. Three years following he became settled in Sangamon County, Ill., his home until 1844. His subsequent travels have been noticed. Mr. Burns first opened up a farm of 120 acres here, which he has given to Mr. Sparrow, his father-in-law. Mr. Burns was married in 1850, in Pulaski County, to Edith Sparrow, a native of North Carolina. He was formerly a member of the Grange, and is now connected with the Agricultural Wheel.

George T. Burton, like so many agriculturists of White County, Ark., is also engaged in fruit culture, and has been exceptionally successful in these occupations. His birth occurred in Indiana, in 1849, and he is one of nine children born to Eli and Mahala (Conley) Burton, the father having been born in North Carolina in 1812, the youngest child of John P. and Mary Burton, who were born in the "Old North State." After living in his native State until he reached manhood, he moved to Indiana, settling in Lawrence County, where he followed farming and coopering and was married in 1834, his wife being a daughter of John Conley, who was born in North Carolina and came to Indiana at an early day. They reared a large family of children: Simpson, Wiley G., Catherine, Rebecca, Isom, John W., William H., George T. and Milton P. The father is a Republican in politics, and has held many public offices in the State of Indiana, and is still living. His wife died in 1852. George T. Burton received his education in the State University of Indiana, and in 1872, started out in life for himself, following the occupations of farming and fruit growing, which callings have received his attention up to the present time. After his marriage, in 1877, to Miss Mary E. Bundy, a daughter of William and Sarah (Cobbell) Bundy, of that State, he came to White County, Ark., and bought a farm of 160 acres, seventy-five acres of which he devotes to corn and fruit of various kinds, being especially successful in the cultivation of strawberries and grapes. He takes a deep interest in all matters pertaining to the good of the county and is agricultural reporter of White County for the Government. He is an earnest member of the Baptist Church and politically is a Republican. His children are: Eli N., Morton, Ethel B. and Benjamin H. Mr. Burton is a Mason and is a demitted member of the Grand Lodge of the State.

Robert W. Canada, a well-to-do farmer and stockman, residing near Beebe, Ark., has been a resident of White County for a period of time. He was born in Madison County, Tenn., April 3, 1829, and is a son of Hugh and Melissa R. (Duckworth) Canada, who were born in North Carolina, in 1808 and 1810, respectively. They were married in 1828, and in 1832 removed from Madison to Haywood County, Tenn., and here the father's death occurred in 1856. Their children are Robert W., Catherine (born January 1, 1831, and died at the age of four years), William J. (was born on May 16, 1833, and lost his life in the Confederate service, being killed in the battle of Atlanta, in 1864, and is now filling an unknown grave), Joseph V. (was born April 16, 1835, and died February 17, 1879, a farmer of White County), James R. (was born July 27, 1837, and died at El Paso in December, 1879, a merchant by occupation), John F. (who was born February 8, 1840, and died at Okolona, Miss., in 1863, being a soldier in the Confederate army), Alpha C. (was born April 16, 1842, and died August 8, 1881, the wife of A. L. Fisher, a farmer of Union Township), Mary E. (was born February 21, 1844, and is the wife of Richard Hill, a farmer of El Paso, Ark.) and Miles C. (who was born on September 20, 1846, and is now a farmer near Stony Point). Robert W. Canada spent his youth on his father's farm and attended the old subscription schools of his youth. At the age of twenty-one he began life for himself, and spent the first few years of his freedom as an overseer. This he followed in connection

HISTORY OF ARKANSAS.

with farming until coming to White County, Ark., and a few months later entered 160 acres of land three miles east of El Paso, which he began to develop. Four years later he sold this farm and bought eighty acres near Beebe, but after residing here a term of four years he went to Illinois, and there made his home during 1865. In 1867 he made the purchase of his present farm of 100 acres, and by good management has increased his acreage to 500, and has 200 acres under cultivation, his land being well adapted to raising corn, cotton and fruits. Small grain does well also, and strawberries grow to perfection and are one of his most profitable crops. Since his residence in the State he has cleared over 200 acres of land and has built more good barns than any other man in the section of White County. Although his principal occupation has been farming he has been engaged in other occupations at different times, and in 1873 erected a livery stable in Beebe, the first establishment of the kind ever erected there. He managed this a few months and at the same time acted as constable, and later served as justice of the peace for eight years. In 1882 he kept a grocery in Beebe and during this time, and for three subsequent years, he acted in the capacity of postmaster of the town, having received his appointment in 1881. He has been a Republican since that party has been in existence, but he has never been an office seeker. He is a member of Beebe Lodge No. 145, of the A. F. & A. M., and has held all the offices of his lodge with the exception of Senior Warden. He is a member of the Agricultural Wheel, and is one of the influential men of the county, and although he differs from the most of the citizens in his political views, yet he is highly esteemed and his opinions respected. When Gen. Grant was elected to the presidency Mr. Canada was the only man in Union Township who voted for him. He has always been an advocate of schools and has contributed liberally to the building of churches, school-houses and to the general improvement of the county. October 28, 1851, he was married to Miss Mahala Hendrix, a native of Hardeman County, Tenn., born October 24, 1838, a daughter of William and Nancy

(Clements) Hendrix, who removed from their native State of South Carolina to Tennessee in 1856, and were among the pioneer settlers of White County. The children of Mr. and Mrs. Canada are Sonora E. (born October 27, 1852, and died December 7, 1856), Almeda (born November 10, 1855, and died June 3, 1857), William R. (born April 26, 1858; is a merchant in business with C. A. Price, of Beebe), Joseph B. (was born September 17, 1860, and is a farmer of Union Township), Martha A. (was born October 15, 1869, and is a school teacher, residing with her parents) and Mary M. (who was born September 24, 1874, and died August 29, 1876). Mr. Canada has given all his children good educational advantages, and he and his family attend the Methodist Episcopal Church, South, he having been a steward in that church for the past thirteen years. Mr. Canada's mother still lives and makes her home with him.

R. W. Carnes, sheriff, Searcy, Ark. This gentleman was elected to his present office in September, 1888, and has filled that position in a capable and efficient manner ever since. He owes his origin to Carroll County, Tenn., where his birth occurred in 1849, and is the second in a family of five children born to John D. and Sarah (Dunn) Carnes, natives of Tennessee. The father was a physician and surgeon and died in Tennessee in 1857. He took quite an active part in politics in the early history of the country. The mother came to White County, Ark., in 1868, settled on a farm near Searcy, and here her death occurred in 1885. Of their family five are now living: R. W., Barbara A. and Alice (now Mrs. Magness), still residing in White County. R. W. Carnes passed his early life in duties upon the farm and in securing an education in the common schools of Tennessee. In 1868 he came to White County, following farming until 1882, when he engaged in general merchandising at Centre Hill, White County, and there continued for three years. In 1885 he embarked in the same business at Searcy, and continued at that for some time. He is not very active in politics, but votes independently and for the best man in the county, and in national affairs votes with the Democratic party. He is also deeply

WHITE COUNTY.

interested in educational affairs and is a member of the school board. Socially he is a member of Searcy Lodge No. 49, A. F. & A. M., and has been Worshipful Master of the lodge. He was married in White County in 1875 to Miss Anna Montgomery, a native of White County and daughter of J. W. and Ophelia A. (West) Montgomery, the former of North Carolina and the latter of Monroe County, Ark. The father is now deceased. Mrs. Montgomery resides on a farm. Mr. Carnes lost his wife in 1880 and was left with two children: Anna Belle and John D. His second marriage took place in White County in 1884, to Miss Elnora Neelly, a native of White County and daughter of Samuel D. and Sally (Montgomery) Neelly, natives of Tennessee and North Carolina, respectively. Her parents came to White County in 1855, and there their deaths occurred a number of years ago, the mother in about 1874, and the father in 1885. They were the parents of three children: Sally Mattie, Neelly and an infant. Mr. Carnes has seen many changes in the country since coming here in 1868, and has always taken an interest in the country. He is one of the prominent and representative men of the county.

William H. Carodine, known to be reliable and honorable, is a liveryman and planter of White County, and a native of Mississippi, being born October 3, 1843, in De Soto County. His father, William Carodine, was born in Tennessee, but immigrated to Mississippi, where he married Miss Emily Hall, also of Tennessee. Soon after their marriage they came to Arkansas (in 1860) and settled first in White County, but subsequently moved six miles west of Beebe, and in 1873 moved two miles south of this town, where the remainder of their life was spent. William H. was reared on a farm and passed his boyhood days in the pioneer schools, obtaining a good education there and in the common schools of Mississippi and Arkansas. In 1862 he started out in this world for himself, their first venture from home being to enlist in the Confederate army, under Col. Glenn McCoy's brigade, in which he served four years. He was in the battles of Prairie Grove, Pilot Knob, Jefferson City, Boonville, Lexington, Independence,

and at Wilson's Creek, in Missouri. He was with Price on his raid through Missouri, and also at the battle of Helena, where he was slightly wounded, but during his entire service in the war he was never once captured. At the time of the final surrender he was home on a furlough. At the close of the struggle Mr. Carodine rented a farm and began working it with nothing but his own exertion to depend on, yet it is not strange that he succeeded, for with his great determination of purpose, the lack of "filthy lucre" would not prevent him at least from making an attempt to cope with the many hardships incident to his start in life. In October, 1867, he was married to Miss Elizabeth Massey, a native of Tennessee, but whose parents came to Arkansas in 1858. To their union three children have been born, two of them now living: Mary Jane, William (deceased) and Jones D. Shortly after his marriage Mr. Carodine purchased his father's homestead and conducted that place for several years, but in 1878 he traded his farm for town property in Indiana, which he still owns. It consists of a lot and good residence in Bainbridge, Putman County, Ind. In 1878 he bought what is known as the Massey place (160 acres) and took up his residence at that place, remaining there until the fall of 1888. He then purchased the rolling stock in the livery business, which he is now successfully conducting. In connection with his other property he now owns eighty acres of land, two miles east of Beebe, and of that farm fifty acres are cultivated. The farm is in an excellent locality, and is adapted to all kinds of crops. Since his residence in White County he has opened over 160 acres of land, and has done his full share in developing the country round him, and it is to his credit, be it said, that very few have done as much. In 1875 Mr. and Mrs. Carodine took an extended trip through Texas, for the latter's health, and after an absence of a year they returned, her health being greatly improved. Mr. Carodine thought Texas a very fair country, but concluded that, as far as he had been able to judge, Arkansas had no superior. He is a member of Beebe Lodge No. 146, A. F. & A. M., also at one time was a Wheeler. In his political views he

HISTORY OF ARKANSAS.

sides with the Democratic party. He has been a member of the school board for a number of years, and with his family worships at the Beebe Methodist Episcopal Church.

W. B. Carter, Searcy, Ark. Among the most skilled and reliable druggists of Searcy may be classed Mr. Carter, who is a member of the well-known firm of Carter & Son. This firm is doing a good business and carries a full line of drugs, chemicals and everything kept in a first-class drug store. He came to Searcy in 1851, engaged in the dry goods and boot and shoe business, where the Perry Block is building, then purchased a frame building across the street, and later moved to the north side of the public square, where he erected the second brick building in Searcy. At this time the firm title was Carter, McCanley & Co., under which it continued until some time during the war. From 1861 to 1865 Mr. Carter was out of business, and in 1867 he engaged in general merchandising under the firm name of J. C. McCanley & Co. He continued with him until 1873, when he embarked in his present business on the north side of the square, and in 1884 moved to his present location. Mr. Carter was born in Prince William County, Va., in 1822, and was the eldest in a family of six children born to James P. and E. J. (Davis) Carter, natives of the Old Dominion. The father was a planter and opened up a large farm in Virginia, where he remained until 1838 and then moved to Independence County, Ark., where he entered land and there passed his last days. His death occurred in about 1860. His wife died in 1876. Of their family these children are now living: W. B. (subject) and T. E. Carter (who is married and resides on a farm near Sulphur Rock, Ark.). W. B. Carter was early initiated into the duties of farm life, and received his education in the schools of Virginia. He moved to Pike County, Mo., in 1837, engaged in farm labor, and in 1838 moved to Independence County, Ark., where he engaged in agricultural pursuits. He purchased land in that county, but sold it and in 1851 came to Searcy, then a very small rough place, but soon after a class of settlers moved in and the town was soon built up. Mr. Carter was an enrolling officer

for some months during 1863, was taken prisoner and held during the winter of 1863 and 1864 at Johnstown Island. He was paroled in March of the last-mentioned year and taken to Point Lookout, thence to Richmond, and finally went on foot from Mississippi across the swamps to Southern Ark., where he joined the army. After the surrender he returned to Searcy. In 1867 he engaged in business continuously for thirty-four years, and is one of the oldest and most reliable merchants in Searcy. He is not active in politics but votes with the Democratic party, and held the office of justice of the peace for about four years. He was appointed postmaster under President Buchanan and served four years. He was married in White County in 1853 to Miss E. J. McCanley, a native of Tennessee, and the daughter of James and Mary (Fletcher) McCanley, natives of North Carolina. Her parents immigrated at an early day to Tennessee, and in 1851 came to White County, Ark., where both passed their last days. Four children were born to Mr. and Mrs. Carter: Ella (now Mrs. Patterson, of Little Rock), and W. F. (who is married and resides in Searcy) and two deceased. Mr. and Mrs. Carter are members of the Methodist Episcopal Church, South, and socially Mr. Carter is a member of the Searcy Lodge No. 49, A. F. & A. M., of which he has been secretary and warden for many years. He is a member of Tillman Chapter No. 19, R. A. M., of which he is King. He is also a member of the council, and has been for some time.

Alfred T. Carter, a leading citizen and of an old and highly respected family, was a native of Mississippi, and was a son of Alfred and Drucilla (Willkins) Carter, of Tennessee nativity. Alfred Carter first saw the light of day in 1812, and lived in Tennessee (where he was married) until 1830, when he moved to Panola County, Miss., and in 1859 came to Arkansas, locating in White County, where his wife died in 1871, at the age of fifty-nine. He then married a Mrs. Conner, a widow, who is still living. The senior Carter was the father of seven children by his first wife, three of whom are still living: S. R. (a farmer of Logan County, Ark.), Alfred T. (our subject) and

WHITE COUNTY.

Sarah (the wife of W. H. Bailey). By his second marriage he became the parent of two children, both living: Fannie and Alfred. Mr. Carter belongs to the Methodist Episcopal Church, as did also his first wife. He died in 1878. Alfred T. Carter was born in Panola County, Miss., on February 3, 1851, but has resided in Arkansas since eight years of age. At the age of twenty he commenced farming for himself, and in the fall of 1870, bought forty acres of land in the woods, and began clearing it. He now is the owner of 280 acres, with ninety under cultivation, which he has made by hard work and economy. On August 28, 1870, he was married to Miss Emma Ward, also a native of Panola County, Miss., and who was born April 22, 1854. They are the parents of eleven children, six of whom are still living: Ella J., Sallie M., Albert J., George O., John T. and Penina. Mr. Carter is a prominent Democrat, and was elected to the office of constable in 1882, which office he held for six years. Mr. and Mrs. Carter belong to the Methodist Episcopal Church, South, of which he is trustee, and officiated as class leader for several years.

J. M. Cathcart, one of the members of the popular and well-known Enterprise Basket and Box Company, manufacturers of fruit and vegetable boxes, etc., was born in Elkhart County, Ind., in 1844, and was the youngest of three children born to B. F. and Joanna (Calkins) Cathcart, the former having been born in that State in 1818, his youthful days being also there. His children are Royal (who died in infancy) and Harrison (who served in Company K, Ninth Indiana Regiment, and was killed at the battle of Shiloh). The mother of these children, who was a daughter of Caleb Calkins, died in 1845, and the father married again, his second wife being a Mrs. Mary (Newell) Ireland, daughter of John and Mary (Crockett) Newell, a native of Kentucky. She bore him one child, J. F., who resides in Arkansas, and is in business with our subject, J. M. Cathcart. After her death he wedded Sarah J. Calkins, an aunt of his first wife, the children of this marriage being Anna and Royal W. and Rosa (twins). Mr. Cathcart is still living, but his par-

ents, James and Paulina, have long been dead. J. M. Cathcart's youth was spent in following the plow on his father's farm in Indiana, and in attending the district schools, but these sober pursuits he put aside upon the opening of the Rebellion, and at the age of seventeen years he enlisted in Company C, Ninth Indiana Regiment, and after participating in a number of engagements he was captured and confined in the county jail at Stanton, Va., one month and in Libby two months. After being paroled he went back to Indiana, and was married there, in 1872, to Miss Anna Snyder, a daughter of William and Lavina (Knight) Snyder, natives of Pennsylvania. Mr. Cathcart was in the railroad business for about thirteen years, as clerk and station agent on the Lake Shore & Michigan Southern Railroad. Resigning his position as agent in 1881, he engaged in the manufacturing business with his brother, J. F., at Bristol, Ind. In 1885 they moved their machinery to White County, Ark., and established the Enterprise Basket and Box Company, known as the Cathcart Bros. They employ on an average about thirty hands, and during the fruit season have a much larger force. Mr. Cathcart is a member of the G. A. R., a Republican in his political views and is one of the aldermen of Judsonia. The junior partner of the firm, J. F. Cathcart, married Miss Flora Boyer, by whom he had two sons, John and James, born in 1880 and 1884, in Indiana. John F. spent his youthful days on a farm raising fruit and in attending the public schools of Indiana. He engaged in the manufacturing business while still a resident of his native State, and after coming to Arkansas in 1885, engaged in the same calling. He is the inventor of the Cathcart's ventilated berry case, which has proved a decided success. His wife, who is a member of the Methodist Episcopal Church, is a daughter of John and Hannah Boyer, the former a Pennsylvanian. Mr. Cathcart is an excellent musician and is the leader of the band in Judsonia.

R. W. Chrisp, farmer, Searcy, Ark. This prominent agriculturist owes his nativity to Gibson County, Tenn., where his birth occurred in 1835, and is the ninth of seventeen children born to the

HISTORY OF ARKANSAS.

union of William and Mary J. (Elder) Chrisp, natives of the Old Dominion. The father was a tiller of the soil, and moved to Rutherford County, Tenn., entered land, and there remained until 1831. He then settled in Gibson County, Tenn., and made that county his home until his death, which occurred in 1863. He was in the War of 1812, and took quite an active part in politics. His wife died in Searcy in October, 1884. Of their family the following children are now living: R. W., Frances W. (now Mrs. Lane, of Gibson County, Tenn.), Horace (married, and resides in Higginson Township) and L. M. (who is married, and resides on a farm in the last-named township). One son, John W., enlisted in the army from Gibson County, Tenn., was Gen. Pillow's commissary, and died of pneumonia in 1863, at Memphis, Tenn. Another son, William B., was a member of the One Hundred and Eleventh Tennessee Infantry, and after the war was a cotton factor of Memphis. His death occurred in 1870. Two other sons, Henry and Starks, were in Gen. Forrest's cavalry, and both died in 1883. R. W. Chrisp was early taught the duties of farm life, and received his education in the subscription schools of Tennessee. In 1857 he came to White County, Ark., then being a single man, and taught the Gum Spring schools during 1858–59. He was married in White County in the last-named year, to Miss Sarah F. Neavill, a native of Jackson County, Ala., and the daughter of Elihu and Margaret (Jones) Neavill, natives of Alabama. Her father was in the Florida War, came to White County in 1844, and was for many years engaged in farming and in the tannery business, becoming quite wealthy. His death occurred in 1851 and the mother's in 1887. They resided in White County for over forty years. After marriage Mr. Chrisp settled in Gray Township on a timber tract of land, which he rented for a few years, and then, in 1867, purchased 240 acres, partly improved. This he sold, and bought forty acres in the timber which he immediately commenced clearing, erecting buildings, and added to this land from time to time until he now has 280 acres, with 100 acres under cultivation, besides a home farm of twenty acres just outside the corpora-

tion. Mr. Chrisp lost his excellent wife, October 9, 1887. The result of this union was the birth of the following children: William H. (married, and resides on the subject's farm), Vinnie R. (at home, attending Galway College), James Everett, Henry Beecher and Benjamin Clark. July 4, 1861, Mr. Chrisp was elected second lieutenant of Company K, but held first position in the Seventh Arkansas Infantry, commanded by Robert Shaver. He was in the battle of Shiloh, after which the company was reorganized, and he came to Searcy to recruit for the Trans-Mississippi Department. He then entered the ranks as private in the cavalry, and was temporarily promoted to the rank of lieutenant-colonel in front of Helena. He was in the Missouri raid, participated in the battles of Pilot Knob, Ironton, Jefferson City, Newtonia and Mine Creek. He returned to White County, Ark., from Fayetteville, and engaged in farming, but later was occupied for about a year in merchandising in Searcy. He has taken an active part in politics, and although originally a Whig, votes with the Democratic party. He has taken an active interest in schools and has been a member of the school board for twenty years. In 1883 he was sergeant-at-arms for the State of Arkansas. He received the nomination for representative, but was declared disfranchised in the reconstruction days. Mr. Chrisp is a member of Searcy Lodge No. 49, A. F. & A. M., and is also a member of Tillman Lodge No. 19. He has been Worshipful Master of Searcy Lodge, and has held office in Chapter. He is practically a self-made man and all his property is the result of his own industry. Although fifty-five years of age he has never drank a drop of liquor.

Arthur Smith Claiborn, eminently fitted and well worthy to be numbered among the successful farmers and stockmen of White County, Ark., is a son of John B. and Perlina E. (Thomason) Claiborn, the former a Tennesseean of Irish descent and the latter a native of North Carolina. They were married in Tennessee, and in 1859 moved to Kansas, purchasing a partly improved farm, consisting of 160 acres, in Prairie County. After considerably improving this land they moved to White

WHITE COUNTY.

County, settling on a tract of railroad land, where the father died seven years later, September 17, 1874, his wife having died October 16, 1870. Their children are as follows: Mary Jane (who became the consort of L. D. Hendrickson, deceased, and is living in Kentucky with her five children), Millie C. (married Jasper Scott, and in 1856 moved to Illinois; her husband was killed at the battle of Nashville, in 1865, leaving her with six children), W. B. (was killed at Franklin, Ky., while a member of the Eighth Tennessee Regiment), Mary F. (was married to R. H. Ferguson, but died after having borne two children), John H. (residing in Texas, and by his wife, who was Miss Mary Ware, is the father of six children), Perlila C. (was wedded to John Hodges, and upon her death left two children), Pleasant T. (died at Jackson, Miss., while serving in the Confederate army), Arthur Smith (our subject), Thomas J. and Samuel B. Arthur Smith Claiborn was born in De Kalb County, Tenn., February 3, 1847, and was educated in the subscription schools of his native county, but it must be acknowledged that his advantages were very meager, and at the time he had attained his twenty-first birthday he had only received three months' schooling. He immediately began business for himself upon attaining his majority, and for two years raised crops of cotton and corn on shares, and at the end of this time was married to Miss Martha J. Hale, a native of Mississippi and daughter of Francis J. and Louisa (White) Hale, who were among the old settlers of Arkansas, having come to the State in 1859. Their marriage took place December 2, 1869, and of eight children born to their union seven are living: Elnora (born October 7, 1870), William B. (born August 20, 1872), James (born July 25, 1874), Mattie J. (born in September, 1876, and died in August, 1877), Annie (born October 16, 1878), Alcora (born March 28, 1882), Arthur S. (born February 27, 1885) and Aver A. (born February 26, 1886). After their marriage Mr. and Mrs. Claiborn settled on eighty acres of land belonging to the latter, and in 1876 Mr. Claiborn became able to purchase 116 acres of wild land, which he has improved and to which he has added

eighty acres. He now has seventy-five acres under cultivation, a good frame house, good barns and one tenant house. He rented his land on shares until this year (1889) but now rents for cash. Mr. and Mrs. Claiborn and two of their children, Elnora and William, hold memberships in the Methodist Episcopal Church, South, and Mr. Claiborn is a Democrat in his political views. He has always been a liberal contributor to the advancement of religious, social and educational institutions, and has also given generously to all enterprises which he deemed worthy of support.

Green B. Clay is a well-to-do farmer and stock raiser of Cadron Township, and was the youngest in a family of ten children of John and Diallia (Morris) Clay. Mr. Clay was a native of North Carolina. His family consisted of the following children: Nancy, Harriet, Louisa, Jackson M., Emily, Sarah, Susan, William H., Martha and Green B. (our subject.) He was reared on a farm in Tennessee, where he was born in 1827, and started out in life when he was sixteen years of age. In 1851 he was married to Mary W. Mizzells, a daughter of Miles and Elizabeth (Rooks) Mizzells. In 1868 Mr. Clay bought a farm in Tennessee. He subsequently sold it and moved to Arkansas, settling in White County, where he bought a farm of 560 acres, clearing about seventy-three acres. Mrs. Clay was the mother of eighteen children, eight of whom are still living: John M., Joseph H., Zacariah M., Francis M., James N., George A., Charles C. and Albert A. He was married the second time to Nancy E. Burton (nee Neal), a widow. To them have been given five children: Walter L., Nathan B., Stephen M., Neoma Parlee and an infant which is not named. Mr. and Mrs. Clay are members of the Missionary Baptist Church. He is a strong Democrat and a member of the County Wheel. He is deeply interested in all work for the good of the church, school or any public enterprise.

J. C. Cleveland, M. D., was born in Independence County, November 19, 1852, and is the son of Joseph and Elizabeth (Butcher) Cleveland, natives of Georgia and Alabama, respectively. Mr.

HISTORY OF ARKANSAS.

Joseph Cleveland moved to Alabama when a young man, where he was married and in 1852, he removed to Independence County, Ark. He served his county a number of times in an official capacity, and in 1873 he represented his county in the legislature. He served eighteen months in the Confederate army, during which time he was taken prisoner and held at Fortress Monroe eight months before he was exchanged. He was with Gen. Price in his raid through Missouri and Kansas. He was a Republican and belonged to the Masonic fraternity, in which he had taken the Royal Arch degree. He died in the early part of the year 1887, at Newport, Ark., at the age of sixty-one. Mrs. Cleveland is still living and a resident of Newport, Ark., and is the mother of eleven children, nine of whom still survive: Martha E. (wife of J. W. Kennedy), J. C. (our subject), Henry P. (a lawyer by profession), Mary A. (wife of J. D. Cantrell), Susan A. T. (wife of L. D. Bownds), James F., Charles E., Samuel and Edward. Dr. J. C. Cleveland began his career as a school-teacher in his nineteenth year, following that profession till 1883, when he began the study of medicine. He graduated from the Missouri Medical College in 1888, first having taken lectures at the Kentucky School of Medicine, Louisville. Dr. Cleveland was married, November 7, 1875, to Miss Nancy E. Vick, a daughter of Dr. T. A. Vick. She died in 1885, having had three children, only one of whom survives, Lavina E., who is still living with her father. Dr. Cleveland was again married, in 1886, to Miss Nannie F. Goad, who is the mother of one daughter: Susan Estella. Mrs. Cleveland is a member of the Methodist Episcopal Church, South. The Doctor is a member of the Masonic fraternity and a strong Republican. He is now a resident of Bald Knob, where he has built up a large and successful practice, and is an enterprising and highly respected citizen.

John D. Coffey is a well-known citizen of White County and was born in Macon, Fayette County, Tenn., June 19, 1838. His father, David P. Coffey, was a Presbyterian clergyman, and first saw the light of this world in Tennessee in November,

1805. He was given all the advantages for an education to be had at that time, and applied himself so assiduously to his studies, that he became an accomplished and finely educated gentleman. He was married in his native State November 12, 1835, to Miss Mary C. Cogville, a daughter of Charlie and Pollie Cogville, and to their union fourteen children were born, of which John D. is the second child and the oldest son. Of that family seven are now living, six residing in this State. The Rev. Coffey immigrated from Tennessee, in 1854, and located near Searcy, where he died in 1883, his good wife surviving him but two years. He was a member of the Masonic lodge, and also a Royal Arch Mason, and was the originator of the first church that was ever organized in Stony Point, the denomination being the Cumberland Presbyterian. This township, where John D. Coffey now resides, derived its title from his father, in whose honor it was named. John D. served in the late war on the Confederate side, and enlisted in 1861, in Douglas County, in Brown's Tennessee Regiment. His first hard fight was at the battle of Shiloh, and he also engaged in numerous other engagements. He was captured at Port Edson, but was soon after paroled, and at once returned home to claim his promised bride, Miss Malicia G. Harris. After his marriage Mr. Coffey returned to the war and accompanied Price on his raid through Missouri, and received his final discharge from service in 1865. To Mr. and Mrs. Coffey have been born a family of eight children: John H., Mary, Josephus, Lucy E., David P., Hugh, James S., Minnie C. Mr. Coffey has a good farm of forty acres, finely stocked, and with all the conveniences and modern improvements to make the home comfortable. Himself and wife are members of the Presbyterian Church, and highly respected by every one.

John Reed Coffey is a prominent farmer and miller of White County, Ark., and owes his nativity to the State of Tennessee, the date of his birth being December 19, 1856. His father, Wiley D. Coffey, was born in Bedford County, Tenn., October 6, 1827, where he received his education, and there married Narcissa A. Muse, August 5, 1850.

WHITE COUNTY.

Mrs. Coffey is a daughter of Richard and Margaret Muse, and a very estimable lady. To their union eight children were born, five of them now living: Mary C., John R., Richard H., Sarah H., Joseph H. The other three died in infancy. Mr. Coffey is a teacher and minister, and owns 286 acres of good land with 100 in cultivation. He immigrated from Texas to Arkansas in 1871, locating in White County, which has been his home ever since. When he came to this county his worldly possessions consisted of a team of horses and a wagon, but he is now worth $5,000, and a farm well supplied with all the necessary stock for its successful operation. Mr. Coffey has educated three of his children for teachers. He has held a membership in the I. O. O. F. and in the Wheel, but has severed his connection with the latter order. He served in the Confederate War, enlisting in 1862, in Company A, Forty-fourth Regiment, and received his discharge in the same year. J. Reed Coffey acquired his education at home by the aid of the fire light, and when twenty-one years old began life for himself, working for two years, then returned home and worked with his father to pay a debt that hung like the sword of Damocles over the old homestead. At the age of twenty-eight years he was married to Sarah A. Harriss, their marriage occurring in October, 1885. She was a native of Illinois, and a daughter of Johnson and Keziah Harriss. They are the parents of two children: Clifton B. and Robert L. He owns 400 acres of good land, which lies southeast of Bald Knob and is well stocked with all the necessary appurtenances required to operate a farm. He is a Democrat politically, and as might be supposed by his home surroundings of English descent. Mrs. Coffey is a member of the Baptist Church, and a favorite in her wide circle of acquaintances. Mr. Coffey richly merits the reward which has attended his efforts during life. Active, industrious and prudent, he enjoys wide respect.

William R. Cook, a man of no little prominence throughout White County, Ark., is a wealthy farmer, stockman and fruit grower, residing near Judsonia, and, although born in Tennessee in 1836, he has been a resident of Arkansas since 1848, although he first resided in Independence County. He was the eldest of six children, born to John and Ann (Anderson) Cook, the former of whom was born in that state in 1814, and was educated as a Methodist minister, being a son of William and Margaret Cook. He was married in Tennessee in 1835 and followed farming there until his removal to Arkansas, his wife bearing him in the meantime these children: William R., Mary, Eliza, Lavinia, Arkansas and Andrew. They took up land in Arkansas and here the father died in 1879, and the mother in 1872. The maternal grandparents were Anderson and Dorcas Clark, Kentuckians, who came to Tennessee at an early day. William R. spent his youth in Tennessee but received the most of his education in Arkansas, and in the year 1860 started out in life for himself. A year later he joined Company B, Seventh Arkansas Infantry, First Arkansas Brigade, and took part in the battles of Shiloh, Perryville, Murfreesboro, Big Creek, and was with Price on his raid through Missouri, and with Bragg in Kentucky. He received his discharge in 1865 and after coming home was married (in 1866) to Albina, a daughter of Thomas and Margaret (Price) Bownds, and by her became the father of four children: Ida, Ella, Maggie and John (the latter dying in 1881). Mr. Cook was the owner of 240 acres of land in Independence County, but sold this and removed to White County, purchasing 460 acres near Judsonia, of which he now has 225 acres under cultivation. He is a steward in the Methodist Episcopal Church, of which his wife is also a member. He belongs to Anchor Lodge No. 384, of the A. F. & A. M., and is Deputy Grand Lecturer of his district. In his political views he is a Democrat. In 1879 he was called upon to mourn the death of his wife, and he afterward espoused Isabel Sisco, a daughter of Zedichire and Thurza Sisco, the father a native of Alabama and the mother of Middle Tennessee. They came to Arkansas about 1838, and here Mrs. Cook was born. The father died in 1858 and the mother in 1862. Mr. Cook and his present wife have had two children, both of whom are now deceased: Reuben P. and Sterling, the former's death occurring in 1881 and the latter's in 1883.

HISTORY OF ARKANSAS.

Joshua J. Crow was attending school in this county at the time of the outbreak of the war, when he laid down his books, left family and friends to join the Confederate Army. He enlisted in Taylor's regiment of Texas troops, and later in the Second Trans-Mississippi Department, in the Second Arkansas Cavalry; also took part in the battles of Jenkins' Ferry, Helena, Poison Springs, Little Rock, and a number of other battles and skirmishes. After peace was once more declared he went to West Point and engaged in the mercantile business, remaining there until 1870, when he removed to Searcy and subsequently filled the position of traveling salesman for a wholesale grocery house at St. Louis, Mo., for the next six years. In 1876 he started in the saw-mill business which he still follows. In 1877 he was married to Miss Emma J. Jones, a daughter of B. F. and J. C. Jones, and is the mother of three children: Frank F., Norman and Norton B. Mr. Crow owes his nativity to Mississippi (being born in Marshall County, June, 1844) and is the son of Joshua B. and Lavinia (West) Crow, natives of Alabama. Mr. Crow, Sr., was born in 1810, and when a young man removed with his parents to Northern Alabama, where he resided until his marriage when he immigrated to Marshall County, Miss., and lived there until 1847, then came to De Soto County, same State, and in February, 1849, came to Arkansas, locating in White County. He was a passenger on the second steamboat which came up Red River. He was a Democrat in politics, a member of the Masonic order, and in religious faith belonged to the Missionary Baptist Church, as did also his wife, and was one of the best-posted men in regard to real estate in his county. His death occurred in 1866 and his wife's in the same year, at the age of fifty-three. They were the parents of eleven children, seven of whom are still living: Mrs. J. N. Cypert, Mrs. T. D. Hardy (of this county), Mrs. T. P. Boon (of Los Angeles, Cal.), Joshua J. (our subject), M. C. (of West Point), Mrs. J. R. Hardy (of Mississippi) and Miss Ella Crow (of West Point). The mother of our subject was a descendant of Gen. Israel Putnam, of Revolutionary fame. Himself and wife are connected with the Missionary Baptist Church, in which they take an active part. He owns 1,400 acres of fine farming land, and is a prominent Democrat in his county.

Jesse N. Cypert, is an attorney, at Searcy, Ark. Among the leading firms of attorneys in this city is the well-known one of Messrs. Cypert & Cypert, of which Jesse N. Cypert is the senior member. This gentleman is one of the pioneer settlers of Searcy, Ark., and was born in Wayne County, Tenn., in December, 1823, being one of eleven children, the result of the union of Jesse and Jemimah (Warthen) Cypert, the father a native of North Carolina, born 1781, and the mother of Pennsylvania, born 1783. The grandparents on the mother's side were of Welsh descent, and at an early day moved to North Carolina. Jesse Cypert, Sr., was married in 1802, then moved to Knox County, Tenn., where he farmed and resided until 1819, after which he moved to Wayne County, of the same State, and there his death occurred in 1858. He was a private in the War of 1812, Tennessee Volunteer, Carroll's brigade, and was in the battle of New Orleans under Gen. Jackson. He was sheriff and collector one term, and justice of the peace and member of the county court for a number of years. The mother died in 1857. Jesse N. Cypert's time in early life was divided between working on the farm, clearing and developing the home place, and in attending the subscription schools of Wayne County, Tenn., in a log-cabin with dirt floor, etc. Later he attended the district schools of that State. He then studied law in the office of Judge L. L. Mack, of Wayne County, and was admitted to the bar at Waynesboro, Tenn., in 1849. Subsequently he went to Walker County, Ga., engaged as clerk, and in May, 1858, came to Crittenden County, Ark., and began practicing at Marion. Here he remained for eight months, and in February, 1851, came to Searcy, Ark., where he began the practice of law and this has continued successfully ever since. In connection with this he also carries on farming. During the war, or in October, 1861, he served as captain of the Confederate army, Fifth Arkansas Battalion, and on the organization of the battalion at Pocahontas, Randolph County, Ark., in Octo-

WHITE COUNTY.

ber, Mr. Cypert was elected major. He was east of the Mississippi River, and after the battle of Shiloh he resigned and came home on account of health. Later he entered the commissary department, purchasing supplies for the troops, and was thus engaged until after the surrender of Little Rock. He was taken prisoner in October, 1863, detained at Little Rock about three weeks, and paroled as citizen the same month. He was in the convention that passed the ordinance of secession in 1861, and was a delegate to both conventions. He continued the practice of law after the war, and this has continued ever since. He has taken quite an active part in politics, votes with the Democratic party, and was a delegate to the convention that voted the State into the union in 1868. He was also in the convention in 1874 that furnished the constitution that the State is under now. Mr. Cypert was elected judge of the circuit court in September, 1874, and served eight years, two terms. Socially he is a member of Searcy Lodge No. 49, A. F. & A. M., Tillman Chapter No. 19, R. A. M. He was married in White County, in February, 1855, to Miss Sarah Harlan Crow, a native of Alabama, and the daughter of Joshua B. and Lavinia (West) Crow, natives of South Carolina. Her parents moved to White County, Ark., in 1849, settled on a farm near the present town of Kensett, and here the mother died in April, 1866, and the father in August of the same year. To Mr. and Mrs. Cypert were born three children, two living: Florence (now Mrs. W. M. Watkins, of Searcy) and Eugene (a partner in the firm of Cypert & Cypert, he having read law in the office of his father, and was admitted to the bar in 1884). The other child, Mary Alice, married H. A. Smith, a merchant of West Point. She died in February, 1886, and left one child, Eugene Austin, and the subject of this sketch is rearing this child. Mr. Cypert takes an active interest in all that pertains to the good of the county, and is one of the pioneers of the temperance cause. He ran for the legislature in 1854, on the temperance question and received a good number of votes. He was the first president of the Temperance Alliance, and served in that capacity

for two years. He is a member of the Methodist Episcopal Church, South, and Mrs. Cypert is a member of the Missionary Baptist Church.

J. W. Darden, the efficient and popular lumber manufacturer and flour-mill operator of Rosebud, is engaged in manufacturing all grades of lumber of oak and pine. He commenced this enterprise in 1861 within one mile of where he is now doing business. In connection with this business he is engaged in operating a flouring-mill, his establishment being the second of the kind erected in White County and the first one in this vicinity. He has been a resident of Arkansas since 1860, and since that date has been a resident of Kentucky Township, removing thither from his native State of Tennessee. He was born in Warren County in 1833 and was the fourth in a family of seven children born to Robert and Elizabeth (Woten) Darden, who were also of Warren County, and were there married. In 1855 they moved to Greene County, Mo., where Mr. Darden had a blacksmith shop for some years, and in 1864 they came to White County, Ark., where Mr. Darden followed the same calling and also that of farming, occupying himself with these callings until his death, in 1886, his wife's death occurring some two years previous. The following are the names of the surviving children: J. W., Elizabeth (now Mrs. Clymer, of Taney County, Mo.), Mattie (unmarried and a resident of Faulkner County) and Sarah (now Mrs. Williams, a widow, residing in Faulkner County). J. W. was educated in the schools of his native county and commenced life for himself by trading in stock. He remained with his father for one year after the latter's removal to Missouri, then returned to Tennessee and was married there in 1856 to Miss Nancy Layne, who was a native resident of that State. Her father, George Layne, was a farmer, and died in Tennessee in 1848, his wife, who was a Miss Aramintie Dickerson, removing with her daughter, Mrs. Darden, to Arkansas, and dying in White County in 1867. Upon the beginning of the Civil War J. W. Darden was detailed by the Confederate Government to operate his mill, and in this work he has continued for nearly thirty years. After purchasing land he be-

HISTORY OF ARKANSAS.

gan improving it, and now owns in this and adjoining counties 2,000 acres, with something over 100 acres under cultivation. He is rapidly converting his timber into lumber, and, although he lost about $10,000 by fire in 1875, he has retrieved this loss in a great measure and is now doing well. In politics he casts his vote with the Democratic party, yet is not an active politician. Socially he is an A. F. & A. M., belonging to St. Mary's Lodge No. 170. He also belongs to Tillman Chapter and Searcy Council. His wife is a member of the Baptist Church. To the union of Mr. and Mrs. Darden have been born four children: Allie (now Mrs. Dr. Moon, of Rosebud), William, Elzie and Lula.

Dr. James M. Davie, an able and learned physician, but now retired from the active practice of his profession, is engaged in farming and stock raising on his farm, which comprises 1,000 acres, about one mile southeast of Beebe. He has something like 400 acres under cultivation and a number of acres that is yet in its wild state and very heavily covered with timber. The soil is good and is well adapted to raising all kinds of grain, and besides this property he has about 1,000 acres of equally as good land in Prairie County. He was born in Pearson County, N. C., December 13, 1830, but in 1836 came with his parents to Madison County, Tenn., and there made his home until 1856, at which time he took up his abode in Arkansas. His father, Dr. George N. Davie, was born in North Carolina of Scotch-Irish descent, his wife, Sarah Coldman, a native of North Carolina, being of Welsh lineage. The paternal grandparents, Edward and Margaret A. (Yarbrough) Davie, the former a native of Scotland and the latter of England, eloped from England to America, coming to North Carolina, and were married here. On the Davie side the family are lineal descendants of Sir Humphrey Davy. Dr. George N. Davie was born in 1800, his wife in 1805, their marriage taking place in 1829 and their deaths in 1836 and 1883, respectively, Both were finely educated, and the father was a physician and surgeon of considerable prominence, and his early death left our subject an orphan at the age of six years. His early childhood was spent on a farm and in at-

tending the country schools, later entering higher schools, and at the age of twenty years was a pupil of the school at Huntsville, Tenn., having for a room-mate Dr. A. M. Westlake, of New York, who induced him to take up the study of medicine. They entered Jefferson Medical College, of Philadelphia, Penn., and after an attendance of two years in that institution, graduated in the class of 1854. The two following years Dr. Davie spent in traveling over the States of Arkansas and Texas, and in 1856 located in Hickory Plains, Prairie County, Ark., and there practiced his profession one year. In 1857 he purchased his present farm in White County, but in 1861 gave up farm work to organize a company of 125 men for the State service, and was chosen captain of the same. In 1862, seeing the need of the general army, he disbanded and reorganized his company, and became connected with the regular Confederate service. He was promoted several times, and when the war closed was colonel of the Thirty-sixth Arkansas Infantry. He was badly wounded in the battle of Helena, was slightly wounded at Prairie Grove, and for several months was on post duty at Camden, and with this exception participated in all the engagements of his command. Upon hearing of Lee's surrender he stacked arms, in Texas, and started for home, and in the latter part of July, 1865, was paroled at Little Rock. He resumed the practice of his profession, regained what he had lost during the war, and until 1874 was a successful practitioner of the county, since which time he has devoted his attention to farming with the above results. He is a Democrat on general principles, but is an independent voter, and although often solicited by his friends to run for office, has always refused to do so. He is a demitted member of Beebe Lodge No. 145, of the A. F. & A. M., and also belongs to the I. O. O. F., and was connected with the Agricultural Wheel. In October, 1859, he was married to Miss Emma Z. Bowling, a native of Tennessee, their union taking place in Obion County, but her death occurred in July, 1872, she having borne four children: George C. (an intelligent and well-educated young farmer of the county), Mattie (who died in infancy), Isom

WHITE COUNTY.

(who also died in infancy) and John C.   On April 2, 1874, Mr. Davie led to the altar Caroline M. Bowling, a sister of his first wife, but on December 26, 1881, she died of that dread disease, consumption.   His third union, on December 9, 1885, was to a Mrs. Hinson, a daughter of Major Thomas, one of the early settlers of Prairie County, Ark.

J. C. R. Davis is a prosperous general merchant of Rosebud, where he has been engaged in business since 1875.   His store building, which he erected in 1885, is a substantial frame building, 22x60 feet, and in addition to handling merchandise, he buys and ships cotton.   He has been a resident of White County, Ark., since 1874, coming from his native county of Barbour, Ala., being born in 1852.   He was the youngest of nine children given to John and Mary (Mooney) Davis, the former of whom was born in North Carolina, and the latter in Georgia.   Their wedding took place in the latter state in 1827, and later on they moved to Alabama (1846), and the father opened up a plantation.   He died in 1871 and his wife in 1878.   He and his father-in-law, Jacob Mooney, were participants in the Indian War of 1836, the latter being killed in battle.   J. C. R., our subject, was reared to farm life and was educated in the schools of Alabama, being married there January 6, 1875, to Eugenie Stevens, whom he brought with him to Arkansas.   By exercising judgment and ingenuity and prudence he has become the owner of 800 acres of land, lying in White, Cleburne and Faulkner Counties, and has about 200 under cultivation.   Although he affiliates with the Democratic party he is not an active politician, but being the people's choice for the office of constable, he filled that position during 1877 and 1878.   He is a Mason. In religion he and wife are members of the Missionary Baptist Church.   Their union has been blessed with six children, five of whom are living: John Green (who died in 1877 aged eleven months), Tay B., Ora O., Hattie C., Grover C. and M. E. Mrs. Davis is a daughter of Green and Margarette (McRae) Stevens.   The father was a planter and in 1871 came to White County, Ark.   Here he spent the remainder of his life, dying in 1885. His wife died in Alabama.

James D. Davis is a well-known farmer and stock raiser of Bald Knob, and came to Arkansas, locating in the woods of White County in 1871, when but nineteen years of age.   The first four years he lived with J. H. Ford, while he was clearing up his farm, after which his marriage to Miss Delanie Watters was solemnized.   She was born in Perry County, Ala., May 23, 1854, and is the mother of three children, two of whom are still living: William D. and Susie H.   Mr. Davis first saw the light of day in Perry County, Ala., on November 26, 1852, and is the son of Huriah and Tobitha (Morris) Davis, who were also natives of Alabama, and married in that State, residing there until after the war.   He enlisted in the Confederate army in 1861, in the Eighth Alabama Infantry, and died on the battlefield.   Mrs. Davis then removed in 1873 with her children to Mississippi, where they remained several years, subsequently coming to Arkansas and locating in White County, where they made their home with James D., who had preceded them several years.   In 1888 she went to live with a daughter at Springfield, Mo., where she now resides.   She was the mother of nine children, six of whom are still living: Frances (now Mrs. Goodnight, of Mississippi), William C. (of Logan County), Caroline (wife of William Green, of Logan County), James D. (our subject), Nancy (wife of James Finney, of Springfield, Mo.) and Thomas H. (a farmer of Pope County.)   Mr. and Mrs. James Davis are members of the Missionary Baptist Church, as were also his parents.   In politics he is a Democrat, and also belongs to the Agricultural Wheel.   He has been a very successful farmer and stock raiser, and deals in all kinds of live stock.

John D. DeBois is a distinguished attorney at law and real-estate dealer of Judsonia, Ark., of which place he has been a resident since 1871, coming from Henry County, Tenn., where he was born in 1848.   He was the elder of two children born to John and Mary C. (Guinn) DeBois, the former a native of West Virginia and the latter of North Carolina.   The father was reared in the "Buckeye State" and was married in Tennessee, the latter State continuing to be his home until his death

HISTORY OF ARKANSAS.

in 1851, he having been a harness-maker by trade, and after marriage directed his attention to farming. His wife died in June, 1888, at Judsonia, Ark. John D. DeBois spent his early life on a farm and received his education in the academy of Henry, Tenn., and in the schools of Lebanon, Ohio. Upon his removal to White County, Ark., in 1871 he engaged in the mercantile business at West Point and in 1872 came to Judsonia and for some time was associated with Dr. J. S. Eastland in the drug business. During this time he began the study of law under the preceptorship of Coody & McRae, and in July, 1878, was admitted to the White County bar and has practiced continuously ever since. Since 1880 he has been in the real-estate business and now owns about 1,000 acres of land, comprising six farms, and has from 350 to 400 acres under cultivation. Mr. DeBois is a Democrat and has been a member of the State and County Conventions at different times. Socially he is a member of the Anchor Lodge No. 384, of the A. F. & A. M. In December, 1872, he was married to Miss Mollie V. Hicks, a daughter of John T. and Martha W. (Heigh) Hicks, originally from North Carolina, who came to White County, Ark., in 1854, settling in Judsonia. Mr. Hicks was a physician and surgeon of many years' standing, and while serving in the Confederate army during the late conflict between the North and South, he received a gunshot wound in the knee (in 1863) from the effects of which he died. His wife survives him, making her home in Wylie, Tex. The children born to this marriage are James Tatum, Flora Blanche, Mary Martin, Iola Opal, Duke Howard (who died in January, 1887, at the age of twenty-two months), and Pattie. Mr. DeBois has taken an active interest in school matters and has served as a member of the school board. He belongs to the Methodist Episcopal Church, South, while his wife worships with the Missionary Baptist Church, being a member of that church.

John J. Deener is a native of Virginia, and is a son of John Jacob and Tobitha (Hamolen) Deener, natives of Virginia. Mr. John Deener, Sr., was born February 25, 1790, and learned the millwright's trade when a boy, and lived in Virginia, where he married, until 1836, when they removed to Fayette County, Tenn. He then engaged in farming, in which he was very successful. Mr. Deener died in 1867, and his wife in 1849 at the age of forty-four. They were members of the Methodist Episcopal Church, South, and were the parents of seven children, three of whom are still living: Martha Ann (wife of William A. Old, deceased), John J. (our subject) and James B. The paternal grandfather of our subject was John Jacob Deener, and a native of England, and came to this country during the Revolutionary War in which he took an active part, on the side of the Americans, and served under Gen. Washington and under Gen. Francis Marion. After the war he settled in Virginia, where he died, leaving three sons: George, John Jacob and William. The Deener family as a race are of small stature. John J. Deener, our subject, was born April 22, 1830, and received his education at the Macon Masonic College, and when nineteen years of age he left school and worked on a farm, and also engaged in clerking in a store. During the war he was occupied in teaching school. After the war he went into partnership with Samuel E. Garther, of Williston, Tenn., in the mercantile business, where he remained about six years, then removing to Arkansas and locating on the farm where he has since resided. In 1883 he was elected assessor of the county, and held the office four years, also officiated as justice of the peace for twelve years while in Tennessee. Mr. Deener was married on November 13, 1851, to Miss Sarah A. Gober, who was born in Franklin County, Ga., in 1832. They were the parents of four children: Eliza Hamblin (wife of George W. Dobbins), Lula A. (wife of S. S. Putty), Richard S. (a Methodist Episcopal minister) and John J. Mr. and Mrs. Deener are members of the Methodist Episcopal Church, South, in which they take an active part. Mr. Deener also belongs to the Masonic order, and is a strong Democrat.

G. W. Dobbins, county assessor, Searcy, Ark. Every life has a history of its own; and although in appearance it may seem to possess very little to distinguish it from others, yet Mr. Dobbins' career

WHITE COUNTY.

as a farmer and stock raiser, as well as his experience in the political affairs of the community have contributed to give him a wide and popular acquaintance with nearly every citizen of White County—if not personally, then by name—and serves to make his career a more than ordinary one. His birth occurred in Monroe County, Ark., in 1851, and was the second in a family of three children born to A. M. C. and Frances Ann (Carlton) Dobbins, natives of North Carolina. The father was a prominent physician and surgeon, and after his marriage, which occurred in his native State, he immigrated to Tennessee, and there followed his practice until about 1850. He then moved to Monroe County, Ark., settled at Clarendon, followed his profession there until 1857, when he went to Izard County and settled at Evening Shade. He remained there until March, 1860, when he moved to North Carolina. His wife died in Izard County, Ark., on January 1, 1860, and in the fall of 1861 he enlisted in the Thirteenth North Carolina Regiment and participated in the battle of Seven Pines, where he received a gunshot wound. He was taken prisoner at the second battle of Fredericksburg and confined at Rock Island, Ill., and was also confined at Johnstown Island, where he was paroled in June, 1865. He then returned to North Carolina, remained there until 1867, and then moved to Fayette County, Tenn., where he engaged in his practice. His death was caused by yellow fever in 1878. He was a strong temperance man. His children were named as follows: Frances Ann (now Mrs. Baxter, of Gray Township), G. W. and John M. (married and resides in Marion Township, White County). G. W. Dobbins was educated in the schools of North Carolina, and commenced for himself as a clerk in a store, where he remained two years with a salary of $8 per month. In 1869 he attended the Olin College, in Iredell County, N. C., and in 1870 went to Fayette County, Tenn., where he again engaged in clerking. This he followed until 1875 when, in that and the following year, he, in partnership with J. J. Deener, engaged in the mercantile business, thus continuing for nearly two years. He then followed farming in 1877, and

the same year came to White County, Ark., where he purchased and improved a farm of 180 acres, and now has sixty-five acres under cultivation. He is raising considerable stock. He is not very active in politics but votes with the Democratic party, also with the Wheel or County Alliance, and is a member of the Agricultural Wheel. He was elected county assessor in September, 1888, and has been deputy tax collector twice, in 1885 and 1886. He has also been deputy tax assessor two terms, in 1885 and 1888. He has been a member of the school board four years, and takes an active interest in educational affairs. He was married in Fayette County, Tenn., on August 26, 1873, to Miss Eliza H. Deener, a native of Tennessee, and the daughter of J. J. and Sarah A. (Gober) Deener, natives of Virginia and Georgia, respectively. Both are living at the present time, and reside in White County, whither they moved in 1877. To Mr. and Mrs. Dobbins were born these children: Lula Alma, Jessie Eva, Samuel Harold, George Milas, Mary Sadie, Shelly Gober and an infant. Mr. and Mrs. Dobbins are members of the Methodist Episcopal Church, and he has been church secretary since 1878. He takes a deep interest in church affairs.

Charles L. Douthat received his education at Buchanan, Botetourt County, Va., and when eighteen years old, was employed as salesman for nearly two years, and then worked at the tinners' trade for about three years. He then went to Memphis, Tenn., where he was employed as salesman in a wholesale grocery house, until 1859, when he came to West Point and started in the mercantile business, with a capital of a few hundred dollars, which he had saved out of his salary. In 1861 he enlisted in the Confederate army, in the First Arkansas State Troops, but which soon after disbanded, when he then joined Ben McCullock's First Arkansas Mounted Rifles, and was with that command until the close of the war. He was elected to take an official position, but preferred remaining in the ranks as a private. On coming out of the army, Mr. Douthat was financially broken, and again returned to Memphis, and was employed by a wholesale grocery house as sales-

HISTORY OF ARKANSAS.

man, where he remained about two years, then returned to West Point, and entered into business with W. C. West, and afterward with A. T. Jones, with whom he was engaged for three years, then running the business alone. He has built up a large trade, and carries a fine stock of goods. Mr. Douthat was born in Rockbridge County, Va., in 1831, and was the son of William H. and Susan (Lewis) Douthat, natives of Richmond, Va., and of Irish descent, the ancestors coming to this country before the Revolutionary War. Robert Douthat, the paternal grandfather of our subject, was the owner of the Rock bridge, or Natural bridge, and was the proprietor and builder of a large woolen mill, and brought many workmen from Ireland. William H. Douthat was a prominent Mason of Virginia, and died in 1858, his wife surviving him till 1883, at the age of seventy-two years. They were the parents of twelve children, nine of whom are still living: Mary J., Robert R., Charles L. (our subject), Henry C., Susan, Fielding (now a stock raiser in Montana), Warner L. (in California), Sarah and Annie (who still lives in Virginia). In 1866 C. L. Douthat was married to Mary C. Whitney, who was born in Fayette County, Tenn., in 1842. They are the parents of three children: Effie L., Alma and Charles W., all of whom are at home. Mr. Douthat and family are members of the Methodist Episcopal Church, South. He is a strong Democrat, and a prominent citizen of West Point.

William T. Dowdy, a sharpshooter in the late war, came to White County in 1855 with his father, who bought 320 acres of wild land and commenced improving it, and cleared up forty or fifty acres before the war. His father, Andrew J. Dowdy, was a native of North Carolina and came to Tennessee when he was a young man, where he was married, in 1835, to Sarah Sutherland, of Tennessee origin, and a daughter of Thomas Sutherland. After his marriage he was employed as overseer on a plantation for thirteen years. He was the father of three children: Anna E. (afterward Mrs. Barger), William T. (our subject) and James S. (deceased). William T. owes his nativity to Western Tennessee, being born in 1839, and spending his younger days in that State. He was married in White County, in 1860, to Emeline E. Barger, a native of Tennessee, and who died on December 10, 1860. He was married the second time on April 17, 1866, to Elizabeth Sessums, also of Tennessee. They are the parents of four children, two of whom are still living: Richard A. (editor of the Economist at Searcy, Ark.) and James A. Mr. Dowdy enlisted in 1861 for twelve months, and afterward for four years or during the war, in Company D, of the Thirty-first Arkansas Infantry, and was one of the Confederate sharpshooters who did such valuable service for the Confederate cause. He took an active part in the battles of Corinth, Stone River, Chickamauga and a number of others, and was taken prisoner on July 22, 1864, near Atlanta, Ga., and then to Camp Chase, Ohio, when he was released on parole, February 12, 1865, and went to Richmond, where he received a furlough. He then went to Western Tennessee, where he remained until the close of the war. He then returned home and has since engaged in farming. He owns a farm of 200 acres, with sixty-five acres under cultivation. Mr. and Mrs. Dowdy are members of the Methodist Episcopal Church, South. Mr. Dowdy is also connected with the County Wheel, of which he has been chaplain since first entering the society. He is also a constituent of the Centre Hill Lodge No. 114, of the Masonic order. Mrs. Dowdy was a daughter of Richard J. and Rachel (Little) Sessums. Mr. Sessums was born in North Carolina in 1805 and died in 1863. He was married in 1833, and was the father of five children.

R. A. Dowdy is editor and publisher of The Arkansas Economist, the official journal of the Farmers' and Laborers' Union of Arkansas, Searcy, Ark. Mr. Dowdy has had charge of the paper since its name was so called, or during 1889. It was made the official organ July 26, 1889, at Hot Springs, and it has quite a circulation and is building up a good State circulation. Prior to the above-mentioned date it was a local paper. Mr. Dowdy took charge of the paper in May, 1888; was partner until April 1 of the following year,

WHITE COUNTY.

when he purchased the full interest in it. The paper was organized in October, 1887, under the name of "White County Wheel," and remained thus until after the meeting at Hot Springs, when it was issued under the present name in August, 1889. Mr. Dowdy was born in Des Arc Township, White County, Ark., in 1868 and is the eldest in a family of four children born to the marriage of William T. and C. E. (Sessums) Dowdy, natives of Tennessee and Kentucky, respectively. The father came to White County, Ark., in 1859, settled in Des Arc Township, and here met and married Miss Sessums. Both are now living and reside in White County. R. A. Dowdy received his education in the district schools, and then took a course in Quitman College in 1885. After leaving college he engaged in teaching in Cleburne County for a few terms but later engaged in editorial work on his present paper. Socially, Mr. Dowdy is a member of the Farmers' and Laborers' Union, and takes a deep interest in all things pertaining to the good of the county.

T. A. Duncan enjoys the reputation of being not only a substantial and progressive farmer, but an intelligent and thoroughly posted man on all matters of public interest. In his dealings with his fellow-men he has been upright and honorable, and his character will stand any investigation which may be given it. His native birthplace was Jackson County, Ala., where he first saw the light of day in 1830, he being the eldest of eight children born to Jesse and Nancy E. (White) Duncan, who were Tennesseeans, the father reared at Nashville and the mother near Winchester. They were married in Tennessee and at an early day removed to Alabama, and here Jesse Duncan followed the occupation of millwrighting and erected one of the first mills in the county, also opening a large plantation. He died in 1884 and his wife in 1883. Their children are: T. A. (living in White County, Ark.), W. R. (who is married and resides in Texas), James H. (married and living in Alabama), J. C. (married and living in Kansas), Mary (Mrs. Selby, living near Iuka, Miss.) and Elizabeth (who also resides at Iuka). T. A. Duncan's early life was like the majority of farmers' boys, and he assisted

his father in clearing up the home farm and began that work for himself at the age of nineteen in Alabama. He was married in Jackson County, of that State, in January, 1849, to S. B. Pace, and upon the opening of the war he enlisted from Jackson County in the Confederate army, for three years, or during the war, becoming a member of Berry's artillery. He was in the battle of Peach Orchard Gap (Ga.), Jackson (Miss.), Resaca, and was taken prisoner at Spanish Fort and sent to Ship Island and afterward to Vicksburg. Upon being paroled in 1865 he returned to Jackson County, Ala., and in 1872 came to White County, Ark., and bought a timber tract of 180 acres which he began clearing and upon which he erected good buildings. He has 110 acres of his 400-acre farm under cultivation, all of which he has cleared since coming to the county. He is a Democrat, has been magistrate nine years, and taken an interest in the finance of the county, which was in bad shape at that time, and succeeded in settling affairs. He is also a member of the school board, and has always taken a deep interest in school matters. He and wife are the parents of the following children: William F. (who is married and resides in White County, Ark.), Cassie (who died in 1885 at the age of twenty-eight years, was married to Mr. Holleman), B. E. (who is married and lives in the county), J. J. (married and living in Cleburne County), Minta (who married A. J. Holleman after the death of Cassie, and lives in White County, Ark.), Nancy (Mrs. J. F. Lawrence), C. A. (who married F. W. Raney, and also lives in White County), Mila and Jo (still with their parents). Mrs. Duncan's parents, William and Elizabeth (Wininger) Pace, were both members of old Virginia families, and moved to Alabama about the year 1827, being among the earliest to enter land in that State. The father died in 1870 and his wife one year later.

James Dupriest is a farmer and ginner of Marshall Township, and owns 850 acres of land, of which 300 acres are under fence, 200 in pasture, and 100 acres under cultivation. He is a native of Georgia, his birth occurring in 1821. His father, Martin Dupriest, was also of Georgia

HISTORY OF ARKANSAS.

origin, where he was educated and subsequently married, and to this union was born a family of eight children. James D. was a twin, being sixth in order of birth and a prosperous boy. He lived in Georgia until 1840, when he moved to Alabama with his father, locating in Coosa County and there remained seventeen years. He was married to Sarah Malcolm and moved to Arkansas in 1856, and by her had two children who died in infancy. His wife died in 1864 and in 1865 was married to his second wife, Mrs. Louisa Henry, and to this union has been born a family of seven children: Ebbie, Burton, Thomas, Cathron, Cullen, McFerrin, Joseph. His second wife had one son by her first marriage, Fenton Henry, he being a thoroughly and highly educated man. James Dupriest honors the Democrats with his vote and takes quite an interest in politics though not an enthusiast; he is also a Mason, belonging to the Blue Lodge. Himself and wife worship with the Methodist Church to which they belong.

Dr. J. S. Eastland is one of the foremost physicians and surgeons of White County, Ark., and his practice lies among the wealthiest and most intelligent people of the county. He has been a resident of Judsonia since March, 1872, having, prior to this, been a resident of Richland County, Wis. He was born in Hinds County, Miss., December 18, 1844, and was the second of a family of ten children born to David J. and Mary E. (Cameron) Eastland, the father born in Genesee County, N. Y., and the mother in Hinds County, Miss. When a young man the father went to the vicinity of Schoolcraft, Mich., and at the age of twenty years removed to Mississippi, and was engaged in teaching school in an academy at Cayuga, and was married there about the year 1841. From 1852 until the present time he has been engaged in milling in Richmond County, and is making his home on a large farm which he purchased near Sextonville. Dr. J. S. Eastland was about eight years old when he was taken to Wisconsin, and he received his education in the schools of Richland County. In 1863 he enlisted at Madison, Wis., in Company H, Seventeenth Wisconsin Infantry, and was assigned to the Army of the Tennessee. He

was a participant in the engagements at Chattanooga, Resaca, Buzzard's Roost, Kenesaw Mountain, and was with Sherman in his memorable march to the sea, and in the Carolina campaign. He was at the grand review at Washington, D. C., but received his discharge at Madison, Wis., in June, 1865. After returning home he began reading medicine, and took a course in the Eclectic Medical Institute during the winter of 1869–70. The following year he entered Blakely Hospital of Philadelphia, Penn., and after graduating the same year he came to Arkansas, taking up his abode in Randolph County, but only remained there until 1872, since which time he has been a resident of White County. In September, 1886, he opened a fine drug store at Judsonia, which is in a flourishing condition, and in addition to managing this establishment and practicing his profession, he is employed as surveyor of the Iron Mountain Railroad. He is a Democrat, a member of the board of medical examiners of White County, and socially is a member of Anchor Lodge No. 384, of the A. F. & A. M., and was Worshipful Master of the lodge for some years. He was married in White County, in 1873, to Miss Samantha W. Boatwright, a native of White County, and a daughter of Charles W. and Virginia (Subbaugh) Boatwright, who were natives of Virginia. In 1856 they settled at West Point, White County, Ark., but Mr. Boatwright is now residing at Jonesboro, Ark. The mother died in 1889. When Dr. Eastland first came to White County the country was, in a great measure, unsettled, and there was a great deal of sickness among the settlers, but it is now much healthier. Mrs. Eastland is a member of the Baptist Church.

J. W. Edie. Among the early settlers of Judsonia will be found the name of J. W. Edie, who came from Buchanan County, Iowa, and settled in the town in 1873. After following the lumber business for some twelve years he began making a specialty of sash, doors and blinds, and does an extensive business. He was born in Harrison County, Ohio, December 6, 1834, and is the eldest of two children born to Thomas and Levina (Palmer) Edie, who were born in the "Keystone

WHITE COUNTY.

State." They immigrated to Ohio with their parents in 1819 and 1821, respectively, and were married in that State in February, 1834. The father was a farmer, and followed that occupation both in Ohio and after removing to Iowa in 1853, in the latter State paying much of his attention to the manufacture of lumber also. These occupations received his attention until his removal to Judsonia in 1877, and from that time until his death, in February, 1883, he lived a retired life. His wife survives him. The paternal grandparents, James and Mary (Ward) Edie, were born in Pennsylvania and England, respectively, and settled in the State of Ohio, in 1819; the great-grandfather was a Scotchman. The maternal grandparents, James and Margaret (Arnold) Palmer, were born in Maryland, and moved to Ohio in 1821, from which State they removed to Iowa in 1853, making the latter their home until his death in 1857, at the age of eighty-one years. He was a soldier in the War of 1812. His wife died, in 1868, at the age of eighty-three years. The children of Thomas and Levina Edie are: Margaret (now Mrs. Wagner, of Judsonia, whose husband is in the Government employ) and our subject (who was reared on his father's farm and received his education in the schools of Ohio. After his removal to Iowa with his parents, he resided there until 1856, when he was married, in Buchanan County, to Miss Rebecca J., a daughter of Joseph and Mary (Garner) Chitester, of Pennsylvania. The father was a millwright, and in 1845 moved to Shawneetown, Ill., and, in 1850, to Iowa. Since 1885 they have resided in Judsonia, Ark., and have passed the sixtieth milestone of their wedded life. After his marriage, Mr. Edie made his home in Iowa until 1873, then came to Judsonia and engaged in business as mentioned above. He is not an active politician, but votes the Democratic ticket, and has been mayor of the town in which he lives three terms, and has also been a member of the city school board. Socially he is a member of Anchor Lodge No. 384, of the A. F. & A. M., and has been Worshipful Master of his order. He belongs to Tillman Chapter No. 19, and Occidental Council No. 1. Mr. and Mrs. Edie are worthy members of the Baptist Church, and their union has been blessed in the birth of eight children, seven being now alive: Silas A. (died in 1878, at the age of twenty-two years), C. F. (is unmarried, and is an engineer on the Denver & Rio Grande Railroad), Ida (now Mrs. McDearman, lives in Judsonia), T. M. (is married, and lives in the town; a carpenter and joiner by trade), Ada Aletha (Mrs. Sims), A. J. (a resident of Little Rock), Eva (Mrs. Croy, of Darke County, Ohio) and Stella. Mr. Edie is public-spirited, and is a member of the board of directors of the Judsonia University.

William H. Edwards. Among the many old settlers of White County, Ark., there is none more highly esteemed than the subject of this sketch, for in his walk through life he has been honest and upright in every particular. He was born in Madison County, Tenn., August 7, 1811, and is a son of Sanford and Mary (Thetford) Edwards, both of whom were born in Greenville District, S. C., the former in 1787 and the latter in 1805. They were married in Tennessee, reared their family in the western portion of that State and there spent their lives, the father's death occurring in 1874 and the mother's in 1869. They were members of the Methodist Episcopal Church and he was a soldier in the War of 1812, and in his political views was an old line Whig, but was not an enthusiast in politics, being one of those quiet men whose life was without reproach. Their family was as follows: Nancy (deceased, was born in 1806 and became the wife of a Mr. Fussell), Anderson (deceased, was born in 1808), William H. (the subject of this memoir), James F. (deceased, was born in 1814 and died in May, 1889, a farmer of White County), Rebecca (deceased, was born in 1817, and was the wife of James Stowbuck, a blacksmith of Tennessee), Ina (deceased, was born in 1819), Joseph (was born in 1822, and is a farmer of White County), Elizabeth (was born in 1823 and is the wife of Enoch Terry, of Texas), Sophronia (deceased, was born in 1828 and is the wife of William Tedford), and Sanford (who was born in 1831 and is a farmer of Tennessee). William H. Edwards received very poor chances for acquiring an education, owing to the newness of the country

HISTORY OF ARKANSAS.

during his youth and to the fact that his services were required on the home farm. On June 4, 1835, he was married to Miss Lucinda Dockins, and to them were born the following children: James M. (a farmer of White County, born in 1836), William L. (born in 1837), George W. (born in 1839) and Mary E. and Rebecca J. (twins, born in 1841, Rebecca being the widow of James Powers). Mrs. Edwards died in 1844 and January 28, 1846, Mr. Edwards married Lucinda Wilson, daughter of James Wilson. She was born in Tennessee in 1825 and by Mr. Edwards became the mother of four children: Sarah Ann (born in 1847 and died the same year), Joseph M. (residing near his father, was born in December, 1848), Susan A. (was born September 26, 1851, and died August 1, 1852), an infant (died, unnamed) and Noah A. (who was born November 15, 1854, and is a farmer of this county). After his marriage Mr. Edwards worked for his father two years and then began tilling his father's farm for himself, continuing until 1852, when he purchased a farm of his own, on which he resided for seven years. Since that date he has resided in White County, and in 1860 purchased the farm of 160 acres where he now lives. He has seventy acres under cultivation and his farm is well adapted to raising all kinds of farm produce. He was reared a Whig, but since the war, in which he served on the Confederate side three years, he has been a Democrat. He became a Mason at Stony Point twenty-six years ago, but is at present a member of Beebe Lodge No. 145, A. F. & A. M., and has held every office in that order. He is also a valued member of the Agricultural Wheel and has always taken hold of every movement that had for its object the social or educational welfare of the community in which he resided. He has ever lived in peace and harmony with his neighbors and he and family are worthy members of the Methodist Episcopal Church.

Thomas J. Edwards. Hayden S. Edwards, the esteemed father of the subject of this memoir, was born in Shelby County, Ky., on April 2, 1811, and was a son of Rev. James P. Edwards, one of the first Baptist ministers that came to the State of Arkansas. He was also a surveyor and came to this State to assist a corps of engineers, and was over a large part of the State. Hayden S. was married to Miss Mary Lumkins, a native of Knox County, Tenn., on January 26, 1832, and in 1853 removed to Arkansas, locating in White County, on the farm now owned by his son, Thomas J., who took charge of the farm and cared for his parents the latter years of their lives. Hayden Edwards was a school-teacher in his younger days, and also served in the Mexican War as wagon master. He was a strong Democrat and a member of the Masonic order, and was connected with the Missionary Baptist Church, as was also his wife. He died in 1887. His wife was born in 1815, and died in 1882, leaving a family of six children, Thomas J., the principal of this sketch, being the only one living. He was born in Ballard County, Ky., on April 17, 1841. In 1861 he enlisted in the Confederate army, under Col. Patterson, and took part in all of the battles in the Missouri raid. He was wounded at Little Rock, and was taken prisoner but soon escaped. After the close of hostilities he returned home and found his family stripped of every thing of value, and as he was without means he was obliged to start from the beginning, but with a will that overcame all obstacles has risen to an eminence of success, and is now the owner of 280 acres of land in the old homestead and eighty south of Bald Knob, and has about 130 under cultivation. In 1884 he was married to Miss Ida N. Maxwell, a daughter of Joseph Maxwell, and who is the mother of one daughter, Mary Stokes, who was born February 5, 1885. Mrs. Edwards is a member of the Methodist Church. Mr. Edwards is a Democrat and a prominent citizen of White County.

James H. Edwards, one of White County's leading citizens, is a son of James and Eliza (Simmon) Edwards, natives of Haywood County, Tenn., who moved to Arkansas in 1850, and located in White County, and later moved to Cleburne County, where Mr. Edwards, Sr., still lives, in his sixty-eighth year. He is a member of the Missionary Baptist Church, and also of the Masonic order. He is still engaged in farming, and

WHITE COUNTY.

owns 460 acres of fine land. His wife died on August 26, 1889, at the age of sixty-two. They were the parents of fourteen children, ten of whom are still living: John F., Thomas H., Tennie (wife of J. W. Blasingim), James H. (our subject), Mary J. (wife of J. R. Fortner), Martha Ann (wife of Frank Epps), Ann Eliza (wife of Richard Davis), Nannie, Benjamin and Henry. James H. Edwards claims White County as his birthplace, his birth occurring on April 26, 1854, and remained on his father's farm until twenty-seven years of age, though part of the time was spent in farming for himself. He married Miss Emma Fortner, a daughter of J. E. and Mary C. Fortner, and who was born in White County, in 1861. Joseph E. Fortner was born in Wayne County, N. C., December 4, 1812, and died in White County, Ark., July 5, 1888. In 1832 he was genuinely and soundly converted to God and joined the Presbyterian Church. After a few years of devotion to that branch of God's church he joined the Methodist Church, in which he kept his membership until God called him home. From North Carolina he moved to Tennessee, and from there to Arkansas, where he lived for thirty-four years, being among the pioneers of this country. He was the father of fifteen children. His seat was never vacant at church, unless sickness kept him away. Mr. and Mrs. Edwards are the parents of two children: Adga May and Hollice Taylor. He owns a fine farm which is well under cultivation, and has been a very successful and highly respected citizen. Himself and wife are members of the Methodist Episcopal Church. Politically he is a prominent Democrat, and also belongs to the County Wheel.

Thomas B. Ellis. Benjamin Ellis was a native of the Old-Dominion, where he was married to Mary Malone, also of that State. They removed to Kentucky in 1807 or 1808, and the following year moved to Alabama, where they made their home until their death, Mrs. Ellis passing away in 1853 and Mr. Ellis in the following year. They were the parents of eleven children: Benjamin R. (married and residing in Shelby County, Tenn.), Sallie M. (Harris), Nancy H. (Norris), Mary H. (deceased), Thomas B. (the subject of this sketch),

James B. and William T. (both deceased), Joseph F. and John W. (residents of Alabama). Thomas B. Ellis was born in Madison County, Ala., in 1820, where he resided for over thirty years, and where he was married to Judith A. Critz, of Alabama, who died in 1850, leaving two children: Mary E. (now Mrs. Hussey, of Searcy, White County) and Olivia C. (now Mrs. Goodlow, also of that place). Mr. Ellis was married the second time, in 1851, to Mary A. Corrington, of Marshall County, Miss., who died in 1860, leaving three daughters: Sarah A. (Mrs. Menus, residing near Nashville, Tenn.), Martha E. (now Mrs. Lanier, of Searcy), Roberta A. (now Mrs. Dickey, residing near the old homestead). His third and present wife, was Mary A. Montgomery, a daughter of Edward and Tobitha Montgomery, of White County, Ark., to whom he was married in 1860. They are the parents of four children: Virgil B., Nora, Thomas B. and John E. (deceased). Mr. Ellis came to Arkansas in 1856, settling in Des Arc Township, White County, where he bought a farm of 560 acres with 110 cleared, and on which he still lives. He enlisted in 1861 as a forager, in which capacity he served a short time, and was then given an honorable discharge on account of age. He returned to his farm, which he found in a state of decay and dilapidation. He has since resided on the farm and been very successful as a farmer, remaining here until the last year, when he removed to Centre Hill and started in the grocery business. Mr. Ellis is a member of the Masonic order, and belongs to Centre Hill Lodge No. 114, and is Master of his lodge. Mr. Ellis and family are members of the Methodist Episcopal Church. Mr. Ellis is a prominent Democrat, and held the office of constable shortly after the war.

James Figg was born in Gates County, N. C., January 31, 1804, and received a practical education in the schools of his native State. He was married March 19, 1829, to Miss Margaret Lewis of North Carolina, who was born March 19, 1809. To their union ten children were given: Mary J. (deceased), Sophia A. (Mrs. W. H. Hallford), F. C. (Mrs. Samuel Gray, deceased), John L. (now residing in Alabama), one child who died in

HISTORY OF ARKANSAS.

infancy (unnamed), Martha R. (who married F. M. Rice), George A. (deceased), Emma J. (Mrs. L. Byrd), Joseph J. and Mary E.   Mr. Figg was a man who took an active interest in political affairs, being a Whig up to the time of the war, and a strong secessionist. A farmer and mechanic by occupation, he owned 120 acres of land highly cultivated at the date of his demise. He was a Master Mason and had held office as Tyler in Newton Lodge No. 224, in Alabama, and was a member of Mount Pisgah Lodge No. 242 in Arkansas at the time of his death, which occurred February 10, 1873. He and wife were members of the Methodist Church, South, and he was one of the prominent factors in organizing the church in the neighborhood where he lived; ever taking an active interest in all church and educational matters. Joseph J. Figg received his education in Alabama, and at the age of twenty-one immigrated to Arkansas and settled in White County, where he is now residing. Reaching an age where he realized that it was not good for man to be alone, he selected for his life's companion Miss Mary F. Andrews, who was born February 16, 1853, a daughter of Benjamin and Elizabeth Andrews. Their marriage was consummated January 13, 1875, and five children have blessed their union: Lelia V. (born May 20, 1877), James L. (born February 2, 1879), Robert G. (born June 20, 1881), Maggie E. (born November 22, 1883), and one who died in infancy. Mr. Figg is a farmer and school-teacher, and owns 120 acres of hill and bottom land, with twenty-five acres under cultivation. He is Master Mason, and has held office as Junior Deacon for one term in Mount Pisgah Lodge No. 242; he was also formerly a member of the Wheel, but has recently resigned. During his connection with that order he acted as secretary of the lodge; he has held the office of justice of the peace for three consecutive terms in the township in which he resides, serving in an acceptable manner. Mrs. Figg is a consistent member and an earnest worker of the Baptist Church.

W. E. Fisher. It has long been acknowledged that, no matter what a man's occupation in life may be if his energies are directed toward advancing the interests of the community in which he resides, he is a useful and respected and prominent man. W. E.'s early life was surrounded with many hardships and privations, and his early education was acquired by reading at night by the flickering light of a brush fire after his day's work was done. Upon commencing life for himself the occupation he had been taught when young naturally became his by adoption, and he now owns 353 acres with about 155 acres under cultivation. Mr. Fisher was born in Wilson County, Tenn., November 25, 1819, and on August 11, 1840, he was married to Miss Martha Adkinson, her death occurring on September 19, 1852, after having borne a family of seven children: Anderson L. (born August 23, 1841, was married to Miss Martha Canada, became the father of six children, and is a farmer of White County), David (born in 1843 and died in infancy), David L. (born September 19, 1844), Cordelia M. (was born December 23, 1846; first married John Winford, by whom she became the mother of three children, and after his death she wedded John Drenon), Amanda J. (was born February 14, 1849, and married Thomas Martin, a farmer of Pope County, becoming the mother of seven children), Eliza J. (was born February 16, 1851, and married Paton Burris, who left her a widow with one child, and she afterward married Frank Massey, a farmer of Searcy County). In January, 1855, Mr. Fisher wedded Mrs. Susan Brown, of Carroll County, but she too died on May 31 of the following year. He espoused his third wife, Miss Harriet Agours, of Fayette County, Tenn., June 24, 1857, and their children are as follows: Mary E. (born June 30, 1863, is the wife of S. J. Crabtree, editor of the Arkansaw Hub at Beebe, by whom she has one child living and two children deceased), Martha E. (was born April 2, 1858, and is the wife of James Martin, who keeps a meat market in Brinkley), Laura E. (was born February 23, 1865, and wedded John Watson, and they also have one child living and one deceased), Harriett A. (was born October 25, 1867, and is the wife of John Shelton, only one of their two children being now alive), George W. (born September 27, 1859), Joseph E. (born

WHITE COUNTY.

April 7, 1861), Maggie (deceased), Sallie (born November 13, 1871) and Jimmie (born July 16, 1873). All Mr. Fisher's children have received good school advantages and are intelligent young people. Our subject removed with his family to Arkansas on November 23, 1860, and located about three-quarters of a mile west of the farm on which he is now living, where he purchased 162 acres of land, and after making his home here for about nine years he bought the farm on which he is now residing. Mr. Fisher affiliated with the Democrat party until 1885, when he united with the Agricultural Wheel, and has been a member of the State Deputy Organization and has also served faithfully and well in the capacity of State lecturer. At the present time he is chairman of the State Central Committee. He is a man who has always taken a deep interest in public affairs, and is well informed in all matters pertaining to county, State and national matters, taking that side in politics which he deemed best calculated to promote the interests of the people. He has served his county in the State legislature and filled this position to the entire satisfaction of his constituents. He holds membership in Beebe Lodge No. 144, of the A. F. & A. M., and has served as Senior Warden and is a Royal Arch Mason of El Paso Lodge. He and wife are members of the Methodist Episcopal Church, South, as are also eleven of their children. Mr. Fisher is a son of Anderson Fisher and Sinie Johnson, the former of English ancestry, his people having come from England prior to the Revolutionary War. Anderson Fisher was a scout under Gen. Jackson in the War of 1812, and for a few years prior to his death drew a pension, although he had refused to do so up to that time. He died in 1876 at the age of eighty-three years, four months and six days. He was the father of ten children: Jeremiah, Eliza, Sarah, James, W. E., Leonard B., Elizabeth, John H., Anderson M., Lucinda A., and Cordelia, who died in infancy, the remainder of the family growing to manhood and womanhood.

J. B. Foreman is a successful planter of South Carolina nativity, and has been a resident of White County, Ark., since 1859. He was born in York District, in 1836, and was the third in a family of seven children born to the marriage of James T. and Elizabeth Luraney (Rowell) Foreman, who were also born in York District, S. C., and were there married. The father was a planter and the year following his wife's death, which occurred in South Carolina, October 6, 1859, he removed to White County, Ark., where he became the owner of 620 acres of timber land. He died on this farm March 26, 1873, and left three children to mourn his loss: William Rowell (who is married and resides in Howard County, Ark.), Elizabeth L. (who is a Mrs. Mann and lives in the county) and J. B. The latter left South Carolina, a young man, and came direct to White County and purchased 160 acres of land on credit, but before getting it in shape to be tilled was compelled to rent land. In 1862 he joined Company B, Gen. McRae's regiment, and was in the battles of Helena, Prairie Grove, Little Rock and Cache River, and then joined the cavalry under Col. A. R. Witt, and was in the Missouri raid, taking part in the battles of Pilot Knob, Jefferson City, Independence, Kansas City and thence to Fayetteville. Upon his return home he resumed farming, and has opened up sixty acres of land. He is a Democrat, a member of the Agricultural Wheel, a Mason, belonging to St. Mary's Lodge No. 170 of the A. F. & A. M., and he and his wife are members of the Methodist Episcopal Church, South. He was married in White County, in October, 1860, to Martha Ellen, a daughter of Valentine and Alice (Carr) Harlan, who were born in Georgia, the father a farmer and carpenter by trade. He came to White County, Ark., in 1857, and here died in 1873, his wife dying November 18, 1877. Mr. and Mrs. Foreman have these children: James V. (a resident of Kentucky), William Edward (in Kentucky), Ann H., Martha E., Wade H., Bernie P. and Alice E. Mary E. died August 30, 1886, when nearly five years old.

John C. Fussell, farmer and stock raiser. The life of this gentleman affords an example which might well be imitated by the young men of the present day, for his capital on commencing life

HISTORY OF ARKANSAS.

for himself was limited, and throughout his career he has been industrious and frugal. He was born in Madison County, Tenn., February 23, 1845, and was brought to Arkansas by his parents in 1859, they having been married in 1840. They first settled on railroad land in White County, but later pre-empted 160 acres of wild land and began building a home, but traded this in 1876 for eighty acres where our subject, John C., now lives. Wyatt Fussell, the father, prior to coming to Arkansas, was a business man of Jackson, Tenn., and kept one of the best livery stables in the place. He was marshal of the town for several years, and in his political views was an old line Whig. He and wife, whose maiden name was Elizabeth Mattox, were members of the Baptist Church, and their deaths occurred in Arkansas, August 12, 1889, and Tennessee, in 1853, respectively. Of six children born to them four lived to be grown: William N. (who is a physician of Denmark, Tenn.), John C., Elmira (deceased, the wife of J. J. Rogers, a farmer of Lonoke County) and Mary E. (the wife of J. B. Shelton, of White County). John C. Fussell was reared to a farm life, and although his facilities for acquiring an education were very poor, he acquired a thorough knowledge of the three R's. Until twenty-five years of age he worked for his father and sisters, then was married to Miss Mary E. Powers, a daughter of A. M. Powers, a farmer of Tennessee, who came to Arkansas in 1860. Their union resulted in the birth of three children, two of whom are living: James W. (a young man residing with his father) and Betty O. Jennie died in childhood. Mr. Fussell is a man who has always been interested in the welfare of his county, and always supports enterprises which tend to benefit the same. He is a member of Stony Point Lodge No. 20, of the Agricultural Wheel. His wife is a daughter of A. M. and Eliza (Moore) Powers, who were Tennesseeans, and as above stated came to Arkansas in 1860, locating near Beebe, where he became the owner of a large number of slaves, and resided for fourteen years. He and his wife reared a family of eight children to manhood and womanhood, their names being as follows: Mary E. (Mrs. Fus-

sell), Robert (a mechanic), Nancy (wife of William L. Edwards, a farmer of White County), Martha (wife of James Edwards, also a farmer), Jennie (widow of William Hartbrooks), William (a farmer of Beebe) and Sophia (is wife of John Lestie, of Lonoke County).

Uriah E. Gentry is a native of South Carolina and a son of Cornelius and Mary (Johnson) Gentry, also natives of that State, where they lived until after their marriage, removing thence to Georgia when our subject was a child. Later they became located in Tennessee, and in 1836 in Alabama, where the father died in 1842 at the age of thirty-nine. After this unhappy event Mrs. Gentry went to Mississippi with her family and located on the head waters of the Tom Bigbee River, going in 1856 to Texas, and remaining until 1868 when they came to Arkansas, settling in Independence County. The family consisted of nine children the following being the only ones living at this time: Susanah (now Mrs. Provence), Thomas, Uriah E., M. V. and Parthenia (wife of Elisha Bass). Uriah E. Gentry was born in Spartanburg, S. C., on July 12, 1830, and continued with his mother until twenty-two years of age when he commenced for himself as a farmer. In 1863 he enlisted in the Confederate army, in the Twenty-ninth Texas Cavalry, in which he served only a short time, having received a wound; after this he was put on detached duty. Upon the close of the war he rented a farm in Texas for two years, but coming to Independence County, Ark., here bought a farm and remained until 1874 when he sold out and located in White County. He now owns a farm of 200 acres with a large portion of it under cultivation, and has also helped his boys in getting a substantial start in life. Mr. Gentry was married after reaching manhood to Mary Davis, who died in 1864, leaving a family of children, two of whom only are living: Robert C. (a farmer of this county) and Louisa (the wife of a Mr. Saulefor, of Independence County). In 1865 he was married to Miss Winnie Bass, who died in 1868, having borne two children: Thomas R. and Jerry L., both farmers of this county. In 1869 Miss Elizabeth Thomas became Mr. Gentry's third wife. She died in 1872. In 1873 his fourth

WHITE COUNTY.

matrimonial venture resulted in his marriage to Miss Estelle Churchwell. They are the parents of six children: Carrie L., Mary T., Sallie, Jessie B., Ora B. and Mattie J. Mr. and Mrs. Gentry are members of the Methodist Episcopal Church, South. The former belongs to the Masonic order, and is a prominent Democrat. He is recognized as one of the leading men of his township and enjoys a well-deserved popularity.

M. N. Gentry, groceryman, Searcy, Ark. The family grocery trade of Searcy is well represented by honorable commercial men, who are full of enterprise. Among those who hold a leading position in this line is Mr. Gentry, firmly established in his business and enjoying an excellent trade. He carries a full line of queensware, groceries, etc., and started his house in 1876. In April, 1882, he was burned out, and in the same year erected a good one-story brick building, 100x25 feet. Mr. Gentry moved to Independence County, Ark., in 1868, remained a short time, and in the same year moved to West Point, White County, where he resided until 1869. He then moved to Gray Township and followed farming. He owes his nativity to Tishomingo County, Miss., where he was born in 1856, being the third in a family of four children, the result of the union of N. J. and Jane (Eaton) Gentry, natives of South Carolina and Alabama, respectively. The father when a boy moved to Alabama, was married in that State, and followed agricultural pursuits for a livelihood. In 1856 he moved to Red River County, Tex., remained there until 1866, then moved to McLennan County, where he resided until 1868. He then moved to Independence County, Ark., and later to White County, purchased land, improved it, and in 1876 engaged in business under the firm name of Ward & Gentry, which title continued until 1878, after which it was changed to Gentry & Son, remaining so until 1887. The father died in June of that year. Socially he was a member of Searcy Lodge No. 49, A. F. & A. M. The mother is still living, and resides at Searcy. Since 1887 the firm title has been M. N. Gentry. The children of the above-mentioned couple are named as follows: W. C. (married, and resides in Navarro County, Tex., engaged in farm-

ing), J. T. (married, residing at Hillside, Tex., and is a railroad agent), M. N. and Mary (who resides in Searcy). Mr. Gentry was reared to farm life, and received his education in the schools of Texas, and in White County, Ark.; attending one year in Searcy. He assisted his father in clearing and developing the home place, and remained on the farm until he engaged in business in 1876. Socially he is a member of Searcy Lodge No. 49, A. F. & A. M., and served as Junior Warden for six years, Senior Warden for one year, and Worshipful Master for two years. He is at present one of the masters of ceremonies. He served four years as a member of the city council, one of which was known as the Dade council, and during that year sheds were erected over the springs. Mr. Gentry takes an active interest in everything for the good of the county. He aids in all enterprises for the public good, and is one of the substantial citizens.

C. S. George, clerk of the county and probate court, Searcy, Ark., is well known to the residents of White County, as one, who, in all his relations to the public, has proven himself faithful to the trusts committed to him. Whether in his private or official capacity no taint of dishonor can be found. He was born in Coahoma County, Miss., in January, 1853, being the fourth of eight children, born to C. L. and Catherine M. (McDermott) George, natives of Kentucky and Ohio, respectively. The parents were married at Helena, Ark., and later settled in Mississippi, where the father followed agricultural pursuits. His father took an active part in politics, was clerk of Phillips County, Ark., was also assessor in the early history of the county, and county judge of Coahoma County, Miss., and in 1867 moved to Lawrence County, Ark., where he purchased an improved farm. From there he moved to Searcy, in 1876, lived a retired life, and there died in November, 1881. His excellent wife still survives and resides in Searcy. C. S. George was reared to the arduous duties of the farm, and received a fair education in the schools of Mississippi and Arkansas. He commenced for himself as deputy clerk of Lawrence County, Ark., in 1871, served two years and

HISTORY OF ARKANSAS.

moved to White County, Ark., in 1876, locating at Searcy. He then entered the office as deputy county clerk in 1880, served eight years, and in 1888 he was elected clerk of the county, having the honor of being the only one elected on the Democratic ticket. He has been connected with the records of White County longer than any one else now living. He is a member of the Masonic Fraternity, Searcy Lodge No. 49, is also a member of Tillman Chapter No. 19, R. A. M. Mr. George was married in Searcy, in February, 1880, to M. B. Isbell, a native of White County, and two children living are the fruits of this union: Herbert L. and Leland S. Those deceased were named: Lillie (who died in 1882) and Charley (who died in 1884). Mr. George is a member of the school board, and takes an active interest in all that pertains to the good of the community. Mrs. George is a member of the Methodist Episcopal Church.

Robert N. Gill, though one of the younger citizens of the county, has risen to a worthy place among its farmers and merchants. He was born in Tennessee in the year 1855, and is the oldest in a family of five children in the family of W. F. and Ollie A. (McDowell) Gill. The former was a native of Tennessee, and spent his life in farming, which occupation proved very successful to him. Moving to Marshall Township, White County, Ark., in 1853, he purchased 300 acres of land, and at once proceeded to carefully cultivate this property. His wife died in Arkansas in 1875, leaving five children: Robert, James N., Ellen, Molly, and Georgia A. Mr. Gill subsequently married again and reared a family of four children; he was called to his final home in 1889. Robert N. passed his early life on a farm, and received a good education in the schools of Arkansas. He was married in 1874 to Miss Johanna Thompson, daughter of Henry Thompson, and a native of Arkansas. To their union six children have been born: Frank M., Ora B., Olie E., Johnie M., Jessie Lee and Elmer. Mr. Gill is an expert mechanic, and has built many houses in the country, which are excellent specimens of his skill. In 1887 he embarked in merchandising business in Romance, where he carries a large and carefully

selected stock, and is building up a substantial and lucrative trade, also owning a fine farm of 120 acres, of which seventy-five acres are under cultivation. He has observed a very great change in the country since taking up his residence here, and in the general growth and advancement has borne a faithful share. In politics Mr. Gill is a Democrat, and with his wife worships at the Methodist Episcopal Church, South.

Emmet O. Gilliam was the fifth son in a family of six children, of William and Mary (Spencer) Gilliam, natives of Virginia and North Carolina, respectively. William Gilliam was at one time a resident of Mississippi, and later became settled in Tennessee, finally coming to White County, Ark., where he opened up a farm of 160 acres, in Gray Township. After remaining here for three years, he sold out and moved to Des Arc Township. The children of himself and wife were named: Albert A., William S., Robert H., Leona L. (deceased), Emmet O. (our subject) and Edward C. Emmet O. Gilliam was born February 8, 1860, in White County, on the farm where he now lives. Consequently he is numbered among the community's younger citizens. In 1880 he took charge of the old homestead, consisting of 160 acres, of which 100 acres are under a high state of cultivation. Mr. Gilliam is a strong Democrat, and although a young man in years, takes an active and influential interest in politics. His energy and determination promise to render him one of the leading men of his county.

James Monroe Gist, M. D., medical practitioner and a resident of Beebe, Ark., was born December 31, 1833, in Carroll County, Tenn., being a son of Joseph B. and Dorcas (Mitchell) Gist, the former of English descent. In 1739 the Gists first came to America and Dr. Gist can trace his ancestry back five generations. Grandfather Mitchell was a participant in the battle of New Orleans and in 1858 came to White County, Ark. He was united in marriage to Miss Sarah Scott in 1812, while a resident of Kentucky. Dr. James M. Gist received his early education in the private schools of his native county and began his medical studies under Dr. J. W. McCall, of Carroll County, and

WHITE COUNTY.

took his first course of medical lectures in the medical department of the University of Tennessee at Nashville, during the winter of 1857-58 and 1859–60, graduating in the latter year. In 1858 he had removed to Arkansas and after his graduation he returned here and settled at Austin, Prairie County. In the spring of 1860 he moved to Stony Point, White County, being there united in marriage June 5, 1861, to Miss Mary Eleanor Thomas, a native of Marshall County, Miss., a daughter of John Franklin and Nancy Thomas, both of whom were of English descent, the former a native of North Carolina and the latter of Mississippi. To the Doctor and his wife two children were born: Nancy Dorcas (born January 10, 1867, was married to J. E. Fisher in 1885 and died, July 9, 1887, at her home in Texas, of cardiac rheumatism, having given birth to a daughter, Myron Gist Fisher, December 6, 1886), Minnie Laura (the younger daughter, was born October 22, 1869). When Dr. Gist first came to Arkansas game was very abundant, the country being very wild and unsettled. There were two log school-houses in the southern part of the county in which religious services were often held, but the morals of the people were at a very low ebb. In the summer of 1862 the Doctor joined the Confederate army as a private in Col. Dandridge McRae's regiment, but was detached from his company and assigned duty in the hospital serving in the Trans-Mississippi Department, in which service he remained for a period of eight months, being discharged by reason of disability. He returned to his home at Stony Point where he was living at the time of his enlistment, and again engaged in the practice of his profession. In 1865 he embarked in mercantile pursuits with H. B. Strange at Stony Point, carrying a general stock of goods, but the firm dissolved partnership in 1872. Dr. Gist then engaged in the drug business for about eight years. In 1873 he was elected by the Democratic voters of his county to represent them in the State legislature, serving two terms in the regular session and in the extra session called by Gov. Baxter in 1884. In the spring election of 1876 he was chosen mayor of Beebe and has served at different times two or three terms. The Doctor has held a membership in the Masonic fraternity for a number of years, and has attained the Chapter order. He and wife are members of the Christian Church and are charitable and hospitable.

George W. Goad, planter and stock raiser of Denmark, Ark. This enterprising agriculturist is a son of John and Elizabeth (Hardin) Goad, natives of Kentucky, born 1806 and 1809, respectively. The father was of English descent, and his ancestors came to America prior to the Revolutionary War. They first settled in Virginia, but as the country developed moved farther west, and were among the first settlers of Tennessee. Benjamin Hardin, the great-grandfather of the subject of this sketch, was a participant in the War for Independence. John Goad and Elizabeth Hardin were married in Graves County, Ky., in the year 1826, and to their union were born the following children: Susan (born August, 1827), George W. (born July 21, 1830), Mary (born 1833), Nancy (born 1836), Sarah Ann (born 1839), John (born 1841), James J. (born 1844), Elizabeth (born 1847), an infant (died unnamed) and Louisa S. (who was born in 1853). Seven of these children grew to maturity. Elizabeth died in the spring of 1852, John died in 1861, Louisa died in 1864 and Mary died in 1853. John Goad left his home in Kentucky to move to Arkansas, and located in Denmark, White County, of that State, on February 3, 1846, after a tedious journey overland of two months. His was the first family to settle in that part of White County. In 1847 he took a claim of 320 acres, improved it and resided upon the same until 1875, when he sold out. He then settled upon Section 31, Denmark Township, and after the death of Mrs. Goad, which occurred in the fall of 1875, he married a lady by the name of Miss Clarissa Pinegar, and resided in Denmark Township until his death, which occurred on December 3, 1887. Five of his children are still living and all married. Susan is now living with her second husband, G. C. Caruthers, and is now residing in Independence County. She had eight children by her first husband, Steven Whilton. Nancy, married Nicholas Lovell and became the

HISTORY OF ARKANSAS.

mother of seven children. Sarah Ann, married George Swick (deceased), became the mother of five children (one living) and is now living with her second husband, Wiley Westmoreland. James J. Goad married Miss Quintilliss Barnes, resides in Jackson County and has one child living. George W. Goad received a limited education in the common schools of Kentucky and at the fireside at home. He was reared principally to the arduous duties of the farm, but also learned the tanner's trade with his father, which business the latter carried on, both in Kentucky and Arkansas. George W. Goad selected for his wife Miss Elizabeth J. Riddle, a native of Tennessee, supposed to be of Irish descent, and the wedding took place on December 25, 1851. Ten children were born to this marriage, six now living: James E. (born September 19, 1852), William (born January 16, 1854, and died March 29, 1864), Mary J. (born February 10, 1855), Harmon M. (born April 23, 1856), Stephen (born May 29, 1857), John (born December 29, 1858, and died April 6, 1864), Lewis W. (born June 16, 1860), an infant (born and died in 1862), Andrew (born February 2, 1863,) and Elizabeth T. (born November 15, 1866, and died August 28, 1868). Mrs. Goad died on November 15, 1866, and Mr. Goad took for his second wife Mrs. Julia A. Wilson, whom he married on August 1, 1867. The following children were the result of this marriage: Margaret (born May 20, 1868), Gabrey (born February 22, 1870), George H. (born January 18, 1872), Jacob (born November 25, 1875), Susie (born August 6, 1880). Of the first children, Mary married William Morgan on December 25, 1873, and has seven children; James married Miss Virginia McCauley, and became the father of seven children; Stephen married Miss Mollie Yarbrough, and has three children; Harmon married Miss Jane Wagoner, in 1882, and has five children; Lewis married Miss Florence Wagoner, in 1883, and has two living children. And of the second marriage, Margaret married Roy M. Hodges, on January 27, 1889, and has one child. Mr. Goad was in the Federal army during the war, served about one year in Col. Baxter's regiment, which was organized at Batesville in the latter part of

1863 and fore part of 1864. The regiment participated in a number of severe skirmishes. Mr. Goad made his first purchase of land in 1855, buying forty acres, upon which he has since made his home. By subsequent purchase he added to the original tract until he owned 480 acres, but now owns 340 acres, with 100 acres under cultivation. He gave his children a liberal portion of land. Mr. Goad is a Republican in politics, is a member of the Agricultural Wheel, and he and wife are members of the Regular Baptist Church.

Joseph H. Grammer is a native of Virginia, and was the eldest in a family of five children, born to P. W. and Mary B. (Tyus) Grammer, both of whom were also Virginians by birth. P. W. Grammer was reared on a farm in the Old Dominion, and in 1836 moved to Haywood County, Tenn., where he died in 1853, his wife preceding him one year. They were the parents of the following named children: Joseph H., Rebecca, Edmond W., B. F., and one whose name is not given. Joseph H., the subject of this sketch, first saw the light of day in Petersburg, Va., in 1829, removing to Tennessee with his parents when seven years of age. He commenced farming for himself in 1851, and in 1853 was married to Miss Josephine W. Pettey, a native of Alabama, and a daughter of G. G. and Elizabeth (Capell) Pettey, of Virginia birth. Two years after his marriage Mr. Grammer came to Arkansas and settled in Des Arc Township, White County, where he bought 320 acres of land, near the present site of Centre Hill. To himself and wife eight children have been born, three being deceased: William Henry (deceased), Emmett L., William N., Nora., Fannie E., Hattie Lee, Jennie B. (deceased) and Jennie D. (also deceased). They also have three grandchildren. Mr. Grammer is a strong Democrat, and has been called upon to serve in various official capacities. He held the position of deputy sheriff of White County, was postmaster of Centre Hill for a number of years, and was appointed postmaster of Mount Pisgah, in April, 1889, by President Harrison. Mr. and Mrs. Grammer and children are members of the Methodist Episcopal Church, South. The former has been engaged in farming

WHITE COUNTY.

all his life, and in connection therewith has given his attention to the mercantile business for a number of years, commencing that branch of trade in 1872, at Centre Hill, and in 1889 at Mount Pisgah; his family, however, still residing on the farm. Mr. Grammer is a member of the Masonic order, and belongs to Centre Hill Lodge No. 114, and to Chapter No. 19. He has been instrumental in aiding many worthy movements hereabouts and helped to build the first church and first school-house in White County.

B. F. Grammer, a Tennesseean by birth, a farmer by occupation, a Methodist in his religious preferences, a Democrat in politics and a veteran of the Civil War, has been a resident of White County since December, 1856, a period of sufficient length to render him well and favorably known. His parents were P. W. and Mary B. (Tyus) Grammer, both natives of Virginia, as were also their parents. B. F. Grammer was united in marriage in January, 1861, to Miss Sarah J. Neal, who was born in Fayette County, Tenn., a daughter of James and Mary (Smith) Neal, also of Tennessee origin, and who came to Arkansas in about 1852. Mr. Grammer enlisted in 1862 for three years' service during the war in the Thirty-sixth Arkansas Infantry, and participated in the battles of Oak Grove and Pleasant Hill, whither his regiment was sent as reinforcement to Gen. Dick Taylor who had been in a siege of eighty-three days. His next engagement was at the ford of the Saline River, after which he was sent to Marshall, Texas, on garrison duty. Upon the close of the war he returned home and again engaged in farming. Mr. and Mrs. Grammer are the parents of seven children, all boys: John B. (married, and resides at Centre Hill), James H. (attending school), Elmer, Horace, Edwin L., Marvin F. and Tyus C. Mr. Grammer has a farm of 125 acres, which he has cleared himself, besides some timber land. Himself and wife and three oldest sons are members of the Methodist Episcopal Church, South. His acquaintance throughout this territory is a wide one and he enjoys universal esteem and respect.

Philip Yancey Graves. The estate upon which Mr. Graves now resides, and to which he has given such close attention in its cultivation, embraces 520 acres, a well-improved farm, substantial and convenient buildings being a leading feature of these improvements. He is a son of John and Mark (Yancey) Graves, the former a native of North Carolina, and the latter of Tennessee, their marriage taking place in the latter State, where the father died in 1841. Philip Y., his son, inherits Scotch blood from his paternal ancestry, and was born in the State of Tennessee, on October 8, 1830, and after his father's death, being the eldest of the children, the support of his widowed mother and three younger children devolved almost entirely upon him. He worked out by the day and month, and at the age of fifteen years, began working on a tract of timber land, on which his father had held a claim, and which was partly improved. He began clearing off the timber and making it into shingles and clapboards, for which he found a market at Somerville, Macon, Moscow and other places. After clearing off the timber from about five acres, and erecting thereon a good log-house, he was compelled to give up all claim to the land, as others had a clearer title than he. In 1855, in company with Joseph Hollis, he purchased some cypress timber near La Grange, Tenn., and this was made into shingles and sold at that place for the academy and college, which were in process of erection at that time. He followed this occupation in Shelby and Hardeman Counties, but in 1857 he gave this up and moved to Tippah County, Miss., where he rented land and engaged in general farming. About one year later he removed to Arkansas, and was married in Mississippi County, of this State, to Mrs. Elizabeth Hollis (*nee* Tingle), the widow of Joseph Hollis, his former partner. In the fall of 1859 he returned to Mississippi, but owing to rheumatism contracted from exposure while pursuing the shingle business, he was compelled to give up work for about four years. From 1861 to 1865 he farmed in Marshall County, then returned to Arkansas and purchased 160 acres of land, four miles north of Beebe, upon which were some log buildings and other improvements, twenty acres being under cultivation. He now has 150 acres under the plow, and seven acres in an orchard

HISTORY OF ARKANSAS.

consisting of peach, apple and plum trees. He finds a market for his fruit at Beebe, his peaches averaging about 50 cents per bushel, and the apples 60 cents. He also ships to St. Louis. His land is well adapted to raising any kind of grain or grasses, and he has raised as high as twenty-two bushels of wheat to the acre. Mr. Graves is a Democrat, a member of the Agricultural Wheel, and he and family are members of the Cumberland Presbyterian Church, at Antioch, Ark. Mrs. Graves had five children by her first husband, two of whom are now living: Arminta (married in 1866, R. W. Bell) and Caroline (who became the wife of S. S. Hayney in 1868, and is now Mrs. F. W. Rodgers). The children of Mrs. Graves' second marriage are: Penelope (born March 22, 1859, is the wife of N. M. Parker, who has a farm near Beebe, but works at the carpenter's trade. They have three children: Fred D., John W. and Gertrude). Ella was married to John H. Pendleton, a native of Tennessee, in 1881, and has two children: James D. (born March 6, 1884) and Bettie Estelle (born November 13, 1885).

Alfred Greer enjoys a deserved reputation as a prominent planter of White County. Born in Davidson County, Tenn., February 22, 1820, he received his education in Alabama, near La Fayette. His father, Elijah Greer, was a Virginian by birth and when about twenty-two years old immigrated to Kentucky, where he married Miss Mary Acors, of that State. To them a family of fourteen children were born, twelve of whom grew to maturity, Alfred being the thirteenth child. Elijah Greer manifested a great interest in politics, and served in the War of 1812 as a fife-major. He was a farmer by occupation, and moved from Kentucky to Tennessee in 1810, going in 1830 to Georgia, and settling in Pike County. He resided in that State until his death, in 1841, his wife surviving him only three years. Alfred was married October 13, 1839, in Alabama, to Miss Elizabeth J. Waters, a daughter of William and Feriberry Waters, and their union has been blessed by the birth of ten children, three boys and seven girls: William V., Elisha J., Hiram A., Mary F., Nancy, Feribey, Lucinda, Susan F., Georgia F. and

Margaret E. who died in 1846. Mr. Greer owns 160 acres of land, with seventy-five under cultivation. He is a member of the Wheel, in which he has held the office of chaplain for three months. He served in the late war, and enlisted in 1864 under Capt. Choshea, as a home guard, and at the final surrender, returned at once and resumed his occupation of farming, which he has continued with good results since that time. Mr. Greer and wife are members of the Baptist Church, in which the former has acted as deacon. He was one of twenty-four who organized Mount Olive Church, and many other enterprises, which have proven of substantial worth, may be attributed in a large degree to his energy and support.

James E. Gregory. There are a number of men prominently identified with the agricultural affairs of White County, but none among them are more deserving of mention than Mr. Gregory, who was born in Rutherford County, Tenn., on September 5, 1837. He was reared in his native county, and after attending the common schools until nineteen years of age, he took a one-year's course in Bethel College, Carroll County, Tenn. After entering on the active duties of life, he clerked one year for Woods & Herrell, of Bell Station, Tenn., and in 1859 came to Arkansas, and spent nearly one year in this section of the State, hunting and enjoying himself in his own way. Upon returning to the State of his birth, he again clerked several months, then returned to Arkansas for the purpose of purchasing land for his friends, but before they could make a settlement the war came up and Mr. Gregory enlisted, November 4, 1861, in the Seventh Tennessee Cavalry, and served three years as second lieutenant of Company F, known as Fork Deer Rangers, being under that intrepid soldier, Gen. Forrest, and with him participated in many battles. He was captured three times, first at Brays Station, Tenn., January 18, 1863, and for four months was kept a prisoner at Alton, Camp Chase and Fort Delaware, and was exchanged at City Point, Va., May 4, 1863. His second capture was in November at Corinth, Miss. After the battle of Harris-

WHITE COUNTY.

burg he returned home and never rejoined the army. From that time until the present, with the exception of 1865, 1866 and 1867, when he was engaged in milling, he has followed farming as an occupation. In 1872 he came to White County, Ark., and purchased 214 acres of land, two miles west of Beebe, on the Iron Mountain Railroad, and after living the life of a bachelor for one year he was married, March 17, 1873, on his father's birthday (he being sixty-one years old), to Miss Mary Burns, and by her became the father of the following family: Maud Lee (deceased), Odem S., Richard, Isabella and Elena. On February 6, 1882, he was called upon to mourn the death of his wife, and after remaining a widower until November 7, 1888, he led to the altar Mrs. Henrietta McClelland, the widow of Newton McClelland, of Crockett County, Tenn. Since locating on his present farm he has cleared about ninety acres of land, and in all has 140 acres under cultivation, his farm comprising 260 acres of exceedingly fertile land. He is a member of the Agricultural Wheel, the I. O. O. F. and the K. of H., and being interested in the cause of education, he is a member of the school board of his district. His parents, Madison and Julia E. (Mason) Gregory, were born in Rutherford County, Tenn., March 17, 1812, and May 2, 1817, respectively, and were married in their native county about 1835, remaining there until 1846, when they removed to Haywood County, making their home there until their respective deaths. The father was an extensive planter and slave holder, and at the time of the Civil War was the owner of thirteen negroes. His plantation comprised 480 acres, and 300 were under cultivation. He and wife were Methodists, and he died at the home of our subject on August 15, 1881, his wife preceding him to the "Silent Land" July 18, 1880. Their children are as follows: James E., Mary F. (deceased), Sarah E. A. (wife of Young Wortham, a farmer of White County), the next in order of birth was an infant who died unnamed, Isabella (wife of James H. Hubbard, a farmer of Parker City, Tex.), Susan P. (deceased, was the wife of James Hart, a farmer of Crockett County, Tenn.), Emeline (wife of John Blades, a druggist of Pet-

tey, Lamar County, Tex.), Mosella (wife of Henry Graves, a farmer of Pettey, Lamar County, Tex.), Madison (a farmer, residing near Alamo, Tenn.) and Joseph H. (a farmer of Johnson County, Tex.). Edwin Gregory, the paternal grandfather, was a Virginian, and was one of the early settlers of Rutherford County, Tenn., whither he moved in 1808, there following the occupation of farming. The maternal grandfather was Joseph Mason, a Revolutionary soldier, and a native of Tennessee. He was for many years a planter, and also kept a tavern, his establishment being midway between Nashville and Murfreesboro. He educated himself after having children large enough to go to school, all attending the sessions together. He filled the office of esquire forty-nine years in succession; all cases stood as he rendered judgment, but one. He freed sixty-seven slaves, and owned 1,500 acres of land. His father was one of the first settlers of Nashville, Tenn. He raised eight children: Elizar, Julia, Polley, Allen, Rinier, Martin, Susan and Isabellar, all lived to be grown and have families. Joseph died in November, 1868.

Dr. Albert Griffin, physician and surgeon, of El Paso, and a graduate of Shelby Medical College of Nashville, Tenn., is a native of Louisiana, and was born in Assumption Parish September 6, 1836, the son of Solomon and Charlotte T. (Edney) Griffin, originally from North Carolina. They were married in West Tennessee in 1834, and the same year moved to Louisiana, where Mr. Griffin engaged in the sugar business, owning a large refinery and plantation. His death occurred in 1837 at the hands of some slaves. Immediately after her husband's demise Mrs. Griffin returned to Williamson County, Tenn., and resided there until 1840, when she was married to Dr. Bruce, a native of North Carolina, but who had been for years a resident of Tennessee. She accompanied him to his home in Haywood County, and died there in 1872. Dr. Bruce was a prominent physician, and his record is one that will be an honor to his children and their offspring. By her last marriage Mrs. Griffin-Bruce was the mother of seven children, five of them now living. Albert Griffin, the subject of this sketch, was the only child of his

HISTORY OF ARKANSAS.

mother's first marriage. He received his primary education in the schools of Brownsville, Tenn., supplementing this course by an attendance at Andrew College at Trenton, Gibson County, Tenn. He then took one year's course in the Emory and Henry College, in Washington County, Va., leaving that school at the age of twenty years with an excellent English training. In the spring of 1857 young Griffin began the study of medicine under the efficient tutelage of his step-father, Dr. Bruce, with whom he continued for one year, adding to this one year's instruction with Drs. Taliaferro & Turner. In the fall he entered Shelby College, from which he graduated in 1859, as before intimated. The year 1860 witnessed his marriage to Miss Mary E. Laws, a native of Tennessee, and a daughter of James P. Laws, of White County. Dr. Griffin enlisted in Carroll's Partisan Ranger Regiment during the war, but was detailed to attend the sick at home by the request of the people of his county. He has been a member of his school board for years, and Mrs. Griffin belongs to and is an active worker in the Methodist Episcopal Church. Dr. Griffin has a beautiful little home in the suburbs of El Paso, which is made cheerful with carefully attended flowers and shrubs. He is a Democrat, and exerts no little influence in local politics, having held various positions on committees in his party. He takes an active interest in schools, churches, etc., is an enterprising citizen and a valuable acquisition to any place.

Elijah Guise has been a resident of White County, Ark., since 1868, and his example of industry and earnest and sincere endeavor to succeed in life, especially in the occupation of farming, is well worthy of imitation. He was born in Hardeman County, Tenn., in 1846, and was the youngest of a family of seven children born to Enoch and Nancy (Patterson) Guise, both of whom were born in the State of Alabama. They were reared and married, however, in Tennessee, and were engaged in farming there until their respective deaths, in 1863 and 1866. Enoch Guise was a minister of the United Baptist Church, and in his early days of labor for the cause of the Master, he was compelled to take long rides in order to preach at his different appointments. His children are: Gann (living in White County), Rebecca (Mrs. J. H. Sellers), Alvira (Mrs. Daniel Campbell), J. L. (residing in White County), Rachel (Mrs. James Sellers) and Elijah. The latter, after remaining with his father until he was eighteen years of age, began farming for himself, in his native county. He was married, in Shelby County, Tenn., in 1866, to Miss Lenora Ann Singleton, a native of De Soto County, Miss., and a daughter of Dr. A. J. and Margaret L. (Guinn) Singleton, both of whom were born in Georgia and Tennessee, respectively. They were married in Mississippi, moved to Tennessee and thence to Arkansas, in 1859, settling in Izard County, from which county he enlisted, in 1861, in the Eighth Arkansas Regiment, Infantry, Company A, and afterward took part in the following battles: Greenville, Corinth, Iuka, Chattanooga, Murfreesboro, Lookout Mountain and siege of Vicksburg. He was one time taken prisoner, but shortly afterward exchanged, and rejoined his family in Mississippi, and in the latter part of 1865 went to Memphis and was in business in that city for one year. He then farmed near there until 1868, when he purchased land in Big Creek Township, Van Buren County, Ark., and there erected a mill. In 1869 he removed to Cleburne County and there died, in 1882, still survived by his wife, who is a resident of White County. A. J. Singleton was also a minister of the Primitive Baptist and a physician of repute. After coming to Arkansas, in 1868, Mr. Guise bought a partly improved farm of 160 acres, and this farm has greatly improved in the way of buildings and in the amount of land he has cleared, having now forty acres under cultivation. He is a Democrat in politics and has held a number of local offices, and is a member of the Primitive Baptist Church. He and wife have had three children: Joseph Andrew, Lillie Ann (who died at the age of two months, in 1867) and Emma Florence (who died in 1874, when five years of age).

John M. Hacker is a farmer and fruit grower of Harrison Township, White County, Ark., and was born in the "Hoosier State" in 1831, being the third in a family of eight children born to John

WHITE COUNTY.

and Cynthia (Becler) Hacker. The father was born in the State of Tennessee and inherited Irish and Scotch blood from his ancestors. He was the second of five children and after spending his younger days in Tennessee he moved to Indiana, going thither after the celebration of his marriage, which occurred in 1827. The children born to him in his adopted State are as follows: Malinda, Joseph D., George W., Margaret A., Mary E., Conrad D., James K. and John M. In 1832 the family moved from Indiana to Illinois, settling on a farm in the southern part of the State, and at a still later period moved to St. Louis, where the father engaged in the mercantile business until 1843, when he moved to Jefferson County, of the same State, where he died four years later. He was survived by his wife until February, 1888, when she, too, died. The early childhood of John M. Hacker was spent in Illinois and Missouri, but his education was received principally in the latter State. Being of an enterprising disposition, he determined to start out in life and seek his own fortune, and accordingly, in 1853, went west to California and spent some time in mining in Eldorado County, becoming thoroughly familiar with western life and the hardships and privations which the miners were compelled to undergo in those days. After his return to Franklin County, Mo., he engaged in farming and in 1862 was married to Martha F. Johnson, daughter of Thomas J. and Mary F. (Falweele) Johnson, who were Virginians, the grandparents having been early settlers of that State. The paternal grandfather was in the War of 1812, and Gen. Joseph E. Johnston was an uncle of Mr. Hacker. Mr. and Mrs. Hacker have a little daughter, born in August, 1881. They are quite well-to-do and own 112 acres of good farming land in Missouri, 130 acres in Harrison County, Ark. (which is under fruit culture), and the farm on which he now lives, comprising 130 acres, seventeen of which he devotes to strawberries. He has an orchard of about 4,000 trees and he has just purchased a farm of forty acres in Fulton County, on which he expects to raise fruit. He is a member of Anchor Lodge No. 384, A. F. & A. M., and he is deeply interested in churches and schools, he

and wife being members of the Missionary Baptist Church.

James William Hall was born in Calhoun County, Miss., on January 12, 1850, and is a son of Hiram and Sarah (Holifield) Hall, natives of Madison and Gibson Counties, Tenn., respectively, the former of English birth. The father moved to Chickasaw County, Miss., in 1844, and engaged in farming and cotton ginning there until January, 1869, when he sold out and moved to De Soto County, and eventually became the owner of large tracts of land in that county. Here he died on January 17, 1888, his wife having departed this life in 1859. Of seven children born to them four are living: John Calvin (who was captured in the battle of Fort Donelson in 1862, and died in prison at Indianapolis, Ind., in the same year), Samuel H. (living), Henry T. (deceased), James William, Sarah S., Senath A. (who became the wife of John W. Wynn, and the mother of two children; she died in 1876 at the birth of her second child, who died at the same time as the mother). The first child, Virginia, is living in Crawford County, Ark., and Hiram E. James William Hall followed the life of the farmer's boy, and received a fair education in the subscription schools. May 8, 1870, he was married to Margaret A., a daughter of G. W. McKinney, of Monroe County, Miss., and for a number of years after he and a brother operated and managed a mill which their father had erected, our subject having an interest in the business, which was fairly successful. On October 7, 1872, he removed to Arkansas and located upon the farm on which he is now living, his worldly possessions at that time consisting of $200 in cash, two mules, a wagon and some household furniture. His original purchase of land comprised 160 acres in a wild state, but he has now 440 acres and 100 acres under cultivation. His children are: Beulah Ann (born March 5, 1871, and died June 22, 1872), Sarah Cornelia (born December 24, 1872), Hiram Luther (born on December 3, 1875, and died November 12, 1886), Helen Caroline (born May 24, 1878) and Georgia Etta (born January 12, 1886).

Jacob Alah Hammons, planter and stockman, Hammonsville, Ark. Among the many successful

HISTORY OF ARKANSAS.

agriculturists of White County, none are more worthy of mention than the subject of this sketch, who owes his nativity to Autauga County, Ala., where his birth occurred on March 7, 1822. His parents, John and Hannah (Dodson) Hammons were honored and respected citizens in the community in which they lived, and the father was a native of Virginia, his birth occurring in that State in 1784. The paternal ancestors came to America prior to the Revolutionary War, and some of them were soldiers in that world-renowned struggle. Grandfather Dodson was a native of England, and came to America before the Revolutionary War. Grandmother Dodson was a native of Germany. John Hammons was a soldier in the War of 1812. Jacob Alah Hammons received a limited education in the subscription schools of Cherokee County, Ala., and was one of eleven children born to his parents: John W. (born in 1817), Elizabeth (born 1820), Jacob A. (born 1822), Jane (born 1824), Martha (born 1826), Luzella (born 1828), Lavina (born 1830), Mary and Susan (twins, born 1832), William P. (born 1835) and Thomas. Luzella died in 1868. In 1846 Jacob A. Hammons went to Cherokee County, Ga., where he assisted in erecting a mill which he afterward operated. In 1847 he returned to Cherokee County, Ala., purchased a tract of eighty acres of land, about ten acres of which was under cultivation, but with no other improvements, and there remained until 1849. He then came to Arkansas, followed agricultural pursuits, and in 1852 was united in marriage to Miss Jane Goodman, a native of Cherokee County, Ala., born on May 18, 1837. Two children were born to this union: John W. (born July 19, 1855) and Minerva L. (born October 6, 1858). In 1856 Mr. Hammons purchased a tract of land with about four acres under cultivation, and a small log-hut being the only improvement on the place excepting the fencing. Mr. Hammons erected a log house, 16x16, in which he lived for about a year, and then erected another log house, 18x18, in which he resided until 1870. He then erected the fine frame house which is such an ornament to his farm, and in which he has resided since that time. One hundred and twenty acres of the first purchase are under cultivation, and he is now the owner of 320 acres of land. Some of his land has been under cultivation for thirty-five years, and although it has never been fertilized, it produces fine crops. In 1864 he enlisted as a private in a company of Col. McRae's regiment, and served one year, participating in the Missouri raid under Gen. Price. Mr. Hammons is a member of the Masonic fraternity, and he and wife are members of the Methodist Episcopal Church, South.

John William Hammons, merchant and farmer, Hammonsville, Ark. For a number of years past the town of Hammonsville has been noted far and wide for its excellent mercantile establishments, and particularly that of Mr. Hammons, who is one of the representative business men of the place. Aside from this he is also engaged in farming, and is the owner of 106 acres of land. He was born in Van Buren County, Ark., on July 19, 1855, and is the son of Jacob D. and Jane (Goodman) Hammons. In 1857 the father moved to White County, Ark., and there reared a large family of children, seven now living. John W. Hammons was reared in White County, Ark., and received his education in the private schools of that county. He assisted his father on the farm for some time, and then commenced business for himself by teaching school, which profession he followed for some time. In 1874 he made a prospecting tour through California and Oregon, in which States he sojourned for nearly three years, and while there followed various lines of industries, viz.: mining, farming, saw-milling, teaming, etc., obtaining some knowledge of farming and mining as conducted in those States. In 1877 he returned to Arkansas, and there resumed the profession of teaching, organizing a school at Hammons' Chapel, near what is now the village of Hammonsville. This he conducted for two years, during which time he also followed agricultural pursuits, having purchased 160 acres, which he hired help to clear and improve. On January 28, 1878, he was united in marriage to Miss Mattie Nelson, daughter of George Nelson, and her death occurred in 1878. In 1879 Mr. Hammons married Miss Mollie J. Nelson, of White County, Ark., and a sister of his former wife. By this marriage

WHITE COUNTY.

six children were born: Edgar L. (born June 13, 1880), John R. (born November 4, 1882), Eva (born in 1883), Grover Cleveland (born March 2, 1885), Troy M. (born November 23, 1886) and an infant son (born in August, 1889). Edgar died in November, 1881, and Eva in 1884. In 1879 Mr. Hammons moved to his farm, followed tilling the soil, and also speculated in patent rights. He also ran a well-auger. In 1885, in partnership with J. T. Phelps, he erected a store building at Hammonsville, and engaged in merchandising under the firm title of Phelps & Hammons. The partnership lasted but a short time, and in 1887, in company with Messrs. Moore & Rollon, at Quitman, Cleburne County, Ark., he again engaged in merchandising. In 1888 he bought the interest of his partners, and located at Hammonsville, where he has since remained. About September Mr. Hammons completed the building in which he now does business, and it is a large, commodious structure. His stock of goods consists of a good line of dry goods, boots and shoes, clothing, groceries, drugs and plantation supplies. In politics he is a stanch Democrat, and has held the office of justice of the peace. At present he is the postmaster at Hammonsville.

Abraham Hancock. John Hancock was a native of North Carolina, and was born July 26, 1804, and was married in 1828 to Miss Martha Harrington, who was born in North Carolina June 10, 1809. In 1836 he moved to Madison County, Tenn., and there engaged in his trade of blacksmithing until 1858, and after a residence of several years in Van Buren County came to White County, where he now resides with his aged wife. Mr. Hancock is of Irish descent and an own cousin of Gen. W. S. Hancock. He has held the office of sheriff in Van Buren County, but has never aspired to office. His wife is of English descent, and both are adherents of the Baptist faith. To them have been born a family of nine children, all living, in which Abraham, the subject of this sketch, is the eldest. He is a native of North Carolina, and was born November 22, 1830. He was reared on a farm and learned the saddle and harness-maker's trade, which has been his principal

work, but is also a good carpenter. He was given a good education in the common schools of his native State, and at the age of twenty-one began life for himself, first as office boy in a bank and later as clerk for a cotton ginner. He was married on March 20, 1851, to Miss Leana C. Jones, and to their union one child was born, Martha R. (now the wife of J. J. Martin, a farmer of Faulkner County, Ark.) Mrs. Hancock died in September, 1857, and in March, 1858, Mr. Hancock was united in marriage to Miss Rebecca A. Bertram, a native of Tennessee. To this union five children have been born, two of whom are now living: John S. (a farmer of White County, and who married Elizabeth Landers, a daughter of Thomas Landers, of White County) and Vera A. (born March 14, 1883). Those deceased are William H., Paralea A. and Lena. In May, 1861, Mr. Hancock enlisted in Company B, Twelfth Tennessee Infantry, and served until the surrender in 1865. He participated in the battles of Belmont (Mo.), Shiloh (Tenn.), Richmond (Ky.), Murfreesboro (Tenn.), Chickamauga (Ga.), Missionary Ridge, and at the latter place was wounded by a gunshot, and was helpless for one year. At the battle of Shiloh, he was shot through the hip, and from that wound he still suffers. The last engagement that he took part in was the encounter at Franklin, where he was injured, and which disabled him for some time. During the entire war Mr. Hancock served as orderly-sergeant, his military record being one without a blemish. He received his parole in 1865, and at once returned home; here he resumed his trade of harness making until 1871. He then came to White County and purchased a farm of sixty acres. One year later he moved to El Paso and worked at his trade there, and has since been engaged at farming and carpentering up to the present time. Mr. Hancock has erected some twelve or fourteen ginpowers in White County alone, and there are many marks of his handiwork in different parts of the country. He is a Democrat in his political views, but is an independent voter. He has held the office of constable and deputy sheriff in Tennessee, and in 1885 was elected to the position of justice

HISTORY OF ARKANSAS.

of the peace of Royal Township, which office he is at present filling. Mr. Hancock is an honorary member of El Paso Lodge No. 65, A. F. & A. M., and was secretary of said lodge for eight years; he is also a member of Lodge No. 6, and is E. S. W. P. of that lodge. Mr. and Mrs. Hancock are members of the El Paso Baptist Church, and the former always gives his support to all laudable enterprises for the public good. Mr. Hancock is a member of New Hope Wheel No. 32, in which he was the efficient secretary for years, and is an ardent worker for his order.

Edward Harper, an influential citizen of Romance, is the son of the late Edward Harper, Sr., who was born in North Carolina in 1774, and was an only son of Samuel Harper. His parents died when he was a small boy and he was left with an uncle. He married, in about 1801, Elender Scallorn, a native of Maryland, after which he moved to Alabama, where he engaged in farming, thence moving to Tennessee and in 1855 came to Arkansas, settling in Prairie County, where he died three years later. His wife died in 1862, leaving a family of eleven children: Overton W., Jefferson B., Andrew J., Durinda, Edia, Malinda, Pomelia, Edward (our subject), Joseph A., William A. and Sarah A. Edward, Jr., was born in Alabama, in 1821, and spent his early life in Western Tennessee, where he received a good common-school education. He taught school in Tennessee for a number of years, and was married in 1851 to Mary Kyle, who was a daughter of Marvin and Sarah (Dement) Kyle, originally of Alabama and Virginia, respectively. To this marriage the following children were given: Martha S. (now Mrs. J. B. Matthews), William K., Edward L., Julia T., James H., Ellen O. (deceased), Jefferson D., Sidney K., Marvin A., John F. and Adolphus. In 1856 Mr. Harper came to White County, Ark., where he purchased 240 acres of land, and now has nearly 100 acres cleared and under cultivation. Himself and wife are members of the Methodist Church. Mr. Harper belongs to the Masonic order, affiliating with Mount Veran Lodge No. 54, and has taken the degree of Royal Arch Mason. Mr. Harper is a highly respected citizen, and has

held the office of justice of the peace for twelve years.

Rev. Henry F. Harvey, one of the leading planters and a popular minister of White County, Ark., is a native of Tennessee, and was born in 1842. His father, Jesse F. Harvey, was born in Alabama, in 1818, where he received his education, and afterward immigrated to Mississippi with his parents, there marrying Miss Mary C. Wyatt, in 1841. To their union was born a family of twelve children, of which Henry F. is the oldest. Jesse Harvey and his estimable wife were respected members of the Church (Methodist), and always manifested a great interest in all worthy enterprises. Henry F. was educated in Mississippi, and moved from that State to Arkansas with his parents in 1869. His marriage with Miss Sarah J. McCleskey was consummated on November 26, 1867. Mrs. Harvey was the daughter of John and Nancy McCleskey, and was born in 1849. To their union eight children have been born, six boys and two girls, seven of whom are now living: John F., Mary Ida, Luther B., William P., Eugene B., Walter W., Samuel J. and Mattie M. Mr. Harvey owns 232 acres of land, with 125 cultivated. He is a member of the Masonic Lodge, and has held the office of secretary of Lodge Chapter, Centre Hill No. 45, also affiliates with the Wheel, in which he held the office of State Chaplain for one year. He has been a member of the council for twelve years. He served in the late war on the Confederate side, and enlisted in 1861, under Gen. Buckner of Kentucky. His first hard fight was at Fort Donelson, where he was captured and carried to Camp Morton, Indianapolis, and imprisoned for seven months. He was then exchanged and again captured in Virginia, near Petersburg, and taken to Point Lookout, Md., and incarcerated for seven months, then exchanged at Richmond, where he received his parole. After the war he returned home at once and began teaching school, which he continued for one year, and then commenced farming and preaching, his present occupation. He is an eloquent and brilliant speaker, and makes many converts to his faith (Methodist), to which he and wife belong.

Richard D. Harris, familiarly known as "Uncle

WHITE COUNTY.

Dick" Harris, was the eldest son in a family of thirteen children born to Newton and Nancy (Spencer) Harris, natives of North Carolina. Newton Harris, the father, was born in 1801, and married in 1821; he was the son of a soldier in the Revolutionary War. He was the father of the following children: Richard D. (our subject), D. C., Louisa, Roland (deceased), Victoria M. (deceased), Milton, M. D., Newton (deceased), Wesley (deceased), Sidney (deceased), Steven D. and Dolly. Richard D. Harris first saw the light of this world in Tennessee in 1824, and was married October 20, 1846, to Arcissie Bowman, a daughter of Maj. William and Cassander (Wade), who were of Maryland nativity. Mr. Harris settled on a farm in Tennessee after his marriage, and in 1862 enlisted in Company C, of the Forty-seventh Tennessee Cavalry, and participated in the battles of Corinth, Richmond (Ky.), Perrysville, Murfreesboro, Chickamauga, Kenesaw Mountain and Franklin. He received his discharge in 1863, on account of deafness and a weakness in the back. He then entered the cavalry under Forrest, but served only a short time when he returned home badly disabled. He had eight brothers in the Confederate army, one of whom, Leven, only was wounded. His first wife died October 2, 1858. She was the mother of nine children: Cassander (deceased), Ella (now Mrs. John Banks, of Tennessee), Molly (now Mrs. Reid), John D., E. A., Abbilow (McDinworthy), Decksy (Turnage) and Effie. Mr. Harris came to Arkansas, settling in White County, in 1871, where he purchased a quarter section of land, of which there were about sixty acres cleared. He was married the second time in 1881 to Elizabeth McDougald, a daughter of Alexander and Ellen (Wade) McDougald. Mr. Harris is a strong Democrat, and cast his first presidential vote for James K. Polk. Mr. and Mrs. Harris are members of the Presbyterian Church, but most of his children are Methodists.

Hubbard P. Heard, a most successful agriculturist and stock raiser, of White County, received his education in this county, where he grew to manhood, and remained at home until the organization of the Third Arkansas Confederate Cavalry, in the early part of 1861. His regiment took part in sixty-five engagements, and of the 104 men which started out, only eight returned, and he had many narrow escapes. He was in the siege of Corinth, at Beauregard's retreat into the river, at the battles of Shiloh, Thomas' Station (where three flag bearers and the colonel of his regiment were killed), Missionary Ridge; also at the capture of Knoxville, and many others, including those in the Georgia campaign, where he was in constant fighting for sixty days. He was taken prisoner near Holly Springs, and carried to Cairo, Ill., where he was kept for nearly three months; then he was exchanged with 1,100 Confederate soldiers. After peace was declared he returned home, and at the death of his father commenced farming, and in 1880 he engaged in the saw-mill business, which occupation he followed for five years, since which time he has given his attention exclusively to farming and stock raising, and owns 400 acres of land, with 150 under cultivation. Our subject was born in Heard County, Ga., August 1, 1840, and is the son of Hubbard P. and Mary (Ware) Heard. The paternal grandfather of Hubbard P., Jr., Thomas Heard, was a soldier in the Revolutionary War, and also in the War of 1812, and was county judge of Heard County, which was named in honor of him. Hubbard Heard, Sr., was born in 1800, and was married in Georgia, and came to Arkansas and located within ten miles of Augusta, Woodruff County, in 1840, and in 1849 removed to White County, where he was engaged in farming and stock raising the rest of his life. He was a prominent Democrat and a constituent of the Masonic order, and both he and his wife were members of the Methodist Episcopal Church, South. Mrs. Heard died in February, 1862, at the age of sixty-one, leaving six children, five of whom are now living: Eliza (widow of John Griffin), Sophia (widow of John Wesley), Amanda (widow of James Asque), Martha (widow of David Duke) and Hubbard P. (the principal of this sketch). After the death of his first wife Mr. Heard married Mrs. Sarah Pierce, who is now deceased. The senior Heard died in White County in 1866, and was highly respected by all who knew him, and had been a very successful

HISTORY OF ARKANSAS.

farmer, but met with heavy losses financially during the war. Hubbard P. Heard was married in 1870 to Miss Jennie Martin, a native of Tennessee, and who was the mother of five children, four of whom are still living: Dora V., Joseph W., Hubbard, Jr., and James H. He was married to his second wife, Olive B. Markham, in 1884, who lived but three years after their marriage, and was the mother of one daughter, who died soon after her mother. Mr. Heard is a Democrat in politics and in secret societies belongs to the Masons.

Col. V. H. Henderson, Searcy, Ark. In preparation of this brief outline of the history of one of the most influential citizens of White County, appear facts which are greatly to his credit. His intelligence, enterprise, integrity and many estimable qualities, have acquired for him a popularity not derived from any factitious circumstance, but a permanent and spontaneous tribute to his merit. He is at present proprietor and manager of Searcy College and is also actively engaged in the real-estate business. He owes his nativity to Haywood County, West Tenn., where his birth occurred in 1833, and is the fourth in a family of nine children born to the union of T. C. and Eunice (Haraldson) Henderson, both natives of South Carolina. The parents moved to Tennessee at an early day, thence to St. Francis County, Ark., in 1849 and located in what is now Woodruff County, where the father followed agricultural pursuits. He died in Mississippi in 1844, and the mother afterward came to Arkansas and thence to Texas in 1858. Col. V. H. Henderson came to Arkansas at the age of sixteen years, engaged in merchandising in Cotton Plant in 1857 and continued at that until the beginning of the war. In that year he enlisted at the above-mentioned place in Capt. Stephen's company, was elected second lieutenant, but served only a short time when he was discharged on account of ill health. He then engaged in the pursuit of farming on a large scale, and in connection carries on merchandising extensively at Cotton Plant. He came to White County in 1884 for the purpose of recruiting his health, which had become impaired, and purchased a farm of 240 acres, which he improved and which is now known as the Griffin Springs, a great watering place. He also raises some fine stock and is extensively engaged in the real-estate business. He has been active in building up the town and is deeply interested in educational matters. Socially, he is a member of the Masonic fraternity, and in politics, although not active, votes with the Democratic party. He selected for his companion in life Miss Sarah J. Simpson, a native of Mississippi, and was married to her in Woodruff (then St. Francis) County, Ark., in 1857. Her death occurred in 1871, leaving one child as the result of this union: Robert C., who is now married and resides at Cotton Plant. Col. Henderson was married to his second wife, Miss Martha A. Davies, a native of North Carolina, in 1872, and the fruits of this union are four children: Freddie Davis, Mary Virgie, Carl C. and Ross K. Col. and Mrs. Henderson are members of the Presbyterian Church.

John T. Hicks, attorney, Arkansas. This gentleman is the junior member of the well-known law firm of House & Hicks, and practices in this and adjoining counties. He was born in Searcy, Ark., on July 21, 1861, and was the second in the family of six children born to William and Martha A. (Lytle) Hicks, natives of North Carolina, born near Hillsboro. The father, when about eighteen years of age, came to Searcy, Ark., read law at that place, and was admitted to the bar. He then began practicing and followed this during life. He took an active part in politics and was senator from this district in 1866. Prior to that he was county judge. He was a prominent Mason, was a Chapter member of Searcy Lodge No. 49, and was a member of Tillman Chapter No. 19. He met the mother of the subject of this sketch while attending college, and was married to her in Fayette County, Tenn., in 1857. Six children were the result of this union, two of whom are living: John T. and Willie (who resides in Searcy). The father was a progressive man and took an active part in building up the town and county. He was also deeply interested in educational matters, and as a man, well and favorably known. He was a member of the Episcopal Church. During the late war, or rather at the beginning of the late war, Mr.

WHITE COUNTY.

Hicks had strong Union proclivities, but after the State seceded, he joined with the State, recruited a company, and was promoted to the rank of colonel. He was in the battle of "Whiting Landing," was wounded by a shell at Helena, and was with Gen. Price on his raid through Missouri. After the war he returned to Searcy, resumed his practice, and died August 13, 1869, at the age of forty-one years. He was the son of Howell T. and Sally (Roberts) Hicks, natives of North Carolina, who came to Searcy in 1846, settled in Gray Township, and engaged in tilling the soil. The grandfather died in 1858, and the grandmother in 1881. The maternal grandparents of the subject of this sketch, John C. and Sarah (Graham) Lytle, were natives of North Carolina. At an early day they moved to Tennessee, where the father followed farming, but also continued the trade of a mechanic. The grandmother died in Tennessee, and her husband came to Searcy (1870), where he is now residing. John T. Hicks was liberally educated in the schools at Searcy and at Fayetteville, Ark., after which he took a course at the University of Virginia. After this he took a law course in 1881-82 and was admitted to the bar in 1883, after which he commenced practicing. He was married at Searcy in 1883, to Miss Minnie Snipes, a native of White County and the daughter of Dr. J. A. and Elizabeth (Murphy) Snipes, natives of North Carolina and Virginia, respectively. Both are residing at Searcy. Mr. and Mrs. Hicks have two children: Everette B. and Willie B. Mr. Hicks takes an active part in politics and was mayor of Searcy from 1884 to 1887. Socially, he is a member of Searcy Lodge No. 49, Masonic fraternity, and is Junior Warden in that order. He is a member of Tillman Chapter No. 19, R. A. M. He is a member of the Episcopal, and she of the Methodist Episcopal Church, South.

N. B. Hilger, a native of this county, is a son of John and Catharine (Yenglan) Hilger. John Hilger was born in Monhan, Germany, on the Rhine, in 1802, and spent his school-days in that country and was married there. A few years after his marriage he emigrated to America with his family, locating in White County, Ark., where he entered a quarter section of land, and at the time of his death, in 1853, owned 900 acres of land. His wife was born in 1807 and died in 1878, leaving thirteen children: John, Bardoia, Philip and Shibastas (who were born in Germany) and Elizabeth, Catharine, Louisa, Louie, Minerva, Nancy, Mary, N. B. (our subject) and Margaret (who were born in this county). N. B. Hilger was married, in 1868, to Frances Elliott, who died the following year, leaving one child, also deceased. In 1873, he married Lucy A. Crump, a native of Alabama, and who is the mother of three children, two of whom are living: Noah and Laurie. He owns the old homestead on which he lived when a boy, and has 440 acres of land, about half of which is under cultivation and which he helped to clear. Socially, he is a member of the Masonic order and is school director of his district, and is a successful farmer and raises good stock, and is well and favorably known throughout the township.

Rev. William H. Hodges. The father of our subject was James L. Hodges, a native of South Carolina, where he was born about 1787, and was the son of William and Elizabeth Hodges, also of South Carolina. Mr. Hodges, Sr., was married, in about 1810, to Sarah Comings, and they were the parents of eleven children: Francis, Nancy, Thomas, Elizabeth, William H., Sarah, Margaret, James, Mary, Martha and Benjamin F. William H. was born in South Carolina on March 22, 1822, and came to Mississippi with his parents when but eight years of age, where he was reared on a farm. He was married, in 1844, to Sarah F. Roseman, a daughter of Samuel and Frances (Hill) Roseman. After his marriage he settled on a farm, where he resided until 1869. As the result of this union the following children were born: James S., Casandria E. (deceased), Thomas H., John F., William A., Benjamin F. (deceased), Marshall L., Sarah F., Archie N. (deceased), Emmett L. and Joseph T. They also have twenty-seven grandchildren. Mr. Hodges commenced preaching the Gospel in Choctaw County, Miss., in 1863. In 1869 he came to Arkansas and settled in White County and in Cane Township, on 240 acres of land, of which he now has about 100 acres under cultivation. Mr.

HISTORY OF ARKANSAS.

Hodges is pastor of the Bethlehem Missionary Baptist Church. He has been a very active worker in his labors and has organized four churches in this neighborhood.

John G. Holland, one of the editors and proprietors of the Beacon, owes his nativity to Wake County, N. C., where his birth occurred on December 10, 1845. He is the son of Willis B. and Lucinda (Barbee) Holland, natives of Wake County, N. C., the former born in 1818 and died in 1869, and the latter born in 1814 and died in 1888. The parents moved from North Carolina to Henderson County, Tenn., in 1851, and nearly two years later to White County, Ark., where the father followed several different avocations—farming, surveying and civil engineering. He was also deputy county surveyor for several years. Both he and wife were members of the Missionary Baptist Church; he was a Royal Arch Mason, and of the Council degrees, and in his political views affiliated with the Democratic party. Of the five children born to this union, John G. Holland is fourth in number of birth. He received a liberal education in the schools of White County, and during the late war served a few months in the Confederate army in the capacity of private. At the age of twenty-one years he turned his attention to the reading of law under Judge Cypert, and in 1867 was admitted to the bar. He practiced his profession until 1882, when he turned his attention to the newspaper business. He was associate editor of the Arkansas Beacon, and in 1883 became partner. In December of the same year John R. Jobe became a partner in the paper, and they have so continued ever since. In 1877 he was mayor of the city of Searcy, continuing in that capacity one year. In 1885–86 he was justice of the peace. He is at present president of the school board of Searcy. In 1877 he was elected assistant clerk of the lower house of the General Assembly, and in 1879 was elected to the position of chief clerk in the same; in 1881 he was elected secretary of the senate, and has served in that capacity ever since. On January 14, 1879, he married Miss Ella M. Henley, daughter of B. F. and Mary J. Henley, and she died in April, 1889, leaving five children: Lillie C., Della,

Percy, Bessie and Lewis F. Mr. Holland is a member of the Missionary Baptist Church at Searcy, and is clerk of the same. He is a Council Mason, is a member of the K. & L. of H., and in his political views affiliates with the Democratic party.

W. G. Holland, M. D. In recording the names of the prominent citizens of White County, the name of W. G. Holland, M. D., is given an enviable position. He was a faithful student in his chosen profession, and truly merits the prominence accorded him in the medical fraternity, as well as the confidence and respect shown him by the entire community. He owes his nativity to Tennessee, and was born in Henderson County, April 6, 1847. His father, Dr. James C. Holland, was born in Wayne County, N. C., December 12, 1807, and he received his education in his native State, and in 1833 he was united in marriage to Rebecca, daughter of Frederick and Lucy Collier, and by her became the father of six children: Julia F., Eliza, Maria R. (deceased), Charles E. (deceased), W. G. and his twin brother (who died in infancy). Mrs. Holland died at Searcy, May 10, 1861, and for his second wife, Dr. Holland chose Miss Ellen Kirby of Tennessee. Dr. Holland was both physician and silversmith by occupation for over fifty years. He immigrated to Arkansas from Tennessee in 1853, and located in Searcy, where he resided until his death in 1887. He was a man of considerable influence, and a politician to some extent. He was a devout member of the Methodist Church, as was also his wife. He held a membership in the Masonic lodge for over forty years, being a member of Searcy Lodge No. 49, and Tillman Chapter No. 19, where he discharged the duties of secretary and treasurer up to the date of his death. W. G. Holland received a good practical education in the schools of Searcy, but obtained his medical knowledge in the University of Louisville, Ky., during the years 1869-71. After his graduation Dr. Holland returned to his home and built the foundation of his present large and lucrative practice. He was married December 8, 1872, to Annie Goad, a daughter of Henry and Mary Goad, and their union has been blessed with three

WHITE COUNTY.

children: Mary E., William E. (deceased), and an infant, who died unnamed. Mrs. Holland died August 10, 1887, and in 1889 Dr. Holland was united in marriage to Rachel V. Fancette, their marriage occurring September 1. Dr. W. G. Holland served in the late war, entering in 1864 under Gen. Shelby. He was wounded at Pilot Knob, September 28, 1864, and also captured and taken prisoner to Alton, thence to Rock Island and Richmond, Va., where he was exchanged in March, 1865, receiving his parole at that point. He at once returned home and entered the literary school for three years, and began the study of medicine in spring of 1868. Dr. and Mrs. Holland are members in high standing of the Methodist Church.

A. B. House is accounted a prosperous farmer and stockman of Red River Township, and like the majority of native Tennesseeans, he is progressive in his views and of an energetic temperament. He was born in Maury County, in 1822, and is the youngest in a family of nine children born to Joseph and Alcy (Bedwell) House, the former of whom is a native of North Carolina, born in 1775. When a lad he was taken to Tennessee, and about the year 1800, was married in that State and engaged in farming and raising stock, his land amounting to 200 acres. He died in 1862, and his wife in 1845, both having been earnest and consistent members of the Cumberland Presbyterian Church. Their children are: Mary (deceased), Reuben (who is married and lives in White County, Ark.), John (married and lives in Tennessee), Patience (Mrs. Haines, now deceased), Charlotte (the wife of John Myers, is also dead), William (and his wife, formerly a Miss Bedwock, are deceased), Marcenie (is the wife of Mr. Brazele and resides in West Tennessee), Jane (and her husband, D. House, are both dead) and A. B. (the subject of this memoir). The paternal grandfather was John House, and the mother's father was Reuben Bedwell, a native of Tennessee. A. B. House resided in his native State until he arrived to manhood, then came to White County, Ark. He reared his family in his native State, and with the assistance of his wife, Eliza Wilkes, whom he married

in 1840, he succeeded in giving them good educations. Their names are: Thomas (who married Mary Minifee, by whom he has two children, resides in Arkansas), Joseph (who married Ina Dowdy and lives at Little Rock, the father of four children), James P. (married Lou Parcell, but is now a widower and lives in Augusta with his one child) and Mary (who married Mr. Harville. She died, leaving one child, who was reared by his grandfather). Mrs. House died after their removal to Arkansas, in 1884. She was a daughter of Thomas and Ruth Wilkes, and was one of a family of thirteen children. After coming to Arkansas Mr. House settled on a woodland farm of 140 acres, and now has eighty acres under cultivation. He raises some of the finest stock in the county and many of his animals have won first premiums at the county fairs. He is a Democrat and a member of the Masonic order and he and his present wife, who was Martha McMillan and whom he married in 1884, are members of the Cumberland Presbyterian Church, his first wife being also a member of this church.

Andrew J. Hughs is the son of Harden Hughs, a highly respected man who was born in Tennessee, in 1791, and took a prominent part in the French and Indian Wars of 1813 and following. He was married in 1813 to Miss Sallie Jones, and they were the parents of eight children: Thomas, Katie, Polly, Betty, Andrew J. (the principal of this biography), Marian, Louisa and Harding. The senior Hughs immigrated to Arkansas and settled in White County, in 1842, where he purchased a quarter section of land and on which he lived until his death, which occurred in 1858, his wife surviving him until 1871. Andrew J. owes his nativity to Tennessee, his birth occurring in 1828, and was fourteen years of age when his parents came to Arkansas. He was married on January 30, 1850, to Miss Sarah Marsh, who was born in Tennessee, January 7, 1831, and was the daughter of Roland and Sarah (Webb) Marsh. Her parents both died in Tennessee, in 1835, and she then came to Arkansas with her brothers, John and Harvey Marsh, who located in White County. Mr. and Mrs. Hughs were the parents

HISTORY OF ARKANSAS.

of eleven children, four of whom are deceased: Francis M. Mary M. (deceased), Thomas F., Harden M., Martha (now Mrs. Asia Buchanan), Sarah Jane (now Mrs. Woodell), John A. (deceased), Ulysses M., Rachel A., Cymantha and Emma. They are also the grandparents of sixteen children. Mr. Hughs has 300 acres of land, with 180 acres under cultivation, which he and his father before him have farmed for the past forty-five years, and which Mr. Hughs says is as fine a piece of land as there is in the State. He and his wife have been members of the Methodist Church for over thirty-five years, and take a very active part in all church work. He also belongs to the County Wheel. He takes an active interest in all public matters, and was on the Review in 1866 and helped to reconstruct the State.

D. W. Holiman is a citizen in good standing, and is held in high esteem by his associates. He was left an orphan at the age of four years, and cared for and reared by his older brothers and sisters, on a farm in Mississippi. At the age of twenty-one he started out for himself, and came to Arkansas, and located in Van Buren County, and four years after removed to White County. In 1876 he married Lucinda Bouliand, a daughter of J. W. and Martha A. (Harvey) Bouliand, originally of Kentucky, and who came to Arkansas at an early day, and settled in White County. His nearest town and market at that time was Little Rock. Mr. Holiman was the youngest son in a family of ten children, born to Willis and Eliza (Virnan) Holiman, natives of South Carolina, and parents of the following children (and two others deceased, whose names are not given): James P., Malinda, William H., John, Martha, Bell, Willis and D. W. (our subject, who was born in Mississippi in 1849). D. W. Holiman and wife are the parents of four children: Martha J., Willis W., Eddie Lee, Hettie J., all of whom are at home. He has a farm of 258 acres, with fifty under cultivation. In religious belief, he and his wife are members of the Baptist Church, in which they take an active part. He is also a member of the County Wheel. Mrs. Holiman has seen a great change in White County during her lifetime, having been

born and reared in this county. Mr. Holiman is a strong Democrat, and a good citizen.

George Irwin is a general farmer and fruit grower of Harrison Township, White County, Ark., and although a native of Kentucky, born in 1822, he has been a resident of this State for the past thirteen years. His father, Joseph Irwin, born in Kentucky in 1782 in a small neighborhood stockade, called Fort Hamilton, in the western part of Nelson County, was of Scotch-Irish descent, being one of a family of nine children born to John Irwin, who came from Ireland before the Revolutionary War. Joseph spent his youthful days on a farm, and on March 30, 1808, was married in Kentucky to Sarah Thompson, and by her became the father of the following sons: Hardin, James, Joseph, George, John and Benjamin. In 1828 he moved to Indiana, and died in Knox County, in 1858, having been a member of the Whig party, and he and wife members of the Baptist Church. His wife's death occurred in Parke County, Ind., in 1862. George Irwin acquired a fair education in the subscription schools of his native county, but at the age of seventeen years he left home and went to the pineries of Wisconsin, and until the spring of 1850 followed the lumbering business. In 1850 he resolved to seek his fortune in California, and after reaching the "Eldorado of the West," he engaged in mining, and succeeded far beyond his expectations. At the end of two years he returned to Indiana, and settled down to the peaceful pursuit of farming, and there, in 1854, was united in the bonds of matrimony to Catherine Black, a daughter of Thomas and Lavina (Dudley) Black, of Sullivan County, Ind. After remaining in Indiana some ten years, Mr. Irwin immigrated to Dallas County, Iowa, and twelve years later came to White County, Ark., buying, almost as soon as he reached the county, 160 acres of land where he now lives. He has sixty acres under cultivation, and owing to the attention which he gives to the minutest details of his work he is doing well. He belongs to the Agricultural Wheel, and although formerly a Republican in his political views, he is now a Prohibitionist. He and wife are members of the Baptist Church, and are the parents of these children: May (Mrs.

WHITE COUNTY.

Charles Briggs, residing in White County), Broughan (who died in 1887), Dudley, and Grace, the youngest, who was eighteen years old in March, 1889.

James M. Jackson, of Russell, Ark., was born in Perry County, Ala., February 18, 1853, and is the son of Lorenzo D. Jackson, of North Carolina. The former's birth occurred in 1811, and at the age of twenty-two years he moved from North Carolina to Alabama, where he was residing at the time of his death, in 1865, when fifty-four years old. He was a farmer by occupation, and quite successful in his chosen profession. In his party views he sided with the Democrats, though not a political enthusiast. He was a member of the Baptist Church and a zealous worker in religious and all charitable enterprises. His wife, Anna (Winston) Jackson, was a daughter of James Winston, and a native of North Carolina. Her marriage with Lorenzo D. Jackson was consummated in 1833, and after her husband's demise she resided with her son, James M., until her death in 1886. To Mr. and Mrs. Jackson a family of eight children were born, three sons and five daughters, four of whom are now living: Anna (wife of L. D. N. Huff, of White County, Ark.), Fannie (first married to Britt Perry, now the wife of Henry C. Strange, of White County), Mary S. (Mrs. John Huff), James M. (the subject of this sketch) and Lacy J. (wife of Reuben Bennett, now deceased). William L. died in the Confederate army, and was one of the first volunteers of the war. Thomas was killed at the battle of Sharpsburg, in the Confederate army, and Martha died in Alabama. James M. received his education in the common schools of his native State, and at the age of eighteen came from Alabama to White County, Ark., where he launched his own canoe, and began life for himself. His choice of an occupation was farming, to which he had been carefully drilled by his father. Mr. Jackson now owns 160 acres of good land in a fair state of cultivation, divided into two farms. He is also interested in a large grist-mill and cotton-gin at Russell. Active, energetic and industrious in his efforts, he is on the high road to prosperity. He was first married, January 10,

1877, to Miss Nannie, daughter of William and Emily Plant. Mr. Plant is a native of Tennessee, but moved to Arkansas in 1859, his being one of the oldest families in this county. Mrs. Jackson died November 20, 1877, leaving one child, William D. In 1886 Mr. Jackson was united in marriage with Miss Virginia L. Shelton, of Arkansas, and at that time a resident of Jackson County. To this union two children have been born: Robert L. and Frank Earl. Mr. Jackson served as township bailiff and deputy sheriff for two and a half years, discharging the duties of that office faithfully and to the entire satisfaction of all concerned. He is a Democrat in politics, and a member of the Baptist Church at Russell, Ark. In societies he is identified with the Masonic order, is a Knight of Honor and a member of the Triple Alliance Mutual Benefit Association. He is a liberal contributor to his church, and the needy are never sent from his door empty-handed. Indeed too much praise can not be accorded Mr. Jackson for his upright course, for he is noble-minded, generous, and of that caliber of men who build up a community to places of thrift and enterprise.

J. R. Jobe, who is one of the editors and proprietors of the Beacon, owned by Holland & Jobe, became connected with the paper in December, 1884, and has continued with it ever since that time. He was born at Ringgold, Ga., on August 24, 1855, and was the fifth in a family of thirteen children born to David and Sarah (Hardin) Jobe, natives of East Tennessee and Georgia, respectively. The father was a farmer by occupation and came to Columbia County, Ark., in 1857, settled on a farm, remained there one year and then removed to Des Arc, Prairie County, Ark., where he followed mercantile pursuits until 1861. He then moved to Pope County, Ark, remained there until 1863, when he moved to White County and settled in Union Township, where he followed agricultural pursuits until his death, which occurred in May, 1888. His excellent wife, still living, resides at Russellville, Pope County. J. R. Jobe's early life was divided between assisting on the farm and in attending the district schools of White County, although he greatly improved his education by

HISTORY OF ARKANSAS.

personal application in later years. He started out on the highway of life at the age of twenty years, engaged in farming until he was elected county clerk in 1882, and in October moved to Searcy, where he filled the above-mentioned office to the satisfaction of all for two years. He then purchased the interest of the Beacon from Rev. Z. T. Bennett, who was the founder of the paper in 1878, and has been connected with it ever since. He is active in politics and votes with the Democratic party. He was married in White County in November, 1878, to Miss Cora E. Harris, a native of Tennessee, and the daughter of Dr. D. C. and Susan E. Harris, natives of Tennessee, who came to White County, Ark., in 1874. Her mother died in 1879, but her father resides at Beebe, and aside from being a practicing physician is also engaged in mercantile pursuits. By his marriage Mr. Jobe became the father of three children: Edgar Wilmett, John Bertram and Lucille. Mr. Jobe was elected in January, 1886, to fill an unexpired term of city recorder and ex-officio treasurer, and has filled that position satisfactorily since that time. He is also corresponding secretary of the Arkansas Press Association, and is now serving the second term.

Wiley A. Johnson, the senior member of the well-known and representative firm of W. A. Johnson & Son, wagon manufacturers of Beebe, Ark., was born in Indiana, October 12, 1832, being the son of Daniel S. and Nancy (Parker) Johnson, natives of New York and Pennsylvania, respectively. Daniel Johnson's younger days were spent in the State of his birth, but when grown to manhood he went to Indiana and there married in 1822. He was a tailor by trade, and a few years before his death served as county clerk of the county in which he resided, in Tennessee. His demise occurred in 1833, at the age of thirty years, Wiley A. Johnson at that time being only one year old. After his father's death the latter moved to Weakley County, Tenn., with his mother, who remained in her widowed state for sixteen years, at the end of which time she was united in marriage with Mr. George Winston, but only lived one year after that event. The parents were members of the Methodist Episcopal Church, and were held in high esteem by all who knew them. Wiley A. Johnson was educated in the schools of Dresden, Tenn., proving a bright and intelligent scholar, and when seventeen years old became an apprentice to a blacksmith. After completing his apprenticeship, at the age of twenty, he at once went to work for himself, and for several years was employed in different shops all over Western Tennessee. In 1856, settling at Union City, Obion County, he was there married to Nanny Curlin, a native of that county, on October 14, 1856, and to them one child has been born, William W. Following his marriage, Mr. Johnson settled in Union City, and carried on his business of blacksmithing and wagon-making for nine years, moving thence to Trenton, Gibson County, where he remained for three years. After living in Verona, Miss., and Sulphur Rock, Ark., he came to Beebe in 1885 and formed the present firm, now having a large and substantial trade. Mr. Johnson and son are among the leading business men of this section, and enjoy the respect of all, both as business and social factors. They are public-spirited and lend their support to those enterprises that are intended for the good or growth of the country. In his religious belief, Mr. Johnson clings to the Methodist faith, of which church his wife is also a devout member. The paternal grandfather of the subject of this sketch, Collert Johnson, was probably a native of Pennsylvania, and a wealthy planter of Indiana. He had several sons who figured prominently in the early wars, and when last heard from were residing in Southern Indiana. Included in Mr. Johnson's maternal relations, of whom he knows but little, were two uncles, Lorenza and Gideon Parker, both holding high offices in the Florida War.

Thomas P. Jones, a distinguished citizen of White County, and a native of South Carolina (his birth occurring in Abbeville District, October 13, 1830), is the son of Clayton and Nancy (Miford) Jones, natives of the same State and district. Clayton Jones was of Welsh descent, and first saw the light of day July 11, 1802. He honored the Democratic party with his vote, and in his relig-

WHITE COUNTY.

ious belief was a member of the Baptist Church. He was a farmer, and quite successful in the accumulation of wealth, and a very prominent citizen, contributing liberally to all church and charitable works. In short, he was a good man in all that the term implies. He died February 2, 1885, at the age of eighty-three years, sincerely mourned by his many friends and acquaintances. Mrs. Jones received her education in South Carolina, and from an early age was a consistent member of the Missionary Baptist Church. She was a faithful wife and an indulgent mother, loved by all who knew her, and at the time of her death (in her fifty-fourth year) was residing in South Carolina. To the union of Mr. and Mrs. Jones five children were born: Elizabeth (wife of Jackson Clements, deceased, and now residing in Anderson District, S. C.), T. P. Jones (living in White County, and the subject of this sketch), Samuel C. (who died in South Carolina), James S. (deceased in Mississippi) and Clayton W. (died in Virginia). Thomas P. Jones received the limited advantages for an education that the schools of the period afforded, and began for himself at the age of twenty-four, being employed as a farmer in his native state. In June, 1854, he was united in marriage to Margaret A. Tribble, of South Carolina, and a daughter of John and Essa Tribble, of Welsh and Irish descent, respectively. The result of their marriage was eleven children, ten of whom are now living: James M. (a farmer of Cross County, Ark.), Thomas C. (also of Cross County), Martha J. (wife of Thomas J. Futrell, a prosperous farmer of Cross County), Christopher E., William N., Emma J., Laura T., Dixie A., Leona A., Samvann and George A. (killed by machinery in 1877). Mr. Jones moved from South Carolina to Georgia in 1854, whence, after a residence of two years, he returned to Pickens District. At the end of two years he came to Jefferson County, Ala., and there resided until the opening of the Civil War. His family returned to South Carolina at the commencement of hostilities, and remained there until joined by Mr. Jones at the final surrender. Removing from South Carolina to Cross County, Ark., in 1868, and thence to White County,

in 1882, where he is at present residing, he now owns a farm well improved and very productive, besides 240 acres of woodland, in two farms. Mr. Jones' second marriage was to Mrs. Tabitha Berry, the widow of Fenwick Berry (deceased), of Cross County, Ark. Mr. Jones enlisted in the Confederate army in December of 1861, in Blount's Battalion, Alabama Volunteers. He participated in the battles of Shiloh, Lookout Mountain, Missionary Ridge, the battles around Corinth, and other engagements of minor importance; was captured at Missionary Ridge and taken to Rock Island, where, for nineteen months, he endured all the horrors and privations of prison life. He was exchanged at the mouth of Big Red River, in May of 1865, the last exchange of prisoners during the war. He was a gallant soldier, nobly espousing the cause, and truly merited the many marks of commendation and praise that he received from his superior officers. At the close of hostilities he returned home and came to Arkansas, as above stated. Mr. Jones is a stanch Democrat, though not an enthusiast in political matters. He is a Master Mason and a Knight of Honor, and a prominent and influential member of the Missionary Baptist Church. A leader, and not a follower, in worthy enterprises, he contributes liberally to all charitable objects, and enjoys the confidence and respect of his fellow-men.

H. C. Jones, M. D., was a son of H. C. and Nancy (Akin) Jones, natives of North Carolina and Alabama, respectfully. The father went to Alabama from his native State, where he married, and in 1846 moved to Mississippi. Himself and wife were the parents of the following children: Silas S. (deceased), Rufus C., Happach (now Mrs. Braddock, of Texas), Josephine (now Mrs. Maddox), H. C. (our subject), Perry Q., Nancy and Adel J. (now Mrs. Leppard). Mr. Jones died in February, 1868, but his widow still survives him and lives in Mississippi. H. C. Jones, Jr., was born in Itawamba County, Miss., at old Correllville, now Baldwyn, where he resided until 1871, when he removed to Arkansas and settled in White County. Having previously obtained a good medical training, he commenced practicing here in 1873, and has met

HISTORY OF ARKANSAS.

with that success which close attention to business and careful, painstaking effort always merit. Dr. Jones, was married in 1869 to Sarah Q. Alford, a daughter of Thomas and Sarah Alford, of St. Clair County, Ala. They have a family of three children: Angie, Mark P. and Irena, all of whom are at home. Mr. Jones is an active Democrat; his wife and family are members of the Baptist Church. Dr. Jones is a very successful physician, and enjoys an extensive practice. He is also an excellent school worker, taking the lead in his township in all school enterprises, and is a local politician of some note.

Arthur Clifford Jordan, M. D. Among the younger members of the medical profession in White County, Ark., is he whose name heads this sketch, already well established as a physician of merit and true worth, and regarded with favor by those older in years and experience. He was born March 10, 1860, and is a son of John B. and Ella (Emmons) Jordan, of Scotch and English descent, born in Alabama and New York, respectively. They were married at Blackhawk, Miss., in 1858, and became the parents of three children: Arthur C., John Preston (born February 19, 1865, is a bookkeeper in the city of Memphis), Lena Lee (born in 1870, lives with her mother who is now widowed, her husband having died in October 1885). Dr. Arthur Clifford Jordan was reared in his native county (Holmes County, Miss.), and acquired a fair education in the Yazoo District high school. At the age of sixteen years he matriculated in the Literary Department of the University of Nashville, Tenn., and after attending school there for two years he began the study of medicine, being guided in his studies by his father, who was an able practitioner at Blackhawk. After holding the position of principal of the Masonic Male Academy, of Carrollton, Miss., for two terms, and teaching in the public schools of Holmes and Carroll Counties, he (in 1884) entered the Medical Department of the Vanderbilt University, and was graduated as an M. D. in 1886. In March of that year he returned to his home in Mississippi, and completed his preparations for his removal to Arkansas. He settled in Beebe in May of that year, commenced practic-

ing, and has continued it with such success that an unusually brilliant future is predicted for him. He has performed many of the intricate operations which pertain to major and minor surgery. The Doctor is a Democrat and has served as alderman of Beebe, and is a member of the board of school directors. January 12, 1888, he was married to Miss Florence Merrill, who was born in Michigan October 25, 1871, and by her has one child, Mable Clare (born July 27, 1889). The Doctor and his wife belong to the Methodist Episcopal Church, South, and are among the honored residents of Beebe. His maternal grandfather was a major in the Revolutionary war.

J. S. Kelley, retired, Judsonia, Ark. Not very far from the allotted age of three-score years and ten, Mr. Kelley has so lived that no word or reproach against his character as a man has ever been heard; for his whole ambition has been to do his duty in every capacity, as a father, husband, citizen or friend. Progressive in all matters, he has kept outside of the political arena, though a Republican in politics. Like many of the older inhabitants of this community Mr. Kelley is a native of Vermont, his birth occurring in 1822, and is the son of Daniel and Mary (Ballard) Kelly. The father was born in Rhode Island, but when a boy immigrated to Vermont with his parents, and was reared in that grand old mother of States. Later he moved with parents to Vermont, and there met and married Miss Ballard, the daughter of David Ballard, a native of the last-mentioned State. After his marriage Mr. Kelley settled near Rutland, followed farming and there reared to maturity the following children: David, Erastus, Alonzo, Smith, Daniel, Julia, J. S., Moses and Elisha. The father died in Vermont in 1859, and his widow followed him to the grave in 1865. J. S. Kelley was taught the principles of farm life when young and secured a fair education in the district schools of Vermont. He was married in that State in 1846 to Miss Mary Hall, a daughter of David and Esther (Wheaton) Hall, natives of Pittsford, Vt., and two children were the fruits of this union: Emma A. and Ella A. (twins). The former is now deceased, but the latter is the wife

WHITE COUNTY.

of Rev. James Tompkins, of Galesburg, Ill., and now resides in Chicago. She is the mother of four children. J. S. Kelley left Vermont in 1854 and settled near Wheaton, Du Page County, Ill., where he followed agricultural pursuits until 1872. He then moved to Judsonia, White County, Ark., and in 1875 his wife died at Hot Springs. In 1876 he was married to Miss Willie Key, daughter of James and Elizabeth (Brown) Key, who settled in White County, Ark., in 1859. Mrs. Kelley was second in a family of nine children, who were named as follows: Cassie M., Willie P., Alpha B., George F., Etoils S., Benjamin F., Harriet C., Lena G. and Maud M. The parents of these children are still living and reside in Judsonia. By his marriage Mr. Kelley became the father of four interesting children: Fannie J., James C., Elmer L. and Ira W. Elmer died at the age of eighteen months. Mr. Kelley was a member of the Masonic lodge and also of the I. O. O. F. lodge in Illinois. When first coming to White County he engaged in the milling business, but later engaged in the livery business, which he continued for a number of years. He is now living a retired life. Mrs. Kelley is an honored and much-esteemed member of the Methodist Episcopal Church.

James M. Key, retired farmer, Judsonia, Ark. This much-esteemed citizen owes his nativity to the Old Dominion, where his birth occurred in 1814, and is the youngest in a family of fourteen children born to the marriage of John and Elizabeth (Watson) Key, natives also of Virginia, the father's birth occurring in 1760. James M. Key was early taught the principles of farm life, and when twelve years of age went to Philadelphia, where for six years he attended school, there and at Burlington, N. J. In about 1833 he went to Alabama, and after remaining there a short time, removed to Tennessee, where he was married, in 1836, to Miss Mary Scruggs, a native of Virginia, and daughter of Robert and Mary Scruggs, who were also natives of that State. To the marriage of Mr. Key were born the following children: Hettie, John, Sidney, Mary A., Myra A., James R., Fannie W. and Floyd B. Mr. Key lost his

wife in 1848, and was married again, in 1854, to Miss Elizabeth M. Brown, daughter of Colonel William R. and Sarah P. Brown. The result of this union were the following children: Sarah M., Willie P., Alfred B., Sallie E., Benjamin F., Harriet C., Lena (deceased), Maud and May. Mr. Key settled in White County, Ark., in 1858, followed agricultural pursuits on a farm consisting of from 300 to 400 acres, and there remained twelve years. He then moved and purchased a farm of 160 acres, seven miles from Judsonia, where he remained until 1888. He then retired from active pursuits and moved to Judsonia, where he expects to spend his declining years. He has seen many changes in the country since residing here, and is one of the county's most respected and honored citizens. He votes the Democratic ticket; is a member of the Methodist Episcopal Church, South; has been magistrate and takes great interest in all that pertains to the good of the county, schools, churches, etc., having helped to found the first churches in this part of the country. In early days Mr. Key took great interest in hunting and was quite a marksman. He had two sons in the late war. His wife is a member of the Missionary Baptist Church.

Blount Stanley King, farmer and stock raiser, Little Red, Ark. The entire life of Mr. King has been one without any material change from the ordinary pursuits of farm toil, and yet not devoid of substantial results as an agriculturist. He is a native-born citizen of White County, his birth occuring in October, 1845, and is one of seven children born to the union of James and Susan (James) King, the father a native of East Tennessee, and probably of German descent. The ancestors came to America prior to the Revolutionary War, and the grandfather participated in that world-renowned struggle. Mrs. Susan (James) King was a native of North Carolina. The parents came to Arkansas on January 6, 1829, and settled in Caldwell Township, White County, Ark., where Blount S. King received a limited education in the common schools. He was reared to agricultural pursuits, and has followed that calling all his life, meeting with substantial results. On June 4, 1871, he was

HISTORY OF ARKANSAS.

united in marriage to Miss Sarah Pinegar, and the fruits of this union were three children. Jerome L. was born April 1, 1874, but the other children died in infancy. Mrs. King died on September 5, 1875. On December 24, 1876, Mr. King took for his second wife, Miss Caroline Virginia Clark, a native of Kentucky, born May 10, 1855, and whose parents came to Arkansas from Kentucky, in 1856. This second union resulted in the birth of the following children: Noah Lot (born October 13, 1877, and died August 31, 1886), Austin Ward (born August 22, 1881), Willia M. (born October 7, 1883), Daniel D. (born July 31, 1885, and died April 23, 1888), and Florence Orenia (born on August 14, 1888). Mr. King came into possession of his farm by will from his father, eighty acres, with about eighteen under cultivation, and well adapted to agriculture or horticulture. He takes an interest in all matters relating to the good of the county, and his children are having as good educational advantages as his means will admit. He is a member of the Agricultural Wheel, and he and his wife are members of the United Baptist Church.

John Thomas King, planter and stock raiser, Little Red, Ark. A lifetime devoted with perseverance and energy to the pursuit of agriculture, have contributed very materially to the success which has attended the efforts of Mr. King, a man of substantial and established worth. He was born in 1849, and is the son of James and Louisa (James) King whose marriage took place in 1846. This union resulted in the birth of six children: Newton (born in 1847), John Thomas (born in 1849), Pinkney McDonald (born in 1851), Joseph (born in 1853), Jesse (born in 1855) and William (born in 1857). Previous to this James King married a sister of his second wife, Miss Susan James, in 1829, and by her became the father of seven children: Sophia (born in 1830), Richard (born in 1832), Jasper (born in 1834), Robert (born in 1837), Marion (born in 1839), Allen (born in 1842) and Blount S. (born in 1845). John Thomas King owes his nativity to White County, Ark., and his education was obtained in the subscription schools of that county. He was reared to agricultural pursuits, and when grown was united in marriage to Miss Mary Jane

Pinegar, a native of Tennessee, born in 1848, and the daughter of William and Clarissa (Redmond) Pinegar. The wedding of our subject took place July 17, 1864, and ten children were born to them: Jesse (born in 1866), James (born in 1868), Eliza (born in 1870), LaFayette (born in 1872), Frances (born in 1874), Laura (born in 1876), Rosa (born in 1878), Viola (twin, born in 1880), Minnie (born in 1882) and David (born in 1884). Viola's twin sister died at birth. John T. King received by deed from his father eighty acres of land in Jackson Township, which he began to improve. In 1879 he purchased the old homestead which adjoined his eighty acres, and made the purchase just prior to the death of his father, receiving a deed from the latter and a dowery from his step-mother, she being his father's fourth wife. The father died on November 4, 1879, at the age of seventy-seven years. Our subject lived on the old home place, consisting of eighty-five acres, until 1886, when he moved to his present home in Denmark Township, where he now owns 275 acres of land with 100 acres under cultivation. His eldest son, Jesse King, was married to Miss Louisa Turley, a native of Arkansas, and the daughter of Samson and Mary Jane (Howell) Turley, and the result of this union has been two children: Commodore (born in 1886) and Fred (born in 1888). His son James was married November 21, to Miss Laura E. Middleton, daughter of Dr. P. A. and Amanda (Moseley) Middleton. Mr. and Mrs. John T. King are members in good standing in the United Baptist Church and are much respected by all acquainted with them. Mr. King is a member of the Agricultural Wheel No. 76. He is giving his children good educations and takes a deep interest in all school matters. His son Jesse is a professor of penmanship and LaFayette is well advanced in the English branches and is taking a commercial course at the Commercial College at Batesville, Ark., the present winter.

E. C. Kinney, editor and proprietor of the Judsonian Advance, is a newspaper man of experience, and his connection with this paper dates from 1880, he being its organizer. He managed the paper until 1885, then sold out to B. W. Briggs, and then engaged in the general mercan-

WHITE COUNTY.

tile business, selling out in the fall of 1889. September 18 of that year he again resumed control of the Judsonian Advance, and its advance under his management has been more noteworthy and rapid than formerly. At the present time it is recognized as a journal of decided merit, its editorials being written with a clearness and force which indicate a writer of ability. He was born in Livingston County, N. Y., in 1843, and is the eleventh of twelve children. born to Ezra and Louise (Clough) Kinney, the former a native of Connecticut, and a minister of the Methodist Episcopal Church. In 1817, during the early history of Livingston County, N. Y., he became one of its settlers, and experienced many of the hardships and inconveniences which are incident to early pioneer life. He died in 1855, and his wife in Walworth County, Wis., in 1868. E. C. Kinney was reared in Mount Morris, N. Y., and in youth learned the harness-maker's trade, and followed it some ten years. Upon the breaking out of the Rebellion he enlisted at Rochester, N. Y., in the Fifty-eighth New York Infantry, Company E, as a private, and was promoted to corporal-sergeant, and in 1862 to second lieutenant. After participating in the battle of Manassas, he was on detached duty for some time, but was taken sick, and after remaining in the hospital at Annapolis, Md., about six months, he, in 1863 returned to Mount Morris, N. Y., and began following his trade. In 1865 he removed to Painsville, Ohio, and was married there in 1866, to Miss Anna R. Abbott, a native of Salem, Mass. Becoming dissatisfied with his location in Ohio, he determined to push westward, and in 1868 settled in Independence, Buchanan County, Iowa. Two years later he became connected with a circus, and was thus enabled to travel over the greater part of the United States. In 1870 he became connected with Sprague, Warner & Griswold, and later with Kinney & Co., and when with the latter company, traveled with a team from Chicago to New York City, making every town on the route selling goods. In 1878 he left Iowa and went overland to Davidson County, Dak., and homesteaded land, remaining there a sufficient length of time to see the full growth of

Mitchell and Alexandria. In 1880 he came overland to White County, Ark., arriving here on May 17, and engaged in the hotel business. He has followed horticulture ever since his arrival in the county, and owns two fruit farms adjoining Judsonia, also one near Little Rock. He is an active Republican, and was president of the first Republican convention ever held in White County. He is the present mayor of the town, and has held other offices of public trust. Socially he is a member of Anchor Lodge No. 384, of the A. F. & A. M., and has been secretary of his order. His children are: George (a printer), Myrtie, Earl and Carlie.

Hon. H. C. Knowlton. If industry united with a strong and determined perseverance can accomplish the desired ends, Mr. Knowlton should be, and is one of the well-to-do planters of the county. He came to the county in 1870, from the State of Tennessee, but was born in Vermont in 1825, being the youngest in a family of three children born to James and Lydia (Cheney) Knowlton, who were natives of the Bay State. They were married in that State in 1813, afterward settling in Vermont, where he worked at the blacksmith's trade until about 1829, at which time he moved to Lenawee County, Mich., and settled on a farm between Adrian and Tecumseh. He was one of the pioneers of this county, and became one of its wealthiest farmers. In 1842 he went to Anderson, Ind., and made that his home, and here his death occurred in 1847, his wife's death following his in 1860, her demise occurring in Tennessee. H. C. Knowlton learned the trade of a general mechanic in his youth, and after moving to Hardeman County, Tenn., in 1845, followed his trade until the opening of the war. He was married in Hardeman County, four years after his arrival in the State, to Miss Mary Agnes Stone, a native of Fayette County, Tenn., and a daughter of William H. and B. P. (Johnson) Stone, the former a Virginian, and the latter a native of North Carolina. At the age of eighteen the father went to Missouri, and assisted in surveying that State, then went to North Carolina, and was married there in 1818, after which he moved to Tennessee and engaged in farming,

HISTORY OF ARKANSAS.

making this his calling until his death in 1866. His wife died in 1877. In 1870 Mr. Knowlton came to White County, Ark., and purchased an improved farm of 200 acres, and at the present time has sixty acres under the plow. Although not an active politician, he supported the Democratic party until he affiliated with the Labor party in 1884, and in 1887 was elected on that ticket to the State legislature, serving one term. He is a strict temperance man, a member of the Agricultural Wheel, and socially is a member of Mount Pisgah Lodge No. 242, of the A. F. & A. M., and is treasurer of his order. The following are the children born to himself and wife: Mary C. (Mrs. Dr. Wells, of Marion Township), Horace C. (a farmer of the township), R. S. (a resident of Oregon), C. M. (who died in 1886), E. E. (who is married and lives in the township), J. D. (married and living in Big Creek Township), W. H. (married and living in the township), Lelia F. (Mrs. Cate) and W. B. (who died in 1875). Mr. and Mrs. Knowlton are members of the Methodist Episcopal Church, South.

Enoch Langley, who is an able representative of the ginning interests of the county as well as the agricultural class, is of Georgian nativity, being born March 31, 1847, and was the third of seven children born to Enoch and Elizabeth (Stone) Langley, who were also of Georgia, and whose births occurred in the years 1824 and 1828. They were united in the holy bonds of marriage in 1843, and as a result of this union seven children came to gladden their hearts: Nancy, Oswell, Enoch (our subject), William B., Mary, Jepha and Kattie. Enoch Langley, heeding the call of his country, enlisted in 1864, in the Thirty-fifth Georgia Infantry and participated in the battles of Cross Junction and the battle of the Wilderness. After the close of the Rebellion he returned to Georgia and, in 1868, was married to Josephine Hopper, who was born July 5, 1852, and a daughter of Thomas C. and Martha (Hendrix) Hopper. Soon after this event Mr. Langley settled in Floyd County, Ga., and farmed for awhile, but in 1874 immigrated to Arkansas and settled in Des Arc Township, White County, and in 1880 bought 235

acres of land in Cadron Township, which he commenced to improve, and he now has 120 acres in a high state of cultivation. Nine children call Mr. and Mrs. Langley father and mother: John M. (born January 9, 1869), James T. (born November 26, 1870), Martha E. (May 30, 1874), Larah B. (January 10, 1878), Luther C. (April 27, 1878), Alice I. (July 18, 1882), Enoch P. (November 28, 1884), Isam I. (December 9, 1887), Oscar B. (April 13, 1889). Mr. Langley is giving the ginning business, in which he has been very successful, his most watchful and careful attention. He is a member of the Agricultural Wheel, and politically a strong and stanch Democrat, and anything relating to his adopted county or to any public enterprise receives his most hearty support.

Rev. Isom P. Langley, pastor of the First Baptist Church of Beebe, owes his nativity to Arkansas, and was born in Clark County, September 2, 1851. His parents, Samuel S. and Mary J. (Browning) Langley, were natives of Arkansas and Alabama, respectively. Samuel S. Langley was born October 29, 1831, in Clark County, and is the son of Miles L. and Sally (Butler) Langley, natives of North Carolina, who came to Arkansas in 1818, and were married in this State in 1819. The maternal grandfather, Francis J. Browning, was a native of Georgia, and was born in 1800. His wife was a native of Alabama, and they were of English descent. The maternal ancestors were all finely educated, and figured as prominent men during their life. Francis J. Browning was a teacher and farmer, also a great and earnest worker in the Baptist Church, having served as a delegate to the first Baptist association that ever met south of the Arkansas River. This meeting was held at Spring Creek Church, near Benton, Saline County, August 12, 1835, and he was also one of the originators of Mount Bethel Church, six miles west of Arkadelphia, in 1835. At the time of his death, and for a number of years before it, he had been occupied as a teacher. He died in 1884, his wife having been called to her final home in 1879. Miles L. Langley died in 1831, and his wife in 1848. They were among the first settlers of Clark County, and endured all of the privations and

WHITE COUNTY.

hardships incident to that time. To them a family of seven children were born: John (was in the Mexican War, also in California during the gold excitement, and is now a prosperous farmer of Clark County, Ark.), Joseph (deceased, was a leading farmer of Clark County, where his family now live; his death occurred in 1882.), William (deceased, was a farmer, and lost his life by a tree falling on him, 1864, and at the time a soldier in the Confederate army), Miles L. (deceased, a very prominent Baptist minister. He was a member of the State Constitutional Conventions of 1864 and 1868, and was a chaplain in the State Senate. He died December 27, 1888.), Isom P. (is a prosperous farmer of Clark County, Ark.), Jensey (deceased) and Samuel S. (the father of the subject of this memoir, who is still living, and is a prosperous farmer of Pike County, Ark. He served four years in the Confederate army as second lieutenant, and was prisoner of war for nineteen months at Johnson's Island. He was also captain, and was acting commander at Helena. He and his estimable wife are earnest workers of the Baptist Church, and he is a Master Mason of considerable note). Rev. Isom P. is the eldest in a family of thirteen, ten of whom are now living: Thomas (deceased), Porter (deceased), Mary C., Andrew V., Permelia G., Abi (deceased), Samuel S., Jr., Annie, infant not named, Sallie, Robert, Penn and Frank. Our subject was reared to farm life, and spent his school-days in the schools of his county, and later took up the study of physiology and phrenology, under the tutorship of Miles L. Langley, his paternal uncle, and a man of very fine attainments; at the same time, and under the same teacher, he studied the English language. At the age of twenty-two he began the study of law under Gen. H. W. McMillan, of Arkadelphia, and Judges M. P. Dobey and H. H. Coleman. He completed his law course, and was admitted to the bar in 1875, and practiced his profession at Arkadelphia and Hot Springs until 1885, when he was obliged to discontinue it on account of throat disease. He joined the Baptist Church at the age of sixteen years, was licensed to preach in 1868, and ordained in 1869, since which time he has been engaged in the work of the min-

istry. He has filled the pulpits of Arkadelphia, Hot Springs, and that of the First Baptist Church of Little Rock, but a large share of his time has been devoted to churches where there was no regular pastorate. In 1880 he formed a partnership with Capt. J. W. and J. N. Miller, the firm name being Miller, Langley & Miller, editors of the Arkadelphia Signal, conducting the same with marked success until 1881. Mr. Langley then withdrew from the firm, and started the Arkansas Clipper, in 1882, a Greenback Labor paper, of which he was sole owner. This he published until 1883, then sold it and went to Hot Springs, and in company with a Mr. Allard founded and edited the Daily and Weekly Hot Springs News. In 1886 he became the editor of the Industrial Liberator, the official organ of the Knights of Labor, and made that paper a decided success, in the meantime having sold the Hot Springs News. He resigned his position in June, 1886, and engaged in the insurance business. He also purchased a controlling interest in the National Wheel Enterprise, acting as its editor until December 17, 1888, when he retired from the newspaper business, and in doing so deprived the literary and newspaper world of one of its brightest lights. In 1885 Mr. Langley became a member of the Local Assembly 2419, K. of L., at Hot Springs, the first assembly ever organized in the State, acting at present as one of the national organizers of that order. He is a member of Union Lodge 31, A. W., and was a delegate to the State convention that met at Litchfield in 1886. While at that convention he was elected as one of the delegates to the National Wheel, which met at the same time and place, and was its acting secretary. It was at this assembly that he wrote the constitution for the National Wheel, and at this same meeting was elected National Lecturer, and in that capacity wrote the demands of the National Wheel that were adopted at McKinzie, Tenn., November, 1887, and in all the conventions he has taken a very prominent part, and in behalf of the National Wheel made the response to Senator Walker's address of welcome at Meridian, Miss., December 5, 1888. That speech which elicited such favorable comment from the press,

HISTORY OF ARKANSAS.

was the crowning effort of his life, and placed him at the head of the list of deep thinkers and eloquent speakers in the labor ranks. On October 20, 1887, he became President of the Famous Life Association, of Little Rock, and served one year, managing its affairs with extraordinary ability. In 1886 he was nominated by a labor convention as a candidate for Congress against Judge J. H. Rogers, of the Fourth Congressional District, and polled more than twice the labor votes of his district. As a stump speaker he has no superior in the State. He has always figured prominently in schools, and was the secretary of the board that reorganized the splendid school system of Arkadelphia. Mr. Langley has done all kinds of work, from the hoeing of cotton to the highest calling man can perform, and is one of the best posted men in the State. In August, of 1870, he was married to Miss Martha A. Freeman, a native of Arkansas, and a daughter of Thomas J. Freeman. He was born in Little Rock, 1821, and settled in Clark County in 1840, where Mrs. Langley was born in 1851. To these parents have been born a family of five children, all living: Florence R., Charles E., Ada J., Katie and Lessie. Father, mother, and the three oldest children are members of the Baptist Church. Socially Mr. Langley affiliates with the I. O. O. F., and has filled all the offices of that order. He is a typical Arkansan, and perhaps is without his peer in public value in the State, considering his age.

Fayette T. Laster, well known to the residents of Russell, Ark., is a native of West Tennessee, his birth occurring in Decatur County, May 27, 1866. His father, William W. Laster, also of Tennessee, was born in 1837, and there married in 1860 to Sinthey A. Wright, of Tennessee, her birth occurring in 1840. Soon after their marriage they came to Arkansas and settled in White County, where they remained until their respective deaths. Mr. Laster was claimed by the grim destroyer, Death, 1886, and his faithful wife only survived him a few months, less than a year. To the union of Mr. and Mrs. Laster three sons were born, of whom only one, Fayette T. (the subject of this memoir) is now living. Albert and John both

died in Tennessee. Mr. Laster was a farmer, a hard-working and law-abiding citizen, and by his unostentatious manner gained many friends. At the date of his demise he had succeeded in amassing quite a comfortable amount of property and money. Fayette T. moved with his parents, when quite a boy, to Arkansas, where he grew to manhood with nothing but the monotonous routine of the pioneer's life to occupy his attention. His educational advantages were from necessity limited, as the schools at that time were far from satisfactory. He started out for himself at the age of twenty-one and began farming and stock raising, in which he is still engaged, and is meeting with very fair success. He now owns 200 acres of excellent bottom land, well improved and in a high state of cultivation. On September 28, Mr. Laster was united in matrimony with Ida (Lee) Mote, adopted daughter of John and Hattie Mote, and own daughter of Arcy and Martha C. Lee. To Mr. and Mrs. Laster's union two children have been born: Elva Theola (born September 10, 1878, and died December 6, 1888) and Belle Alrietia (born November 4, 1889). Mr. Laster is independent in his political views, casting his vote for the best interests of himself and the country at large. He is a prosperous young farmer, of industrious and frugal habits, and has gained the good will of his fellow-citizens.

Winfield Scott Lay is a native Arkansan, his birthplace being Van Buren County, where he received his education. He enlisted at the age of seventeen in the Confederate Cavalry (Twenty-seventh Arkansas), in which he served until the close of the war, being with Gen. Price on his raid through Missouri. Subsequently he attended school, remaining two years, and in 1868 came to Searcy, where he engaged as a clerk in a store and followed this for three years, then commenced business for himself on a capital of $600, and is now one of the leading business men in Searcy. In 1884 he was burned out, losing several thousand dollars worth of goods, but immediately built up again, and the following year did the largest business he has done before or since, selling $52,000 worth of goods. He was born on November 24, 1846, and is a son of William H. and

WHITE COUNTY.

Polly (Bacon) Lay, natives of Virginia and Tennessee, respectively. William H. Lay went to Knox County, Tenn., when a young man, where he was married and resided until 1839, when he came to Arkansas and located in what was then Van Buren County, but which is now Cleburne County, where he farmed until his death. In his political views he was a strong Democrat, and while in Tennessee served several years as deputy sheriff, and afterward as sheriff. The Lay family is of English descent, the paternal grandfather of our subject coming to this country from old England. Mr. and Mrs. Lay were members of the Methodist Episcopal Church, South. They were the parents of eight children, seven of whom are still living: Allen S., Elizabeth Witt, Emma Simmons, Sarah Fulko, Mattie Manus, Winfield Scott (who heads this sketch), and W. L. (now a resident of South America). W. S. Lay was married in Searcy on September 13, 1870, to Miss Nannie Stevenson, a daughter of the Rev. Alexander Stevenson, pastor of the Cumberland Presbyterian Church, at Searcy, and who was born in White County in 1853. Mr. Lay is one of eight stockholders in the Searcy and West Point Railroad, of which he is also a director and secretary. He is a strong Democrat, and a wide-awake business man, and has one of the largest trades in his line in Searcy.

Hon. F. P. Laws, president of the local board of immigration at Beebe, Ark., also engaged in selling wagons, buggies and farming implements, has probably done more to develop the resources of White County than any other one person, and is a very popular man wherever he is known. He is a native of Missouri, and was born in what is now Benton County May 10, 1840. His father, Joel J., was a native of North Carolina, and was born February 17, 1812, in Wilkes County, and was considered one of the best farmers of his section. His wife, the mother of the subject of this sketch, was also of North Carolina nativity, her birth occurring about 1814. Her name was Martha Grissum, and was of English ancestry, as was also her husband. She was a bright and highly cultured lady. Mr. and Mrs. Laws were married in North Carolina

in 1838, and the same week left for Missouri, settling in what is now Benton County, and there lived for about two years. They then moved to Farmington, St. Francis County, but at the time of Mr. Laws' death, in 1848, they were residing in Ste. Genevieve County. He was a life-long Democrat, though not an active politician. In his religious faith he was not identified with any particular church, but was a man of high moral character, honor, and strict integrity, and one who always left a pleasant impression and a desire to enlarge acquaintance with him. After her husband's death Mrs. Laws married again, her second marriage taking place in 1850 to Mr. Harvill Shepherd, a farmer of Ste. Genevieve County, and by him became the mother of four children. She was left a widow in 1858, and is at present living with her third husband, Mr. Humphfrey, a farmer of Miller County. Hon. F. P. Laws is the oldest in a family of four children as follows: Hon. F. P., Jane (Mrs. A. J. Humphfreys of Crawford County), Mary (married, living in Miller County, Mo.), Marion J. (married, and a well-to-do farmer). F. P. was reared to farm life, and received such advantages for an education as the schools of that period afforded. At the age of seventeen he left his step-father's home and started out to make his fortune, facing the world with nothing to back him but his courage and determination to succeed. He went first to Franklin County, Mo., and engaged in the lumber business for about four years, and was very successful. In 1861 he enlisted in the Confederate army, and served for one year. He then returned to Washington, Mo., and resumed his work in the lumber business, and while there fell in with his friend, Mr. Morris, of New Orleans, and from him secured the contract to furnish the heavy square timbers for the first grain elevator ever erected in the city of St. Louis. This contract was successfully carried out, and was the means of his securing lucrative employment in the way of large contracts. During the years 1872–73 he built sixty miles of fence for the 'Frisco Railroad, but the panic of 1873, in which so many were financially embarrassed, left him without regular work until 1875. He next traded for a tract of land fourteen

HISTORY OF ARKANSAS.

miles north of Beebe, Ark., and moved to Beebe at once, but the same year sold the saw-mill and land, continuing the timber business in Beebe, also building several houses there. Ever since his residence in White County he has been interested in all movements for the good of the county, and is a liberal contributor to all worthy enterprises. He engaged in the real-estate business in 1888, and when the Beebe Board of Immigration was organized he was elected president, and has since given his time and attention to that work. In September, 1883, Hon. F. P. Laws was elected on the Democratic ticket as a Prohibitionist to the office of county and probate judge, and in that capacity did more for the county in the way of internal improvements than had ever been done before by any one county judge. He built a good fire-proof jail on the latest improved plans, bettered the condition of the county farm by erecting three new and comfortable houses, and took special care of the county poor. He repaired all the existing bridges, and built five new ones in different parts of the county, where they were greatly needed, also bought a copy of the field notes of the county and placed them on file in the county clerk's office. At the expiration of his term of office he left the county without a saloon in it. Judge Laws organized the Beebe Artesian Well Company, in August, 1889, and is acting president of the same, and fills the same position in the Southern Building & Loan Association. October 17, 1864, witnessed Judge Laws' marriage with Miss Lorinda J. Johns, a native of Missouri and a daughter of one of the oldest families of Franklin County. To their union six children have been born, only one now living: Nellie, a charming young lady of fourteen. Mamie, Eddie, Charlie, Jennie and Bessie are deceased. Judge Laws was made a Mason in Pacific Lodge No. 159, A. F. & A. M., in 1864, at Pacific Mo., and with his wife and daughter is a member of the Methodist Episcopal Church, South. He was a lay delegate to the general conference of the Methodist Episcopal Church, South, which met at Richmond, Va., in 1866, and was a delegate to the annual conference which met at Searcy December 11, 1889.

George W. Leggett, the well-known dry-goods merchant, of Floyd, has been engaged in the mercantile business since 1878, first in Mount Pisgah, and two years later in Floyd, where he is at present engaged. He was born in Hardeman County, Tenn., in 1849, and was a son of E. S. and Polly (Whitford) Leggett. E. S. Leggett owes his nativity to Tennessee, being born in that State in 1811, and is son of Daniel Leggett, who settled in Tennessee at an early day. He engaged in the mercantile business in Tennessee in 1849, and later came to White County, Ark., where he still continues in business. Mrs. Leggett was a daughter of David Whitford, of Tennessee, and died in White County in 1885. George W. was married in 1875 to Lue Bailey, who died in 1885, leaving one child, also deceased. Mr. Leggett was married the second time to Miss Vincie Greer (a daughter of O. and Coraline Greer, of this county). They are the parents of two children: Vincie Pearl and Henry L. Mr. Leggett was appointed postmaster under President Garfield, and has held the position ever since. He carries a large stock of general merchandise, and does the largest business in his line in the place, having a trade of about $1,500 to $25,000 per year. He also owns a farm of 140 acres, eighty of which are under cultivation. In politics Mr. Leggett is a strong Democrat.

Dr. John L. Leggett, known to be one of the most progressive farmers in his township, and well qualified to discharge the trust reposed in him by the people, commenced the study of medicine shortly after the war, under Dr. M. F. Dumas, and upon obtaining his certificate in 1876, located at Little Red, White County, and commenced practicing. On coming out of the army he was without means, but taking up the study of medicine he became very proficient and very successful as a physician, but in 1883 he turned his attention to the mercantile business and to farming, and now owns a fine farm of 250 acres on the Red River, mostly bottom land, with 150 acres under cultivation, and is one of the most extensive farmers in Jackson Township. The Doctor was born in Madison County, Tenn., October 9, 1844, and is a son of E. S. and Polly (Whitford) Leggett, natives

WHITE COUNTY.

of North Carolina and Tennessee, respectively. E. S. Leggett came to Madison County, Tenn., when a boy with his parents, and after his marriage was engaged in farming in that State until 1860, when he removed to Arkansas, locating in White County. He has filled the office of justice of the peace for a number of years, is a Democrat and belongs to the Baptist Church, as did also his wife, who died in 1876, being the mother of ten children, five of whom are still living: F. M., J. B., George, Martha (now Mrs. Rushing) and John L. (our subject). The senior Leggett is still a resident of White County, and is eighty years of age. Dr. Leggett enlisted in the Confederate service, in 1861, in the Eighth Arkansas Infantry, in which he served one year. He then came home and joined the Tenth Missouri Cavalry, and took part in the memorable Missouri raid, and also in a number of hard-fought battles. In 1866 he was married to Miss Bettie Martin, a native of Alabama. They were the parents of ten children, eight of whom are still living: Mary (wife of D. C. Middleton, a farmer of this county), William L., Lewis T., Icy, Ida, Charles, Lida and Isaac. Mrs. Leggett is a member of the Missionary Baptist Church. Dr. Leggett is one of the most enterprising men of his community, and a leading Democrat, and has served as postmaster at Little Red since 1876.

John H. Leib. Near the little town of Lancaster, Ohio, on November 13, 1836, John H. Leib first saw the light of day, being one of ten children born to the marriage of John and Elizabeth Leib. John Leib, Sr., was born in York, Penn., in the year 1800, and his wife was born the same year in Juniata County, Penn. They were united in marriage in Bremen, Fairfield County, Ohio, in 1823, and spent fifty-seven years in happy wedded life. Mr. Leib died in 1883, at the age of eighty-three years, and at the time of his death was in Russell, Ark. His wife had gone to her final rest in the year 1880, aged eighty years. They resided in the States of Ohio, Indiana and Illinois, and were quite successful in the accumulation of wealth, being quiet, industrious people. For many years Mr. Leib was an old line Whig, but at the

dissolution of that party he united with the Republican, though was not active in party measures or campaigns. In their family of ten children only five are now living: James (a farmer of Lagrange County, Ind.), Benjamin (farmer, resident of Crawford County, Ind.), John H. (the subject of this sketch), Anna E. (living in White County, Ark., and Mary J. (Mrs. William Poindexter, of Crawford County, Ind.). Lydia, John and Augustus were born and died at Bremen, Ohio. Hamilton deceased at Russell, and George S. died at Chauncey, Ill. John H. resided at Bremen, Ohio, until sixteen years of age, at that date removing with his parents to Lagrange County, Ind. His education was limited to the common schools of the period, and though they were far from satisfactory, he managed to acquire a thorough knowledge of business, and is now a well-informed man. In November of 1861 Mr. Leib entered the United States army as a volunteer in the Forty-eighth Indiana Infantry, in Col. Eddy's regiment. He enlisted as a private, but was soon promoted to the office of first lieutenant in Capt. Mann's Company G. His ability was recognized and commented on by his superior officers, and in 1865 he was given the title of captain, commanding a company until the close of the war. He participated in the siege of Corinth, Vicksburg, and in the battles of Iuka, Corinth, Raymond, Champion's Hill, Jackson and Black River Bridge in the State of Mississippi, Altoona and Bentonville in Georgia, also in Chattanooga, Tenn. He was with Gen. Sherman on his famous march to the sea. After the close of hostilities, Mr. or rather Capt. Leib returned home and engaged in farming and stock raising, which is still his occupation. He is a Royal Arch Mason, having reached the seventh degree, and is a liberal contributor to schools, churches and all public enterprises.

Benjamin W. Lewis. David and Elvira (Hagler) Lewis, the parents of the subject of this sketch, were natives of North Carolina and settled in Tennessee at an early day, rearing a family of thirteen children: Benjamin W., Nancy F., J. L., Elizabeth, Lucy, Polly, Lucinda, John L., Elvira, Sarah, William, Richard (also a resident of Kane Town-

HISTORY OF ARKANSAS.

ship, White County) and Martha. Mr. Lewis died in Tennessee in 1870, and his wife in 1852. B. W. was born in Western Tennessee, where he grew up on a farm and was educated in the common schools. He was married on January 2, 1851, to Mary E. Hastings, a daughter of John M. C. and Elizabeth (Sexton) Hastings, of North Carolina nativity, and who immigrated to Tennessee at an early day. After his marriage Mr. Lewis settled on a farm in Henry County, Tenn., where he lived until 1870, when he removed to Arkansas, and settled in Gray Township, White County, and three years later bought a farm of 160 acres in Cane Township, where his home now is. He enlisted in the fall of 1862 in the Forty-sixth Tennessee Infantry, commanded by Col. J. M. Clark, and was in the service five months. Mr. and Mrs. Lewis have a family of eight children, all of whom were born in Tennessee: Nancy J. (now Mrs. Osborn), John D. (lives in this township), William L., James W. (deceased), L. D., Henry W., Elvira (wife of Dr. V. W. Ware, of this township) and Benjamin F. In politics he is an active Democrat, and takes a strong interest in all work for public improvement, and has been school director for the past five years. Himself and wife are members of the Methodist Episcopal Church, of which Mr. Lewis is one of the trustees.

Jefferson Pinkney Linder is one of the enterprising and industrious agriculturists of this region, and is a son of Abraham W. and Itea (Templeman) Linder, the former of whom was born in Spartanburg District, S. C. He was of English descent, his grandfather having emigrated from England to America before the outbreak of the Revolutionary War, and took an active part in that struggle on the side of the Colonists. He settled in North Carolina, and there reared his family, his son John, the grandfather of our subject, being born there. He was married in that State and at an early day removed to South Carolina, where his son Abraham W. was educated and grew to manhood. He was also married there and eight of his children were born there prior to the year 1844, after which they moved to Alabama and settled in Benton County, where four more children were given them. Their names are as follows: John A. (born July 18, 1823), Calvin D. (born July 1, 1825), Elizabeth Ann (born July 10, 1827), Delilah E. (born September 9, 1829), James Templeman (born April 17, 1832), Lewis M. (born October 24, 1834), Austin A. (born March 17, 1837), Jefferson Pinkney (born August 10, 1839), Mary A. (born October 6, 1841), Arcena S. (born March 21, 1844), Virgil Taylor (born June 3, 1848) and Martha C. (born on March 8, 1851). The father and mother of these children were born on September 23, 1803, and February 27, 1807, respectively, and in 1857 they came to Arkansas. Abraham Linder and his sons were opposed to secession, but Lewis M. and Austin A. espoused the Confederate cause after the ordinance of secession had been passed, and served as members in a company of Arkansas Volunteer Infantry. Lewis M. died of measles while at home on a sick furlough, and Austin was mortally wounded at the battle of Helena, Ark., on July 4, 1863, and was taken from the field where he fell by the Federals to a hospital at Memphis and there died. Jefferson Pinkney Linder (our subject) was reared to farm life and received his education principally in the subscription schools of Alabama, whither his father had moved from South Carolina. He embraced religion at the age of twenty-one years, and is now a member of the Presbyterian Church. On December 4, 1861, he was married to Miss Lucinda Jane Shelton, a daughter of John F. and Martha Payne (Milam) Shelton, of Shelby County, Tenn., her birth occurring in that county on May 8, 1846. The names of their children are here given: Thomas Jefferson (born March 28, 1863), Laura Eudora (born August 24, 1865), Margaret Itea (born December 26, 1867), John Robert (born January 6, 1870), Charles Henry (was born on February 1, 1873, and died August 1, 1875), McWilliam (was born on August 4, 1875,) Oscar B. (was born on September 5, 1877), Albert Lee (born February 8, 1880), Mertie Velmer (born March 23, 1882, and died October 9, 1884), Vida May (born June 16, 1884, and died August 3, 1886), Burrilah (born on February 14, 1887). Thomas J. was married to Miss Fannie Dennis, of Henderson County, Tex., on December 23, 1886, and is now

WHITE COUNTY.

farming in Monroe County, Ark. Laura E. became the wife of S. N. Trotter, and lives in Monroe County, Ark. Margaret Itea bore one child by her husband, J. W. Acree, but is now separated from him by mutual consent. Mr. Linder has been noted for his industry and thrift, and on commencing life these constituted his capital stock and well he has made use of them, being now the owner of 360 acres of land, his first purchase being only eighty acres. He has 100 acres under cultivation and makes a specialty of stock raising, his mules being of a fine grade, and he also has some very fine horses of the Tone Hal breed. Mr. Linder was troubled for some time with a scrofulous white swelling on one of his legs which finally resulted in the loss of that member, the operation being performed in 1879. He is a man possessing a fund of useful information and is a Democrat in his political views. Himself and wife and four children are members of the Baptist Church.

Elder Benjamin H. Lumpkin, a prominent Baptist minister of White County, is a son of Robert and Jane (Harden) Lumpkin, and owes his nativity to Arkansas, his birth occurring May 2, 1849. Robert Lumpkin was a native of Georgia, and his wife of Ballard County, Ky. They were married in the latter State and came to White County in February, 1835, settling near Denmark, said county, where Mr. Lumpkin died in 1855. He was a Universalist in belief and a farmer by occupation. Mrs. Lumpkin was a member of the Methodist Episcopal Church for many years, and closed her eyes to the trials and tribulations of this world in 1857. Mr. Lumpkin in his political views was a Democrat, and manifested an active interest in party campaigns. To the marriage of Mr. and Mrs. Lumpkin, eight children were born, three sons and five daughters: Louisa (wife of Elder J. M. Butler, a Baptist missionary to the Cherokee Indians), Susan M. (Mrs. Ramer, of Shelby County, Tenn.), Sophia E. (now Mrs. J. F. Burket, residing in Northern Arkansas), Benjamin H. (subject of this sketch), John (died while in the Rebel army at Bowling Green, Ky.), Noah (deceased in boyhood, in White County), Charity (wife of Thomas Simmons, a farmer of Fulton

County, Ark.) and Rebecca (died in White County, Ark., in 1868). Benjamin H. passed his early life near Denmark, Ark., and received but meager advantages for an education in his youth, but is now a well-read gentleman, and conversant on all important subjects of the day. He began preaching at the age of twenty-nine years, and by his earnest and eloquent expounding, has made many converts to his faith. He began farming at the age of fifteen years, which he continued until he reached the age of thirty. In 1883 Mr. Lumpkin embarked in the mercantile business in connection with his preaching, and has been very successful in that departure. He carries a stock of carefully selected groceries, valued at $15,000. Mr. Lumpkin was married July 19, 1870, to Rachel F. Ruminor, of White County, and a daughter of James Ruminor. By this marriage five children have been born, two sons and three daughters: Allie F., Hayden A., Maggie A., Benjamin T. and Lena Rivers (deceased). Mr. Lumpkin was elected justice of the peace in September of 1888, for a period of two years, and is discharging the duties of that office in a manner that proves beyond a doubt his ability to satisfactorily fill that position. He is a member of the Missionary Baptist Church in his religious belief, and a stanch Democrat in politics. Mr. Lumpkin contributes liberally to all worthy enterprises, and lends his valuable support to all church, school and charitable movements. In societies he is identified with the Masonic order, in which he is a member in high standing.

Dr. J. F. McAdams, physician and surgeon, Searcy, Ark. There are few men of the present day whom the world acknowledges as successful more worthy of honorable mention or whose life-history affords a better example of what may be accomplished by a determined will and perseverance than that of Dr. J. F. McAdams. This gentleman was born in Shelby County, Ala., in 1830, and was the fourth of seven children, the result of the marriage of James and Sarah (Foreman) McAdams, natives, respectively, of South Carolina and Tennessee. The father was a planter, and when a young man went to Alabama, where he married

HISTORY OF ARKANSAS.

Miss Foreman and settled on a farm within five miles of Columbiana, where he lived for over fifty years. His death occurred in 1867, and his wife died in February, 1889. Of their family the following children are living: Isaac F. (resides in Dallas, Tex.), J. F., Elizabeth (now Mrs. Edwards, of Shelby County, Ala.), Sarah (now Mrs. Horton, resides in Shelby County, Ala.), and Dr. Henry Clay (who is married and resides in Shelby County, Ala.). Dr. J. F. McAdams was reared to plantation life and secured a good practical education in the schools of Shelby County, Ala., subsequently taking a three-years' course in Talladega, Ala. After leaving school he engaged in teaching, and at the same time commenced reading medicine at the Mobile Medical Institute, graduating in the class of 1861. After this he practiced some and in the spring of 1862 came to Searcy. He was the leading physician of the county during the war, and remained at home by request. He was married in Perry County, Ala., in 1859, to Miss Sarah J. Crow, a native of Perry County, Ala., and daughter of Joseph W. and Elizabeth (Hopper) Crow, natives of Alabama. Her father was a successful agriculturist and his death occurred in 1865. His wife died in 1876. When coming to Searcy in 1862 Dr. McAdams found the town very small, and where fine business streets now are was then undergrowth. The Doctor opened his office in the public square and began practicing, which he continued all through the war without molestation. He is not very active in politics, but votes with the Democratic party. Socially, he is a member of Searcy Lodge No. 49, A. F. & A. M. To his marriage was born one child, Frank Waldo, who is book-keeper for F. Lippman, at Olyphant, Ark. Dr. McAdams has seen many changes since first residing here, both from an educational and moral standpoint. The customs of the people have also changed. He and Mrs. McAdams are members of the Baptist Church.

Maj. John C. McCauley, Searcy, Ark., is one of the well-known and esteemed pioneer residents of this county, having come to White County in 1851. He was born in Orange County, N. C., February 24, 1834, and was the second in a family of nine

children born to James and Mary A. (Freeland) McCauley, both natives of North Carolina. The father grew to manhood near Chapel Hill, N. C., settled on a plantation and made that his home until 1836, when he moved to Tennessee. He first settled in Fayette County, then Tipton County, and kept a hotel at Concordia, Tenn., in 1851. Later than this he came to White County, settled in Gray Township, speculated in land (being also a contractor), and erected a great many houses in Searcy. He there closed his eyes to the scenes of this world in December, 1888, at the age of seventy-nine years. His excellent wife died in 1883. The father was a member of Searcy Lodge No. 49, A. F. & A. M., and was charter member of the same. Of their family, seven children are now living: E. J. (now Mrs. E. J. Carter, who resides in Searcy), Maj. John C., Mary A. (now Mrs. William T. Holloway, of Searcy), Martha E. (now Mrs. Joseph R. Hall, resides in Tipton County, Tenn., near the old homestead), James (is married, and resides on the father's homestead near Judsonia), Catherine B. (now Mrs. John D. Sprigg, resides at Searcy), and George C. (who married Miss Emma Black, resides at West Point, White County). The paternal great-grandfather, John McCauley, was a captain under Gen. Marion in the War of the Revolution. He was at Antrim Island in the war against England, retreated and took secret passage on a Colonial vessel, in which he safely crossed the ocean to America. He landed in North Carolina, and made that State his home. Grandfather John McCauley was a soldier in the War of 1812, and held the rank of colonel. He represented Orange County, N. C., in the legislature for many years, and his death occurred in that State. On the mother's side, the family was of Scotch descent. Maj. John C. McCauley was nearly seventeen years of age when he came to White County, and received his education under the tutelage of Dr. James Holmes, an able educator. After coming to Arkansas he commenced studying law under Scott McConaughey, but in 1852 engaged in merchandising, which business he has since continued, with the exception of four years during the war (1861–65). He has had different

WHITE COUNTY.

partners, the present firm being McCauley & Son, which has continued since 1865, and carry everything to be found in a general store. In 1861 Mr. McCauley raised Company K, First State Guards, and entered the State's service January 1, 1861. Later he was transferred to the Seventh Arkansas Infantry, and remained there during the war. He was in the bombardment of Columbus, Ky., and was at Bowling Green and Shiloh; was twice wounded, and was confined in the hospital at Tupelo, Miss., and Blount Springs, Ala. After the battle of Shiloh the company was reorganized, and the subject of this sketch was the only one of the company re-elected, and he was promoted to the position of major. He was in Farmington, took the battery and then rejoined Gen. Bragg in his invasion of Kentucky. After the battle of Chickamauga, Ga., he was promoted to the rank of lieutenant-colonel, and after the battle of Missionary Ridge he was detailed and put in charge of a company to recruit men. He was captured by the Third Missouri Cavalry near Batesville and taken to the military prison at Little Rock, where he was paroled by Col. Chandler at the house of Mrs. Green, remained two months, and was then taken to Johnston Island, where he was exchanged on January 9, 1865. He surrendered on May 9, 1865, after which he returned to White County and engaged in merchandising. He has taken quite an active part in politics, and votes with the Democratic party. He was deputy postmaster for many years before the war, and was postmaster under President Hayes, filled the same position under President Cleveland, and occupies that position at the present time. He has been Master of the Masonic Lodge No. 49, Searcy, for six years, is a member of Tillman Chapter No. 19, and has been High Priest and King; is also a member of the Council, having been Thrice Illustrious. Maj. McCauley was married in Tipton County, Tenn., in 1855, to Miss Eliza J. Hall, a native of Tennessee, and the daughter of Thomas S. and Mary Hall, natives of North Carolina. Her father was a farmer and tanner, and both he and wife died in Tennessee. They were related by marriage to Stonewall Jack-

son. To Mr. and Mrs. McCauley were born four living children: Aurora (now Mrs. Fancette, resides in Searcy), Charles E. (widower, and is postal clerk on the Iron Mountain Railroad between St. Louis and Little Rock), Ernest J. and James Thomas. Mr. McCauley and wife are members of the Old School Presbyterian Church, and he is deacon and Bible-class teacher in the same.

James A. McCauley, farmer and ginner, White County, Ark. Permanent success in any calling in life is largely dependent upon the energy, perseverance and enterprise of an individual, and this, together with honest, upright dealing, will eventually bring him to the front. Mr. McCauley was originally from Tipton County, Tenn., where his birth occurred in 1842, and was the fifth of seven children, the result of the union of James and Mary (Freeland) McCauley, natives of Orange County, N. C. The parents were married in Chapel Hill, N. C., and in 1836 moved to Tipton County, Tenn., where the father tilled the soil until 1851. He then came to White County, settled at Prospect Bluff, now Judsonia, and in connection with his former pursuit, ran a steam saw-mill, one of the first in the county, and doing the grinding for several counties. In 1885 he moved to West Point, White County, and there his death occurred on December 15, 1888. His wife received her final summons in Searcy, in 1882. James A. McCauley attained his growth on the farm, received his education in the schools of Searcy, and on April 13, 1861, he enlisted in Company K, Seventh Arkansas Infantry, as a private, for one year. He was in the battle of Shiloh, and after this disastrous engagement he re-enlisted for three years or during service, in the same company and regiment. He was in the battles of Perryville and Murfreesboro, and at the reorganization of the company he was promoted to the rank of second lieutenant. This was after the last-named battle. The regiment was consolidated with the Sixth Arkansas Infantry, and Mr. McCauley was transferred to Gen. Kirby Smith. He was put in Turnbull Camp, Washington, Hempstead County, for four months, drilling troops, and was then transferred to Dobbin's brigade, McGee's regular cavalry. He was with

HISTORY OF ARKANSAS.

Gen. Price on the Missouri raid and was paroled at Jacksonport, Ark., in 1865, after which he returned to White County. Mr. McCauley then embarked in mercantile pursuits in Searcy, in 1866, but the following year sold out and returned to the farm. His marriage occurred in White County, on December 13, 1865, to Miss Nancy A. Bond, a native of White County, and the daughter of John W. and Emily (Smith) Bond, natives of North Carolina and Georgia, respectively. The father moved to Arkansas Territory in 1836, and was residing there when it was admitted into the Union. He was the first county clerk of White County, was one of the prominent and first merchants of Searcy, and started his store in the woods. His death occurred in 1887. His wife died in 1869. Mr. McCauley settled where he now resides in 1856, and in 1874 he purchased 715 acres of land, and now has 315 under cultivation. He raises grain and cotton. Mr. McCauley has been running a cotton-gin ever since he settled on the farm, and has been quite successful. In his political views he is a cotton-mouth Democrat. To his marriage were born ten children: James Walton, Emma, Holmes, Stonewall, Lee, Hardee, Pat Cleburne, Jeff Davis, Allen and Mary. Mr. and Mrs. McCauley are members of the Presbyterian Church.

George C. McCauley is not unknown to the many readers of the present volume. He learned the miller's trade when a boy, and operated a grist-mill and cotton-gin at Judsonia for six years, after which he engaged in farming on the old Beeler place, where he remained nine years. Moving thence to West Point, he engaged in farming and in the cotton-gin business, in which he is still engaged, enjoying the confidence and liberal patronage of his many acquaintances. On October 24, 1877, he was married to Miss Emma Black, a daughter of W. G. Black, who was born in 1860, in Searcy. They became the parents of three children, two of whom are still living: Mattie May and Maud E. Mr. McCauley is a strong Democrat, and a liberal donator to all enterprises for the benefit of church or educational work. He was born in Tipton County, Tenn., on February 5, 1851, being the son of James and Mary Ann Mc-

Cauley, natives of North Carolina, who were reared near Raleigh, where they were married and made their home for some time. After residing awhile in Tennessee and Missouri, they finally came to Arkansas in 1851, settling in White County. Mr. McCauley was one of the most successful farmers that ever found a home in Arkansas, being the owner of 1,200 acres of land at the time of his death, which occurred in December, 1888, at the age of seventy-seven years; his wife had died in 1882, in her seventy-second year. Both were members of the Presbyterian Church, and were the parents of ten children, seven of whom are still living: Elizabeth (the wife of W. B. Carter, of Searcy), John C. (the present postmaster of Searcy), Mary (wife of W. T. Holloway), Martha (wife of J. R. Hall), James A. (farmer of this county), Catharine B. (wife of Capt. J. D. Spriggs, now deceased) and George C. (our subject).

R. H. McCulloch, farmer and stock raiser, Searcy, Ark. In reviewing the lives of those individuals mentioned in this volume no adequate idea of the agricultural affairs of White County, or of its substantial citizens, would be complete, which failed to make mention of Mr. McCulloch, or of the substantial property which he owns. Originally from Murfreesboro, Rutherford County, Tenn., his birth occurred August 26, 1849, he passing his boyhood days and early manhood in Tennessee. He was educated in Andrew College of that State, and after leaving school began the study of pharmacy, subsequently going to Giles County, Tenn., where he was engaged in agricultural pursuits from 1870 to 1871. The next year he became book-keeper at Plum Bayou, in Jefferson Township, on the Arkansas River. In March, 1873, he came to Gray Township, White County, and finally locating at Beebe, entered the employ of Strange & Ward as book-keeper, with whom he remained for two years. Deciding to settle in Union Township, he purchased a farm of 120 acres, with sixty-five under cultivation, and now has eighty-five acres of it improved. On October 27, 1884, Mr. McCulloch moved to Searcy, having the previous September been elected clerk of the circuit and chancery court, and also recorder, and

WHITE COUNTY.

served efficiently in that capacity until October 30, 1888, when he was engaged as traveling salesman for Mitchell & Bettis, of Little Rock, continuing on the road until March 1, 1889. He then moved to his present farm, having bought in 1887 eighty acres, with thirty acres under cultivation. He now owns a good place of 200 acres, with 115 acres under substantial improvement, besides a timber tract of 169 acres. Mr. McCulloch is the eldest in a family of five children born to Dr. P. D. and Lucy V. McCulloch, both being natives of Tennessee. The father was a physician and surgeon by profession, and in 1876 moved to Hot Springs, Ark., where he still resides. He has been active in the Masonic order, having just retired as Grand Knight of the Grand Templars of the State. He represented the Grand Lodge of Tennessee in all its various offices. The mother of R. H. McCulloch died in July, 1865, in Gibson County, Tenn. In their family were the following children: R. H., P. D. (married, and resides in Lee County; is an attorney and an extensive planter), E. A. (married, and an attorney in Lee County) and Lydia B. (now Mrs. J. T. Hogg; resides in Trenton, Tenn.; her husband is traveling salesman for a Memphis firm). R. H. McCulloch was married in White County, Ark., November 25, 1874, to Miss Anna E. Cobb, a native of Tennessee (Haywood County), and the daughter of T. T. and Mary (Rose) Cobb, of North Carolina origin, who immigrated from that State in 1832 and 1833, respectively, to Tennessee. In 1858 they came to White County, Ark., settling in Union Township, and there the father's death occurred in 1881. The mother died about 1860. Mr. McCulloch lost his excellent wife in 1876, and was married again in White County, June 30, 1878, to Mattie L. Cobb, a Tennesseean by birth, and the daughter of S. P. and Eliza (Rose) Cobb, originally from North Carolina. The parents moved to Tennessee in 1832, coming thence to White County, Ark., in 1870, and settling near Beebe, where the father followed agricultural pursuits. Both parents are now living. To Mr. and Mrs. McCulloch were born five children: Samuel R., Philip D., Bertha C., Maggie and R. H., Jr. Mr. McCulloch is a member of Searcy Lodge No. 49, A. F. & A. M.;

was Worshipful Master of Beebe Lodge No. 145 for about ten years; is a member of Tillman Chapter No. 19, R. A. M., and belongs to Searcy Lodge, K. of H., at Searcy. He has been for a number of years a member of the Grand Lodge, and for the past three years has been secretary and treasurer, and chairman for two years.

Miles C. McDowell, actively occupied as a farmer and stock raiser, of Marshall Township, White County, Ark., is the son of Harvey and Ruth (Walker) McDowell, and was born in Tennessee in 1854. Harvey McDowell, also a native of Tennessee, dates his existence from July, 1806, as a son of Joseph and Olive McDowell. He spent his younger days on a plantation, and in the schools of Tennessee, and was married in April, 1834, to Ruth Walker, becoming by her the father of the following family: Ollie (Mrs. W. F. Gill, now deceased), Parthena (Mrs. L. Jones, also deceased), Louisa (widow of Mr. Greegs), William (married), Gideon, Robert, John, Harriet C. and Miles C. (the subject of this memoir). Harvey McDowell died soon after the war, his last days being spent in Missouri, where he had moved with his family from Tennessee. After his father's demise, Miles C. came to Arkansas in company with his mother, and purchased land in White County which he soon after sold, and subsequently acquired another 120 acres in the same township, one mile south of Romance. This farm he bought in 1888, and now has forty acres in an excellent state of cultivation. His farm is well and carefully stocked, and in many respects is the equal of any in the country. His mother, who is residing with him, is an estimable lady, and is hale and hearty for a person of her age. Mr. McDowell takes decided interest in all those movements which promise good to the county, and never fails to give his support to any worthy cause.

George W. McKinney is one of the most enterprising and progressive farmers of White County and one who has done a great deal in changing the country from a dense wilderness to what is now a prosperous and thrifty community. Born on May 9, 1826, in Monroe County, Miss., he came to Arkansas in 1870, and settled on the farm that he now owns, buying 120 acres on which was a

HISTORY OF ARKANSAS.

small log-cabin and about ten acres cleared, but shortly after he purchased 200 acres more, and erected a good house, barns, fences, etc., having here 135 acres under successful cultivation, and all the necessary improvements of the present day. Mr. McKinney is a model farmer, as everything around his place indicates; negligence and degeneracy being traits unknown about his home. He is the son of John and Rosanna (Land) McKinney, natives of North Carolina and Tennessee, respectively, who were married in the latter State and shortly afterward moved to Mississippi, there becoming engaged in farming. Mr. McKinney was a Democrat, and soldier in the War of 1812, also serving as magistrate of his county for several years. His death occurred in 1832, his wife surviving him until 1872. They were the parents of nine children, five now living. The oldest son, J. G., is a prosperous farmer in Texas. Susan C. (Mrs. Chesley Malone, at present resides in Calhoun County, Miss.), Andrew J. (is a farmer of Chickasaw County, Miss.), and one daughter (Mrs. R. E. Brewer). George W. was reared to farm life, and received a good education in the common schools of the period. He cared for his aged mother until her death, giving her all the comforts necessary to her declining years, and in his twenty-fourth year was married to Miss Helen C. Gibbs of Mississippi birth, by whom he became the father of eight children, six now surviving: W. T. (a farmer of Royal Township, White County), John M. (also a farmer in Royal Township, White County), George W. (at home), T. A. (a farmer of Royal Township, White County), Margaret A. (wife of James W. Hall, a prominent farmer of Royal Township), J. R. and Julia E. (now Mrs. Thomas S. Kitchen). Mrs. McKinney died in 1889, and Mr. McKinney chose for his second and present wife, Mrs. M. E. Malone, a native of Mississippi. At the time of the war Mr. McKinney was justice of the peace and consequently did not enter the service until 1863, when he enlisted in Col. Duff's regiment, remaining until the final surrender. He was in McCullough's brigade in the cavalry service, and participated in several brisk skirmishes, but was never wounded.

He was ordered to Mobile with Col. Duff, and advised by that colonel to go to his family. While in Mississippi Mr. McKinney held the office of justice of the peace and overseer of roads and men. He is a member of El Paso Lodge No. 65, A. F. & A. M., and was made a Mason in 1865, also belonging at this time to New Hope Agricultural Wheel No. 32, T. A., and is treasurer of the Wheel. He is at present a member of his school board, and takes an active interest in schools, churches, and gives his influence and help to all public enterprises. In his political views Mr. McKinney is a Democrat, but casts his vote irrespective of party and where he considers it will do the most good, supporting always the best man for the position.

D. L. McLeod, who, though comparatively young in years, has had an experience such as but few men enjoy, is now a prosperous planter and fruit grower of White County. When only fourteen years of age he became a "sailor boy," and in 1869 received the honor of being made captain in the merchant service. He was born in Prince Edward's Island, Canada, April 27, 1841, and is the son of Donald McLeod, also a native of Canada, who there married Miss Annie Henderson, her birth also occurring on Prince Edward's Island. A family of six children blessed this union, five of whom are still living. Donald McLeod was principally engaged in agricultural pursuits during life, in which he was very successful. Himself and wife were members of the Presbyterian Church, in which he had been deacon for a number of years, rigidly upholding the tenets of his belief. His wife died some years previous to his demise, which occurred in 1886. From January, 1864, D. L. McLeod served as chief quartermaster in the United States navy, receiving honorable recognition for the manner in which he discharged his duties. His term of service in the navy expired in May, 1867, but he at once returned to the sea and engaged in the merchant service continuing until 1879. One noteworthy event marks his career during this time: A beautiful marine telescope was presented to him in 1873, awarded by the King of Norway for a brave and noble deed in rescuing a

WHITE COUNTY.

Norwegian crew, on the Atlantic Ocean. Mr. Mc-Leod was married, in 1874, to Susie K. Kitchen, a daughter of William and Jane Kitchen, and a native of Ontario, Canada. To this union two children have been born: Lillie J. (born in Akyobe, India, April, 1875, and died in 1880), William (born in February, 1877, and died at sea May, 1878, and is buried at Belfast, Ireland) and Arthur R. (who is now seven years old). In 1880 Mr. Mc-Leod became a resident of Iowa, where he remained for three years engaged in fine stock raising, in Fayette County, but in 1883 he moved to Arkansas and located at Judsonia, White County, where he still lives, successfully occupied in fruit growing. He owns 240 acres of excellent land, and has a fine residence, which he has erected during his abode here. He is a Master Mason in good standing and is also president of the Arkansas Fruit Growers' Union, which was organized in 1886. Besides this he is first vice-president of the State Horticultural Society, and, with his wife, belongs to the Baptist Church.

Dandridge McRae, attorney at law. Searcy, Ark., has every reason to be proud of both its law courts and the members of the bar who support them. Among the leading firms of attorneys in Searcy, is the well-known one of Messrs. McRae, Rives & Rives, who are notable representatives of the learned profession. Mr. McRae has also been expert for the United States treasury department, appointed in 1889, and this business is to gather statistics for that department. He was born in Baldwin County, Ala., on October 10, 1829, and the eldest in a family of eleven children born to the union of D. R. W. and Margaret (Braey) Mc-Rae, the father of West Florida Parish, Miss., and the mother of South Carolina. The parents were married in Alabama in 1828, and were the owners of a large plantation, which he carried on although he was a lawyer by profession. He took quite an active part in politics, was sheriff of Clark County, and represented that county in the legislature. His death occurred in March, 1849. After the death of her husband and the same year, Mrs. McRae came to White County, Ark., settled in Little Red River Township, entered land, im-

proved it, bought several claims, and in 1859 moved to Pulaski County, near Little Rock, and made that her home until 1861. After this she visited the Lone Star State, but returned, and her death occurred at the home of her son, Dandridge McRae, in Searcy in 1867. Those members of the family living are: Dandridge, Rebecca (Mrs. Col. G. F. Bancum, of Little Rock), Ann (wife of A. T. Jones, near West Point, White County, Ark.) and Mrs. Mona Rawles (at Perryville, Perry County). Dandridge McRae was early trained to the arduous duties of the farm, received his education at home under a private tutor, and later entered the University of South Carolina, from which institution he graduated in the class of 1849. He then aided in opening up the farm in Red River Township, but in 1853 moved to Searcy, and there commenced reading law. He was admitted to the bar by Justice C. C. Scott, of the supreme court, in 1854, and commenced the practice of law immediately afterward. In 1856 he was elected county and circuit clerk of the county, and served six years. In 1861 he was actively engaged in organizing troops for the State, and in the same year was sent by the military board to muster Gen. N. P. Pierce, brigadier of State troops, while even at that time the Missourians were driven from the State by the Federal Generals Lyon and Siegel. Gen. Ben. McCulloch in command of the Arkansas and Indian Territory, issued a proclamation to the people of Arkansas to go to the border and repel invaders. Many companies organized reported to Mr. McRae, and at the request of the General, the former took command and moved into Missouri, toward Springfield, to make a diversion, while the General moved to Carthage to relieve Gen. Parsons of the Missouri State Guards. Upon his return to Arkansas Mr. McRae organized a regiment under the direction of Gen. McCulloch, and was made colonel of the same. He served until 1862, was with Gen. McCulloch at Wilson's Creek, Pea Ridge and Corinth. He returned to Arkansas in 1862, raised another regiment by June, and was assigned by Gen. Hindman the command of a brigade. This brigade served until 1862, when Mr. McRae was promoted in December, to the

88   WHITE COUNTY, ARKANSAS - BIOGRAPHICAL AND HISTORICAL MEMOIRS

* *

HISTORY OF ARKANSAS.

rank of brigadier-general, and served in that capacity until the close of the war. He was in the battle of Helena, captured the only fort taken, also Jenkins' Ferry, Prairie Grove, and returned to Searcy, White County, in 1865. He engaged in the practice of law until 1881, and was then deputy secretary of State for four years. In 1885 he was acting commissioner for Arkansas, at the World's Fair at New Orleans, and in 1886 was the commissioner. Mr. McRae was appointed expert on December 26, 1888, by United States treasury department for gathering information. He was vice-president of the bureau of emigration of Arkansas in 1887. Socially, he is a member of Searcy Lodge No. 49, A. F. & A. M., and was Worshipful Master of the same; is a member of Tillman Chapter No. 19, and a member of the Council. Mr. McRae was married in De Soto County, Miss., on January 10, 1855, to Miss Angie Lewis, a native of Mississippi, who bore her husband two children: Annie (now Mrs. Neeley, residing in Searcy) and Minnie (now Mrs. J. F. Rives, Jr., residing in Searcy).

Thomas Jefferson Malone, planter and stock raiser at Pleasant Plains, Ark., is the son of Stephen and Sarah (Parks) Malone, natives of North Carolina, being born December 16, 1816, in Henry County, Tenn. He was reared in the arduous duties of the farm, received his education in his native county, and on December 20, 1846, he was married in Fayette County, Tenn., to Miss Pinie E. Ozier, a native of North Carolina, where she partly received her education. In about 1848 Mr. Malone purchased a tract of land, consisting of 160 acres of unimproved land, and this he went to work to improve. After clearing about twenty-five acres and erecting good buildings, he sold this property and came to Arkansas. To his marriage were born six children, four of whom are now living: Sarah Frances (born in 1847), William Thomas (born in 1849, and died in 1857), Alice Jane (born in 1858), an infant (died unnamed), Charles Calvin (born May 7, 1861) and Lititia (born in 1863). Sarah Frances married W. Yarbrough, a native of Tennessee, is the mother of three children, and now resides in White County. Calvin C. married Miss Ella Boen, a native of Alabama, and now resides with parents. Martha Ann married James Kilo, a native of Arkansas, and has one child. They also reside with the parents. Mr. Malone came to Arkansas in 1856, located in Independence County, and there made their home for one year, he engaged in tilling the soil. In 1857 he came to White County, located on his present farm, and there he has since made his home. The original tract contained about 194 acres, which were uncultivated at that time. Mr. Malone has purchased other tracts at various times and has always sold to advantage. He has put all the improvements on his place and has about fifty-three acres under fence. The soil is of good quality and furnishes nearly all the necessaries of life, corn and cotton being the principal crops. Vegetables of all kinds grow in abundance, and he also raises some tobacco which is of good quality. Mr. and Mrs. Malone are members of the Methodist Episcopal Church, and have held membership since 1843. They live true Christian lives and have the love and esteem of a large circle of friends. Mr. Malone is a member of Cedar Grove Lodge, A. F. & A. M., and is also a member of the Agricultural Wheel No. 88. The parents of Mr. Malone were natives of North Carolina, and were married in that State. They were of Scotch-German descent and their ancestors on both sides came to the United States prior to the Revolutionary War. Grandfather Malone served seven years in the Colonial War and drew a pension for some years previous to his death, which occurred at the age of eighty-one years. Grandfather Parks also participated in that war, serving in the capacity of colonel, and died about 1804. To Stephen and Sarah (Parks) Malone were born thirteen children, all of whom grew to maturity.

Mrs. Malinda J. Malone, proprietress of a well-kept hotel at Auvergne, Ark., is a daughter of Henry R. and Mary E. (Follis) Bray, the former a Baptist minister and a native of Virginia, and the latter born in the "Palmetto State." They were married in Alabama in 1832, and shortly afterward moved to Lynnville, Tenn., where they made their home for twelve years, Mr. Bray being engaged in

WHITE COUNTY.

conducting a large woodyard, blacksmith's shop and also attended to his ministerial duties. In 1850 Rev. Bray removed with his family to Alabama, where he followed the occupation of farming and preaching until 1860, when he settled in Madison County, Ark., and two years later moved to Cotton Plant, in Phillips County, where he resided five years. In the fall of 1867, he came to Jackson County, and purchased 250 acres of land and was here residing at the time of his death in July, 1870, his wife's death occuring five years later. Mrs. Bray was a daughter of William and Mary (Dickinson) Follis who were natives of South Carolina, and removed to Alabama at an early day. The father's ancestors were Virginians and of Irish descent. Mrs. Malone is the eldest of a family of nine children and is the only one now living, her birth occurring on November 23, 1837. The remainder of the family were: William R. (born March 14, 1839; he was twice married and died January 3, 1888, two children and his last wife surviving him), Mary E. (was born August 1, 1841, and was married to Gabriel Couch of Jackson County, Ark., and died in 1871), Sarah A. (was born in 1843, and was the wife of G. C. Harrison, by him becoming the mother of three sons; she died in 1882), Charity E. (was born 1845 and was twice married, her first husband being William Johnson and her last Newton Bleakley; she died in 1880, leaving two sons, Charley W., who resides with Mrs. Malone and William, who lives in New Mexico), Iradel (was a farmer of Texas, but in 1881 moved to Jackson County, Ark., and died the same year), Martha (was the wife of Levi Blakely and died in 1871 leaving no issue), Boldon (died in 1877 at the age of eighteen years) and a little sister, Katie (died in infancy). Mrs. Malone was reared in Lynnville and in that town and in Rogersville, Ala., received her education. In 1854 she was married to B. T. Malone, she at that time being only fourteen and a half years of age and he nineteen. Their children are named as follows: John T. (a miller at Athens, Ala., has a wife and two children, Charlie and Dollie), Henry E. (a man of Thornton, Miller County, Ark.; is married and has had five children but now has only three, Emmet, aged nine; Lulu, aged

seven, and Lucile, aged five), Emma (is a young lady at home), Mollie L. (was born in 1863 and is the wife of J. A. Canada, a merchant of Beebe; she died in 1885 and her husband and one child survive her), Dollie (was born August 1, 1872, and died May 7, 1886), Mattie (was born August 2, 1866, and died August 6, 1877), Linnie (was born January 1, 1877 and died April 1, 1879), James W. (was born August 3, 1858 and died June 2, 1859) and Charles (born August 2, 1876, and died in infancy). After their marriage Mr. and Mrs. Malone resided in Tennessee until 1859 and after a short residence in Northern Alabama they settled in Mississippi and there made their home for ten years. In 1869 they removed to and purchased a large plantation in Jackson County, Ark., and there also managed a mercantile establishment up to 1877, when they sold their land and moved to Beebe, purchasing considerable town property at that place on which they erected good buildings. Mr. Malone was also engaged in merchandising; in his political views was an active Democrat and held the offices of magistrate and notary public for a considerable length of time. He was a leading member of the Baptist Church and was a member in good standing of the Masonic fraternity. Mr. Malone died in 1884 and his widow immediately put her shoulder to the wheel, increased her stock of dry goods and carried on the business at Beebe, and also erected a store at Auvergne which she put in charge of her son Henry E., her eldest son conducting the business at Beebe. In 1877 Mrs. Malone located in Auvergne and took charge of the Auvergne academy and for one year filled the office of matron of that institution. In September, 1888, she opened a hotel which she is at present successfully conducting and since the death of her husband she has so successfully conducted the property he left that it has greatly increased in value. She is a lady of great force of character and more than ordinary powers of mind and has reared her family in such a manner as to win the respect of all with whom she comes in contact. She is a member of the Missionary Baptist Church and her family are also church members.

Jeremiah E. Manasco. The Manasco family,

HISTORY OF ARKANSAS.

or rather that branch to which the subject of this sketch belongs, were early settlers of Arkansas, having originally come from Alabama, and were in all probability of French descent. Mr. Manasco, our subject, was born in Tipton County, Tenn., in 1833 or 1834, and is a son of James and Ruby E. (Crawford) Manasco, both of whom died about the year 1841, and although he was the youngest of a family of nine children, he was left to shift for himself, and became a bound boy to his brother John, and was reared by him to manhood on a farm. He suffered the trials of the orphan, and although his school advantages were very limited, and he was compelled to work very hard, he remained faithful to his bondsman till he reached his twenty-first year, when he drifted out into the world to try his own powers. He first engaged as a farm hand, doing all kinds of heavy work, becoming in the meantime thoroughly familiar with the details of farm work. In 1857 he was married to Miss Mary J. Flanagan, a native of Tennessee, and by her became the father of six children, three of whom lived to be grown: John F. (a railroad man of Little Rock), William J. (a resident of Tennessee), Preston V. (deceased), Amandeville W. (living) and twin girls, Emily and Martha (who died in infancy). The mother of these children died in September, 1869, in full communion with the Methodist Episcopal Church. After remaining a widower two years, Mr. Manasco married Miss Virginia P. Wooten, a native of Tennessee, and of their large family of ten children all are living: Nellie Naomi, May L., George W., Calla D., Bedford F., Reuben B., Fanny, Helen, Bertha and Leonora M. In 1864 Mr. Manasco joined the Twelfth Tennessee Cavalry, but owing to weak eyes soon left the service. Before the war and afterward till January, 1872, Mr. Manasco carried on farming in his native State, and in this calling succeeded far beyond his expectations, but sold his property in December, 1871, and in 1872 removed to Prairie County, Ark., where he rented land and farmed for three years. Since that time he has resided in White County, and in 1875 purchased 160 acres of land, on which were erected some log-cabins on fifty acres of cleared land. He set ener-

getically to work to improve his property, and soon had one of the finest homes in White County. In June, 1885, he had the misfortune to lose his residence and nearly all its contents by fire, but he has since rebuilt, and now has one of the most substantial residences in the county. By subsequent purchases he has increased his lands to 245 acres, and has 100 acres under cultivation. The land is well adapted to raising all kinds of grain, but his principal crops are corn, cotton and oats. Mr. Manasco is public-spirited and enterprising, and has always favored worthy movements. He is a member of El Paso Lodge No. 65 of the A. F. & A. M.

John S. Marsh, one of the well-known farmers and stock raisers of White County, is the son of Roland and Sarah (Webb) Marsh, his birth occurring in Warren County, Tenn., July 28, 1825. Roland Marsh was born and educated in North Carolina, emigrating when quite young to Tennessee in company with his parents, where he met and married Miss Webb, also of North Carolina nativity, and the daughter of Elisha and Sarah Webb. To the union of Mr. and Mrs. Marsh five children were born, four of them now living, and residents of Arkansas. They are Harry, Pollie, Sarah, Rachel and John S. Mr. Marsh was a farmer, and quite successful in the accumulation of wealth. He died in 1835, and his estimable wife only survived him about a year. Both were members of the Baptist Church. John S. passed his boyhood days in the schools of Warren County, Tenn., and in 1845 was united in the bands of matrimony to Annie Potter, also of Tennessee. Ten children blessed their marriage: Rollin, Tillman, Sarah J., Thomas M., Jackson R., Martha, William H., Martina and Martisia (twins) and Johnnie. Mrs. Marsh died in 1873, and in 1879, Mr. Marsh chose for his second wife Sarah Gordon, a resident and native of Tennessee. In 1849, when the subject of this sketch immigrated to Arkansas from Tennessee (locating in White County), he found himself the possessor of a single wagon and a yoke of oxen, the two comprising his worldly all. He now owns 120 acres of land well cultivated, and having exercised great care in the selec-

WHITE COUNTY.

tion of his stock, has some excellent animals. His farm, though not as large as some in the county, is perfectly complete in all its appointments, and its general appearance is indicative of peace and prosperity. Mr. Marsh takes a great interest in all educational matters, and is determined that his children shall be deprived of nothing that tends to advance their intellectual training. He is one of the organizers of the first church established in Mount Pisgah, and is an influential member. His wife and entire family are all members of the Methodist Church. He belongs to Lodge No. 460 of the Masonic order, in which he has held the office of treasurer.

John W. Matthews was the eldest son in the family of Robert and Annie (Howard) Matthews, the former of whom came upon the stage of life's action in Alabama, in 1802. His parents were Walter and Rachel Matthews, of South Carolina origin, but who moved to Alabama at an early day. Robert Matthews was married about 1830, and followed the occupation of a farmer all his life. Coming to Arkansas in 1836 (his family following him in 1852), he settled in White County; his wife had died shortly before his removal. Mr. Matthews enlisted as a soldier during the Civil War in 1863, and served until his death, which occurred at Rock Port in 1864. Himself and wife had a family of three children: John W., Sarah J. and Delia F. John W., the only surviving member, was born in Alabama in 1832, and was married in 1858 to Nancy Brady, daughter of William and Mirah (Cordal) Brady. Mr. and Mrs. Matthews are the parents of nine children: Mirah Ann (now Mrs. Pruett), Mary Jane (married S. M. West), James C., William R., John W., Joseph E., Benjamin F., Ester A. and Nancy N. Mr. Matthews enlisted in 1861 in Morse's company, Fourth Battalion, Arkansas Infantry, and took part in the battles of Cotton Plant, Ark.; Columbus, Ky., and a number of other engagements. He now owns a fine farm of 313 acres of land, 175 acres of which are under cultivation. Mrs. Matthews is a member of the Baptist Church. Mr. Matthews is treasurer of the County Wheel, and is an influential and highly respected citizen.

Burwill M. Merrill is a member of the go-ahead, enterprising firm of Merrill & Reed, dealers in real estate in Beebe, Ark., a native of the "Empire State." He was born in Chautauqua County in 1835, as the son of George and Eliza (Millard) Merrill, natives of Massachusetts and Canada, respectively. George Merrill was born in 1809, and died in 1884, his wife, who was also born at an early date, dying at Burwill's birth. The latter, the only child of his father's first marriage, when about five years old, moved to Michigan with his parent, who became a very successful farmer in the "Wolverine State," giving his careful and undivided attention to that occupation. By his second marriage Mr. Merrill became the father of two children, only one now living: Letitia (wife of John Gordon, a farmer of Floyd County, Iowa). Burwill M. Merrill was given such advantages for obtaining an education as the excellent schools of Michigan afforded, and at the age of twenty-one assumed the responsibility of his father's farm, the care of which he continued until the latter's death in 1884. In 1854 he was married to Miss Lydia Wilson, a native of Canada, and to their union two children were born: Letitia (the wife of J. C. Covert, manufacturer of store fronts and other building materials, at Belmont, Iowa) and De Forest (a mechanic at Detroit). Mrs. Merrill died in 1867, having been a devoted wife and mother, and a member of the Baptist Church. Mr. Merrill chose for his second wife Miss Alviria Cross, who also died in Clinton County, Mich., in 1884, having become the father of two children: George W. (who died at the age of eighteen, unmarried) and Florence L. (now the wife of Dr. A. C. Jordon, a prominent physician of Beebe, Ark., with which daughter Mr. Merrill now resides). He came to Arkansas in 1885, that he might find a home in a more genial climate, also desiring to try small fruit raising in this favored section. Purchasing sixty acres in White County, one mile west of Beebe, he at once turned his attention to the cultivation of small fruits and grasses. Mr. Merrill has tried all kinds of grasses, and is thoroughly convinced that the soil of White County will produce liberally any of the various kinds grown so bountifully in the

HISTORY OF ARKANSAS.

East and North. Red clover, three feet in length, was raised on his farm one season, which was something of a curiosity. He is now successfully raising regular crops of clover and timothy. Strawberries and root crops yield immensely. Garden vegetables are especially productive, sweet potatoes yielding 350 bushels per acre. Mr. Merrill is a member of Beebe Lodge No. 47, I. O. O. F., and has passed all the chairs in the subordinate lodge. He has been a member of the Methodist Episcopal Church for many years, and is a public-spirited, enterprising man, giving his hearty support to all movements that betoken the good or growth of the county.

Christian Miller is a farmer and fruit grower of White County, Ark. This gentleman was born on Bornholm Island, Hasley, Denmark, in 1842, and is the second in a family of ten children, the result of the union of John and Elizabeth Miller, natives, also, of Denmark, and who died in their native land. Their children were named as follows: Mary, Christian, Sena, John, Petra, Lena, Otto Line (deceased), Andrew, James and Julyno. Four of these children came to this country, two of whom reside in Wyoming. Andrew and the subject of this sketch came to Arkansas and settled in White County. The latter spent his youth in his native country, was educated there and came to America in 1865, but first settled in New York. Later he moved to Illinois, remained there until 1871, and then, as stated above, came to White County, Ark., and settled in Harrison Township. He purchased eighty acres of timber land, improved it, and has added to the original tract until he now owns 240 acres, with 130 acres cleared and 100 acres devoted to horticulture. Mr. Miller was married in Illinois in 1871 to Miss Mary Hahn, daughter of Saro Hanson and Eline Christian Hahn, natives of Denmark. Mary Hahn came to America in 1861, first settling in Illinois. Mrs. Mary Hahn's marriage to Christian Miller was in 1871. After his marriage Mr. Miller moved to Arkansas, where he has remained ever since. He has about sixteen acres of land devoted to the raising of strawberries, ten acres in raspberries, and an extensive peach orchard of sixty acres. He is one of the most ex-

tensive shippers in Judsonia. He is also the owner of a good town property in Judsonia. Socially, he is a member of Anchor Lodge No. 384, A. F. & A. M., and he and wife are members of the Missionary Baptist Church, of which he is a deacon. He is active in church and educational matters, and, in fact, takes a decided interest in all enterprises for the good of the county.

John S. Mitchell, M. D., whose professional career is one in which he may take just pride, is a son of a veteran of the Mexican War, James S. Mitchell, and has been a resident of White County since 1858. James S. Mitchell was born in Monroe County, Ky., on August 14, 1793, and was married shortly after his return from the War of 1812, in which he was actively engaged, to Miss Sarah Scott, a Tennesseean by birth, born January 18, 1795. They were the parents of seven children: Dorcas (afterward Mrs. Gist), Frances (Wilson), Mary (Dies), Matilda (Barger), John S. (our subject) and Louis B. (who is also a physician of Monroe County. Mrs. Mitchell's family were also originally from Tennessee. The Mitchells were connected with the celebrated Boone family of Kentucky. John S. was born in Kentucky November 14, 1824, growing to manhood on a farm, and accompanying his father to Henderson County, Tenn., when a boy. He was married December 30, 1849, to Miss Sarah J. Dotson, daughter of Thomas and Charlotte (Pipkin) Dotson, who were married in 1815, and became the parents of four children. After his marriage, Dr. Mitchell returned to Tennessee, living there nine years. In the spring of 1858 he came to White County, where he bought a farm of two hundred acres of unimproved land, clearing the same himself, and placing over half of it under cultivation. Himself and wife have been blessed with seven children, five of whom are living: Irena F. (Swinford), James B., William B., John T. (deceased), Albert G., Sally A. and Virgil. Dr. Mitchell also has ten grandchildren. He is a strong Democrat, and served as justice of the peace during the war and until the reconstruction. A Master Mason, he belongs to Centre Hill Lodge No. 114, and to Centre Hill Chapter. Dr. Mitchell and wife are connected with the Christian Church.

WHITE COUNTY.

Two of their children only are living at home at the present time.

Nathaniel Lee Mitchell. The entire life of Mr. Mitchell has been passed in an industious manner, and not without substantial evidences of success, as will be seen from a glance at his present possessions. His birth occurred on April 11, 1828, and he is a son of Charles B. and Nancy (Miller) Mitchell and a native of Boonville, Cooper County, Mo. His paternal ancestors came to America in 1760, and the paternal grandfather, Thomas Mitchell, was born in the State of Virginia. The Millers came to America prior to the Revolution, probably about 1750. Owing to war troubles Great-grandfather Miller was forced from his home, and without his family, which consisted of his wife and infant, he was compelled to flee elsewhere for protection. Grandfather Miller was born in North Carolina, about 1780. Nathaniel Lee Mitchell received his early education in the district schools of his native county, and afterward entered the high school of Boonville, his school-days ending in the State University at Columbia, Mo., in 1850. In 1850 he crossed the plains to the gold region of California, and there worked in different mines for about one and a half years, his labors being attended with fair results, and he then returned to his home in Missouri, and the following year became second assistant of Solomon Houck, who was engaged in freighting goods between Kansas City, Mo., and Santa Fe, N. M., making one trip which required about eight months' time. In 1853 he again crossed the plains to California, via Salt Lake City, Utah, and as before only met with moderate success. At the end of two years he engaged in the butcher's business, and in 1857 bought a farm in Yolo County, consisting of 160 acres of improved land. In addition to managing this farm, he engaged in teaching, but in 1859 concluded to return home, so sold his property, and after returning home, engaged in collecting notes, and in 1861 rented a farm near Sedalia. The troubles incident to the war coming up at this time, he left his farm and enlisted in Company G, Second Missouri Volunteer Cavalry, Confederate States Army, under Gen. Price, who was at that time commanding the Confederate army in Southwest Missouri. Almost immediately after joining he was called to duty in the commissary department, and was given the rank of captain. After holding this position two years he resigned, and returned to duty with his company as a private soldier, and was at various times under the famous cavalry leaders: Price, Forrest, Chalmers and Armstrong. He surrendered with his command at East Port, Tenn., and was paroled at Columbus, settling soon after at Panola, Miss., where he became acquainted with Miss Susan A. Hall, to whom he was united in marriage on November 30, 1865. She is a Mississippian by birth, and is a daughter of Porter and Mary Hall (the father of Scotch-Irish descent, and a native of South Carolina). Some of his ancestors were soldiers in the Continental army during Revolutionary times. After their marriage Mr. and Mrs. Mitchell rented and farmed land for one year, and in 1866 immigrated to Missouri, and took up their abode on a farm near Kansas City, on which they resided three years. In 1870 they came to White County, but eleven years later moved to Washington County, where they purchased a forty-acre tract of land. Since 1884 they have resided on their present farm. Their children are: Mary M. (born August 30, 1866, and died in September, 1872), Charles Porter (born May 18, 1868, and is now studying medicine under the tutelage of Dr. McIntosh, of Beebe. He was married November 15, 1888, to Miss Mattie Byram, a native of Arkansas, and a daughter of William W. and Margaret (Williams) Byram), and William Nathaniel Mitchell (born January 6, 1871). These children have received good educational advantages, and are a credit to their parents. Mr. Mitchell is a Democrat, serving his party for years as justice of the peace, and he and his wife, and their son Charles and wife, are members of the Methodist Episcopal Church, South. Mr. Mitchell is favorable to educational and religious advancement and in fact all worthy movements. He became a Mason in 1859, joining Cooper Lodge No. 36, and now holds a demit from that lodge, bearing date January 23, 1886.

Josiah J. Moncrief, M. D., Hammonsville, Ark.

HISTORY OF ARKANSAS.

This able and successful practitioner owes his nativity to Harris County, Ga., where his birth occurred on April 13, 1858, as the son of George W. and Emily A. (Calhoun) Moncrief. The father is a native of Georgia, and of French descent, his ancestors having emigrated to America prior to 1770, and settled in Georgia. The grandfather, Lebanon Moncrief, was a soldier under Gen. Jackson, and was at the battle of New Orleans in 1812. The maternal ancestors were of Irish descent. Dr. J. J. Moncrief moved with his parents to Alabama in 1857, acquired a good English education, and in 1881 entered the office of D. Dunlap, M. D., where he commenced the study of medicine in St. Clair County, of that State. In 1887 he attended a course of lectures in the Medical Department of the University of Arkansas, situated at Little Rock, and later located at Tupelo, Jackson County, Ark., where he practiced medicine for a short time. In April of 1889, he came to Hammonsville, where he located, and where he contemplates making his home. The Doctor is a member and secretary of Hammonsville Lodge of the A. F. & A. M. He also holds membership in the Methodist Episcopal Church, South.

William Bird Moon, M. D., is a native of Georgia; born June 12, 1821. He was reared and educated in his native State, receiving his medical education in Louisville Medical Institute, now the Medical University of Kentucky, following which he began practicing physic in 1845. After having remained in Georgia eight years he moved to Alabama and continued in active practice for nineteen years, coming thence to White County, Ark., in 1872, where he purchased real estate, upon which he now lives. Dr. Moon was married October 19, 1845, to Roena Cathrine Spratlen, daughter of Henry and Mary Spratlen, natives of Georgia. The Doctor and his wife are the parents of eleven children: Mary Caroline (born August 15, 1846, married S. S. Pearson in 1867, and died January 27, 1878), Francis L. (born April 21, 1848, married H. M. Ware, died March 26, 1876), Jacob Oliver (born July 31, 1856, died October 31, 1877), Susan C. (born June 20, 1854, married D. G. Copeland, and died March 27, 1888), James Calhoun (born

October 8, 1864, died August 27, 1865), Theodosia Earnest (born May 31, 1866, died October 6, 1873), William David (born February 11, 1850, married Allie E. Darden), Ana P. (born April 19, 1852, married H. McKay), Emma Wilkinson (born September 6, 1858, married W. E. Powel), Robert Urial (born July 22, 1860, married G. H. Neely), and Alice Virginia (born September 5, 1862, married G. C. Layne). Dr. Moon is a son of Jacob and Mary Ann (Staples) Moon, who were also of Georgia nativity. Their ancestors came originally from Virginia. Jacob Moon was born September 28, 1795, and died August 13, 1877, and his wife, whose natal day was December 6, 1799, died November 16, 1876. Dr. Moon's brothers and sisters are: Lavina (born December 28, 1817, died in 1840), David Staples (born November 16, 1819), John Chapel (born August 15, 1824, died April 9, 1855), Thomas (born February 24, 1827, died March 21, 1852), Mary Ann (born February 18, 1829), Susan E. (born July 9, 1841). Dr. Moon is a devoted Democrat. He and his wife are members of Missionary Baptist Church, and take active interest in all laudable enterprises. He is deacon of his church.

William D. Moon, M. D., is a worthy son of one of the most esteemed residents of this county. His parents were Dr. William B. and Roena C. (Spratlen) Moon, natives of Georgia, who moved to Alabama in 1853, as stated in the biography which immediately precedes this. William D. Moon first saw the light of day in 1850, improving to the utmost the advantages enjoyed for receiving an education in the common schools of Alabama. In 1877 he attended the medical college at Louisville, where his father had studied, and in 1878 commenced practicing in White County, Ark., which locality has been his parents' home for some years. His later career has been an encouraging and highly satisfactory one. Dr. Moon was married in the fall of 1872, to Allie E. Darden, daughter of J. W. and Nancy H. Darden. They have a family of four children: Robert E. Lee (deceased), Lena L., Yandell and William Darden. Dr. Moon and wife are members of the Missionary Baptist Church. The former is a Democrat in pol-

WHITE COUNTY.

itics and is a highly respected citizen. Yandell is named after the Yandells in Louisville, Ky., who were fellow-students and teachers of the Doctor's grandfather, and several of them belonged to the medical faculty when the father was attending medical lectures in 1877.

Moore & Lyon are proprietors of the largest livery, sale and feed stables at Searcy. The senior member of the firm, James L. Moore, is a son of Robert W. and Sally (Carter) Moore, natives of North Carolina and Tennessee, respectively. In 1858 the father moved to Arkansas and settled in White County, where he died March 24, 1884. His wife still survives him and resides in Cleburne County with her daughter and younger children. James L. Moore came originally from Tennessee, where his birth occurred July 27, 1857. A year after this event his parents moved to White County, Ark., where he has since made his home, gaining by his upright course a wide and honorable acquaintance. He was engaged in farming until 1887, when he moved to Searcy and embarked in the livery business, the patronage accorded this establishment being liberal and of increasing dimensions. Jack F. Lyon, associated with Mr. Moore in the conduct of the stables referred to, was born in Mississippi, on September 5, 1858, as one of a family of William and Lydia (Arnold) Lyman, of Alabama origin. Mr. and Mrs. Lyman moved to Tennessee in 1864, where the former engaged in farming and remained until 1883, then becoming located in Cross County, Ark. Here he died three years later. Jack F. Lyon removed to White County in 1881, and was occupied in stock raising for the following six years. In 1887 he settled at Searcy and entered into the livery business in company with Mr. Moore. Mr. Lyon has two brothers similiarly occupied in Wayne, Cross County, and another brother is engaged in farming in Cross County. Messrs. Moore & Lyman are doing the largest business, in their line, of any firm in Searcy, and are very popular, being affable and obliging in their intercourse with the public.

M. M. Morris, proprietor of cotton-gin, gristmill and planing-mill, Searcy, Ark. There are few men of the present day whom the world ac-

knowledges as successful, more worthy of honorable mention, or whose history affords a better illustration of what may be accomplished by a determined will and perseverance, than Mr. Morris. He owes his nativity to Kanawha County, W. Va., where his birth occurred February 25, 1828, and is the third in a family of nine children born to the union of P. H. and Ann (Summers) Morris, natives of West Virginia. The father was a miller by trade, but in connection carried on farming, and became the owner of a large plantation. His death occurred in 1842. The mother is still living, makes her home in West Virginia, and is in perfect health, although eighty-three years of age. Their children were named as follows: Floyd W. (married, and resides in West Virginia), Henry (was killed in White County, by a mule, in 1868), M. M. (subject of this sketch), F. T. J. (married, and resides in Garner, White County, Ark.), F. F. (married, and resides in West Virginia), Nancy Jane (now Mrs. Poindexter, of West Virginia), William (married, and resides in West Virginia), George L. (married, and resides near Searcy) and Harriet Ann (now Mrs. Crisp, resides in the Lone Star State). M. M. Morris was reared in a town in West Virginia, received his education in the subscription schools of that State, and there learned the blacksmith trade. On January 13, 1850, he came to Searcy, engaged in blacksmithing in front of the Gill House, and continued there a number of years. Later he erected the first steam-mill in White County, on Red River, near Searcy, and one year later, or in 1851, at Searcy Landing. Mr. Morris ran the mill over one year, and then sold it. He next engaged in cutting wood, and the same year erected a mill and went to work. He was married on October 22, 1852, to Miss M. J. Story, a native of Tennessee, and the daughter of Henry and Annie (Moore) Story, who were originally from Tennessee. Her parents came to Independence County, Ark., settled in Batesville, in 1844, and here the father followed merchandising the principal part of his life. His death occurred in 1845 or 1846, but his wife survived him many years, and made her home with her son, M. M. Morris. She died in 1868. To Mr. and Mrs.

HISTORY OF ARKANSAS.

Morris were born seven children: M. G. (married to Miss Pruitt, and is the father of five children), T. J., W. F., Mary Ellen (widow of Andrew Mc-Ginnis), George L., Henry (died in 1875), Charley and Hattie. Mr. Morris lost his excellent wife in April, 1885. He has been continuously in business for nearly forty years, and, although starting with little or no means, he is now one of the successful and progressive men of the county. He owns sixty-eight acres of land joining Searcy; has about 400 acres under cultivation, and has some fine buildings on his farms, one costing $3,300. He has all the latest machinery for running his farm, and follows agricultural pursuits more extensively than any other man in Gray Township. He is not active in politics, but votes with the Democratic party. Socially, he is a member of Searcy Lodge No. 49, A. F. & A. M. He takes an active interest in all matters relating to the good of the county, and has been a member of the Methodist Episcopal Church for many years. His wife was also a member of the same church. During the late war Mr. Morris was boss workman of a Texas Brigade shop, in Texas Brigade, Col. Taylor's regiment.

George L. Morris, one of the representative men of White County, came to this locality when nineteen years of age. When the war-cry sounded he joined the Confederate army, under Col. McRae, remaining in service until the declaration of peace, mostly on detached duty as wagon master and marshal of trains. After the war he engaged in farming, and, though financially embarrassed when leaving the army, he has, by hard work, good management and economy, become the owner of one of the best farms in White County, 800 acres of land in extent, with 400 of these thoroughly cultivated. Mr. Morris was born in Putnam County, W. Va., in 1840, and is the son of Harry and Annie (Summers) Morris, natives of Old Virginia. Mr. Morris, Sr., was a farmer, miller and distiller. He departed this life in 1840, when about forty years old. Mrs. Morris afterward married Richard Chandler, now deceased. She is still living, somewhere in the neighborhood of eighty-nine years, and has been a consistent and faithful member of

the Baptist Church for seventy-five years. Mr. and Mrs. Morris were the parents of nine children, eight of whom are still living: Floyd (a farmer of Putnam County, W. Va.), M. M. (resides in Searcy), William (an attorney of West Virginia), Ferdenand, Nancy (now Mrs. Poindexter), Harriett (now Mrs. Crisp, of Texas) and George L., our subject, who was united in marriage on May 20, 1868, to Sarah Sewell, a daughter of Frank Sewell, and was born in Tennessee on October 6, 1850. They were the parents of nine children, eight of whom are still living: M. M., John W., Eura May, George W., Minnie Lee, Eura, Kate and Henry. Mr. and Mrs. Morrison worship with the Methodist Episcopal Church, of which Mr. Morris is steward. To him this society is largely indebted for their church edifice, he furnishing the ground on which it stands, and also a part of the material. He is engaged in raising mules and cattle, which he ships to the Southern markets.

James R. Neal is a citizen of Centre Hill, popularly and well known as a prosperous farmer of White County. He is a native of Fayette County, Tenn., and was born in 1840, being the son of William D. and Mary A. J. (Parham) Neal, also of Tennessee origin. William D. Neal's birth occurred August 14, 1809, and in business was a prominent planter of Tennessee. He was married August 19, 1831. His father was also a native of Tennessee, who lived and died there. He had a family of eight children: Betsey, Ann, William D. (the father of our subject), Meredith H., James M., Polly, Nancy and John H. Our subject's maternal grandparents, Thomas and Nancy Parham, were natives of Georgia, and came to Tennessee in 1820. William D. Neal was the father of fourteen children: James T., Martha J., John W., William M., James R. (the principal of this sketch), Elica T., Samuel A., Nancy E. (now Mrs. Clay), Sarah A. (Hicks), Eunice M. (Harrison), Susan H. (deceased), David J., next an infant (who died before it was named) and Newton H. Mr. William D. Neal came to Arkansas in 1842, settling in Searcy County, and in 1853 moved to White County, where he bought a farm of 160 acres, all timbered land, and cleared about sixty

WHITE COUNTY.

of these. James R. Neal spent his early boyhood on the farm and attended the subscription schools. He was married to Mary J. Holland, a native of North Carolina, as were also her parents and grandparents on both sides. James R., his father and four of his brothers were all in the Confederate service. He enlisted on September 13, 1861, in T. H. McRae's regiment, for twelve months, at the end of which time he enlisted for three years or during the war. He participated in the battles of Prairie Grove, Helena, Little Rock and many others, and received his discharge June 5, 1865. He was married while in the service and while home on a furlough. After the war he settled on a farm in this county where he has since resided. To this union were born seven children: Alice C. (Brumlow), Kiddee S., Lucy A. (deceased), Mary J. (Harrison), John W., Ella F. and Henry W. Mr. Neal is a Mason, and belongs to Centre Hill Lodge No. 114. Himself and wife are members of the Missionary Baptist Church; he has a fine farm of 160 acres, with fifty improved and in a high state of cultivation. He is a prominent Democrat, and takes an active interest in all public improvements, or all work for the good of the community.

John H. Neal, Searcy, Ark. This much respected citizen and pioneer came to White County, Ark., in 1850, and settled in Searcy, where he followed merchandising. In 1851 he embarked in the grocery and general merchandising business, and this continued until 1854, he being one of the pioneer business men of Searcy. In 1854 he engaged as clerk in dry-goods business houses, and this continued until 1861. He was born in Maury County, Tenn., in 1830, being the youngest in a family of nine children, born to James and Sarah (Dodson) Neal, natives, respectively, of North Carolina and South Carolina. The father was a planter, and at an early day moved to Tennessee, where he died, in Fayette County, in 1845. The mother died the same year. In their family were the following children: William D. (married, and came to Arkansas in 1844, settled in Searcy County, and followed farming. He enlisted in Van Buren County, in 1861, and re-

ceived a gunshot wound through the thigh. He was taken to Camp Dennison, Ohio, remained as a prisoner until exchanged, and returned in 1863; he died in 1869), Meridith H. (came to White County, in 1852, and lost his first wife the same year. He was a Methodist Episcopal, South, preacher, and returned to Memphis in the fall of 1852, taking charge of South Memphis Church. In 1874 he returned to White County, Ark., and in 1877 went to Tennessee, where he died in 1883), James M. (married, came to White County, October, 1850, and settled in what is now Des Arc Township, where he opened up a farm. His death occurred in 1852), Nancy (married P. L. Downey and moved to Searcy County, Ark., in 1846. Her death occurred in about 1857 or 1858), Elizabeth L. (married W. R. Johnson and moved to Searcy County, Ark., in 1846. She died in Fulton County, Ark., in 1877), Mary G. (married J. J. Crouch, a Methodist minister, and came to Searcy County, Ark., in 1849. He was a pioneer preacher of that county. Her death occurred in 1850), Martha A. (now Mrs. Evans, the only surviving daughter, lives in Izard County) and an infant named Sarah. John H. Neal was reared to farm life, received his education in the schools of Fayette County, Tenn. He commenced for himself at Searcy, Ark., in business, in 1850, and continued thus employed for some time. He was married in Searcy, Ark., in 1852, to Miss Mary A. Clay, a native of Louisiana, but reared in Missouri, and the daughter of Lewis A. and Mary Clay, natives of Virginia. Her father came to White County, Ark., at an early day and died in Searcy in 1874. The mother died some years before. To Mr. and Mrs. Neal were born five children, three now living: Augustus E. (died in 1887, at the age of thirty-three years), James A. (died in 1865, at the age of ten years), John D. (is a prominent educator, and is teaching in the public school at Newport, Ark., where he has taught for six years), Henry Clay (is married and resides in Corsicana, Texas, and is engaged in commercial pursuits) and Mary A. (who is now Mrs. Hale, resides at Texarkana, Ark.). Mr. Neal lost his wife in November, 1863, and was married again, in White County, in

HISTORY OF ARKANSAS.

1864, to Mrs. Kiddy A. Neal (*nee* Holland), a native of North Carolina, and the daughter of Willis B. and Lucinda (Barbee) Holland, natives of Wake County of the same State. The father was a planter by occupation, and in February, 1851, immigrated to Henderson County, Tenn., where he continued his former pursuit, and in connection taught school. In 1852 he came to White County, Ark., resided in Gray Township for three years, and in 1854 moved to Des Arc Township, settling where Centre Hill is now located. He sent in the petition and established the postoffice at that place, and was made the first postmaster. In 1860 he moved to Van Buren County, and in 1863 returned to White County, where he remained until 1865, and then moved to Searcy. His death occurred at that place on March 7, 1869. His excellent wife survived him until January 22, 1888. The father was county surveyor, surveyed and resurveyed a great deal of the country. Socially, he was a member of Searcy Lodge No. 49, A. F. & A. M., was also a member of Tillman Chapter No. 19, R. A. M., and was High Priest of the same. He was also a member of Searcy Council No. 12, and aided in the organization of Centre Hill Lodge No. 114. He was a charter member and was Worshipful Master of that lodge. There is a lodge, Holland Lodge No. 158, in Van Buren County, which was named for him. To Mr. Neal's second marriage were born no children. Socially, Mr. Neal is a member of Searcy Lodge No. 49, A. F. & A. M., and was the second Mason initiated into that lodge, having joined in 1852. He has been a Worshipful Master of the lodge, and assisted in organizing Centre Hill Lodge No. 114, and was Worshipful Master of that. He is a member of Tillman Chapter Lodge No. 19, R. A. M., and has been High Priest in the same. He is also a member of Searcy Council No. 12, and has thrice been Illustrious Master of it. Mr. Neal is a member of the Eastern Star Chapter No. 5, and is one of the representative men of the county. Mrs. Neal is a member of the Eastern Star, has been Worthy Matron several times, and was elected First Grand Matron of the State, in 1876, and served one year. She is a member of the Baptist Church, and he a member of the Methodist Epis-

copal Church, South, and both have been members for thirty-six years. During the war Mr. Neal was postmaster and justice of the peace, and after the war (in 1871) he engaged in the undertaking business, which he has carried on successfully ever since that time.

John A. Neavill, Searcy, Ark. There are many citizens represented within the pages of this volume, but none more deserving of mention than Mr. Neavill, who is not only one of the pioneers of the county, but is universally respected by all who know him. He was born in Jackson County, Ala., in 1826, and was the eldest in a family of nine children, born to the union of Elihu and Margaret (Jones) Neavill, the father a native of Alabama, and the mother of North Carolina. Elihu Neavill was married in his native State, in about 1825, settled on a claim and followed agricultural pursuits there until 1844, when he came to White County, Ark. He settled near where his son James A. now resides, entered land, erected a tanyard, and in connection carried on farming and the tannery business until his death, which occurred April 17, 1888. He was a resident of the county for over forty years, and had the esteem and respect of all. He was in the Florida War, was orderly-sergeant and was in service twelve months. He was of French descent, and the mother of Scotch-Irish. Of their family the following children are the only ones living: James A. (subject), Elijah (married and resides in Cane Township), William H. (married, and is the marshal of Searcy) and Mary (now Mrs. F. W. Smith, of Gray Township). James A. Neavill was early taught the rudiments of farming, and received his education in the subscription schools of Alabama and White County, Ark. He was eighteen years of age when he came to Arkansas, and he was employed for a number of years in assisting his father in clearing up the farm. After this he began farming for himself near where he now resides. He was married in White County, Ark., in 1853, to Miss Smith, a native of Mississippi, who bore him two living children: John and William B. The latter is married and resides in Gray Township. Another child, Mary, was the wife of

WHITE COUNTY.

John Gilliam, and died August 9, 1884. Mrs. Neavill died in 1856, and Mr. Neavill selected his second wife in the person of Mrs. Mary (Barkley) Britt, widow of Mr. Davis Britt, a native of Middle Tennessee, and the daughter of Andrew and Hannah C. (Walker) Barkley. The father was a native of Tennessee, and his ancestors were the earliest settlers of that State. He followed agricultural pursuits and opened up a large tract of land. His death occurred in 1862. The mother was a native of North Carolina, and died in Tennessee, Rutherford County, in 1887, at the advanced age of ninety years. To Mr. and Mrs. Neavill was born one child: Andrew A. After his marriage, which occurred in 1875, Mr. Neavill moved to his present residence, and is now the owner of a good farm of 125 acres, with about seventy acres under cultivation. He is active in politics, and votes with the Democratic party. He is a member of the Agricultural Wheel, takes an active interest in educational matters, and has been a member of the school board. He has also filled the position of constable of his township, and in a highly satisfactory manner. Mrs. Neavill is a member of the Methodist Episcopal Church, South. Grandfather Neavill was in the War of 1812, and was at the battle of New Orleans with Gen. Jackson. Mr. Neavill (subject of this sketch), came to Arkansas in 1844, and can hardly realize that it is the same country now, on account of the many and rapid changes made since that time. Searcy was in the woods, and there were but three houses between that town and Beebe. Off the main traveled roads there were no settlements, and Mr. Neavill has killed many a deer on land now under cultivation, at a distance of 175 yards. He still has in his possession his trusty gun. During the war he was with Gen. Price, in his raid through Missouri, and enlisted in Capt. Black's company, participating in the following battles: Pilot Knob, Ironton, Newtonia, Blue Gap, etc. He was with Gen. Price until reaching Fayetteville, Ark., when he returned to White County.

Charles E. Newman, farmer, fruit grower and educator of White County, Ark., was born in Madison County, Ill., on Feburary 17, 1844, and is the eldest of six children born to William E. and Martha A. (Harrison) Newman, the former a native of Madison County, Ill., the latter originally of Kentucky. William E. was also of a family of six children. His father was a native of Pennsylvania, and one of the early settlers of Illinois, locating in the territory as early as 1804. They trace their family name back five generations to Ireland. William E. Newman lived and died in the county in which he was born. His birth occurred in February, 1821, was married in 1843, and died June 17, 1886. He and his wife were members of the Cumberland Presbyterian Church, and became the parents of the following named children: Charles E. (the subject of this sketch), Eliza (now Mrs. Fields, living near the old homestead), Mary (Kimball, now deceased), Henry (still living near the old homestead), Ida (deceased) and Mattie (married October 5, 1887, now living in Montgomery County, Ill.). The mother of these children still resides at the old home, and is a daughter of William and Mary (McClure) Harrison, Virginians, who at an early day removed to Kentucky, in which State she was born, being one of four children: Maria, Martha, Elizabeth and Benjamin. Charles E. obtained his education in the common schools of Illinois, and assisted his father on the farm. August 9, 1862, he enlisted in Company D, One Hundred and Seventeenth Illinois Volunteer Infantry, under Col. R. M. Moore, and went to the front to do battle for his country, participating in a number of battles and skirmishes during his three years' service. He received his discharge June 3, 1865, and upon returning home, commenced teaching school in the same room he left three years before to wear the blue. After spending two years teaching, he took Horace Greeley's advice and went West, locating near Paola, Miami County, Kas., again engaging as a pedagogue, remaining in the same school seven years. He was married November 9, 1871, to Amanda L. Porter, daughter of John and Amanda (Hampton) Porter, people from Ohio, in which State Mrs. Amanda Newman was born June 11, 1849. Mr. Newman was engaged in horticulture in Kansas, in connection with teaching, but

HISTORY OF ARKANSAS.

the grasshopper scourge of 1874 caused him to return to Illinois, where an educator received better pay and a longer school term. He followed teaching until 1884, when, September 3, of that year, he came to Arkansas, and settled at Judsonia, where he has followed farming, fruit growing and teaching. He has sixty-five acres of good second bottom land under cultivation, devoted to general farming and fruit growing. He takes an active interest in the political issues of the day. In religious faith himself and wife are Cumberland Presbyterians. They have three children: Lillian (born September 3, 1872), Edna (born September 26, 1877) and Ethel (born February 3, 1887).

Elijah B. Norvell. Although in his active career through life Mr. Norvell has not amassed the wealth which has fallen to the lot of many others, yet he is in comfortable circumstances, and has gained to an unlimited extent the confidence and esteem always awarded integrity, honor and industry. His birth occurred in Bedford County, Tenn., April 5, 1841, and is a son of David and Martha (Bomar) Norvell, who were also born in that State, and were of Scotch-Irish and Dutch descent. By occupation the father was a farmer, and for several years he served his county as bailiff and deputy sheriff. He died in the State of his birth in 1858, his wife dying at her home in White County, Ark., in 1869. Their children are: David (a physician of Johnson County), Elijah B., B. B. (a farmer of Texas), Mary (wife of Charles Devers, a farmer of Johnson County), William (a farmer of Boone County), R. H. (a mechanic of Texas) and Martha (wife of James Holiday, of Johnson County). Like the majority of farmers' boys, Elijah B. Norvell was compelled to work hard in his youth, and received very little schooling, but being possessed of a bright intellect, and through his own exertions he obtained a very good general knowledge of the world of books. In 1861, when he was in his nineteenth year, he joined the army, enlisting in Company B, Forty-fourth Tennessee Infantry, and during his service of nearly three years, he was in the battles of Shiloh, Hoover's Gap, Tullahoma and others, being wounded in the first-named engagement. After his return home he worked as a rail-

road hand for about three years, then engaged in the liquor business in Tennessee, continuing one year, and in 1866 came to Arkansas, conducting the same business at Stony Point a year longer. Since that time he has been engaged in farming, the first two years renting land, after which he purchased a farm of forty acres on Bull Creek, which he improved and four years later sold. In 1886 he purchased eighty acres of his present farm, and now has 120 acres, of which fifty-five are under cultivation. The soil is fertile, and is well adapted to raising corn, cotton, oats and all kinds of fruit. He has given considerable attention to experimental farming, trying different kinds of seeds and fertilizers, and has succeeded far beyond his expectations, and the past year had perhaps the best cotton in Union Township. In 1881 he purchased property in Beebe, and was a resident of that town for three years in order to give his children the benefit of the city schools, but farm life being more congenial to his tastes, he has since lived in the country. He has been a member of Lodge No. 35 of the Union Wheel ever since its organization, and in 1885 was a delegate to the National Wheel, which met at Little Rock, and to the State Wheel, which convened at the same time and place. Although formerly a Democrat in politics, he has been a member of the Union Labor party for the last few years. In 1869 he was married to V. A. Mossey, a native of Shelby County, Tenn., and a daughter of Jerry Mossey, a farmer and later a merchant of Beebe. Of a family of seven children born to them, four are now living: Robert H. (who is at present attending the schools of Beebe, and is in every respect an exemplary young man, was born in October, 1871), Virginia (was born in 1878), George's birth occurred in 1880, and Ruth was born in 1883. Mr. Norvell and his family worship in the Methodist Episcopal Church, and he has filled the office of steward.

T. J. Oliver, farmer and stock raiser, Searcy, Ark. A lifetime of hard, earnest endeavor in pursuing the occupation to which he now gives his attention, coupled with strict integrity, honesty of purpose and liberality in directions, have had a result to place Mr. Oliver among the truly respected

WHITE COUNTY.

and honored agriculturists of the county. To this he has continually added improvements of a high order, until now about the place everything is in excellent condition. He was born in Maury County, Tenn., in 1833, was the eleventh in a family of thirteen children born to Hezekiah and Mahala (Shumac) Oliver, natives of the Old Dominion. The father was a tiller of the soil, and in 1820 moved to Maury County, Tenn., where he entered land, and made that his home a number of years. Later he moved to West Tennessee, where his death occurred in 1867. His wife died about 1848. He was in the War of 1812. T. J. Oliver was reared to farm life, and received his education in the schools of Tennessee. When it became necessary for him to start out in life for himself, he very naturally and wisely chose the occupation to which he had been reared, and from that time to the present his success has been such as only a thorough acquaintance with his calling and years of experience might lead him to achieve. At the age of twenty-one he commenced farming in Madison County, Tenn., and purchased a timber tract, which he improved. He was married in Gibson County, Tenn., in 1860, to Miss Mary E. Scott, a native of Arkansas, born in Fayetteville, and received her education at the Memphis (Tenn.) State Female Academy. She is the daughter of Dr. Scott, who was assassinated at Memphis in 1864. After his marriage Mr. Oliver settled in Madison County, and in 1861 enlisted in the Twelfth Tennessee Infantry for twelve months, from Gibson County, Tenn., and participated in a number of skirmishes. On account of ill health he was discharged in 1862, and returned to Tennessee, where he engaged in farming. In 1883 he came to White County Ark., purchased an improved farm of 100 acres, with eighty under cultivation, and on this has many good buildings. He is not very active in politics, but votes with the Democratic party at State elections. He is a member of the I. O. O. F. He and wife are members of the Methodist Episcopal Church, South; he has been Sunday-school superintendent for six years, and is one of the progressive men of the town. To his marriage were born these children: Edgar (married, and resides at

Greer, Ark.), Benetta (now Mrs. Witt, of Conway), Roland C., Eugene, Wilber, Herbert Earl and Bertram.

William De Berry Overstreet, now residing on Section 34, Caldwell Township, White County, Ark., is a son of William and Caroline (Jumper) Overstreet, the father a native of South Carolina, and of English ancestors. His forefathers probably came to America before the War for Independence. The maternal ancestors were of English-German descent. The parents of our subject were married November 23, 1832, in Alabama, came to Arkansas in 1860, located near Little Red post-office, in Harrison Township, and there rented land and farmed until 1864, when they moved to Caldwell Township. Here they still continued to till the soil and here the father died October 28, 1832. Their family consisted of the following children: Samuel D. H., David J., Elicas S., Mary Ann, John H., Martha H. C., Eliza F., William De Berry, Dora A. and Paralee J. All the children were born in Tishomingo County, Miss., with the exception of Paralee, and all grew to maturity with the exception of her. William De Berry Overstreet comes of a long-lived race, some of his ancestors living to be over ninety years of age. He was born October 19, 1850, and his educational advantages were enjoyed in the subscription schools of White County. He attended part of a term near what is now known as Little Red Post-office, also part of a term at Clear Water, then Clear Springs school-house, the whole time of attendance not being more than two months. Mr. Overstreet is a diligent reader, is observing, and is probably better posted on the majority of subjects than many who have had better educational advantages, having made the best use of his opportunities. At the time of the death of his father he was the only son at home, his brothers being away in the Confederate army, and the support of the family, consisting of the mother and three sisters, devolved upon his shoulders until 1865. Then his brother, John H., returned from the war and took part of the duties upon himself for about a year. By the end of that time he was married and the duties again fell upon the shoulders of William,

HISTORY OF ARKANSAS.

who took care of his sisters until they were married. He is now the counsellor of the family. Mrs. Eliza F. Gordon lost her husband in 1878 and was left with four helpless children, but Mr. Overstreet again came to the assistance, and Mrs. Gordon is now living upon his farm and receives help from him. Her children are now almost large enough to contribute toward her support. October 28, 1870, Mr. Overstreet was united in marriage to Gabriella Lumpkin, a native of Jackson County, born in February, 1857, and the daughter of George W. and Sarah (Martin) Lumpkin, who died when their daughter was but a child. She was then taken by her uncle, Hoyden Edwards, with whom she lived until her marriage. To this union have been born ten children, five of whom are now living: William David (born September 13, 1871), Mary Anna (born May 1, 1873), Dora Lee (born January 7, 1875, and died September 18, 1878), Lula May (born February 20, 1877), Laura Della (born February 10, 1879), Mattie Maud (born February 22, 1881), John Marvin (born October 29, 1885) and three infants, who died unnamed. Mr. Overstreet made his first purchase of land in 1871, and this consisted of 160 acres. He has made all the improvements on his farm, and has one of the most comfortable and home-like places in the county. He has three dwellings on his farm, one occupied by his aged mother and another by Mrs. Gordon. He has good barns, cribs, sheds, etc., and is a thrifty, industrious farmer. He also has a fine peach orchard, which supplies the family with this luscious fruit, and also leaves a surplus for the market. He raises principally cotton, corn, oats and grass. He has a fine grade of cattle, being a cross between the Durham and the native stock, and is also raising some fine hogs, a cross between the Poland-China, the Berkshire and the Chester White, which experience has taught him is a very profitable venture. In politics Mr. Overstreet is a Democrat, but has never been an office seeker. In his religious belief he is a Methodist, and has been a member of that church for twenty-two years. He is a liberal supporter of schools, churches and all laudable enterprises, and is much respected by all acquainted

with him. Mrs. Overstreet is also a member of the Methodist Episcopal Church.

Rev. William M. Owen, pastor of the Missionary Baptist Church, Shady Grove, one mile from Bald Knob, is a native of Tennessee, and a son of Felix and Permelia H. (Plant) Owen, of Kentucky and Alabama origin, respectively. Felix Owen came from Kentucky to Fayette County, Tenn., when a young man, and remained there until 1849, when he again moved with his family to Arkansas and located in White County, when the country was but sparsely settled, and with the aid of his family cleared up a farm, on which he lived until a few years before his death (which occurred in 1883, at the age of seventy-four), when he removed to Judsonia. Mrs. Owen is still living at this place and is the mother of eight children, six of whom are living: William M. (our subject), Sarah C. (wife of Rev. E. T. Church), Robert H. (in business in Judsonia), Green B. (a Baptist minister of this county, also engaged in farming), Elizabeth and Melinda (wife of John O. Kelley, of this county). Rev. William M. Owen was born in Fayette County, Tenn., on October 29, 1839, and was educated at the common schools and by self-study at home, and when arriving at the age of manhood (twenty-one), began life as a farmer. In June, 1861, he joined the Third Arkansas Cavalry, remaining in this company until the close of the war, having had part in the battles of Corinth (where he was taken prisoner and held captive at St. Louis and Alton, Ill., for four months), Chickamauga, Atlanta, and many others. After the war he returned home and again commenced farming, in which he has ever since been engaged. In 1867 he joined the Missionary Baptist Church, and in ten years thereafter (1877) was licensed to preach, and the following year was ordained, and since his ordination he has been faithfully engaged in preaching the Gospel, having under his charge three or four churches at a time, and has also been instrumental in organizing a number of new churches, among them the one at Bald Knob. In 1866 he was married to Miss Laura Coffman, a native of Alabama, who died in 1875. She was the mother of four children, only two surviving

WHITE COUNTY.

her: Leander and Mark. In 1877 he was married the second time, to Mrs. Edwards (nee Patty), a widow. They are the parents of three children: Gracie M., Willie E. and Edith M. Mrs. Owen, with her two oldest children, belongs to the Missionary Baptist Church.

Littleberry B. Parker is a prominent farmer of White County, and first saw the light of day in Northampton County, N. C., on February 8, 1831, and is a son of Saul and Miriam (Hicks) Parker. Saul Parker was born in England and came over to this country when a boy, and participated in the War of 1812 at Craney Island. He subsequently located at Norfolk, Va., and later removed to North Carolina, where he died in 1835, while yet comparatively a young man. He was a brick-mason by trade. His wife was a native of North Carolina and was the mother of seven children, four of whom are still living: Samuel (a farmer and ex-sheriff of Jasper County, Miss.), Tabitha T. (wife of Jesse Lassiter of Northampton, N. C.), Jacob J. (a farmer and brick-mason, of Lonoke County) and L. B. (our subject). After the death of her husband, Mrs. Parker removed with her family to Calloway County, Ky., subsequently to Madison County, Tenn., and in 1852 came to Arkansas locating in Lonoke County, where she died in 1881, at the age of eighty-four years, and was a member of the Methodist Episcopal Church. L. B. Parker remained with his mother until eight years of age, when he was bound out to James B. Wheeler, a cabinet-maker and farmer of Northampton County, N. C., with whom he remained until Mr. Wheeler's death, which occurred four years later, when he was hired out to a farmer for $1 per month, part of which was to be paid him in money and the balance in clothes. He remained there one year and was then (1844) hired out for a year for $10 for the year, but quit in April and joined an emigrant train and worked his way to Kentucky, where he found employment at $5 per month, and remained there until 1847 when he went to Madison County, Tenn., where he was engaged as a mail-carrier during the year 1847. He then farmed for a short time, after which he was employed on a flat-boat

running to New Orleans. One year later he came to Arkansas, locating in White County. At the outbreak of the war he joined the Confederate army in the Fourth Battalion Arkansas Infantry. He served until the surrender of Island No. 10, when his battalion was the only one which escaped by wading back through the water twelve miles to the boat, which they carried to Fort Pillow. Mr. Parker becoming disabled received his discharge at Corinth. He then returned to Arkansas and located in Prairie County, but after the cessation of hostilities he came back to White County locating on the farm which he now calls home, and which was then in the woods. He is the owner of 320 acres, with 100 under cultivation. In January, 1852, he was married to Miss Hannah E. Longmire, who was born on March 22, 1839. Mr. and Mrs. Parker never had any children of their own, but have reared three orphan children: George W. and James Coleman and Mary F. (who is now the wife of William Tidwell). Mrs. Parker is a member of the Presbyterian Church. Mr. Parker has taken the Council degree in the Masonic order, and has represented his lodge in the Grand Lodge of the State several times. He is a strong Democrat and a respected and valuable citizen.

John T. Patterson is one of the well-to-do and successful agriculturists of White County, Ark., and although he has only resided here since 1881, coming from Tennessee, he has become well and favorably known. His birth occurred in Franklin County, Ala., in 1834, and he was the third of a family of nine children born to James and Catherine (Gray) Patterson, the former born in the "Old North State" and the latter in the "Keystone State." James Patterson went to Alabama when the country was new, and opened a plantation which he afterward sold, moving thereafter to Hardeman County, Tenn.. with his wife, whom he married in Alabama. They settled on a farm in Tennessee in 1844, and here the father spent his declining years, his death occuring in 1873. He served in the Seminole War. His wife passed from life in 1888. Their children are: Mary Jane (Mrs. Ethridge, resides in Tennessee), William (lives in Kentucky), John T., Hugh (residing in

HISTORY OF ARKANSAS.

Conway County, Ark.), Jacob (who died in Tennessee, in 1863), Joseph (who also died in that State in the same year) and Enoch and Franklin (both residents of Tennessee). Joseph Gray, the maternal grandfather, was born in England, and served in the Revolutionary War. John T. Patterson spent his youthful days in attending school and in farm work, and after attaining his twentieth year he began working for himself. He was married in McNairy County, in 1855, to Miss Emeline Brown, a native of North Carolina, and a daughter of Isaac and Millie (Dunn) Brown, who were born, reared and married in the State of North Carolina. In 1844 they removed to McNairy County, where they settled on a farm, on which the mother died, in 1855. The father moved to Bell County, Tex., in 1858, and there is now making his home. From the time of his marriage until 1858, Mr. Patterson lived in Tennessee, then spent two years in Texas, after which he returned to McNairy County. On March 4, 1862, he enlisted in Company C, Thirty-second Illinois Infantry, United States army to defend the Constitution of the United States, but left his wife and two children in the South, with little hope of ever returning to them, but through the kind providence of God returned to them in safety. He was wounded at Shiloh on April 6, 1862, and was confined in the hospital at Savannah, Tenn., for some time, being honorably discharged on July 31, 1862, after which he returned to his home and resumed farming. Since 1881 he has been the owner of 160 acres of land in White County, Ark., and has fifty under cultivation. He is an active supporter of the Republican party, and not only has he been a prominent supporter of schools, but he is a member of the school board. Socially, he is a member of Rock Springs Lodge No. 422 of the A. F. & A. M., of which lodge he has been Worshipful Master for some years. He and his wife are members of the Missionary Baptist Church, and are the parents of the following children: Green Harrison (deceased), Melissa (Mrs. Martindale), Alice (Mrs. Holmes), Isabelle (Mrs. Stringfellow), Arca (Mrs. Langley), Elizabeth, Cordelia, Elzora, Cora Lee and Florence. Two children died in infancy.

Rev. J. A. Pemberton is an elder of the Cumberland Presbyterian Church and by occupation is a farmer, and being one of the old settlers of White County, has figured prominently in public affairs. His native county is Wilson, Tenn., where he was born on December 13, 1825, and is the only one now living of a family of five daughters and three sons born to Thomas J. and Mary (McHaney) Pemberton, who were born in Virginia in 1804 and 1800, respectively. They were married about 1822, and followed the occupation of farming, both being members of the Missionary Baptist Church. Mr. Pemberton took part in the Creek and Florida War, and assisted in the removal of the Creek and Seminole Indians to the western reserves. He died February 26, 1871, and his wife in August, 1861. The Pemberton family came to the New World prior to 1700, from their native country, England, and settled in Virginia, and the great-grandfather was one of four sons of the first settler. When the Revolutionary War came up the grandfather Pemberton was only twelve years of age, so of course did not take part in that struggle. He was one of the first settlers of Tennessee, and in this State reared his family, his son, Thomas J., being a relative of Gen. Pemberton of the Southern army, in the late Civil War. Andrew McHaney, the maternal grandfather, was born in Ireland, and as a boy joined the American army and took part in the Revolutionary War, serving from the beginning until the close. He was in Col. William Washington's command, and was present at the battle of Cowpens and witnessed the personal encounter between Washington and Tarleton, in which the latter fled with a sword gash in his hand. After the war was over he settled in Tennessee, where he became a wealthy planter, and died at the age of sixty-five years. Rev. J. A. Pemberton, our subject, attended subscription school in the old-fashioned log-houses of his day, and at the age of twenty-one years began an independent career. In 1846 he married Miss Sarah C. Harrison, and with her removed to Arkansas in 1857 and entered 160 acres of land a few miles northwest of where Beebe now is. When the war came up he, in July, 1861, enlisted in the Tenth Arkansas Infantry, and

WHITE COUNTY.

was made captain of a company which he had assisted in organizing. While in the infantry service he participated in the battle of Shiloh, but in the latter part of 1862 he became a member of the cavalry, and was at Helena, Little Rock, Pine Bluff, Pilot Knob, and was with Price until that General's command was divided at Fayetteville, in 1864. The same year he was captured at Augusta, and was held a prisoner of war until peace was declared. After his return home he continued to farm near Antioch until 1879, then came to Beebe to live. He became a member of the Cumberland Presbyterian Church in 1865, and since 1874 has been a minister of that denomination and has preached in Beebe and vicinity. He has been a very active worker for the cause of his Master and has expounded the doctrine of his denomination in nearly all the principal churches of White County. He was a member of the General Assembly that met at Bowling Green, Ky., in 1876, and for the last two years has been the representative of the Arkansas Synod. He has never been an office seeker, but since his residence in Beebe has been a member of the board of aldermen, and during the reconstruction period was a member of the board of supervisors of White County. He is a Royal Arch Mason and is a member of Beebe Lodge No. 145. He and wife have never had any children of their own, but have given homes to a number of orphan children, and have reared three from infancy. Mrs. Pemberton is a daughter of J. P. and Ann C. (Sweeney) Harrison, who were born in Virginia, the former of whom was an active soldier in the War of 1812.

Joshua W. Pence, an old settler and prominent citizen, of White County, and postmaster of Egbert, is of Tennessee nativity, and a son of George J. and Rebecca (Webb) Pence, natives of South and North Carolina, respectively. George J. Pence was born in 1802, and was married in Alabama in 1825, and remained there until 1829, when he removed to Warren County, Tenn., and six years later to Williamson County of that State. In 1839 he immigrated to Wilson County, where he died in 1852. He was a member of the Christian Church and a man of decision and strong will

power, and was an old-time Jacksonian Democrat. Mrs. Pence was born in 1806, and in 1855, after her husband's death, came to Arkansas, locating in White County, on the farm on which our subject now lives, and where she died on July 16, 1888. She was a member of the Baptist Church, and was the mother of thirteen children, three of whom are still living: Louisa (widow of William Allen), Joshua W. (the principal of this sketch) and Marion T. (a farmer of Prairie County). Joshua W. was born in Warren County, Tenn., May 18, 1830, and when twenty-two years of age, commenced farming for himself, which occupation he has since followed, and in 1855 commenced farming the place on which he still lives, his mother living with him during the last twenty years of her life. He now has a fine farm of 252 acres, with about seventy-five under cultivation. In June, 1862, he enlisted in the Eighth Arkansas Infantry, but remained only a short time, being discharged on account of disability. Upon his discharge he returned home and found his farm in a state of dilapidation. In 1866 he was elected justice of the peace, which office he held for sixteen consecutive years, and was appointed postmaster of Egbert in February, 1887, which position he is still holding. He was married in February, 1854, to Miss Damaris L. Grissom, a native of Tennessee, who died in 1874, leaving nine children, six of whom are still living: Matilda (now Mrs. Hood), George L. (farmer and justice of the peace, of Dogwood Township), Oren D., Oscar D., Ira R. and Lillie A. Those deceased are Wiley H., Joshua M. and Barbara E. In 1874 he was again married to Mrs. Freeman (nee Belton, a widow, and who died in 1883, leaving no children), and on December 19, 1888, he married his third and present wife, Mrs. Ellen M. Rimer (nee Strodder, also a widow). Mr. Pence and wife are members of the Christian Church. He is a prominent Democrat and a member of the Knights of Labor, and of the County Wheel. He joined the Freemasons in July, 1867, of which he is still a member in full fellowship, in West Point Lodge No. 24. December 23, 1873, he joined the Grange No. 137, and has since filled several prominent offices in that society, such as Master, Over-

HISTORY OF ARKANSAS.

seer, Chaplain, Steward, etc. He and wife also belong to the Famous Life Association of Little Rock, Ark., their policy of membership being limited to the amount of $3,000.

N. B. Pettey. Among the early settlers of White County was our subject, N. B. Pettey, who came to this county with his widowed mother in 1855. Mr. Pettey was a son of George G. and Annie E. (Chappell) Pettey, natives of South Carolina and Virginia, respectively, and was born in Limestone County, Ala., August 26, 1839. Mr. George G. Pettey settled in Alabama at an early day, and later moved to Mississippi, where he died in 1850. Five years later his widow moved to Arkansas with her family, where she died in 1861. N. B. Pettey was raised and educated in Tennessee, Mississippi and Arkansas, and at the age of sixteen went to Hickman County and engaged in clerking, where he remained two years. In 1856 he came to White County, Ark., landing at Negro Hill in September, where he worked at farm labor in the summer season and attended school in the winter. He then went to Searcy and accepted a position as clerk for W. B. Carter, where he remained until 1861, when he enlisted in July of that year in Company E of the Third Arkansas Cavalry, enlisting for three years, or during the war, as private. Mr. Pettey was in the battles of Shiloh, Murfreesboro, and was with Bragg in his invasion of Kentucky, and was in the Georgia campaign. He was captured as a prisoner November 1, 1864, and was taken with Sherman to the coast, and up to Point Lookout, where he was paroled February 21, 1865, and returned and joined his command prior to the battle of Bentonville, N. C. He arrived home at Searcy on June 7, 1865, and took up farming. In 1871 he was elected deputy sheriff, and the following year elected sheriff of the county (White), serving three successive terms. In 1879 Mr. Pettey bought an improved farm of sixty acres, near Centre Hill, and commenced farming, and also engaged in merchandising, which he followed some two or three years. He served as postmaster under President Cleveland's administration. Mr. Pettey was married on September 20, 1866, to Jennie Dannelly, a native

of Mississippi, and daughter of Rev. George A. and Annie E. (West) Dannelly, originally of South Carolina and Alabama, respectively. Rev. G. A. Dannelly immigrated to Phillips County, Ark., at an early day, then to Jackson County, where he joined the Methodist Episcopal Conference at Batesville in 1856. He is now in Woodruff County. His wife died in 1865. Mr. and Mrs. Pettey are the parents of two children: George G. and Napoleon B. Mr. Pettey has seen the complete development of the county and has taken an active interest in all work for the good of the community. He is a prominent Democrat, and a member of the I. O. O. F. Mrs. Pettey is a member of the Methodist Church. Her grandfather Dannelly was a member of the Masonic order, of which he held the office of Grand Master of the Grand Lodge of the State, and was Grand Lecturer of the State some five or six years, and was District Deputy Grand Master in 1871. He was also prominently connected with the order of the I. O. O. F.

John Andrew Phelps is a merchant doing business and residing in El Paso, and to him may be applied that often much abused phrase, "self-made man," for he started out in life for himself at the early age of fifteen years, and has attained his present enviable place in business and society. He was born in Haywood County, Tenn., on January 16, 1852, and is one of two children (the other member being J. T. Phelps) born to Philip P. and Arkansas (Overton) Phelps, both of English descent, the former a native of Kentucky and the latter of Virginia. They were married in Tennessee about the year 1850, and in Hardeman County of this State; the father died eight years later. John Andrew Phelps followed various employments until the year 1875, when he began clerking in a mercantile establishment belonging to D. H. Thorn, of Jonesboro, Ark., and during a three years' stay with this gentleman became thoroughly familiar with all the details of the work. During this time Mr. Thorn was sheriff of the county, and Mr. Phelps acted as his deputy, and in this capacity rendered valuable service. Upon leaving Mr. Thorn he rented land in Craighead County of the Hon. W. H. Cate, who, taking a fancy to our sub-

WHITE COUNTY.

ject, gave him an excellent chance and furnished him with stock to till his land. During this time he also acted as foreman of Mr. Cate's cotton-gin, and upon leaving this gentleman, took with him about $500 in money which he had earned. On April 3, 1879, he was united in marriage to Miss Avey Broadway, by whom he has one child, John Andrew, who was born on November 30, 1884. In 1879 Mr. Phelps engaged in merchandising in El Paso in company with his brother, J. T. Phelps, and M. L. Booth, under the firm name of Booth & Phelps, continuing in business with those gentlemen until 1882, at which time Mr. Booth withdrew from the firm and the two brothers continued alone under the firm name of Phelps & Bro. This partnership was dissolved in 1883, and the firm then took the name of Phelps & Co., and from 1885 to 1888 Mr. Phelps was in business alone. The firm has since been known as Warren & Phelps, and they carry a large and well-selected stock of general merchandise, and in connection they carry on a harness and saddlery shop, and in this establishment employ none but the best workmen. They are also extensive dealers in cotton, and in the year 1888 they shipped 1,330 bales to St. Louis and Memphis. In invoicing their goods in July, 1889, they found in accounts and stock on hand $40,000, their average stock amounting to $12,000. Mr. Phelps is a Democrat, a member of El Paso Lodge No. 65 of the A. F. & A. M., and in his business relations is shrewd and enterprising. He and wife are rearing a little girl named Mamie Canada, whose mother died in 1881, when she was but two weeks old. Her father is Thomas J. Canada, and her mother was a Miss Ada Booth.

Joseph T. Phelps is a prosperous merchant of El Paso, Ark., and in his relations with the public has ever proven trustworthy and reliable. By his superior management and rare business ability and efficiency he has done not a little to advance the reputation the county enjoys as a commercial center, and is well liked and esteemed by all. He was born in Hardeman County, Tenn., June 25, 1854, and is the son of Philip and Arkansas (Overton) Phelps, who were Virginians, but were married in Tennessee, and lived the lives of farm-

ers in that State. The father was an Englishman by descent and was a man who, had he lived, would have become wealthy, but he was cut down in the prime of life, in 1858, at the age of thirty-five years. In 1860 his widow married P. Rainer, a farmer of Tennessee, who came to Arkansas about 1870, and are residing in Craighead County. The mother, as well as her first husband, were members of the Old School Presbyterian Church, but she is now a member of the Methodist Episcopal Church. Joseph T. Phelps was left fatherless at the age of three years, but was reared to a farm life by his step-father, and in his youth acquired a fair education in the common schools of Tennessee and Arkansas, paying his own tuition. At the early age of fourteen years he began life on his own responsibility, and for about three worked as a farm hand, earning sufficient money to take a course in a higher grade of school. Upon leaving his step-father he could neither read nor write and had very little clothing. He made his home with an uncle, with the agreement that he should work one-half the time and go to school the remainder, but his uncle failed to live up to the contract and he left him. He next made his home with a lady who treated him kindly, and later with a Mr. Turner, who took considerable interest in him, and at the age of sixteen years, through the recommendation of this gentleman, he succeeded in obtaining a good position with a Mr. Parker, of Bolivar, Tenn., and remained with him six months, attending school and working in his store, doing chores to pay for his board. After teaching school for a short time, he obtained a situation as clerk in a dry-goods store at Bolivar at $10 per month, a position which he held for six months; then became newsboy on the Mississippi Central Railroad, continuing for three months. In the fall of 1872 he came to Craighead County and he and his brother bought a house and lot in Jonesboro, and followed the occupation of saw-logging a sufficient length of time to get enough logs to build a house, but the mill burned and their property was lost. Their next bad luck was the discovery that the title to their house and lot, for which they paid $100, was worthless, but nothing daunted, they

HISTORY OF ARKANSAS.

went in debt for forty acres of land, and their first year's crop paid for the property. At the end of one year our subject sold out to his brother and began teaching a subscription school, which was a great success. He next engaged in clerking in a store in Jonesboro, but came to El Paso after a few months, and spent eight months in school at that place. After cutting cord wood for about three months, he hired to M. L. Booth as a farm hand, at $20 a month, working one year. December 21, 1876, he was married to Miss Martha Booth, a daughter of his former employer, and her birth occurred in Haywood County, Tenn. This union has been blessed with six children, four of whom are living: Roberta H. (born August 2, 1878 and died August 2, 1888), Reuben C. (born February 8, 1880), Philip L. (born June 19, 1883, and died December 20, 1884), Joseph H. (born October 15, 1884), Oklahoma (born February 6, 1887) and an infant (born March 29, 1889). After his marriage, Mr. Phelps made one crop on his father-in-law's farm, but in the fall of 1878 he began the mercantile business with a Mr. A. P. Poole, under the firm name of Poole & Phelps. This partnership lasted two years, then Mr. Phelps sold out and engaged in business with M. L. Booth, the firm name being Booth, Phelps & Co., for one year. During his business connection with Mr. Poole, he was appointed postmaster at El Paso, and served in this capacity for six years. He is now engaged in merchandising under the name of M. L. Phelps & Co. His life has been an eventful one, and notwithstanding the many difficulties which have strewn his pathway, he has been successful and is of material benefit to any community in which he resides. He and his wife are members of the Missionary Baptist Church, and he is a member of El Paso Lodge No. 65 of the A. F. & A. M., in which organization he has held all the offices with the exception of Worshipful Master.

Wiley D. Plant. Hilary Plant was born in South Carolina, July 7, 1812, and, when quite young, moved to Alabama, where he met and married Mercy Tatum, a native of Alabama. Shortly after his marriage Mr. Plant immigrated to Ken-

tucky, thence to Arkansas, where the remainder of his quiet, uneventful life was passed. Mr. Plant was a stanch Democrat, and a consistent member of the Methodist Church, South, for many years. He was a quiet, law-abiding citizen, charitable, industrious and frugal, and at the date of his death, in 1880, had amassed quite a fortune. Mrs. Plant is now a resident in White County, Ark., aged eighty-five years. To the union of Mr. and Mrs. Plant ten children were born, five sons and five daughters, four of them now living: Nance B. (widow of George Hamby, of Jackson County), Charles F. (a farmer of White County), Wiley D. (the subject of this sketch), Green L. (a planter of White County), Andrew W. (died in Woodruff County), Robert L. (died in Conway County), Mary A. (widow of George M. Smith, deceased in White County), Susan M. (died in Jackson County) and Sarah F. (wife of N. E. Kidd, died in Woodruff County). Wiley D. Plant was reared in White County, and received excellent advantages for an education, which he was not slow to improve, and is a well-informed man. He is a typical Arkansan, and a native of that State, his birth occurring in Conway (now Faulkner) County, January 19, 1847. He began for himself at the age of twenty-one years, first as a farmer, which was his occupation for a few years, but realizing that his vocation lay in another direction he turned his attention to the mercantile business, in which he has been successful. He located at Bradford, White County, where he is now one of the prominent men of the community. His stock consists of general merchandise, valued at $8,000, and by his courteous manner and straightforward dealing he has established a permanent and lucrative business. Mr. Plant is well worthy the liberal patronage bestowed on him, for he endeavors in every possible way to please his customers, considering their interests his, and the petty, disagreeable traits of so many merchants are entirely foreign to his characteristics and nature. In May of 1885 Mr. Plant led to the hymeneal altar Mrs. Sarah E. Moore, daughter of William and Prudence McKnight. To their union two bright children have been born, Bessie and William D., who, with their childish prattle, make

WHITE COUNTY.

the house bright and joyous, and gladden the hearts of their devoted parents. He is a Democrat in politics, takes an active part in the elections, and is a strong partisan. He is a believer in the Methodist faith, though not a member of any denomination. He is a leading citizen, contributes liberally to all public movements; is a prominent personage in his town and community, active and progressive.

Henry W. Pope is a prominent farmer and stock raiser of Cane Township, a native of Georgia, and a son of Micajah and Hattie (Bruce) Pope. Micajah Pope was born in Virginia, November 21, 1808, and was a son of John and Mary (Morris) Pope of Virginia origin, and was married in 1827. John Pope moved to Georgia in 1818, and settled on land where Atlanta now stands. Mrs. Pope, the mother of Henry W., was a daughter of Daniel and Sallie (Prenct) Bruce, who were the parents of eleven children. Our subject was born December 28, 1835, and was married December 27, 1855, to Mollie E. Rea, a daughter of Rev. W. T. Rea and Rhoda (Brown) Rea. Mrs. Rea was a daughter of William and Nancy Pruet. After his marriage Mr. Pope found employment in teaching, following this for several years. All of his brothers were in the Confederate army, and Henry W. was mustered in, but was unable to stand muster, and was discharged. In 1867 he removed to Jefferson County and taught school, and two years later came to White County. In March, 1878, he came to Cane Township, and commenced farming on a quarter-section of unimproved land, and, by his energy, has 100 acres of it under cultivation. To this union have been given twelve children: Sarah F. (now Mrs. Earnest, and the mother of six children), Mollie H. (now Mrs. Langforo, and the mother of two children), William H. (married, and has one child), Mamie (now Mrs. Cagle), John D. (a professor of penmanship), Horace E. (deceased), Ella (deceased), Katie B., Daniel W., Samuel T. (deceased), Albert J. and James E. Mr. Pope is a strong Democrat, and takes an active part in politics, and is now holding the office of justice of the peace of his township. Himself and family are members of the Methodist Episcopal Church, South. He always takes an active interest in the temperance movement.

Frederick R. Price, one of Gen. Price's soldiers in his raid through Missouri, Kansas and Mississippi, is the fifth son of a family of twelve children, born to Russell and Mary (Turner) Price. Russell Price was the son of Joseph Price, who died in South Carolina in 1833. Russell Price was born in 1790, and was married about 1810, and was the father of the following ten children, and two whose names are not given: Delia, Thomas, Jane, Fielding, Frederick R., Minerva, Mahaley, Joseph, Mary Ann and Nancy. He followed farming in South Carolina, and moved to White County, in 1836, taking up eighty acres of land, and where he died two years later, his wife surviving him until 1844. Frederick R. first saw the light of this world in South Carolina, March 2, 1821, and was married at the age of twenty to Lucinda Jones, a daughter of B. Jones, of Cane Township. After his marriage he commenced farming for himself. By this marriage they had eleven children: John T., Russell, Levi (deceased), Polly (deceased), William (deceased), Sarah J. (deceased), Louisa, Fielding, Lucy C. (deceased), Elizabeth and George W. (deceased). Mr. Price's first wife died in June, 1872. He was married the second time, in 1873, to Ruth J. Taylor (nee Chrisman), widow of W. H. Taylor. She was born in 1831, and was the daughter of Isaac S. and Lucinda (Allen) Chrisman, natives of Lee County, W. Va., who came to White County in 1856, both of whom are now deceased. Mr. and Mrs. Price are the parents of one child, Allie O., who was born May 29, 1874. Mr. F. R. Price moved to White County, in 1836, where he has ever since lived. Himself and family belong to the Methodist Church, of which denomination his wife has been a member since eight years of age. He is also a member of the County Wheel, and has been honored with the office of president. In his younger days he was engaged principally in hunting. He is a highly respected citizen, and always has the good of his community at heart.

Amaziah M. Price is what might be called a life resident of White County, having been born

HISTORY OF ARKANSAS.

on the farm which he now calls home, and where he has always lived. It is a fine tract of 240 acres, 100 of which are under cultivation. Joseph R. Price, the father of A. M. Price, was a native of South Carolina, and was a son of Russell and Sarah (Turner) Price, both of South Carolina origin. Mr. Price was married in March, 1846, in White County, to Martha Guthery, a daughter of Joseph and Susie (Wood) Guthery, also natives of South Carolina. To their union were born seven children: Mary A. (deceased), A. M. (our subject), Arva J. (now Mrs. Chumbley), Carrel A., Rhodie J. (married James Hodges, of this county), Monroe and Susan (who married William Chumley). Mr. Price died in 1860, and his wife some ten years later. A. M. Price was born on November 13, 1849, received a common-school education, and was married in 1882 to Miss Susan M. Taylor, a daughter of James M. and Maggie J. (Barker) Taylor. Mr. Taylor is originally from Tennessee, and a son of Alexander and Margaret (Davis) Taylor. Mrs. Taylor was a daughter of Alexander and Margaret (Dodson) Barker. Mr. and Mrs. Price are the parents of two daughters: Lenna (born September 14, 1883) and Bertha (born November 21, 1885). He is a member of the Presbyterian Church, and his wife of the Baptist Church. Mr. Price is a strong Democrat, politically, and takes an active interest in all work for the good of the community.

Carroll A. Price. A glance at the notes from which this sketch has been prepared indicates at once that the mercantile career of Mr. Price has been one of ceaseless activity, and that he has been successful is well known. His parents, Joseph and Mary (Guthrie) Price, were of French and Scotch descent, and were born in North and South Carolina, respectively. After their marriage they came to Arkansas, and became farmers of White County. The father died in 1859 and the mother in 1866, their union having been blessed in the birth of seven children, all of whom grew to manhood and womanhood: Mary Ann (was born in 1846, was married to M. J. H. Jenkins, but was left a widow with six children in 1887), A. M. (was born in 1848, married Miss Susan Taylor,

a native of Tennessee, and has two children), Zennance (was born in 1850, and was married to J. M. Couch, by whom she has two children), Carroll A. (our subject, was the fourth child), Rhoda J. (was born in 1852, became the wife of J. S. Hodges, of Mississippi, and is the mother of seven children), Monroe (was born in 1856, married Nancy Gibson, a native of North Carolina, and by her has four children), Susan (born in 1858, married to W. T. Chumley, of Illinois, and has two children). The paternal great-grandfather was a soldier in the Revolutionary War. Carroll A. Price was born November 13, 1852, and was educated in the private schools of White County, and attended a male academy for two terms, paying his way through this institution with money earned by industry, perseverance and economy. In 1874 he became a salesman for his uncle, Nelson Guthrie, in Pope County, but at the end of one year returned to White County, and engaged in farming and stock dealing, which calling he continued to pursue until 1878, then came to Beebe and engaged as a clerk with D. C. Harris, with whom he remained until 1880. The following year he formed a partnership with J. M. Liles in general merchandising in the town of Beebe, and successfully conducted business at that place until 1887, when they dissolved partnership, Mr. Liles buying Mr. Price's interest. The latter invested his money in real estate, but in the spring of 1887 went east and purchased an excellent line of general merchandise, his stock being now valued at $10,000, and he controls a large share of the patronage of town and county. On September 17, 1883, he was united in marriage to Miss Mary G. Gibbs, of Arkansas, their marriage taking place in the Cumberland Presbyterian Church, in Beebe, Rev. R. T. Wylie officiating. They have two children: Cecil (born July 30, 1884) and Cuthbert A. (born December 7, 1887). In his political views Mr. Price is a liberal Democrat, and he and wife are earnest members of the Cumberland Presbyterian Church, of Beebe. He is progressive in his views, and contributes liberally to all religious, social, educational and political interests.

WHITE COUNTY.

L. M. Pyles, a prominent fruit and vegetable-grower of Judsonia, was born in Maryland, near Washington, D. C., in 1849, and was the eldest son in a family of thirteen children given to William V. and Margaret A. (Ryan) Pyles, also owning Maryland as their native State. Mr. William V. Pyles was a son of William and Massie (Allen) Pyles, who was born in 1825 and was married in 1847 to Margaret A. Ryan, daughter of William and Sarah (Kingsburry) Ryan, of Maryland. To the union of Mr. and Mrs. Pyles were born the following children: L. M. (our subject), Anna S. (deceased), Laura V. (now Mrs. Allen), Emma J. (married Bud Ball), Maggie (now Mrs. Stewart), Fannie (married Robert Padgett), Amanda (Mrs. Middleton), Lucy (now Mrs. Langley), Jennie, William H. and Thornton. Mr. L. M. Pyles was married in 1877 to Laverna Clark, daughter of Alfred and Mary Clark, who were of Ohio origin. After his marriage Mr. Pyles moved to Cincinnati, and thence to Warren County, Ohio, where he started in business as a butcher, which he followed for seven years. His wife died in 1881, in Warren County, leaving two children: Mary M. and William L. After the death of his wife Mr. Pyles returned to Maryland, remaining in that State but a short time, and then came back to Ohio and located in Darke County, where he was married the second time, in Greenville, in 1884, to Almeda Good, daughter of Samuel and Margaret Good, of Ohio. The year following he removed to White County, Ark., and located in Judsonia, where he made the raising of fruit and vegetables a business for two years, and then opened a meat market, in which business he continued for a limited time, and again took up the employment of growing fruit and vegetables, giving his principal attention to the raising of fine strawberries, which he ships to northern markets. Mr. and Mrs. Pyles are members of the Methodist Episcopal Church. He is also connected with the I. O. O. F., holding the office of Noble Grand. Mr. Pyles is a strong Republican and a member of the town council. He owns some property in Judsonia, and is widely known and highly respected as a citizen. His father was one of the three men who were allowed to cross the Potomac on the night of President Lincoln's assassination.

Thomas Jefferson Quick. Since commencing life for himself Mr. Quick has given his attention to two callings, that of farming and stock raising, and in these enterprises has met with well merited success, for he is not only progressive in his views, but is intelligent and thoroughly posted in all public affairs. He was born February 11, 1842, and is a son of Nathan and Pency Emeline (Hubbard) Quick, the father, being in all probability, of Spanish descent, his birth occurring in the "Palmetto State." The mother was a Georgian, and her union with Mr. Quick resulted in the birth of nine children, eight attaining manhood and womanhood: Nancy Melissa (was born in 1838, and was married to W. R. T. Singleton, of Mississippi), William (was born in 1840, and died in 1852), Thomas Jefferson (the subject of this memoir), Martha Adeline (born in 1844, was married to J. M. Butler, of Mississippi, in 1865), Eliza Permelia (born in 1846, wedded to L. R. Butler, of Mississippi, in 1865), James Robert (born in 1848, espoused Miss Mary Allen, of Mississippi, and died in Arkansas, in 1882), Mercy F. (born in 1850, married James E. Timms, of Mississippi) Sarah Ellen (born in 1852, wedded Thomas Hill, also of Mississippi), Amanda R. (born in 1854, became the wife of J. H. Roberts, a Mississippian), Matthew Isom's birth occurred in 1856, and he took for his wife Miss Evaline Summons. Mr. Quick, the gentleman whose name heads this sketch, received his education in the subscription schools of his native county (La Fayette County, Miss.), and has been familiar with farm work from his earliest boyhood. This work continued to receive his attention until he had attained his seventeenth year, when, with the enthusiasm of youth, he enlisted as a private in Company F, Nineteenth Regiment Mississippi Volunteer Infantry, the first battle in which he participated being Williamsburg. On March 3, 1865, he was captured at Petersburg, Va., and taken to Hart's Island, N. Y., where he was kept in confinement for two months and a half. On being paroled he went to New York City, embarking there on a steamer for New Orleans, going

HISTORY OF ARKANSAS.

from there up the Mississippi River to Memphis, from there by rail to La Fayette Station, thence on foot to Oxford, Miss., a distance of seventy miles, to his father's plantation, two miles east of that place, arriving at home May 6, 1865. He assisted his father on the farm for two years, and on January 16, 1867, wedded Miss Mary A. Callaway, of Georgia, and started out in life for himself. November 18, 1869, he came to Arkansas, and settled in White County, residing for one year on a farm he had purchased, then sold out and removed to Van Buren County, and after purchasing a saw-mill near Quitman, operated it for one year. Being dissatisfied with this location, he resolved to return to White County, and here purchased a farm, comprising 320 acres, all wild land. He resided on this until 1884, then sold it, having in the meantime made many valuable improvements, among which was the clearing and putting under cultivation of 120 acres of land. In 1884 he took up his abode in El Paso, but in 1885 purchased his present farm, consisting of 106 acres, on which was an incompleted house and fair stables. He has since completed the house, and has erected a cotton-gin, which has a capacity of six bales per day. On May 4, 1880, his wife died, and September 7, 1881, he married Sallie E. Crosby, of the State of Arkansas, and to them were born two children: Lawrence Bernard (born June 28, 1882, and died October 31, 1882), Clarence Leonard (born June 28, 1882, and died August 12, 1889). The mother of these children died October 17, 1884, and June 21, of the following year, Mr. Quick took for his third wife Mrs. Elizabeth (Arnold) Griffin, a daughter of John and Cynthia (Smith) Arnold, the father about one-fourth Cherokee Indian, and the mother of Irish descent. The following children have been born to Mr. Quick's last marriage: Thomas Fletcher (born July 16, 1886) and Quro (born October 26, 1888). At the present writing Mr. Quick owns 200 acres of land, with eighty acres under cultivation. His land has on it a fine peach and plum orchard, and a vineyard of about 100 vines. Mr. Quick is a member of the Methodist Episcopal Church, South, and also of El Paso Lodge No. 65, A. F. & A. M.

William C. Rainey is an extensive planter and cotton-ginner of Union Township, and was born in Madison County, Tenn., in 1829, being a son of Isaac and Parthena (Rainey) Rainey, who were also people of Middle Tennessee. The father was a farmer by occupation, and a son of Zebulon Rainey, a soldier in the War of 1812. Both parents were members of the Methodist Episcopal Church, and died in Middle Tennessee, after rearing a family of six children: William C., Theophilus (who died in youth), Addison Levi (a farmer of West Tennessee), Samuel (a farmer of West Tennessee), James W. (of Lauderdale County, Tenn.), Henderson A. (of Haywood County, Tenn.), Delicia F. (widow of Joseph L. Hendron, of Tenn.), Amanda (wife of W. Coffman, a merchant of Woodville, Tenn.), Elizabeth (who died at the age of four years), and Martha (who died in 1856, aged eighteen years). William C. Rainey began life for himself when twenty-two years of age, and after working one year as a farm hand and from that time up to 1858 was an overseer. In the fall of 1856 he was married to Elizabeth Coffey, a daughter of Rev. D. P. Coffey of Tennessee, and by her has had a family of eleven children, eight of whom are living: James D. (who was born November 25, 1857), Mary F. (wife of Jeff Walker, was born May 14, 1860), Leonidas E. (was born January 12, 1866), William J. (born February 29, 1868), Thomas (born October 7, 1870), Samuel (born November 30, 1872), Jesse C. (born March 4, 1874), Joseph L. (born December 27, 1879), and Eddie (born February 27, 1877). On December 20, 1854, Mr. Rainey first set foot in White County, Ark., and for two years he acted as overseer for one of the well-to-do planters of this region. After his marriage he moved to Hickory Plains, and in 1857 came to this portion of the county and settled on the land where Beebe now stands. After a one year's residence at this place he sold out and settled in the vicinity of Stony Point, and here has since made his home. His first purchase of land was 160 acres, and in 1856 he erected the first gin put up in the south part of White County, which he is still operating. Prior to 1883 the machinery was run by horse-power but since that time

WHITE COUNTY.

he has used steam. Mr. Rainey is a member of the Agricultural Wheel, and he and wife are members of the Cumberland Presbyterian Church, as are the most of their children, Mr. Rainey and his eldest son being ruling elders in that church. During the war he served in Company D, Tenth Arkansas Regiment, but after May 28, 1862, became a member of Forrest's cavalry and served under him until the close of the war, when his company was disbanded on January 9. He was at Shiloh, Corinth, the gunboat fight on the Big Sandy in Tennessee, Murfreesboro, Guntown, Franklin, and was in the various engagements in which Forrest's cavalry participated.

John F. Randall, a worthy and conscientious representative of White County, was born in Cape Girardeau County, Mo., near the city of Cape Girardeau, March 31, 1832. His father, Willam C. Randall, was born in Lexington, Ky., December 15, 1805, and died in Arkansas, February 4, 1863, aged fifty-eight years. He was a regular apprentice to the boot and shoemaker's trade, and an expert in that profession. He was an old line Whig, and manifested great interest in all party campaigns. In 1831 Mr. Randall was united in marriage with Sarah A., daughter of Anthony and Mary Randol, and a native of Missouri. She received her education in her native State, where the greater part of her life was passed, and at the date of her death, in 1854, she was residing in Stoddard County, Mo. To the union of Mr. and Mrs. Randall twelve children were born, all of whom grew to maturity. Those living are: John F., Sarah E. (wife of James Samuels, of Missouri), Orlando L. (of Hood County, Tex.), Martha J. (widow of Joseph M. Lean). Those deceased are: William O., Carrol V., Mary Z., Eliza A., Charlotte V., Rebecca L., Edward L. and Harvy C. John F. received but limited advantages for education, as the schools of his boyhood days were very few, but he received a practical knowledge of farming, which occupation he has always followed in connection with stock raising. He owns 320 acres of excellent land, highly cultivated, and everything on his farm indicates thrift and prosperity. He was first married in Calhoun County,

Ill., in 1859, to Martha J. Scott of that State, and the result of this marriage was two children, who died in infancy. His second marriage occurred in 1862 to Edna P., daughter of Andrew and Nancy Woodley, of Pike County, Ga., and by her he became the father of three children: William O. and a daughter (dead), and Edward L., now living. He also reared W. R. Randall, a nephew, born June 7, 1860, and Mattie Lee Woodley, a niece, born March 25, 1877. Mr. Randall enlisted in the Union army, July 27, 1862, in Company A, First Arkansas Mounted Rangers. This regiment was reorganized in 1863, at Benton Barracks, Mo., with John E. Phelps as colonel; the regiment afterward being known as the Second Arkansas Cavalry. He acted most of the time as recruiting officer, and in the capacity of scout and escort duty. He participated in the battles of Independence, Jefferson City, Kansas City, Big Blue and many others of minor importance. He received his discharge as first sergeant from said regiment, Company A. For twenty years Mr. Randall has acted as justice of the peace in White County, where he has lived since 1860, and is now filling said office and discharging its manifold duties in a creditable and exemplary manner. He is a Prohibitionist in politics, though not in any way a partisan. He is one of the most prominent members of the Methodist Church, South, and takes an active interest in all the affairs and work of the church, also contributing to all charitable enterprises. He is a member in high standing in the Masonic order.

James F. Ray, M. D., is a substantial and well-known practitioner of Arkansas, his first field for the practice of medicine being in Centre Hill in 1883. His early days were spent in Jackson County, where he was born in 1854, and in White County, and when nineteen years of age he commenced the study of medicine. Dr. Ray was the son of Samuel and Jane (Sorrell) Ray. Samuel Ray was born in Alabama in 1824, and was a son of Samuel M. Ray, a native of North Carolina. He moved to Arkansas in 1854, settling in Jackson County, and in 1860 came to White County, where he followed farming. He enlisted in 1862 and

HISTORY OF ARKANSAS.

served in the Confederate service. Mrs. Ray was born in Alabama, in 1828, and was a daughter of James F. and Flora Sorrell, and died in White County in 1869. They were the parents of three children: James F., John and William. Dr. Ray was married in 1877 to Susan E. Barnett, a daughter of Z. H. and Emiline (Stewart) Barnett, natives of Tennessee. To these parents were given seven children, four of whom are still living: Floyd S., Mary E. (deceased), Arthur Curtis (deceased), Mamie A., Samuel H. (deceased), Ethel I. and Blanch W. In 1885 Dr. Ray moved to Mount Pisgah, where he still lives and practices, and is the owner of a forty-acre tract of fine timber land. Himself and wife are members of the Missionary Baptist Church. When the Doctor first came to this county, bear, dear and wild turkey were abundant. Politically he is a strong Democrat, and although not taking an active part in politics, has held the office of bailiff of the township; he is a highly respected citizen, and enjoys a large practice extending throughout the adjoining townships.

William P. Reaves, a miller and ginner, of Cadron Township, was born in Alabama, in 1850, and was the second son in a family of eleven children of Emery G. and Elizabeth A. (Davis) Reaves, also of Alabama. Their family consisted of the following children: Emily, William P., Amandy, John T., Narsiscey, Nancy A., Sarah E., George W., Sarah J., Thomas and David. Mrs. Reaves died in 1879, and Mr. Reaves was again married, in 1881, to Susan Foster, and they are residing in Alabama, and have a family of small children. William P. Reaves, the gentleman whose name heads this sketch, was married at the age of seventeen, to Majourie O. Monk, a daughter of Silas and Nancy (Youngblood) Monk. Her father was a Primitive Baptist minister. Mrs. Reaves died in 1885, having been the mother of nine children: Tresser T. (deceased), Tulula, Mary M., William Lee, Ransom L., Caroline (deceased), Georgia (deceased), James (deceased) and Effie (deceased). Mr. Reaves came to Arkansas in 1877, and settled in this township, and in 1882 started a saw-mill and is now sawing and converting the pines of

Arkansas into lumber. He was married the second time in 1887 to Anna Drain, the daughter of the Rev. William W. Drain. To this union have been born two children: Isaac E. and Jessie J. Mr. Reaves owns 160 acres of fine timber land, and has twenty acres cleared and under cultivation. He is a member of the Masonic fraternity, belonging to the Rock Springs Lodge No. 422, and also a member of the County Wheel. He is a prominent worker in all matters relative to educational and school work, and is one of the esteemed directors of School District No. 28.

J. F. Redus came with his parents to White County, in 1851, they settling in Marion Township. He was born in Alabama, in 1844, and was the second son in a family of nine children born to Joel S. and Susan J. (Gill) Redus, also of Alabama nativity. The senior Redus had a land warrant for service in the Mexican War, and on which he settled and broke land for a farm, where he lived until he died in 1858, his wife surviving him ten years. The family consisted of the following nine children: W. G. (who resides in this county, and who enlisted in Company B of Thirty-sixth Arkansas Infantry), J. F. (our subject), L. S. (who also served in the Confederate army), L. E. (now Mrs. Simmons, of Cleburne County), John C. (deceased), D. J., Joel S. (deceased), M. G. and T. J. J. F. Redus assisted his father in opening up the farm, and in 1861 enlisted in the Confederate service for twelve months, in Company K, of the Seventh Arkansas Infantry. After the reorganization of the company, he re-enlisted for three years, or during the war. He participated in the battles of Shiloh, Murfreesboro, Perrysville (Ky.), Liberty Gap, Chickamauga, and in the ninety-days' fight before Dalton, also at Lookout Mountain, Atlanta and a number of others. He marched barefooted from Franklin, Tenn., to Pulaski, Tenn. Immediately after the cessation of hostilities, he returned home and again took up farming. He now owns a farm of 160 acres, with eighty-five acres under cultivation. He takes an active part in politics, and is a strong Democrat, and was candidate for county treasurer in 1889, but was defeated by combined efforts.

WHITE COUNTY.

He and entire family are members of the Baptist Church.

Jackson V. Reynolds, a prominent farmer and fruit grower of White County, was born in Tennessee in 1844, and is a son of Samuel and Margaret (Maderis) Reynolds, natives of Alabama. Mr. Samuel Reynolds was born in 1808, and was married in 1831, after which he moved to Tennessee, and in 1851 came to Arkansas, settling in White County, where he bought a farm of 160 acres, on which he lived until his death, which occurred in 1861. His wife survived him twenty years, and was the mother of nine children, three of whom are living: Jackson V. (our subject), Samuel T. and Marquis L. Jackson V. Reynolds was reared on a farm, educated in this county, and was married, in 1866, to Margaret Thompson, a daughter of James and Martha Thompson of Tennessee origin, and who came to Arkansas at an early day. Mrs. Reynolds died in 1880, leaving five children, four of whom are still living: Edward, Minnie, Mary and Florence. After the death of his first wife, Mr. Reynolds married Mrs. Mitchell (*nee* McMurtry), a widow, and by this marriage became the mother of three children: Willie, Effie and Van. In 1862 he enlisted in the Confederate army, serving in Capt. Hick's regiment, but was wounded at the battle of Helena, and received his discharge. Mr. Reynolds has a farm of 237 acres, with 140 acres under cultivation, and devotes the most of his attention to fruit growing.

James P. Rheu, planter, Stevens Creek, Ark. White County, is acknowledged by all to be one of the best agricultural portions of the State, and as such its citizens are men of advanced ideas and considerable prominence. A worthy representative of this class is found in the person of Mr. James P. Rheu. He was originally from Dickson County, Tenn., where his birth occurred on November 23, 1824, and is the son of John and Margaret (Dunnegan) Rheu, natives, respectively, of North Carolina and Kentucky, and both of Scotch-Irish descent. The maternal grandparents probably came to Alabama before the Revolutionary War. John Rheu and family moved to Kentucky in about 1830, lo-cated in McCracken County, where they remained until about 1840, and then moved to Graves County. There he improved a farm, and made his home until death, which occurred in 1855. The mother died about 1827. James P. Rheu was early initiated into the duties of farm life, and received a liberal education for those days. In 1857 he came to Arkansas, located at Denmark, Jackson County, and engaged in merchandising, which he continued successfully for many years. On May 15, 1859, he was united in marriage to Miss Martha V. Edens, a native of Fayette County and the daughter of H. and Ann (Price) Edens, natives of Lincoln County, Tenn., and probably of Irish descent. The maternal great-grandfather of Mrs. Rheu was connected with the commissary department of the Colonial army, and her grandfather Price, was a soldier under Gen. Jackson, in the War of 1812, participating in the battle of New Orleans, also in the subsequent Indian Wars. To Mr. and Mrs. Rheu were born four children: Ider E. (born June 11, 1860), Lelia C. (born October 8, 1865), William F. (born February 8, 1875), and Maggie A. (born February 22, 1876). Ider E. married J. C. Meadows on November 30, 1879, and is the mother of four children: Claude L., Ollie V., Lillian M. and Homer C. Mr. Meadows is a farmer by occupation. Mr. Rheu's other children are at home. In the fall of 1862, Mr. Rheu had become nicely fixed in business, had erected a fine dwelling-house, also a store, and excellent outbuildings upon his place; was also speculating in cotton, and had about ten bales on hand, when his buildings were set on fire, and his store, his entire stock of goods and his cotton were destroyed. After this severe loss he rented land, followed farming near Denmark, and there remained until 1866, when he bought a farm in Jackson County. This tract contained eighty acres of improved land, and there he resided until 1871, when he moved to his present property, arriving there on December 20 of that year. He purchased one hundred acres, with about fifteen under cultivation, and erected their present house the same year. At present he has about thirty acres under cultivation. He is a member of Anchor Lodge No. 49, A. F. and A. M., and has

HISTORY OF ARKANSAS.

served the lodge in the capacity of Senior Warden and Junior Warden, and has also been secretary for seven years of Fredonia Lodge No. 229. He holds a demit from Tillman Chapter No. 19, R. A. M., Searcy, Ark. In his political views he affiliates with the Democratic party. Mrs. Rheu, and her daughter Lelia, are members of the Methodist Episcopal Church, South, and Mrs. Ider E. Meadows is a member of the Missionary Baptist Church.

Mrs. Mary M. Rhoden is the daughter of Jacob Free Coffman (deceased), who, from an early period in the country's history, gave to Independence County (to which he came in 1851, locating on the White River) the best energies of his life as one of the most worthy and respected citizens, and to the community and all among whom he lived, the example of a life well and usefully spent, and the influence of a character without stain. In this county he bought a farm of 400 acres, on which he lived till his death in 1858. His birth occurred February 10, 1805, and he was united in marriage to Miss Catherine Young on March 17, 1826, in Lauderdale County, Tenn. He was the son of Lovell and Sallie (Greene) Coffman, the former a native of Virginia, of German descent, and whose ancestors came to America previous to the Colonial War. Sallie (Greene) Coffman was a relative of Gen. Greene of Revolutionary fame. Mrs. Catherine (Young) Coffman was the daughter of Samuel and Keziah (Hogue) Young. Samuel Young was a native of South Carolina, was of English descent, and his grandfather came to America about 1740 and located in South Carolina where Samuel was born. Keziah (Hogue) Young was a native of South Carolina, her parents being of English descent. The maternal grandfather (Doolittle) was killed by Tories in South Carolina during the Revolutionary War. Jacob Free and Catherine (Young) Coffman were the parents of these children: Sarah Ann K., Samuel Lovell, Mary Margaret, John Tillmore, Daniel A., Martha Jane, Elizabeth C., Amy Evaline, Susan Rebecca and Laura Malinda. Mary M. Coffman was the third daughter of the above-mentioned family, her birth occurring on January

25, 1832, in Franklin County, Ala., and she received a good English education in the subscription schools of her native county. There she grew to womanhood and was united in marriage to John Harrison Rhoden, a native of Alabama, on November 11, 1847, in Lawrence County. To this union were born eight children: Archie C. (born August 2, 1848), Frances Catherine (born November 3, 1849), Martha Jane (born September 6, 1851, and died in December of the same year), Rebecca Walker (born November 2, 1854, and died on September 5, 1858), Sarah E. (born January 25, 1856), Laura Sophronia (born September 6, 1858), John Breckenridge (born October 15, 1860) and Lucy Coleman (born December 20, 1862). All the children were born in Arkansas, with the exception of Archie, whose birth occurred in Alabama. Archie C. married Miss Matilda J. Means, a native of Virginia, and Frances C. married J. W. Moseley, a native of Kentucky, who is now residing in White County; Sarah E. married Lawrence Westmoreland, a native of Georgia, who is now deceased, Sophronia married William Woodall, a native of Arkansas, John B. resides in Texas, Lucy C. married Dr. Joseph H. Fillinger, a native of Virginia, and now residing in White County. The settlement of the Rhoden family in Arkansas was made in 1849 when the country was an unbroken wilderness. Mrs. Rhoden is a member of the Missionary Baptist Church, having united with that denomination in 1849. The family purchased 160 acres when they first settled in this State, and Mrs. Rhoden now owns 120 acres of that farm.

Dr. Willshire Riley is engaged in the drug business at Judsonia, Ark., and has been established there since 1880. He was born in Auglaize County, Ohio, in 1828, and in 1866 settled in White County, and after residing in Searcy one year, he moved to Red River Township, and for some years was engaged in shipping corn at Riley's Landing. He was educated in the schools of Ohio, and in 1849 was married in Mercer County, of that State, to Miss Ruth Lindsey, removing in 1854 to Toledo, where he acted as deputy collector of customs. He also published the Toledo Daily, but in 1856 went to Perry County,

WHITE COUNTY.

Ill., and began practicing medicine, having previously taken a course in the Cincinnati Medical College, graduating in the class of 1856. He remained in Perry County until 1866, then came to Searcy, and has been in business here since that time. He took an active part in politics during reconstruction days, and in 1870 and 1871 was senator, representing White and Pulaski Counties. He has been interested in the cause of education, and has aided all enterprises which were for the good of the community. He is a Douglas Democrat, and he and wife are members of the Methodist Episcopal Church. Of five children born to them, three are living: Horatio (who is married, and resides in Pine Bluff), Kate (Mrs. Hines, resides in Van Buren County) and Willshire (a druggist of Pine Bluff). Dr. Riley is a member of Lodge No. 384 of the A. F. & A. M., and belongs to Tillman Chapter No. 19, and Searcy Council. He is one of the family of six born to James W. and Susan (Ellis) Riley, the former a native of Connecticut, and the latter of New York, and their union took place in Ohio. Mr. Riley was a Government surveyor, and did the most of the surveying of Northwest Ohio and Indiana, but was also a lawyer by profession. He died in January, 1876, and is still survived by his wife, who is a resident of Denver, Colo. The paternal grandfather, Capt. James Riley, was born in Middletown, Conn., and was the author of Riley's Narrative. Being appointed by President Jackson to survey the Northwestern Territory, he came to Ohio in 1819, and laid out the town of Willshire. Being a sea captain he returned to his calling, and died on the ocean while on one of his voyages in 1840.

Elbert A. Robbins, the eldest son of D. and Olivia (Shinpouch) Robbins, natives of Alabama and Mississippi, respectively, dates his existence from December 23, 1857. His father became a resident of Arkansas in 1856, settling in White County, on a farm of 160 acres of land, ten miles south of Rose Bud, where he died in 1865, shortly after returning from the war. His wife survived him nine years, leaving a family of five children: Elbert A. (the subject of this sketch), J. W. [reference to whom follows], C. D., Molly and Samuel. E. A. Robbins started out in the world for himself at the age of fifteen without means or influence. He worked on a farm for three years, with but little success, after which his time was spent in a saw-mill until in April, 1881, when he bought a saw-mill, selling it, however, in October of the same year. In 1882 he farmed, but commenced the mercantile business at Rose Bud, in January, 1883, in partnership with his brother, J. W. Robbins. This he has followed ever since, with encouraging results. Besides his only brother he has one sister, Mollie Holmes, still living. Mr. Robbins professed religion, and joined the Baptist Church in 1887. He was married, in 1878, to Miss Ida Crooms, and to them have been born six children, three of whom are living: Emma, Walter and Maudie; those deceased are Mollie, Elmer and an infant. Mrs. Robbins is also a member of the Missionary Baptist Church. He takes an active part in the Sunday-schools, and exerts his whole influence for the promotion of religious and educational institutions.

J. W. Robbins, a brother of E. A. Robbins, commenced in life on his own account at the age of fourteen, in 1883 entering into the mercantile business in White County. He was born in this county in 1860, his parents being D. and Olivia (Shinpouch) Robbins [reference to whom appears in the sketch which precedes this]. J. W. Robbins was married, in 1886, to Susan I. Thomas, a daughter of W. A. and Jane (Post) Thomas. Mr. and Mrs. Robbins are the parents of two children: Oscar (living) and Laura A. (deceased). Mr. Robbins is a strong Democrat, and takes an active interest in all work for the interest of schools or general public good.

John A. Roberson. Among the farmers and stockmen of White County, Ark., none are more prominent than our subject, who, though he is a native of Rutherford County, Tenn., born November 19, 1835, has been a resident of White County since 1870. He was reared to a farm life and his knowledge of the "Three R's" was acquired in the common schools. He was thrown on the world to fight his own way through life at the early age

HISTORY OF ARKANSAS.

of sixteen years on account of the death of his father, and until his marriage on November 17, 1854, he worked as a farm hand. His wife, Angeline Redmon, was a native of Haywood County and bore Mr. Roberson eight children as follows: George (who died in infancy), a child who died unnamed, William (who is a farmer of White County), James (also a farmer), Anna (wife of Elijah Cupp, died leaving one child), Lela (is the wife of William P. Brickell, a farmer of Phillips County, Ark.), Thomas (farms in Texas) and Edgar (who was born on June 20, 1873). Mr. Roberson departed this life on July 27, 1888, an earnest member of the Methodist Episcopal Church. Mrs. Mary (Coleman) Murphy, a native of Alabama and a resident of Arkansas for about nineteen years, became his wife February 24, 1889. After his first marriage Mr. Roberson farmed and acted as overseer until 1864 when he went into the army and served until the cessation of hostilities. He then became manager of a large farm owned by a wealthy planter of Haywood County, but since 1870 has resided in White County, he being now the owner of 320 acres of land. At the time of his purchase there were sixty-five acres under cultivation, but he now has 110 acres under the plow and has added 130 acres to his original purchase. His land is well adapted to raising all necessary farm products, and for several years past he has devoted much of his time to stock raising. He has been an active worker for the cause of Christianity for many years and socially is a member of Beebe Lodge No. 145 of the A. F. & A. M. His parents, Jesse and Mary A. (Vaughn) Roberson, were born in Virginia and South Carolina in 1815 and 1810, respectively, and were married about 1834. They died in Tennessee, the former in Haywood County in 1851, and the latter in Davidson County, in 1848. Three of their eight children died in infancy: William (lived to be grown and lost his life in the battle in June, 1863, and was buried in a soldier's cemetery), Mary (is the wife of James Tatum, of Bell Station, Tenn.), Fidelia (is the wife of James Collins, an Englishman, residing in Tennessee), Eliza (is the wife of Robert Pitner, a farmer of Tennessee), and John A. (our subject).

A. T. Rodmon has ably served his county as commissioner four years, as school director six years, and also as president of the board of registration. His parents, James and Jennie (Kell) Rodmon, were natives of South Carolina, his paternal and maternal grandfathers being of Irish origin, who came to this country at the same time and settled in South Carolina. Grandfather Rodmon had a family of four children: John, Thomas, Sarah and James. James Rodmon was married in 1828 or 1829, and had a family of five children: A. T. (our subject), Mary A. (who married a man by the name of Blunt), Susan (Ballard), John C. and James C. Mr. Rodmon died on July 13, 1849, in South Carolina, to which State his family moved from South Carolina that year. A. T. Rodmon was married, after attaining manhood, in 1856 in Mississippi, to Miss Mary Williams, a daughter of P. W. and Nancy (McDowell) Williams, and of North Carolina birth. After this event Mr. Rodmon settled on a farm and devoted himself to agricultural pursuits for four years, then moving to White County, Ark., in 1859, and locating on a farm twelve miles south of Searcy. In 1862 he enlisted in the Confederate army and served on detached duty during the war. In 1873 he removed to Kane Township, where he now resides, enjoying at this time a wide and honored acquaintance. Mr. and Mrs. Rodmon have had twelve children, four of whom only are living: Alice M., Nora E., Frank and Clinton J. These are at home and attending school. In 1868 Mr. Rodmon was appointed justice of the peace, and the same year elected county commissioner, which position he held four years. In 1872 he was elected president of the board of registration, and is now school director, having discharged the official duties connected therewith for six years. He is a member of the Masonic order, and has been connected with the I. O. O. F. Himself and wife have been members of the Baptist Church for the past thirty-two years, Mr. Rodmon having held the position of church clerk for seventeen years. He has also acted as president of the County Wheel for six years, besides holding the office of district deputy for two years. Mr. Rodmon is a strong

WHITE COUNTY.

Republican and has taken an active interest in the politics of his county. A highly respected citizen, he worthily deserves the universal esteem bestowed upon himself and family.

Benjamin Rogers, in his active career through life, has amassed considerable wealth, and is now owner of a fine farm, comprising 400 acres, 120 of which he has put under cultivation, clearing ninety acres himself. He has around him every convenience, and his buildings, fences and orchards have been placed on his property by his own hands. From his earliest remembrance he has been familiar with farm life, but his youthful advantages for acquiring an education were very limited. He came with his father to Arkansas, and made his home with him until twenty-six years old, having married, at the age of twenty-four, Miss Anna E. Bailey, a native of Tennessee, and a daughter of J. J. Bailey, a pioneer settler of White County. Mrs. Rogers died in September, 1862, and on January 15, 1865, he married Miss Hannah J. Jackson, a native of Tennessee, and a daughter of H. Jackson, a blacksmith by trade. Eleven children have been born to them, of whom ten are living: Marion F. (born February 24, 1866, and lives on his father's farm), J. M. (who was born October 13, 1868), William H. (born August 27, 1869), Robert E. (born June 23, 1871), Mary E. (born August 6, 1873, and died September 2, 1887), Minnie B. (born January 30, 1875), Bettie H. (born November 13, 1878), Benjamin D. (born February 9, 1880), Calvin J. (born January 27, 1883), Ava L. (born January 27, 1885), and Arthur L. (born April 25, 1887). Mrs. Rogers, the mother of this large family, departed this life February 7, 1889, having been a life-long member of the Missionary Baptist Church, a faithful wife and mother, and her death is not only mourned by her immediate family, but by all with whom she came in contact. In 1861 Mr. Rogers bought 160 acres of the farm where he now lives, going in debt for the same, and notwithstanding the fact that the war came up and scattered his property, he has succeeded admirably. In June, 1862, he joined Company A, Thirty-sixth Arkansas Regiment, and was in the battles of Prairie Grove, Helena, Little Rock, besides numerous skirmishes.

He was not wounded nor taken prisoner during his term of service, and was a faithful soldier to the cause he espoused. Upon his return home he found himself robbed of all his property, except the land for which he was considerably in debt, but he began devoting his entire attention to his farm, and has succeeded in putting himself and family beyond the reach of want. He is a Democrat, a member of Beebe Lodge No. 145 of the A. F. & A. M., and for the past seventeen years has been one of the most faithful members of the latter organization. He is public-spirited, and keeps thoroughly apace with the times on all matters of public interest. He was born in Haywood County, Tenn., on August 1, 1836, and is a son of William and Sarah E. (Powers) Rogers, the former born in North Carolina in 1809, and the latter in 1811. They were married in Tennessee about 1830, and in 1854 came to White County, Ark., and settled on what is well known as the Williams' farm, near where Beebe now stands. Mr. Rogers bought 400 acres of woodland, and until he could build him a log-house his family lived in a tent. Like the majority of the pioneer settlers of early times

> "He cut, he logged, he cleared his lot,
>   And into many a dismal spot
>   He let the light of day."

During his lifetime he cleared over 100 acres of land, and at the time of his death (in 1871) he was one of the wealthy men of the county. In politics he was an old line Whig. His wife died in 1838, and in 1842 he married again, having by this union five children, only two now living, Rufus H. and Robert E., both farmers. His first marriage also resulted in the birth of five children, Benjamin and Elizabeth (wife of Oliver Greene) being the only ones alive.

Thomas J. Rogers, another of the prominent pioneer settlers of White County, has been located here for a period of over forty years, and has not only become well known, but the respect and honor shown him is as wide as his acquaintance. He came to White County in 1848, settled with a brother, Robert J., within three miles of Searcy, which at that time contained two small supply stores, one made of log and the other of plank,

HISTORY OF ARKANSAS.

and a blacksmith shop. Mr. Rogers was born in Chatham County, N. C., in 1826, was the sixth in a family of ten children (all dead but two), born to Absalom and Hannah (Johnson) Rogers, natives of North Carolina. The parents immigrated to Tennessee at an early day and there the father carried on agricultural pursuits. He was one of the jury that convicted J. A. Merrill. His death occurred in Tennessee, in 1840, and his wife died in North Carolina. Grandfather Rodgers is buried in North Carolina, of which State the family were pioneers. Brought up as an agriculturist it would have been quite natural had Thomas J. Rogers followed in the footsteps of his father, but his tendencies inclined elsewhere, and after securing a fair education in the subscription schools of Tennessee and Arkansas, and farming one year, in 1849 he came to Searcy, where he clerked for Bond & Maxwell, general merchants. He remained with this firm until 1851, and went into partnership in a separate house with the firm, taking the management. In 1852 Mr. Rogers purchased the full control and continued in business until 1862, when he had everything taken from him, it all becoming common property. During the war he raised a company and followed guerrillas, but later he moved to Urbana, Ill., purchased property and remained until the close of the war. The people were anxious to know what he was going to do, so in 1865, he returned to Searcy, Ark., but before coming back liquidated his debts at 25 and 50 per cent with Philadelphia houses. He paid it and received their receipts in full, and later paid it in full with interest, in 1867. After this Mr. Rogers engaged in the real-estate business, in which he is now interested, and is the owner of 20,000 acres in White and Cleburne Counties. He has twenty improved farms in these counties, is renting out land and owns a fine body of timber situated on White and Red Bayou, Des Arc. Politically, Mr. Rogers is the father of the Prohibition party in this county and bought the Lever by the thousands, distributing them gratuitously through the country. He fought for the Local Option bill, was successful, and all rejoiced. He is a member of the Masonic fraternity, Searcy Lodge No. 49, and was charter member of the same. He was married in White County, Ark., in 1859, to Miss Susie M. Lewis, a native of Mississippi, and to this union were born seven children, five now living: Thomas B., Hallie B., Angie (now Mrs. Jones, of Memphis, Tenn.), Susie M. and Naomi. The mother of these children closed her eyes to the scenes of this world in 1877. She was a member of the Methodist Episcopal Church, to which Mr. Rogers also belongs, having joined in 1840; he has been a scholar and teacher ever since. In 1852 Mr. Rogers joined the Sons of Temperance, but now considers that their work was largely in vain. In 1880 he was sent to Cleveland, Ohio, to the Prohibition National Convention, became a member of that party, and has been on the executive board ever since; was sent to the National Prohibition Convention, which met at Indianapolis, Ind., in 1888, and assisted in forming the Prohibition platform, every plank of which exactly suited him. The same year he was also delegate to the Arkansas State Convention at Little Rock, which adopted the national party platform.

Hon. John P. H. Russ is a man who needs no introduction to the readers of this volume, for he has been usefully and honorably identified with the interests of this county and with its advancement in every worthy particular for many years. His early paternal ancestors were of Scotch-Irish descent and were among the original settlers of Jamestown, Va., but the two immigrants, Vincent and John, spelled their name Rusk, although the old Scotch way of spelling the name was Russ, a fact which was discovered by Charles E. Russ, the father of our biographical subject, while reading Scotch history, during his attendance at Hillsboro (N. C.) College. He adopted the old way of spelling the name, and as such it has continued to the present time. Charles E. Russ and his brother, John P. H., afterward graduated from Raleigh College, Raleigh, N. C., and the latter subsequently became a prominent politician, and was honored with the office of Secretary of his native State, a position he held several terms, serving in the interests of the Democratic party. Charles E. Russ was strongly opposed to secession, and stumped the "Old North State" and Georgia in

WHITE COUNTY.

opposition to that measure. His wife, Sarah A. Parker, was a daughter of Harrison and Sarah (Parrish) Parker, the former of Scotch-Irish descent and the latter of French. Hon. John P. H. Russ was born in Floyd County, Ga., April 27, 1852, and in 1859 he was taken by his parents to Charlotte, S. C. After a residence of a few months in Florida they settled in Marengo County, Ala., remaining there until 1866, when Denmark, Tenn., became their home. Their first settlement in Arkansas was in the year 1869, when they settled at El Paso, in White County, purchasing a farm of 160 acres, twenty acres of which was heavily covered with timber. Here both father and mother died, in 1884, the former in January and the latter in June. They were members of the Methodist Episcopal Church, South, and Mr. Russ was a Mason, his wife belonging to the Eastern Star Lodge. Their family consisted of four sons and two daughters, two of whom are living besides our subject: James E. (who was married to Miss Belle Andrews, a native of Kentucky, is an attorney at law of Beebe, Ark.) and Laura J. (the wife of Thomas Midyett, a resident of El Paso Township). This couple was married in Tennessee and came to Arkansas in 1870, and are here rearing their family of three sons: Henry, Charley and Bascom. Hon. John P. H. Russ first commenced attending school in Red Mountain, Ala., but was afterward a student in the common schools of Tennessee, and finished his education in the Methodist graded school under the supervision of Prof. J. W. Thompson. June 23, 1872, he was united in marriage to Miss Narcie L. Booth, a daughter of M. L. and Elizabeth (Bushel) Booth [a sketch of whom appears on another page of this work], and their union resulted in the birth of the following family: Mary E. (born May 18, 1873, and died September 4, 1885), Samira M. (born March 14, 1875), Charles L. (born March 23, 1877), Lena Mora (born December 4, 1880, and died March 4, 1889), Walter M. (born February 9, 1882), Otey S. (born February 28, 1884), John T. (born April 2, 1886), and Laura B. (born January 21, 1888). Mr. Russ always voted with the Democrat party until 1883 and, as he says, did more for the party than his Satanic Majesty, the Devil,

ever did, but he left it in consequence of dissatisfaction with the corruption of both the Democrat and Republican parties and identified himself with the Labor movement; and at a meeting of the White County Wheel, May 7, 1884, he was elected a delegate to the State Wheel, which was held at Little Rock, on June 9, of the same year. At this meeting a full county ticket was organized and Mr. Russ, the delegate, was told to use his own judgment as to which to support—a Labor State or a Wheel ticket. The result was the nomination of the Labor State ticket, and Mr. Russ was chosen by the committee as chairman of the committee for drawing up a platform, and wrote the first four planks. He was afterward elected chairman of the State and Labor Central Committee, and when a meeting was called at Litchfield, Jackson County, on July 27, 1884, he again filled out the ticket, and Charles E. Cunning was the nominee for Governor and received 19,706 votes in twenty-three counties organized in the State, out of seventy-five. At this meeting the delegates met under the shade of a tree and nominated a ticket for Congress, their nominee, R. B. Carl Lee, receiving a small vote in the district. At a meeting of the State Wheel at Little Rock, in 1884, Mr. Russ was elected as a delegate to the Labor Convention at Cincinnati, Ohio, the meeting to be held February 2, 1885. At the meeting of the Union Labor party in White County he was chosen permanent chairman, and was a delegate to the State convention with instructions to put in the field a full State ticket, using his judgment in favor of the best man. He did so, and a vigorous canvass was carried on, the result being the election of Hon. C. M. Norwood, an ex-Confederate, one-leg soldier, as Governor, by a majority of from 8,000 to 10,000 votes. In 1886, at a meeting of the State Wheel, he was elected a member of the executive committee of that body, and was re-elected for three consecutive terms. He was also a delegate to the National Agricultural Wheel, the meeting of all Labor organizations, at Meridian, Miss., in December, 1888; was a member of the first National Cotton Committee, also at that place, and the second one, held at Atlanta, Ga. In 1886 he represented the Ar-

HISTORY OF ARKANSAS.

kansas State Wheel, at Raleigh, N. C., and was elected by that body to the Farmers' Union to be held at Shreveport, La., in 1887. At a meeting of the State Wheel held at Little Rock, the same year, he was chosen State Lecturer, and was re-elected in 1888. The following year, at a meeting of the State Wheel at Hot Springs, he was chosen president of the State Wheel of Arkansas, and was at the same time elected a delegate to the National Farmers' and Laborers' Union, which was held in St. Louis, in December, 1889. October 19, of the same year, as president of the above-named body he issued a proclamation dissolving the State Wheel, and adopting the Farmers' and Laborers' Union of America, as agreed at the meeting of all the Labor organizations in 1888. Mr. Russ was president of the first district Wheel ever organized in White County, and filled the same position for the Twenty-seventh, the first senatorial Wheel, comprising White and Faulkner Counties. He discharged the duties of this position also for the Second Congressional Wheel, to which office he was elected in 1884, and he has been re-elected each succeeding year. He has held the office of Lecturer in the subordinate office for five years, and in this capacity has lectured in a great many counties. He is a strict temperance man, and for many years has been a member of the Methodist Episcopal Church, South, and in support of the latter, as well as in the cause of education, he has been exceedingly liberal and free-hearted. He is now acting as deputy sheriff of White County, and although repeatedly urged to run for representative of White County, he has declined, thinking he could do more good for his party off the ticket than on. In 1873 Mr. Russ purchased from the United States Government 160 acres of wild land, and by subsequent purchases has increased his land to 660 acres, of which 122 are under cultivation. His first farm was heavy timber land, but after many years of arduous labor and with the assistance of his worthy wife, who has proved to him a true helpmate, he has become one of the wealthy agriculturists of the county. In the comparatively short time which has elapsed since he commenced doing for himself, he has developed and improved

two fine farms, and has made all the property he now has by the sweat of his brow as, at the time of marriage, he only possessed $23, a horse and a gold watch. At the time of locating, he, his wife and father could carry their effects on their backs, and the furniture with which their house was provided was made of lumber from their own land. Many changes have occurred since this esteemed citizen first located here, and he has witnessed the growth, of what was once a vast wilderness, to one of the most prosperous and influential counties of the State. He and wife have hosts of warm friends, and as they look back over their past careers they can see little to regret, while the future in the life to come stands out brightly before them.

James E. Russ, an attorney at law and notary public, of Beebe, is recognized as a prominent member of the legal fraternity of White County. A native of North Carolina, he was born in Orange County, November 9, 1855, being the son of Charles E. and Sarah A. (Parker) Russ, also of North Carolina origin [a sketch of whose lives appears on a previous page, as well as a history of this illustrious family]. Charles Russ was born in 1819 and his wife in 1826. They were of Scotch-Irish and English descent, and were married in their native State in 1843, moving in 1859 to Alabama, where Mr. Russ conducted an extensive plantation, and managed a large force of slaves until after the war (in which he held the rank of major for four years). He subsequently went to Tennessee and after a residence there of four years, moved again, this time settling in El Paso, Ark., where he followed the occupation of farming until his death in 1885. He was a Universalist in his religious belief, his wife, who only survived him a few months, being a devoted member of the Methodist Episcopal Church, South. Mr. Russ was a member of high standing in the Masonic order, and Mrs. Russ of the Eastern Star. James E. was the fifth in a family of six children, as follows: Laura J. (wife of Thomas H. Midyett, a wealthy farmer of El Paso), J. P. H. Russ (farmer and president of the State Wheel of Arkansas), Charles W. (who died at the age of twenty-two, unmarried), Mary and Robert (who both died in their youth). James

WHITE COUNTY.

E. was reared to farm life, but his opportunities for obtaining an education were very limited, three months being the extent of his entire schooling. At an early age, however, he became a careful student and constant reader at home. When twenty-one he entered upon the reading of law, at the same time managing the farm and supporting his parents. This course he continued until 1883, when he was admitted to the bar at Little Rock, having passed a critical examination before Judges W. F. Hill, T. J. Oliphant and J. M. Rose, committee, with Judge F. T. Vaughn as presiding judge. After passing this examination Mr. Russ formed a partnership with Judge Oliphant, under the firm name of Oliphant & Russ, which relation existed nearly two years. Compelled to withdraw at that time on account of ill health, he passed several months in traveling, later returning to Arkansas, and finally settled in Beebe, where he has since resided, gaining by his upright course and recognized ability, the confidence and esteem of all acquaintances. As a practictioner he has built up an enviable and lucrative clientage, having a general law business in all courts of the State. In January, 1887, he lost his residence and contents by fire, but by energy, economy and strict integrity, has recovered from that disaster almost entirely. In December, 1883, Mr. Russ was united in marriage with Miss Belle Andrews, an estimable lady, daughter of William Andrews, a lawyer of Paducah, Ky. To them have been given a family of two children: Paul Eaton (born in September, 1884) and Jane (born November 2, 1886). Mr. and Mrs. Russ are members of the Methodist Episcopal Church, South, and both are deservedly popular in society circles. The former votes the straight Democratic ticket, but has never been looked upon as an aspirant for political preferment. During the year 1888 he was a member of the real-estate firm of Merrill, Russ & Co.

Christopher N. Saunders, a farmer and stockman of Dog Wood Township, White County, Ark., was born in Virginia in 1822, and is the second child born to Wren and Mary D. (Teatroff) Saunders, who were also Virginians, the father's birth occurring in 1822. His parents, Reuben and

Frances Saunders, were born in that State, and there reared their family, of which State their son Wren is still an inhabitant. He was married in 1840, his wife being a daughter of John Teatroff, and he and wife reared a family of eleven children: Columbia I., Christopher N., Jane (who was a Mrs. Hunt, and is now dead), Reuben, Daniel (who died young), Mary (also died in childhood), Ellen and Logan (both died in infancy), Millard P. (a resident of West Virginia), Artemas and Leanna D. (married). The mother of these children died in 1865, a consistent member of the Christian Church at the time of her death. Christopher N. Saunders spent his youth on a farm, and also received his early schooling in his native State. In 1862 he enlisted in Company F, Twenty-fifth Virginia Cavalry, and the first battle in which he participated was near Richmond. After the war he began farming for himself, and in 1871 was married to Malina Owen, a daughter of William and Keron Owen, natives of Virginia, both of whom are now dead. Mr. Saunders and his wife reared a family of six children: Wren, Minnie, Claudius, Keron, Clifford G. and Charles C. John W. died in childhood, and Mattie Lee died in October, 1889. In 1876 our subject removed with his family to White County, Ark., and in 1881 bought his present farm of 160 acres. He has forty acres under cultivation, and is doing well. He is a Democrat, and he and wife belong to the Christian Church.

Elihu Q. Seaton is the son of George W. Seaton, a native of Alabama, who was born near Huntsville, Madison County, N. Ala., on June 13, 1820, moving when quite young with his parents to Panola County, Miss., where he grew to manhood. In 1841 he was united in marriage to Miss Lucinda Smart, also of Alabama origin, her birth occurring in Florence, Lauderdale County, April 9, 1820. When a young girl she accompanied her parents to Mississippi. George W. Seaton was by profession a farmer, but spent a greater part of his time in teaching school, being a man of superior education and refinement. He was an exemplary member of the Missionary Baptist Church, and took an active part in all church and charita-

124   **WHITE COUNTY, ARKANSAS - BIOGRAPHICAL AND HISTORICAL MEMOIRS**

* *

HISTORY OF ARKANSAS.

ble enterprises, particularly so in his later years. In his political views he sided with the Democrats, and held many offices of trust, discharging his duties in a highly commendable manner, and winning great credit for himself and family. He was a Mason in high standing, and recognized as a prominent and influential citizen. Mrs. Seaton, though a professor of religious faith from a very early age, was not connected with any church. She and her husband were descendants of some of the oldest and best families of Northern Alabama. Removing from Mississippi to Lonoke County, Ark., in 1878, they were residing there at the time of Mr. Seaton's death in September, 1880. Mrs. Seaton then went to Texas, but soon returned to her home in Lonoke County, where she now lives. To their union nine children were born, seven of whom survive: William (a farmer of Panola, Miss.), George S. N. (a planter of Sevier County, Ark.), Sarah S. T. (the wife of J. M. Smith, of Faulkner County, Ark.), Elihu Q. (the subject of this sketch), Albertine, J. (now Mrs. J. D. McPherson, of Collins County, Tex.), Lucy A. (wife of Elias Harrell, of Prairie County, Ark.), Georgiana A. (Mrs. Frank White, a prosperous farmer of Lonoke County, Ark.), Frances H. (widow of William Mason; now the wife of Andrew Lowe), B. A. (the wife of L. J. Pardue, and died in Lonoke County in 1887). Elihu Q. Seaton's educational advantages in youth were limited to the inferior schools of the period, but by constant reading and close observation, he has obtained a good practical education. He began for himself at the age of twenty years, first as a farmer, and then as a teacher in the public schools, where for eight years he instructed the young idea, and gained an enviable local reputation as an instructor. For the last three years Mr. Seaton has been engaged in the mercantile business, and is now located at Russell, Ark. He carries a general stock valued at $2,000, and has been quite successful in this business, and in the accumulation of property. He was married January 13, 1889, to Miss Frances A. Gamble, of White County, and a Kentuckian by birth. To this marriage one child has been born, Benjamin A., on October 11, 1889. Mr. and Mrs. Seaton are mem-

bers of the Cumberland Presbyterian Church, to which they give their support. In all worthy enterprises Mr. Seaton is a leader, not a follower, and has accomplished, by his progressive spirit, many things that might otherwise still be in an embryo state. He is a conservative Democrat, and a member in high standing of the Masonic order. In 1888 he received an appointment as notary public for a term of four years.

Andrew C. Shoffner, M. D., deserves honorable mention as one of the successful practitioners of the healing art in White County, and since 1876 has been actively engaged in alleviating the sufferings of the sick and afflicted, his services being in demand among the best people of the county. He was born in Tennessee, in 1830, and is a son of Martin and Jane C. (Johnson) Shoffner, and grandson of John and Christenia Shoffner. Martin Shoffner was born in North Carolina, in 1806, and inherited German blood from his parents. He was married in 1828, and the children born to his union are as follows: Andrew C., Mary A. (Mrs. Johnson, living in Tennessee), Minerva A. (Mrs. Powell, now deceased), James H. (a resident of Mississippi), Elizabeth J. (Mrs. Howard, living in Mississippi), Susan A. (Mrs. Vick, also a resident of Mississippi), John F. (who was killed in the battle of Chickamauga), Josephine (Mrs. Curl, of Mississippi) and Francis M. (living in De Soto County, Miss.). Martin Shoffner followed the occupation of farming all his life, and spent his declining years in Marshall County, Miss., his death occurring there in 1858, his wife's death having occurred in 1851, both being members of the Cumberland Presbyterian Church. Dr. Shoffner, our subject, spent his youth on a farm in Tennessee, and completed his education at a private school. In 1862 he enlisted in the army, but was shortly after discharged on account of ill health and returned home. He was married in 1851 to Miss Julia A. Vick, a daughter of Ransom and Elizabeth Vick, the former of Virginia, and the latter a Tennesseean. Of a family of thirteen children born to the Doctor and his wife, only one is dead. Those living are: Robert L. (who married Sallie A. Walker, and resides in the county), Cordelia (Mrs.

WHITE COUNTY.

Smith, a resident of Marshall County, Miss.), Jennie (Mrs. Walker, is a resident of Dog Wood Township), Ella (Mrs. Davis, lives in Argenta, Ark.), James M. (lives at Searcy), Laura (Mrs. Beaver, is a resident of Arkansas), Augustus F., Lucy E., Henrietta, Idonia and Addie, all single. In 1866 Dr. Shoffner came to White County, Ark., settling in Searcy Valley, but since 1874 has been a resident of Dog Wood Township, where he has a farm of 100 acres, with fifty under cultivation. He devotes his time to the practice of his profession, and leaves his sons to manage the farm. He is ever interested in all good works, and gives liberally of his means in the support of schools and churches. Politically he is a Republican, and socially, belongs to the Masonic fraternity.

Thomas Smith. Personal popularity results largely from the industry, perseverance and close attention to business which a person displays in the management of any particular branch of trade, and in the case of Mr. Smith this is most certainly true, for he has adhered closely to farming and the stock industry, and helped in so many ways to advance all worthy interests in the community, that he has won the admiration and respect of all. His parents, Matthew and Mary (McCue) Smith were born in Killeshandra Village, Ireland, and to them were given three sons: Peter (born in 1821), Thomas (born in 1822), and James (born in 1824). The father died in 1824, and his widow resided in her native county until 1831, when she with her family moved to the city of Balbriggean, County Dublin, and there lived until her demise in 1840. Seven years later Thomas Smith and his brother James emigrated to America, the elder brother, Peter, having emigrated to this country in 1845. They landed at New York, May 27, 1847, and after a few days' stay in that city they joined their brother Peter in Delaware County, Penn., he having secured work with a farmer, S. T. Walker. They were also fortunate enough to find employment, and from the time they reached Pennsylvania until three and one-half years later Thomas was engaged in farm labor. In 1850 he, with his brother James, removed to Arkansas and settled in Faulkner County (then Conway County), each be-

coming the owner of 160 acres of land, both of which are in the possession of our subject at the present time. In 1850 he was married in the Catholic Church of Old Chester, Penn., to Miss Mary Ann Collins, a native of County Donegal, Ireland, and after their removal to Arkansas they both set energetically to work to clear and improve their farm, which was a heavy timber tract inhabited by all kinds of wild game. Their capital consisted of a pair of willing hands and a determination to succeed no matter what the obstacles might be, and to say that they had been successful would not do the subject justice. The year following their arrival in the State they built them a substantial log-house, and the first letter they received after settling in their new home, was from a friend in Pennsylvania, Mr. Smith walking to the nearest postoffice, a distance of twenty miles to receive it. He has cleared 150 acres of his farm from timber, and now has some of the most fertile land of which the county can boast. Having experienced the many hardships and privations which beset a man in his journey through life, Mr. Smith never turns the more unfortunate from his door, but is always generous, charitable and hospitable. The following family was born to him and his first wife: James (born August 19, 1851), Mary Ann (born in 1853), Sarah (born in 1855), Susan (born in 1856), Thomas (born in 1857) and Edward (born in 1859), all of whom died in infancy, the mother also dying August 1, 1859. In 1861 Mr. Smith espoused his second wife, Miss Elizabeth Hogans, of Arkansas, but her death occurred in 1870, in giving birth to her son, Henry. The children of this union are: William (born January 20, 1862), Alice (born May 9, 1864), Thomas (born October 24, 1865), Hugh (born April 17, 1867), Edward (born April 27, 1867), Robert (born December 9, 1869) and Henry (born January 27, 1870). On January 18, 1871, Mr. Smith's union with his third wife took place, her name being Elizabeth Wilson. Mr. Smith and wife are members of the Catholic Church, and all their children have been baptized in that faith, but were never confirmed. Mr. Smith is a Democrat, and a member of the Agricultural Wheel No. 99.

Joel W. Smith, a prominent farmer of White

HISTORY OF ARKANSAS.

County, is a son of Alexander and Sarah (Follwell) Smith, natives of Virginia. Alexander Smith was married in 1816 or 1817, and had a family of five children: Catharine, William H., James M., Sarah A. and Joel W., our subject. Mrs. Smith died in 1828, in Alabama. Mr. Smith then married his second wife in 1830, her maiden name being Miss Margaret Ellis. They were the parents of nine children: Aaron G. (deceased), Keziah, Alyrah, Mary, George, Margery, Lottie, Victoria and Martha. Joel W. Smith was born in Limestone County, Ala., in 1826. He was reared on a farm, and received but little education, his father dying in 1852. Upon arriving at maturity he was married on November 25, 1845, to Elizabeth F. Lewis, also of Alabama nativity, and a child of William and Jane (Rogers) Lewis, being the second daughter in a family of ten children. Her birth occurred May 8, 1820. Mr. and Mrs. Smith are the parents of six children: Henrietta (Redus), John A., Edward F., Margaret J. (Yearby) Sarah F. (Alford), and Harriet A. (Sowel). Mr. Smith came to Arkansas in 1858, and settled in White County, whence he enlisted in 1862 in Company B of the Arkansas Infantry, under Capt. Critz, Col. Schofer being in command of the regiment. He was taken sick and received his discharge and returned home, but re-enlisted in 1863, under Col. Geyn. He was in the battle of Helena, and was taken prisoner and carried to Little Rock, later to Walton, Ill., and afterward to Rock Island, Ill., being confined until the close of the war. Mr. Smith has a farm of 300 acres, with over 200 under cultivation. He is a member of Centre Hill Lodge No. 114, A. F. & A. M., and himself and wife belong to the Baptist Church. Mr. Smith is a strong Democrat, and has been school director for the past six years, taking great interest in the work.

Frank W. Smith, Searcy, Ark. Another pioneer settler of the county, and a much-respected citizen is the above-mentioned gentleman who came to White County, Ark., in 1853, from Mississippi. He was born in Fayette County, Miss., in 1833, and was the eighth in a family of nine children, the result of the union of John and Rebecca Smith, natives of Tennessee. The father was a planter, and in connection carried on merchandising at Oxford, Fayette County, Miss. In 1830 he moved to Benton County, Ark., remaining there a short time, and then returned to Mississippi in 1831, making that his home until his death which occurred at Oxford, Miss., in 1844. His widow survived him many years, came to White County in 1853, and there her death occurred in the fall of that year. Their family consisted of the following children: Harrison (married, and a farmer of De Soto County, Miss.), Benjamin (married, and resides in Gray Township), Margaret (wife of William Graves, of Howard County, Ark.), Catherine (died in White County, Ark., in 1889; she was the wife of John Boggs), Thomas (married and resides in Gray Township), William (died in White County in 1871), John (married and resides in Gray Township), Frank W. and Mary (wife of James Neavill; she died in 1858). The father of these children participated in the War of 1812. Frank W. Smith's youth in growing up was passed in attending to duties about the home place, and in the subscription schools of Mississippi. He commenced farming for himself in White County, Ark., at the age of twenty-one, and in 1855, in partnership with his brother, John, purchased 160 acres of land which he improved. Later the brothers separated, each doing for himself. F. W. Smith has erected all the buildings, and has added to his farm from time to time until he is now the owner of 400 acres, with 150 under cultivation, and 100 acres or more in pasture. He does mixed farming, raises corn and cotton and also considerable horses and cattle, and is one of the wide-awake farmers of the county. He enlisted in the army at Searcy in 1862, and for twelve months was in Capt. Davis' company, Gen. McRae's regiment. He participated in several skirmishes and later went into the State troops, where he remained but a short time. At the close of the service he returned to the farm. He was married in White County in 1855 to Miss Mary L. Neavill, a native of Alabama, and the daughter of Elihu and Margaret (Jones) Neavill, natives of Alabama. Mr. and Mrs. Neavill came to White County in 1844, settled in Gray Township, and he was one

WHITE COUNTY, ARKANSAS - BIOGRAPHICAL AND HISTORICAL MEMOIRS 127

****

WHITE COUNTY.

of the influential men of the county, being treasurer of the same one term. His death occurred in 1852 and the mother's in 1888. After marriage Mr. Smith settled where he now resides, and there he has since remained. Although not very active in politics he votes with the Democratic party; is a member of the Agricultural Wheel, of which organization he was steward, and he and wife are members of the Methodist Episcopal Church, South. To this union two living children were born: Sarah and Kirby (of which Kirby is married and resides with his father). Mr. Smith came to this county when all was wild and unbroken, and when game was in abundance. Now fine farms cover the country, and everything is in a prosperous condition. He is practically a self-made man; having started with little he is now very comfortably fixed, and can pass the remainder of his life in ease.

William Smith. Faulkner County is rapidly coming into a position as one of the foremost stock counties in the State, and it is but uttering a plain fact to say that to a few men in this community is due the credit for advancing stock interests here and establishing a reputation in this department which is bound to stand for years. Mr. Smith has had not a little to do toward developing the stock matters of this region and if for no other account he is accorded a worthy place in this volume. His parents, Ebenezer and Permelia (Murphy) Smith, were married in Tennessee, in 1823, but the former was born in the State of Mississippi. He was left fatherless when a small boy, his paternal parent dying in Georgia, after which his widowed mother moved with her family to Tennessee, where she died, having borne a family of five sons and two daughters. Ebenezer Smith and his wife became the parents of eleven children, who grew to manhood and womanhood, seven of whom were born in Mississippi and four in Tennessee. After the mother's death in 1855, Mr. Smith married again, his second wife being Miss Elizabeth Chambers of Mississippi, their marriage being solemnized in 1856; six children were born to this union. William Smith, our subject, was reared to a farm life and received a limited education in the subscription

schools of Tishomingo County, Miss. He grew to manhood, and on April 26, 1856, was married there to Miss Melvina Dotson, the wedding taking place at the home of the bride's parents, William and Nancy (Bales) Dotson. Victoria A., their eldest child, was born March 26, 1859, and June 14, 1874, became the wife of D. A. Thornton, a farmer who resides in Faulkner County, by whom she has four children. Sidney, the youngest child, was born August 15, 1860, and died August 24, 1864. September 15, 1886, witnessed the celebration of Mr. Smith's second marriage to Mrs. Mattie E. (Tucker) Beasley, daughter of LaFayette and Jane (Knight) Tucker, who were born in Mississippi, the father being of Irish origin. At the age of twenty-one years, Mr. Smith's father made him overseer of his plantation, and for his services gave him a one-fourth interest in the profits of the farm, and at the end of one year he had accumulated sufficient property to enable him to purchase eighty acres of land, all of which was heavily covered with timber. During the six following years, he cleared thirty acres of this tract, and erected thereon a dwelling-house, and the necessary outbuildings. Owing to the turbulent state of affairs during the war he, with his wife and children and a few articles of household furniture, removed by wagon to near Union City, Ky., making their home there for about ten months, and raising one crop. They next settled in Tennessee, near Island No. 10, and here Mr. Smith left his family and went to Paducah, Ky., where he enlisted in the First Kentucky Calvary, Confederate States Army, and served six months or until the close of the war. He then returned to his family and soon after purchased 100 acres of wild land in Gibson County, and this he resided on and continued to improve until 1870, since which time he has been a resident of the State of Arkansas. The farm upon which he is now residing consists of 243 acres, the original purchase consisting of 160 acres. Only a small portion of this land had been cleared, but at the present writing seventy acres are in high state of cultivation, the soil being well adapted to the raising of cotton, corn, oats and all varieties of vegetables. Both Mr. Smith and his wife are professors of religion, the

HISTORY OF ARKANSAS.

former a member of the Missionary Baptist Church, and the latter of the Methodist Episcopal Church. Mr. Smith is a supporter and member of the Agricultural Wheel, belonging to El Paso Lodge No. 158, is a man of enterprise and progress, and being hospitable and generous is a valuable addition to the county of his adoption.

Abner F. Smith received his education at the high schools of Powhattan County, Va., but left his implements of study and literary pursuits in May, 1861, to take up the instruments of war. Joining the Confederate army he entered the Powhattan Rifle Company and was in the battles of Prairie Grove, Cotton Plant, Helena, Little Rock, Jenkins' Ferry, and a number of skirmishes. After the war Mr. Smith went to Grand Glaize, Ark., and commenced farming, and in 1870 engaged in the grocery business in partnership with John Thurman. Two years later he started alone, but the credit business proved unprofitable to him and he embarked in the timber business, being engaged in getting out ties for the Iron Mountain Railroad. In 1886 he opened up a store in Bald Knob, and is now enjoying a large and lucrative patronage. Abner T. Smith was born in Chesterfield County, Va., in 1843, being the son of William S. and Elizabeth (Edwards) Smith. The former was a railroad contractor and also contractor for public works while in Virginia, but after his removal to Arkansas carried on merchandising at Grand Glaize. He was a Whig in politics, and belonged to the Masonic order at the time of his death, which occurred in 1864, when forty-eight years old. Mrs. Smith has long been a member of the Methodist Episcopal Church, South. She was born in 1815 and is still living in Bald Knob, Ark. In this family were six children, only two of whom are living: Abner F. (our subject) and Alonzo (who is in business with his brother). Mr. Smith was married February 22, 1867, to Miss Fanny Heard, daughter of Baily E. Heard. She died in 1873, leaving three children, only one of whom is living: William B., a student at Searcy College, and who intends entering a law school after graduating at Searcy. June 24, 1874, Mr. Smith married Lucy C. Patrick, who died April 20, 1871, leaving one child:

Edward A. He was married to his present wife, Adeline Allen, March 4, 1876. Mrs. Smith is a daughter of Dr. John Allen, of White County, and is the mother of one daughter: Mamie. Mr. Smith is a strong Democrat and belongs to the Masonic order, also holding membership in the Methodist Episcopal Church, South. While in Jackson County he was appointed justice of the peace by Gov. Garland.

Dr. J. A. Snipes, Searcy, Ark. The career of Dr. Snipes as a physician and surgeon has long been well and favorably known to the many who have tested his healing ability, and his popularity as a druggist is firmly established. He owns a good two-story brick business building, 100x30 feet, carries a full line of drugs, paints, oils, etc., and does a thriving trade. He first engaged in the drug business in the early part of 1885, and since then he has been thus employed. He was born in Orange County, N. C., in 1825, was the third in a family of seven children born to E. P. and Nancy (Burnett) Snipes, natives of North Carolina, the father born in 1800 and the mother in 1801, and in Orange and Chatham Counties, respectively. The parents were married in Chatham County, N. C., in 1821, and the father followed agricultural pursuits there until 1845, when he moved to Madison County, W. Tenn. After residing there until 1854 he moved to Haywood County, Tenn., purchased an improved farm, and still owns 560 acres in Jefferson County, with 350 acres under cultivation. The father is still living, and makes his home with the Doctor. He has been a very industrious, energetic man, was magistrate of several counties, and has been a member of the Methodist Episcopal Church for sixty years. The mother died in Madison County, Tenn., in 1857. The paternal grandparents, Thomas and Martha (Williams) Snipes, were natives of the Old Dominion, and moved to North Carolina when children. The maternal grandparents, Isaiah and Jane (Herndon) Burnett, were natives of North Carolina, and always made that State their home. They died many years ago. The seven children born to E. P. and Nancy (Burnett) Snipes are named as follows: Walter A. (married, and in 1856 came to

WHITE COUNTY.

White County, locating in Marion Township, followed farming, and there remained until 1857, when he went to Jefferson County, and there continued his former occupation; his death occurred in the winter of 1884–85, and he left one child, William E., who is a machinist and resides in Jefferson County, Ark.), Eliza J. (widow of C. B. Horton, resides at the Doctor's), Dr. J. A., Farrington B. (married, resides in Madison County, Tenn., and is a lawyer and farmer), Julia A. (now Mrs. Allen, of Brownsville, Tenn.), Martha M., (now Mrs. J. T. Key, of Searcy, Ark.) and Thomas J. (who enlisted in the army in Jefferson County in 1862, and died of smallpox in Mississippi two years later). Dr. J. A. Snipes was reared to farm labor and was favored with such educational advantages as the district schools of that day afforded. After coming to Tennessee he engaged in teaching and also read medicine for about three years, subsequently attending that far-famed institution, the Jeffersonian Medical College, at Philadelphia, Penn., in 1848. In 1851 he began the practice of medicine in Dyer County, Tenn., thence in 1852 went to Madison County, Tenn., and finally in 1854 came to White County, locating in Searcy, and has practiced his profession in White County continuously for thirty-five years. He is one of the earliest practitioners and is one in whom all have confidence. Aside from his practice he has also been engaged in farming in this and Marion Townships. He resided in the last-named township from 1856 to 1868, and opened up a large farm in Big Creek. He has resided in Searcy since 1868, with the exception of three years, when he resided on his farm in the suburbs. Dr. Snipes was married in Lauderdale County, Tenn., in December, 1853, to Miss Elizabeth J. Murphy, a native of Halifax County, Va., and the daughter of Thomas and Lucy (Coleman) Murphy, natives of Virginia. Her father died in that State, and the mother afterward immigrated to Tennessee (1842), thence to Searcy in 1854, and made her home with the Doctor until 1867, when she was killed in the memorable cyclone of May 27 of that year. By this union five children were born, three now living: Anna B. (now Mrs. W. H. Lightle, of Searcy),

Minnie (now Mrs. John T. Hicks, of Searcy) and Emmett (a pharmacist in the drug store of the Doctor). Mrs. Lightle has four children: Minnie H., Edward J., Bettie K. and Julian. Mrs. Hicks has two children: Everett B. and Willie Burnett. The Doctor's deceased children are named as follows: Everett (died, in 1876, at the age of eighteen years, and Camillus (died, in 1874, at the age of fourteen years). Socially, the Doctor is a member of Searcy Lodge No. 49, A. F. & A. M., and is a member of Tillman Chapter No. 19, R. A. M. He is also a member of the I. O. O. F. Lodge at Searcy. Dr. Snipes has seen the full growth and development of Searcy during the many years of his residence here. What is now Mrs. Chambless' hotel was the court house at that time, and many and great have been the changes. He took an active interest in working for the location of the State University that was finally located at Fayetteville, but union not existing in Searcy, that city failed to get it. The Doctor, his wife and all the family are members of the Methodist Episcopal Church. Dr. Snipes has always been deeply interested in educational matters.

Omal H. Stanley is the eldest son of a family of eight children born to John H. and Elizabeth (Yancey) Stanley. John H. Stanley, born in about 1800, was a native of Halifax, Va., and a carriage-maker by trade, his marriage occurring in 1829. He afterward moved to Jackson, Tenn., where he went into the carriage business, and there he died in 1848, his wife following in 1873. O. H. Stanley learned the carriage-maker's trade of his father when a boy, and upon reaching manhood was married, in Jackson, Tenn., in 1852, to Jane M. Lauffort, originally from Madison County, Tenn., born in 1835. Her father held the office of county clerk in 1848 and for four years following, and in 1852 was elected county treasurer, occupying this official position for two years. In 1856 he moved to Arkansas, where he died in 1862. After his marriage, Mr. Stanley started a carriage shop at Jackson, remaining until 1860, when he removed to Austin, Prairie County, Ark., and carried on business there until 1864, excepting one year, while serving in the Confederate army, in Glenn's

HISTORY OF ARKANSAS.

regiment; he was in the quartermaster's department. Upon receiving his discharge, in 1864, he went to Perry County, Ill., but thirteen months after, or in September, 1865, came back to Arkansas, and settled at Devall's Bluff, where he took charge of the Government shops. Four years later he started a shop in Searcy, tarried two years, then moved to a farm on Dead River, where he remained four years, and in 1874 came to Cane Township, White County, purchasing 160 acres of wild land. This he has partially cleared (about sixty acres), and on it has erected a good house and other buildings. Mr. and Mrs. Stanley were the parents of ten children, nine of whom are still living: Edgar H. (deceased), James R., Jason C., Mary E. (now Mrs. Smith), Elanora, Willie B., Oscar L., Gertrude, Emma L. and Charles W. Mr. and Mrs. Stanley are members of the Methodist Episcopal Church, Mr. Stanley being chairman of the board of trustees. He is a strong Democrat in his political preferences, and takes an active interest in all movements for the good of the community.

J. W. Starkey is a representative and wide-awake farmer of White County, Ark., having been a resident in this county since 1870. He first saw the light of this world in Tuscaloosa County, Ala., in 1853, and was the second in a family of twelve children given to John B. and Nancy (Weaver) Starkey, the former born in North Carolina and the latter in Alabama. They married in the latter State in 1851, and after clearing and living on a farm there until 1866, he immigrated to Itawamba County, Miss. Four years later he settled in White County, Ark.; here he purchased a partially improved farm of 160 acres, and now has 100 under the plow. In 1862 he enlisted from Alabama in the Confederate army, and served three years. His death occurred in White County, January 14, 1889, and at the time of his demise was counted one of the members of the Wheel organization. His wife still lives, and resides on the old homestead. Their children are: Martha A. (Mrs. Weeks), John W. (the subject of this sketch), D. A. (a resident of the county), E. J. (Mrs. Worthen, of Kentucky Township), N. B. (Mrs. Troxell, of

the same township), M. F. (Mrs. Rissell, of the same township), R. C., Ellen, George Robert, Robert Bruce, William Bedford and Ollie B. John W. Starkey learned the carpenter's trade in his youth, in addition to becoming familiar with farm work, and received the greater part of his education in the schools of Mississippi. At the age of twenty-four he began farming for himself, and was married to Mattie Jones, a native of Georgia, purchasing soon after a timber tract of eighty acres, and now has fifty-five cleared and improved. He gives considerable attention to raising stock, and is succeeding in his enterprises. In politics he is a Democrat, and he, with his wife, worships with the Missionary Baptist Church, to which they belong. They are the parents of five children: John T., Alwilda, Nancy Jane, Grover Cleveland and Bersada. Mrs. Starkey is a daughter of Thomas F. and Nancy (Kilpatrick) Jones, who were native Georgians, the father a boot and shoe maker by trade. In 1870 he settled in Brownsville, Prairie County, Ark., but a year later removed to Searcy, White County, and, in 1885, to Texas, where he now resides. His wife died in Searcy, in 1873.

Hon. Lee Thomas Stewart, a man who has held public office every year since he was twenty-one years old, of Beebe, Ark., was born in the county in which he is now residing on April 16, 1863, and is one of seven surviving members of a family of thirteen children born to Robert M. and Catherine (Walker) Stewart, from whom he inherits Scotch-Irish blood. The father and mother were born in North and South Carolina, respectively, and were among the early immigrants to White County, Ark., settling about ten miles from Searcy on the Searcy and Des Arc road. Here Mr. Stewart improved a farm and at the time of his death, in 1868, owned considerable land, of which seventy-five acres were under the plow. When the war broke out he owned fifteen slaves, but of course they were all lost during the Rebellion. R. M. Stewart moved to this State in 1856. He was a member of the Presbyterian Church, and a Mason, standing high in this order and was buried with Masonic honors. He also helped build the first church and school-house in the southern part of White County. The

WHITE COUNTY.

following are the members of his family: Joseph (was born in 1842 and died during the war while in the hospital in Little Rock), Adaline (who was born in 1844 and became the wife of Isaac Chrisman, a farmer residing on the Arkansas River in Lonoke County), J. G. (who was born in 1846, and wedded Mrs. Nancy Carter *nee* Myrick; he is a school-teacher and farmer near Pine Bluff), Bettie (born in 1848, became the wife of Edward Barnes, a farmer and stockman of Texas, and died in November, 1882), D. M. (was born in 1850, he being also a farmer and stock trader, and he was married to Miss Allie Allen), Susan (was born in 1852 and died at the age of twenty-two), Robert G. (was born in 1854, and by occupation is a druggist being now a resident of the town of Dayton, Ark.), W. C. (was born in 1856, and he is a practitioner of dentistry at Dripping Springs, Tex.), Mollie (was born in 1858, and is the wife of Dr. J. D. Harris, of Butlersville, Ark.), Dora and Cora (were born in 1860, and are both deceased, Cora dying in infancy and Dora at the age of twelve years). The next in order of birth is Lee Thomas (our subject) and Rena (who was born in 1865, and died in infancy). Lee Thomas Stewart remained on his father's farm until about fifteen years of age and received the greater portion of his early education in the schools of Searcy, being an attendant at the high school for two years. After returning to the neighborhood in which he was reared he taught a subscription school for three months and the three following years worked as a tiller of the soil. After coming to Beebe he clerked in the general mercantile establishment of D. C. Harris for about eighteen months and then devoted the entire year of 1883 to the study of telegraphy, after which he went to Hoxie, on the Iron Mountain Railroad, where he held the position of telegraph operator for some time. In the winter of 1883 he returned to Beebe and resumed clerking in Dr. Harris' store, but the following year engaged in the same business with T. S. Neylon. This connection lasted for two years, then Mr. Stewart sold his interest and the next six months acted as book-keeper for J. M. Liles, after which he spent six months in the study of law. In Jan-

uary, 1888, he began clerking in the drug store of Dr. Ennis, but in the spring of 1889 was elected to the office of mayor of Beebe over his competitor, a popular gentleman, and is at the present time the incumbent of that office. He was elected by the Democrats to the position of alderman when only twenty-one years of age and served two terms. Mr. Stewart is progressive in his views, liberal in his opinions and labors and contributes willingly to the advancement of the county and State and is an ardent advocate of education. Though thoroughly democratic in his views politically, he respects very highly the opinions of others who differ with him in matters generally.

A. L. Stowell was born, reared and educated in Bureau County, Ill., the former event taking place August 8, 1841. Just after commencing his apprenticeship as a carpenter, the war broke out and Mr. Stowell, full of youthful enthusiasm, joined his destines with the cause of the Union, enlisting in Company B, First Battalion of Yeats' Sharpshooters, and served in Mississippi, being present at the battles of Corinth and New Madrid (Mo.). He was stationed one year at Glendale, near Corinth, after which his regiment returned to Illinois and was reorganized, or rather veteranized, into the Sixty-fourth Illinois Infantry. While serving in this capacity he was with Sherman on his march to the sea, and was at the siege of Atlanta, where he was under fire for sixty days. He carried his knapsack to Washington, D. C., and was present at the grand review. He was as well acquainted with the face of Gen. Sherman as that of a brother, and when the latter came to part with his command, on July 4, 1865, he made the division that Mr. Stowell was in a special speech and wept like a child, so warm a place had these veterans gained in his heart. The company was mustered out of service at Louisville, Ky., and was disbanded at Chicago, Ill., and for three years Mr. Stowell was president of the reunion of this command. He is now vice-commander of his post of G. A. R. After his return from the war he resumed the carpenter's trade, which had been so suddenly broken off, and continued this occupation at McComb, Ill., until 1883, at which time he settled in Beebe,

HISTORY OF ARKANSAS.

Ark., and engaged in fruit growing, making strawberries a specialty. In order to save his fruit he commenced making his strawberries into wine, some five years since, and in this enterprise has established a remunerative business. Mr. Stowell is a member of the I. O. O. F. and in his political views is a Republican. He was married March 19, 1867, to Miss Sarah B. Kissinger, who was born in Pennsylvania in 1843. The earliest facts known in the history of the Stowell family is that they were originally Normans, and removed to England with William the Conqueror, and were there knighted. Two brothers came from that country to the United States, one settling in California and the other in the eastern part of the United States, and all the Stowells in this country are their descendants. The parents of our biographical subject are Joshua and Amanda (Harrington) Stowell, the father being born in the Green Mountains of Vermont. He was a harness-maker by trade, and after residing for many years in Princeton, Ill., he removed to Chicago, where he is now living. The Harringtons were of German descent.

Henry Beverly Strange is a general merchant and farmer, of Beebe, Ark., and is well known throughout the county as a business man of honor and integrity. Like many other prominent men of the county he is a Tennesseean, his birth having occurred in Maury County, September 29, 1830, where he was also reared and educated. At the age of twenty years he started out in life for himself as a book agent, and for two years sold "The Southern Family Physician" and other books, meeting with signal success in this undertaking. In 1859 he came to White County, Ark., and engaged in business at Old Stony Point until 1872, when the Iron Mountain Railway reached Beebe, and in order to get a station at this point Mr. Strange built a depot and gave it to the company. He then moved his goods here and has since done a prosperous general merchandise business, being particularly successful in house furnishing. He has the largest business of any firm in the town, and his residence property is the finest in the place. He also has a store at Ward which nets a good income. He was first married in 1859 to

Miss E. Ward, a native of North Carolina and a daughter of Whitman Ward, who was one of the prosperous farmers of Tennessee. Mrs. Strange died in 1870, leaving one child, Florence, wife of John Walker, five other children she bore having died in infancy. Mr. Strange married Sallie Apple in 1872, she having come from North Carolina to Arkansas at an early date, and their union resulted in the birth of three children, two of whom are living: Hubert (a youth of fourteen) and Vida (about sixteen years of age). Mrs. Strange is a member of the Methodist Episcopal Church, South, and he belongs to Beebe Lodge No. 145, A. F. & A. M., and also to the K. of H. and the A. L. of H. He is vice-president of the American Building, Loan & Savings Association, and is one of the public-spirited men of Beebe and takes an interest in all movements designed for the public good. He is a son of Beverly and Susanna (Martin) Strange, who were Virginians, and removed from that State to Tennessee shortly after marriage, and there engaged in farming. At the time of their deaths both were worthy members of the Methodist Episcopal Church, South.

William H. Strayhorn is a worthy descendant of Gilbert Strayhorn, who was a native of North Carolina, and was engaged in farming all his life. He died about 1835, having been the father of six children: John D., William James, J. K., Margaret and Rebecca. John D., the eldest, was born in Tennessee, in 1800, and was also a farmer by occupation. He married in 1829, Mary A. Stevenson, a Tennesseean by birth, and a daughter of Henry and Ann (Robinson) Stevenson. John D. Strayhorn was familiarly called major on account of being, as a general thing, the commanding officer on celebration days. He was a member of the Old School Presbyterian Church. To himself and wife only one child, a son, William H., was born. William H. Strayhorn first made his appearance upon the scenes of this world in Tennessee, in 1833. He moved to Arkansas, in 1850, with his grandfather Stevenson, who settled in White County; his father died and his mother marrying the second time, in 1840, W. R. Fortner. Mr. Strayhorn, in 1854, took for his wife Mary J. Burket,

WHITE COUNTY.

daughter of William and Rachel (Hughs) Burket, natives of Tennessee, who moved to White County, Ark., in 1848. They have become the parents of eleven children (two of whom are deceased): Josiah, William H., John D., Samuel W., Alexander, Poney, Benjamin, Mary A., Rachel E., Elvira (deceased) and Elizabeth (deceased). Mr. and Mrs. Strayhorn are members of the Cumberland Presbyterian Church. The former settled on the farm upon which he now resides, July 14, 1856, having a place of 230 acres, 150 being under cultivation. He is a strong Democrat, and although not taking an active part in politics he has held the office of justice of the peace for two years, Mr. Strayhorn says he can raise any crop here that can be grown at all, and thinks Arkansas is *the* State of the Union.

Alfred B. Sutton's war experience is perhaps similar to that of many other soldiers, mentioned in this volume, but they are all interesting, and give the present generation some idea of the hardships and perils endured by the gallant and brave boys, thousands of whom now fill an unknown grave. In 1861 Alfred Sutton entered the Confederate service, and fought under Col. McCarver. His first serious engagement was at the battle of Corinth, Miss., from which he escaped serious injury. He was captured at Vicksburg, Miss., and taken to Indianapolis, where he remained for three months, then being removed to Port Delaware, and from there to Point Lookout on the Chesapeake Bay. In the latter place he was incarcerated for nine months and nine days, receiving his parole in December, 1864. He was in several engagements and skirmishes, but escaped serious wounds. After receiving his parole he returned to Camden to his command, and in 1865 was discharged, and at once returned to his home, resuming his former occupation of farming, which he has followed principally ever since. His father, Jesse Sutton, was born in Wilson County, Tenn., in 1817, where he received his education, there marrying Elizabeth Hight, of the same State. Their union was blessed with a family of nine children, of whom Alfred B. is the second, his birth occurring in 1840. He was a farmer by oc-

cupation, owning 500 acres of excellent land at the time of his removal from Tennessee to Arkansas, in 1848. He located in Cleburne County, and there resided until his death in 1887, his wife having preceded him a few years. Mr. Sutton and his estimable companion were devout members of the Christian Church, and he was a man who took a great interest in all enterprises, especially those of an educational nature. Alfred B. received a common-school education in the schools of Arkansas, and in February of 1867 was united in marriage with Miss Sarah Bailey, daughter of Henry and Frances Bailey. To their union have been born a family of three children: Henry, Jesse L. and Nora L. Mr. Sutton is a prosperous farmer, and owns 160 acres in White County, and 200 acres in Cleburne County; of this amount 100 acres are in a high state of cultivation. He is Past Master of the Masonic lodge, and has represented that order in the Grand Lodge two different times, besides having held various other offices. He has served as school director for twelve years, and is a man respected and esteemed by the entire community.

Rev. J. M. Talkington, pastor of the Methodist Episcopal Church, South, at Searcy, took charge of the church at that place in December, 1888, but prior to that time, from 1885 to 1888, was presiding elder in the White River district, embracing about seven counties. He joined the White River Conference at Mount Zion in 1870, and was located in the Searcy circuit, consisting of several pastoral charges adjacent to Searcy and in White County. He remained on that work from 1871 to 1873, after which he received a call to West Point, and after remaining there some time, moved to the El Paso charge, where he was given the presiding eldership one year. He subsequently left the Searcy circuit, went to Lebanon circuit, then returned to El Paso circuit, thence to Helena district, then to the pastoral charge in Beebe in 1884, where he remained two years. From there he went to the Searcy district, remained there until 1888, and in that year received a call to the pastorate of Searcy Church. Mr. Talkington is a native of Jackson County, Ala.,

HISTORY OF ARKANSAS.

where his birth occurred in 1835, and was the oldest in a family of nine children, the result of the union of Andrew Jackson and Mary Ann (Isbell) Talkington, natives of Alabama. The father was a farmer by occupation, opened up a plantation and remained on the same until his death, which occurred in 1856. The mother's death occurred in 1889, at the advanced age of seventy-three years. The father was a soldier in the Florida War. Their children were named as follows: J. M. (the subject of this sketch), Henry F. (married and resides in Union Township), Jane (died in Lonoke County, Ark., in 1887), Elizabeth (died in 1857, in Alabama), Margaret (wife of Joseph Pace, of Alabama), William T. (died in Alabama, in 1857), John (married, and is farming in Alabama), Vincent (died in 1855, in Alabama) and Mary S. (who died in Alabama, in 1855). Rev. J. M. Talkington was educated in the schools of Jackson County, Ala., and came to White County, Ark., at the age of nineteen, where he engaged as clerk for Isbell & Co., general merchants, and remained with them some time. In 1855 he engaged in teaching in Searcy, and followed this profession in White County for ten years. He was married in that county in 1856 to Miss Sarah A. Wright, a native of Independence County, Ark., and the fruits of this union have been eight children: Mary Ann (now Mrs. Arnold, in Gray Township), Julia (now Mrs. Sherrod, resides in Gray Township), Pearl Josephine, Virginia, James M., William Pierce, Cora Ann and John Wesley. While teaching school Mr. Talkington was also engaged in agricultural pursuits, and in 1867 was licensed to preach. From that date up to 1870 he did local work, and in 1877 he purchased a partly improved farm of 170 acres. This he has since improved, and has ninety acres under cultivation, with forty-five acres in fruit. He is deeply interested in horticulture, and now has one of the best fruit farms in the county, raising all variety of fruit that does well in this climate. Mr. Talkington was made a Mason in Searcy Lodge No. 49, A. F. & A. M.; is also a Mason of Tillman Chapter No. 19, R. A. M. In his pastoral work Mr. Talkington has organized many churches in the county,

and has organized some of the principal churches in this and adjoining counties. He has seen a vast change in the county since living here, and the greatest is from a moral standpoint.

Andrew B. Tate, a prominent citizen of Gray Township, is a native of South Carolina, and was born in Chester District, March 21, 1840, being the son of Samuel and Mary J. (Collins) Tate. Samuel Tate was also of South Carolina origin, as was his wife; they were married in Chester District, and moved to Lincoln County, Tenn., in 1841, where the remainder of their lives were passed. They were members in good standing of the Presbyterian Church, and held in high regard by all who knew them. Andrew's grandfather came to America from the Emerald Isle, at the age of twenty-seven and located in Chester District, S. C., where he was recognized as an influential and enterprising citizen. Mrs. Tate's people came from England. To the union of Mr. and Mrs. Tate the following children were given them: William V., Andrew B. (the subject of this memoir), Agnes J., Sarah M., Robert J., Caroline and Tirzah A.; Lavenia G. and James L. (deceased). Samuel Tate died at the age of forty-nine, and his wife in 1866, at the age of sixty-three. The early days of Andrew B. Tate were spent in Lincoln County, Tenn., but when quite young began for himself as a farmer, which has been his principal avocation ever since. His home was in Lincoln County until 1877, when he decided that there was a better opening in Arkansas, to which place he came, locating in White County, and has never had cause to regret the change. He was married on February 6, 1879, to Miss Emma N. Wortham, a daughter of Young Wortham, and to their union two children have been born: Anna B. (born April 18, 1880) and Hettie B. (born April 26, 1885). Mr. and Mrs. Tate, in their religious sympathies, are with the Methodist Episcopal Church, South. Mr. Tate, in his political views is an uncompromising Democrat, and served in the late war, enlisting in the Confederate service in April, 1862, in Col. Stanton's regiment of Tennessee Infantry. On account of disability he was honorably discharged after three months' act-

WHITE COUNTY.

ive service. In social fraternities he is identified with the Masonic order.

A. Byron Tapscott, M. D., although a young man, is one of the leading physicians of West Point, and has a large practice, enjoying a reputation of which many older in the professional experience might well be proud. Dr. Tapscott is a native of Tennessee, and a son of Ira and Mary (Jones) Tapscott, natives of North Carolina and Tennessee, respectively. Ira Byron was also a physician, and a graduate of the Medical College of Richmond, Va. He was a surgeon in Forrest's cavalry, in the late war, and after that struggle practiced in Tennessee until 1872, when he removed to Arkansas, continued his professional duties at West Point. He was a strong Democrat, a member of the Methodist Episcopal Church, and also of the I. O. O. F., and died in January, 1887, at the age of fifty-one years. Mrs. Tapscott is still living in West Point, and is the mother of five children, all living: A. Byron (our subject), Charles V. (an attorney), Emma J., Mary G. and Samuel F. At the age of fifteen Byron Tapscott commenced the study of medicine under his father's instruction, and in 1887 and 1888 attended the Missouri Medical College, at St. Louis. After graduating, he returned to West Point and embarked upon a career as a physician, also opening up a drug store, which he continued until October, 1889. Then he sold out, and has since devoted his whole attention to his rapidly increasing practice. He is firmly Democratic in his preferences, and a member of the Methodist Episcopal Church, South.

Thomas P. Taylor is a prosperous agriculturist and fruit grower of White County, Ark., and was born in Carroll County, Tenn., being the only child of Hiram A. and E. A. (Moore) Taylor, the former a native of North Carolina, and one of a family of six children born to Peter Taylor and wife. In 1848 he moved to Tennessee, and was married there in 1852, his wife being a daughter of Wesley Moore, also of North Carolina. Hiram A. Taylor was a contractor by occupation, held the highest rank in the Masonic order, and he and his wife were members of the Methodist Episcopal Church. He died in Tennessee. Thomas P. Taylor has always resided on a farm, but since seven years of age has resided in White County, Ark., making his home with his mother, who died in 1878, being the wife of A. V. Van Meter. He received fair educational advantages, and in 1882 he was married to Miss Mattie Sharp, a daughter of T. H. Sharp of this State, who died at an early day, his wife's death occurring in 1880. After his marriage Mr. Taylor settled one and a half miles from Judsonia, and has 140 acres of his 700-acre farm under cultivation. He was at one time quite extensively engaged in the stock business, but now only raises enough for his own use. He has seen the county develop in a remarkable manner since his early location here, and has done his share in aiding in this development. He is independent in his political views, and votes for the man rather than the party. Mrs. Taylor is a member of the Methodist Episcopal Church, South, and by Mr. Taylor has become the mother of two children: Irma (who died at the age of three years) and a boy by the name of James.

W. J. H. Taylor is a prominent farmer and stock raiser in Coffey Township, and a son of Newton W. and Ellen (Hickman) Taylor, natives of Alabama and Tennessee, respectively. Newton W. Taylor was born in Alabama in 1820, and was married in 1846, subsequently engaging in farming. In 1860 he moved to White County, Ark., and bought a quarter section of land, on which he resided until his death, in about 1879 or 1880. W. J. H. Taylor came upon the stage of action in Tennessee in 1848. He was married in 1870 to Miss Jennie Madith, of White County, and to them an interesting family of six children has been given: Maggie, Emmett, Albie, Wesley, Pearl and Newton. Since his marriage Mr. Taylor has farmed several different places, but is now located in Coffey Township, whither he came in 1885. He has a farm of eighty acres, with about fifty acres under cultivation, and in connection with farming has operated a cotton-gin until recently. Mr. and Mrs. Taylor are members of the Methodist Episcopal Church, South. The former is a Democrat, and actively interested in schools, having long been school director of his district.

HISTORY OF ARKANSAS.

Manuel Teer is a representative citizen and a large tax payer of White County, owning over 1,000 acres of land, his fine home farm of 200 acres being under excellent cultivation. He enlisted in the Confederate army in 1862, and served throughout the war, taking part in Price's raid through Missouri from beginning to end. He was born in North Carolina on December 29, 1826, and was a son of Ludwick and Mary (Sheppard) Teer. The former's birth occurred in South Carolina in 1790; he was married in 1820, and died in his native State in 1858, a family of four children having blessed the union of himself and wife: Haywood S., Manuel, Francis E. and Susan J. (the widow of the late W. W. Horn). Manuel Teer came to Arkansas in 1857, and settled in White County, where he bought a farm. He was married in 1846 to Miss Martha J. Craig, of North Carolina origin, and a daughter of Abraham and Jane (Steel) Craig, who came to Arkansas in 1857, purchasing an improved farm of 160 acres in White County. Mr. Teer lost his esteemed wife on August 15, 1880. She had been a member of the Methodist Episcopal Church, South, since thirteen years of age. Mr. Teer is connected with the Masonic order, and is a highly respected citizen, having always taken a great interest in the improvement and prosperity of the county. He has been a liberal donator to all religious and charitable institutions during his residence here, keeping thoroughly apace with the progress of the times. Mr. Teer has now retired from active life, and as he has been an industrious, energetic farmer all his life, can now rest in the consciousness of a career well and usefully spent.

Prof. W. H. Tharp, president of Searcy College, Searcy, Ark. A glance at the lives of many representative men whose names appear in this volume will reveal sketches of some honored, influential citizens, but none more worthy or deserving of mention than Prof. W. H. Tharp. This gentleman was born in Fayette County, Tenn., on November 21, 1853, and was the eldest in a family of eight children, three now living, who blessed the union of Dr. W. H. and Susan Payne (Whitmore) Tharp, natives, respectively, of North Carolina and Tennessee. The father was a prominent physician and surgeon, was married in Fayette County, Tenn., and there died, in 1869. The mother died in 1874. She was cousin to Bishop Payne. Grandfather W. H. Tharp was one of the leading and deservedly popular men of Fayette County, Tenn., and was chairman of the county court for many years. He moved from North Carolina when quite a young man. Though young, he was very prominent in his native county, and was a member of the General Assembly of the State. He was, repeatedly, strongly urged to become a candidate for a similar position in his adopted State, but always declined. Prof. W. H. Tharp graduated at Macon Masonic College, in 1871, and, the same year, was in school at Lexington, Ky. In 1872 he entered the U. C. College, at Toronto, Can., and from this college was called in 1873, by the declining health of his mother, whose death, in 1874, made it necessary for him to take charge of the farm and look after his younger brothers, both minors. Here he remained till 1879. While residing on the farm he was, for three years, principal of the Union Hill Academy. In 1879 he was engaged as president of the Male College at Somerville, Tenn. At the end of his year's work he was elected president of Female College, at Somerville, Tenn., where he remained until 1883, and then came to Searcy, Ark. While occupied in teaching at Somerville, he had charge of a county paper called The Falcon, which became very popular throughout the county, but he sold his interest on coming to Searcy, in 1883. Prof. Tharp was married in Tennessee, in 1874, to Miss Lizzie Joe Cocke, a native of Fayette County, Tenn., and the daughter of Thomas R. and Laura (Winston) Cocke, also of Tennessee origin. Her father was a statute lawyer of fine ability, and was county judge for many years, never being defeated. His death occurred in 1886. The mother is still living and resides in Somerville, Tenn. Mrs. Tharp received her education in Somerville Female Institute and Columbia Institute. She is a member of the Ladies' State Central Committee, editor of the children's column of the Arkansas Baptist, and is a smooth and clear writer. She has always been

WHITE COUNTY.

a very valuable assistant to Prof. Tharp in his school work. For the past six years Prof. Tharp has given his time and energies to Searcy College, which he projected, and, together with Prof. Conger, founded in 1883. No institution in the State has more character for thorough work than Searcy College. Prof. Tharp is a man of progressive ideas, and has always taken a deep interest in educational matters. That his work and ability have gained recognition in the State of his adoption is evidenced by the fact that he is at present the president of both the State Teachers' Associations and the Arkansas Summer Normal School. He is also managing editor of the Arkansas Educational Journal, a live and progressive monthly. To his marriage were born two children: William J. and Kathleen. Prof. Tharp and wife are members of the Baptist Church.

J. C. C. Thomas has been from earliest boyhood familiar with the duties of farm work, and is now also extensively engaged in ginning cotton. He was born in Richmond County, N. C., in 1834, and in 1869 came to Arkansas and settled in Independence County, and after farming there one year, came to White County. He acquired a good education in his youth, and after attending the common schools of his native county, he entered Rockingham Academy, which he attended three years. After commencing the battle of life for himself, he removed to Louisiana in 1856, locating near Monroe, and there bought land. From this State he enlisted in the Confederate army the first year of the war, being a member of Company B, Fourth Louisiana Battalion, and served by re-enlistment until the close of the war, participating in the battles of Chattanooga, Missionary Ridge, Lookout Mountain and others. After his return home he spent two years in raising crops, then spent one year in Independence County, and has since resided in White County. He was married here in March, 1875, to Susan L. Watkins, a native of Alabama, and by her has four children living: Sarah A., Grover C., Carlyle and Clifton B. Although Mr. Thomas votes the Democrat ticket, he is not an active politician. His wife is a member of the Baptist Church, and he is a believer in the

doctrine of that denomination. In 1876 he purchased a farm comprising 204 acres of land, but now 360, and has 160 acres under cultivation. He also owns one of the oldest cotton-gin stands in the county, and does quite an extensive business in that line. He is one of eight children born to William C. and Sarah A. (Williams) Thomas, the former born in North Carolina, and the latter in Cumberland Island, Ga. Their union took place in the former State, and the father was well known in the community in which he lived, as a successful planter. He was also a millwright and erected the first cotton-gin in Richmond County, N. C. He died in North Carolina in 1852, preceded by his wife in 1848. Grandfather Thomas was an Englishman, and was a soldier in the Revolutionary War. The maternal grandfather was born in Wales and was a Tory during the Revolution.

John A. Thome, M. D., numbered among the rapidly rising practitioners of White County, received his education in this county, and at Union Academy in Gibson County, Ind., after which he worked on his father's farm until twenty-three years of age. During this period he studied medicine at home, and in 1877–79 attended lectures at Evansville Medical College from which he graduated February 27, 1879. Returning thence to West Point he commenced at once the active practice of his profession, which he has continued with such success as stamps him undoubtedly one of the thorough, capable, professional men of the community. Dr. Thome was born in Gibson County, Ind., November 29, 1854, being the son of Jacob and Isabella (Hayhurst) Thome. The former came originally from Prussia (near Berlin) where his birth occurred on March 26, 1818; he emigrated to this country by way of New Orleans, in 1848, first locating in Evansville, Ind., but in 1865 removed to Arkansas and settled near West Point, on a farm on which he resided until his death on February 26, 1888. Mrs. Thome was born near Troy, Ohio, on January 8, 1833, and is still living in this county with some of her children. They were the parents of nine children, five of whom survive: John A. (our subject), David C., Alice (wife of C. W. Davis), Nathallia

HISTORY OF ARKANSAS.

(wife of J. R. Riner) and Naomi (wife of James Thomas). Dr. Thome was united in marriage on June 22, 1882, with Miss Fouzine McCallister, who was born at West Point November 2, 1864. They have two daughters: Evia I. and Vera B. Dr. Thome is a strong Democrat, and as popular socially as he is in professional circles.

James Wair has been a farmer all of his life and has harvested his fiftieth crop, thirty-one of which have been raised in this county. This experience has given him a wide and thorough knowledge of the affairs of agricultural life. Born in Western Tennessee on December 20, 1814, he was the seventh son of H. and Jane (Ware) Wair. After reaching manhood Mr. Wair was married in June, 1844, to a Miss Bobson, who died in 1858 leaving five children: William, Mary, Martha, Margaret and Tennessee. Following this event he moved to Arkansas in the fall of 1858, and settled in White County, where he bought a quarter section of land. Mr. Wair's second marriage occurred in 1860, Mrs. Elizabeth Low, a widow, and a daughter of Edwin Perergrew, of Georgia, becoming his wife. She departed this life in 1873, leaving six children: James E., Frank B., Lucy V., Ellen T., George H. and Lawrence V. Mr. Wair and each wife were members of the Presbyterian Church. He is a Democrat in politics and a highly respected citizen.

Capt. Calvin Calkins Waldo is a successful gardener and fruit grower, residing in White County, Ark., and like the majority of people who claim New York as the State of their nativity, he is enterprising, intelligent and thrifty. He was born in Genesee County, January 16, 1829, and is a son of Samuel and Mercy (Calkins) Waldo, the former of French descent and a native of Oneida County, N. Y., where he was born in 1794. The family belong to the ancient and honored Waldenses family, and first became represented in America in 1650. Robert and Benjamin Waldo were private soldiers in a Connecticut regiment during the Revolution, and in the battle of Brandywine Robert was killed by a Hessian ball. The maternal ancestors were of Scotch-Irish descent, and were members of the Primitive Baptist Church

and were represented in the Revolutionary War by the maternal great-grandfather of our subject, Joshua Calkins, who served as commissary in Gen. Washington's immediate army from 1775 to 1783. He died in 1838, at the advanced age of ninety-two years. Daniel Calkins, the paternal grandfather, commanded a company in the War of 1812, and served six months, but afterward died of disease contracted while in the service, at the age of fifty-seven years. The parents of our subject were married about 1827, and became the parents of six children: Calvin C., Minerva S. (born March 31, 1831, married Joseph Cooper, of Wyoming County, N. Y.), Permelia (born in 1833, and was married to Moses H. Tyler, of Utica, Ind.), Daniel S. (born in 1835, and married Mrs. Julia Gardner, of Jonesville, Mich.), Lloyd Garrison (born in 1837 and died at the age of four years) and Maria (born in 1839, and married Samuel Cooper, a brother of Joseph Cooper). Capt. Waldo (our subject) received the education and rearing which is accorded the majority of farmers' boys, and after attending the common schools he entered the Perry Center Academy for one year, and at the age of twenty-three years graduated from Middlebury Academy, a normal school of good standing. During the winter of 1851–52, previous to graduating, he taught the district school at La Grange, N. Y., and he afterward taught a four-months' term at Leroy. During the winters of 1853–54 and 1854–55 he taught school at Elyria, Ohio, and in 1856 immigrated to Jeffersonville, Ind., and in February of that year was united in marriage to Miss Polly Jane Raymond, a native of Columbia County, N. Y., and a graduate of Mrs. Willard's Female College of Troy, N. Y. In her girlhood she was a pupil of Mrs. Lyons, at Mount Holyoke, Mass., and was a teacher in the Methodist school at Bardstown, Ky., at the time she formed Mr. Waldo's acquaintance, having previously taught in a female seminary at Murfreesboro, Tenn. After their marriage they engaged in teaching a select subscription school in Jeffersonville, Ind., continuing two years. Mr. Waldo having for some time spent his leisure moments in the study of law was admitted to the bar of Charleston, Ind., moving the same

WHITE COUNTY.

year to Utica of that State, where he again began teaching, holding the position of principal of the schools for the period of one year. In 1859 he opened a female boarding and day school, of which his wife became principal, but deeming the facilities for practicing law much better at the county seat, he removed to Charleston, where he followed the practice of law until the spring of 1861. Upon hearing of the bombardment of Fort Sumter he and others began immediately to raise a company for the three months' service, and Mr. Waldo was elected orderly-sergeant and reported with his company to Gov. Morton, but in consequence of the quota of Indiana being full they were disbanded. Later Mr. Waldo assisted in raising a company for the Twenty-second Indiana Regiment, then assisted Capt. Ferguson in raising a company for the Twenty-third Indiana Regiment. For the money expended and the service rendered in his patriotic and successful efforts to serve his country in her dire need he has never received one cent in compensation, or even a favorable notice. In July, 1861, he, with the assistance of Cyrus T. Nixon, of Charleston, Ind., raised sixty men for Company F, Thirty-eighth Regiment Indiana Infantry, and owing to Mr. Nixon's illness reported in person to Adj.-Gen. Noble, of Indianapolis, who assigned him and his company to camp duty at New Albany, Ind. Here he was elected captain of his company, known as Company, F; Thirty-eighth Regiment Indiana Volunteer Infantry, commanded by Col. B. F. Scribner, but through the latter's instrumentality he was deposed and a favorite, Wesley Connor, put in his stead. Owing to the dissatisfaction caused by these proceedings about two-thirds of the commissioned officers left the regiment, among whom were Judge Gresham, who was at that time lieutenant-colonel of the regiment. Many private soldiers also left the company, the Hon. Lee Clow, now of Hempstead County, Ark., being among the number. After leaving his command Mr. Waldo returned to Charleston, and during the remainder of 1861 and the summer of 1862 he was engaged in the practice of law, but in the latter year was also engaged in assisting the Hon. W. H. Eng-

lish in recruiting a regiment, which afterward became the Ninety-fifth Indiana Infantry. He was commissioned first lieutenant, but relinquished his position to one of the aspirants of the regiment for promotion, and then began assisting in raising another company, known as Company I, Eighth Regiment Indiana Legion, and was chosen orderly-sergeant. The only important service rendered by this regiment was in repelling Morgan in his raid of 1863, after which it was disbanded and Mr. Waldo removed with his family to his native State (New York). Here, after a short time, he enlisted as a private in Company F, Second New York Veteran Cavalry, was commissioned captain of provost guard, and was on duty at Lockport, N. Y. In November he reported to his company, at Geisboro Point, D. C., and February 1, 1864, the regiment embarked on a steamer for New Orleans, La., where they arrived the same month, being five days over due, on account of a severe storm. He was with Gen. Banks in the disastrous Red River campaign, and was seriously injured while making a cavalry charge by his horse stumbling and falling on him, and as a result, was confined to the hospital at New Orleans for thirty days, after which he again joined his regiment, and in February, of the following year, he embarked with his regiment, at Lake Ponchertrain, for Mobile, and while marching overland from Barancas Island to that city, they met Gen. Clerndon, of the Confederate service, whom they defeated, wounded and captured. After assisting in the reduction of Fort Blakely and Spanish Fort, they routed and captured a Confederate cavalry force, which had annoyed them during the siege of Mobile. After the capture of the latter city the regiment was ordered to Talladega, Ala., where Capt. Waldo was detached from his company and sent to Jacksonville, Ala., as quartermaster's clerk, remaining until September, 1865. He was mustered out of service at Talladega, Ala., November 8, 1865, went to Mobile, and there doffed his suit of blue and donned citizen's clothes once more. He returned to Utica, Ind., to which place his family had previously returned. Here his wife suddenly died, as did also a little son, four years

HISTORY OF ARKANSAS.

old, leaving his home desolate indeed. During the succeeding three years he followed teaching and such other occupations as his impaired health would permit, but his health grew no better, and thinking that a change of climate might prove beneficial, he removed to Jo Daviess County, Ill., in the spring of 1869, where he followed teaching and prospected for lead. In 1872 he went to Osceola, Iowa, and was employed by the Sioux City & St. Paul Railroad Company, in detecting and bringing to justice county swindlers, in which he was successful. In the latter part of the same year he returned to Illinois, where he again engaged in teaching school. The following year he went to Salem, Iowa, and was there united in marriage to Miss Elvira Garretson, and in September of that year he removed to Council Bluffs, Iowa, where he purchased a farm adjoining the corporation, and began market gardening and fruit raising. This occupation received his attention for about six years, with the exception of one year which he spent traveling in the interests of the Howe Truss Company, being present at the Centennial Exhibition in 1876. Three years later he again settled in Salem, and in consequence of ill health, again took up teaching as an occupation, and was also engaged in canvassing for a book. In 1882 he became a resident of Arkansas, visiting the famous Ravenden and Eureka Springs in search of health, but returned to Salem in April, 1882, where he was called upon to mourn the death of his wife, June 3, after an illness of about three weeks. She left two children: Grace (born in June, 1874) and Frank S. (born in February, 1876). Since March, 1884, Mr. Waldo has been a resident of Beebe, Ark., and has confined his attention to market gardening and fruit growing. He has been a member of several secret societies, but through indifference, is not an active member of any at the present time. He is a Republican, and holds a membership in the Missionary Baptist Church.

J. T. Walker is a merchant and farmer of Dog Wood Township, and in his relations with the public has won the respect and esteem of all, for he is honest, upright and attends strictly to his business. His birth occurred in Rutherford County, Tenn., and he was the third child born to George and Anna E. (Barkley) Walker, the former a native of Virginia, born in 1807. His early life was spent in his native State, but when still quite young he was taken to Tennessee, and there the nuptials of his marriage to Miss Rebecca Keilouct were celebrated. She died after they had been married only a short time, and in 1842 Mr. Walker espoused Anna E. Barkley, a daughter of Andrew J. and Hannah Barkley, who were Virginians. Mrs. Walker was born in Tennessee, and the following are the children born to her union with Mr. Walker: William B., Andrew J., Henry B., Hannah C. (Mrs. Allen, living in White County), Martha J. (Mrs. Crisp, also residing in White County), Sallie A. (Mrs. Shoffner, a resident of the county), George R. and Mary E. (Mrs. Ferrell, who is now deceased). In 1850 Mr. Walker moved to White County, Ark., and at the time of his death, in 1872, was the owner of about 1,000 acres of land, of which 125 were under cultivation. He was a Republican, and died in the faith of the Presbyterian Church. His widow survives him, and resides in White County with her children. Up to the age of thirteen years J. T. Walker resided in the State of Tennessee, but after coming to Arkansas he acquired a good education in the common schools, and in 1867 started out in life for himself. He opened up a farm, and in December, 1872, was married to Jennie C. Shoffner, a daughter of Dr. A. C. and Julia A. Shoffner, who removed from Mississippi to White County, Ark., in 1870. Mr. Walker and his wife have five children who are living, and one, Daisy, who died at the age of seventeen months: Evelina, Louella, James D., Lorambla and Maxie are those living. Mr. Walker is a Democrat, and in 1878 was elected to the office of magistrate, and held the position four years. He and wife belong to the Baptist Church, and he is deeply interested in the cause of education, and has held the position of school director of his district for about twelve years. He owns about 500 acres of land, with 200 acres well improved, and for some time has been engaged in merchandising at Walker's Store, the place taking its name from him. He is

WHITE COUNTY.

doing well in both enterprises, and fully deserves the success which has attended his efforts. He is a grandson of Bird Walker.

Walker & Ford. This firm comprises one of the prominent and reliable business houses of Beebe, and is composed of Robert C. Walker and J. A. Ford, two of the honorable and upright men of the county. The senior member of the house, Mr. Walker, was born in Marshall County, Miss., March 16, 1850, his parents, Rev. Charles B. and Jane O. (Jelton) Walker, having been born in Virginia and Tennessee, respectively. The father was born May 26, 1811, and moved with his parents to Rutherford County, Tenn., in 1818, where he embraced religion in December, 1829, becoming a member of the Baptist Church the following year. He was ordained a minister of that denomination on November 17, 1839, and on October 4, 1841, was married to Miss Jelton, and with her removed to Arkansas in 1858, locating at Stony Point, where he engaged in general merchandising. Later he followed the same occupation at Beebe, and was here residing at the time of his death, in 1872, his wife's death occurring three years later. The latter was a daughter of Isaac and Anna Jelton, of Rutherford County, Tenn., and for three years after her marriage lived in Lamar County of that State, then made her home in Marshall County, Miss., until 1858, after which they removed to White County. They were abundantly blessed with worldly goods, and Mr. Walker showed excellent judgment in selecting land, and was very prosperous in his mercantile enterprise. Their son, Robert C. Walker, spent his early life in Mississippi, attending school there and in Arkansas, but after becoming thoroughly familiar with the common branches he entered Hickory Plains Institute, attending one year (1868). After teaching a three months' term of school he entered the State University of Fayetteville, as a beneficiary for White County, but at the end of nine months was called home by the death of his father, and did not again enter school, but remained at home to care for his mother, which he continued to do until her death. He was married in 1875 to Miss Sallie Percy, a native of Jackson, Tenn., and to them were born

two children: James (born August 29, 1877) and Ollie (born October 12, 1879), the mother's death following the birth of the latter, October 24. She was a member of the Methodist Episcopal Church, a faithful wife, mother and friend, and her death was deeply lamented by all. In January, 1881, Mr. Walker espoused Miss Mattie L. Scott, of Arkansas, whose father, John Scott, was a farmer of Mississippi and later of Arkansas, but died at Selma, Ala., in 1862. This union resulted in the birth of four children: Sallie (born February 11, 1885), Minnie and Winnie (twins, born July 28, 1886, and died August 2, 1886), and Viola (born October 7, 1887). The first experience Mr. Walker had was in settling his father's estate, he being one of the executors. He was afterward associated in business with Mr. Westbrooks, continuing with him until 1875, following farming from that time till February, 1888. At that date he and Mr. Ford purchased their present stock of goods, and, owing to their genial dispositions and excellent business qualifications, their union has prospered. He and wife are members of the Baptist Church. Mr. Ford, the junior member of the firm, was born in Georgia, December 4, 1851, his native county being Whitfield. His parents, Joseph R. and Palmyra (Cowan) Ford, were also natives of Georgia, and until the war the father was a wealthy merchant of Dalton, and wielded a wide influence in the politics of the State. He was for a long time collector of his county, and represented the same one term in the legislature. He served as orderly-sergeant in the Confederate army during the war, and upon being taken captive was imprisoned for fifteen months at Camp Chase, Ohio. He and his wife are members of the Baptist Church, and are residing at Bellevue, Tex. J. A. Ford is the second of their eight children, the other members of the family being as follows: George (who is circuit and county clerk of Clay County, Tex.), Marion (who is a conductor on the Alabama & Chattanooga Railroad), Edward (a salesman at Poplar Bluff, Mo.), Joseph (a ranchman near Bellevue, Tex.), and Robert L. and Lawrence (who reside with their parents in Texas), Ava (the only sister, is the wife of Robert Miller, a stockman at Gainesville, Tex.). J. A. Ford received

HISTORY OF ARKANSAS.

his education at Dalton, Ga., and Flint Springs, Tenn. At the age of nineteen years he began life for himself, and after teaching school for several years he clerked one year, embarking in business on his own account in 1873, doing a general business. Owing to failing health, he was compelled to give up this work for awhile, and accordingly sold his goods and returned to Georgia, where he was engaged in farming until 1876, at which time he came to Arkansas. After farming three years in Conway County, he came to Judsonia, agriculture receiving his attention here also, and in the fall of 1883 bought a farm near Beebe. In 1886 he became associated with Mr. Campbell in the mercantile business, and until February, 1888, the firm was L. Campbell & Co., since which time it has been Walker & Ford. January 31, 1879, Mr. Ford was married to Miss Lane, a native of Georgia. She was reared in Missouri, and is a daughter of John F. Lane, a prominent attorney at law of Poplar Bluff, Mo. He and wife have four children: George L. (born December 4, 1870), Samuel E. (born September 14, 1881), Joseph Lee (born November 8, 1883) and Palmyra (born August 16, 1887). Mr. and Mrs. Ford are members of the Baptist Church, and he belongs to Beebe Lodge No. 145, A. F. & A. M., and has been a member of the I. O. G. T. He has the interest of the county at heart, and supports all movements tending to promote the public good.

W. T. Wallis has been a resident of White County since 1856, acquiring during this time an enviable reputation as a citizen of energy and enterprise, and a man honest and conscientious in his walk and transactions. A native of Tennessee, he is a son of John and Mary (Bird) Wallis, originally from North Carolina, who had a family of eleven children: John B., Mary, Elizabeth, Myas, Rebecca, Josiah, Nancy, Doctern, Catharine, W. T. (the principal of this sketch) and three whose names are not given, and who were older than W. T. The father of our subject died when he was only two years old, the mother following six months later. W. T. Wallis was born in 1829, and spent his early days in Tennessee, starting out for himself, in 1851, first as a carriage-maker and

then as farmer, to which occupation he has since given his attention. Removing to Mississippi, he was married there, in 1852, to Leamia E. Bromson, and in 1856 came to this county, where he entered 200 acres of land. At the beginning of the war Mr. Wallis enlisted in Col. Monroe's regiment, and served until the close of hostilities, participating in twenty-seven battles and skirmishes. His career as a soldier was honorable and effective. Mr. and Mrs. Wallis are the parents of eight children: John S., William H., Mary E., Martha A., Thomas, Patrick L., Annie E. and Lucinda V., all married and living in Arkansas, and most of them in this county. Mr. Wallis and wife belong to the Missionary Baptist Church, the former owns 1,000 acres of land, and has about 150 acres under cultivation, his stock numbering some two or three hundred head of cattle.

Caleb Parker Warren. The connection of Mr. Warren with the interests of White County has proven to be a fortunate thing for its residents and especially for the citizens in and near El Paso, as a perusal of the sketch will testify. He is a son of Thomas and Rebecca (Wright) Warren, who were born in North Carolina, and immigrated to West Tennessee about 1820, and were there married in 1833. They came to Arkansas in the fall of 1856, and located in the country then known as Royal Colony, purchasing 160 acres of wild land, on which they erected a double log-house, this being the first of the sort in the colony. In 1861 Mr. Warren enlisted as a private soldier in Dr. F. M. Christian's company, known as the Border Rangers, remaining in that capacity and with that command for four years and ten days. He took part in a number of battles and skirmishes, one in particular being the battle of Chickamauga, in which his company dismounted and fought as infantry. He was also at Shiloh and Corinth, and was under the famous Confederate cavalry commanders: Forrest, Wheeler, Hampton and Armstrong, but a greater portion of the time was with Forrest and Wheeler. His first experience in warfare was at Lost Creek, Mo., in 1861, and he surrendered with his command at Charlotte, N. C., at which time there was a request made by the commanding

WHITE COUNTY.

officers of both armies for volunteers to go to Chesterville, S. C., to guard and serve the rations to the Confederate soldiers as they were paroled, the Government allowing the cavalry to retain their arms and horses. Mr. Warren finally arrived at home, June 15, 1865, having ridden his horse all the way. His first venture in business after his return was to invest in some cotton, making his purchase with money loaned him by a Mr. Hadley, who at that time had charge of the penitentiary at Little Rock, and his enterprise met with fair success. The next year he put in a crop on land deeded him by his father (160 acres), and to the thirty acres which were already under cultivation he improved and added ten more. These he devoted to cotton and corn in equal parts, but the second year he left his crop to be gathered by others and embarked in merchandising at El Paso, under the firm name of Warren & Son, his father furnishing the capital and receiving half the profits. At the end of eight years our subject became the sole proprietor, paying over to his father all the money he had furnished, and took into his employ O. P. Poole, and at the end of one year gave him an interest in the business. Mr. Poole's wife and three children were killed in the terrible cyclone of 1880; he and his little daughter, Martha J., being the only ones of the family to escape with their lives, but Mr. Poole was so badly injured that existence became unendurable, and in July of the following year he ended his weary life. Mr. Warren has since acted as guardian of his daughter, and has placed her in Ouachita Baptist College, Arkadelphia, Ark. Mr. Warren's wife, who was formerly a Miss Mary A. Harkrider, was born in Tennessee, and is a daughter of John and Eunice Harkrider, native Dutch. Their family are as follows: Mattie M., John Thomas, Rebecca Eunice, Mary P. and Cora V. These children have received excellent educational advantages, and the eldest has graduated from Searcy College, Arkansas, and is at present principal of the public school at El Paso, Ark. Thomas, after having spent several terms at the State University, Fayettville, Ark., took a course at Goodman & Eastman's Business College, Nashville, Tenn., and is filling the position of book-keeper for Warren & Phelps, the present style of the firm. The three youngest daughters are at Ouachita Baptist College. The family worship in the Missionary Baptist Church, and Mr. Warren is a member of the A. F. & A. M., El Paso Lodge, No. 65. He was born in Tennessee, January 21, 1840.

Thomas Warren. He whose name heads this brief sketch, is one of White County's pioneers, and is an active and enterprising agriculturist, alive to all current issues, public spirited and progressive in all matters tending to benefit the community. His life has been an active one, and by his own industry and intelligent management, has secured a substantial footing among the citizens of White County. He was born in Edgecombe, County, N. C., September 22, 1814, and about the year 1820 he removed with his father, Caleb Warren, to the State of Tennessee, and was there reared to farm life. The schools of Tennessee were not of the best at this time, and were only conspicuous for their scarcity, therefore the educational advantages which Thomas received were of the most meager description. He learned to read a little, but never did an example in arithmetic in his life. In the year 1834 he was wedded to Miss Rebecca Wright, a daughter of John Harrison and Nancy (Whitiss) Wright, and a native of North Carolina, born on June 16, 1815. Their marriage resulted in the birth of ten children, whose names are as follows: Martha Ann (born November 22, 1834; was married December 31, 1853, to William J. Canada, who was killed while serving in the army. His wife died in 1869, leaving three children: Martha J., born in November, 1855, Thomas, born in December, 1857, and Joseph, born in 1859), Sarah E. (was born September 25, 1837, married Isaac Dougan, and bore him two children, both deceased), Caleb P. (born January 22, 1840), Matilda N. (born on March 22, 1842, and married Dr. M. Costen, of El Paso), Clarissa E. (birth occurred on the 31st of August, 1844, and her marriage took place in 1861; she and her husband had two children, William P. and Barbara), Nancy C. (was born March 31, 1847, and in 1862 she was married to Joseph Grissard; she died in Septem-

HISTORY OF ARKANSAS.

ber, 1869), William T. (the next in order of birth, was born August 17, 1849, and died in infancy), Josiah W. (was born June 21, 1851, and died five years later), Mary K. (was born December 31, 1853, and died in December, 1856), Rebecca T. (was born April 18, 1856, was married to Rufus Blake in 1872, and became the mother of eight children, four of whom are living). Prior to leaving Tennessee, Mr. Warren purchased three slaves, paying $600 and $800 apiece for two women, and $1,000 for a man, but on coming to Arkansas in 1856, his slaves had increased to six. He located on a quarter section of land which had been deeded to him by his father, and subsequently added, by purchase, three other quarter sections of land, and at the opening of the Rebellion was the owner of large landed estates, and had fourteen slaves. At the time of his location in Arkansas the country was in a very wild and unsettled condition, but, with the energy which has ever characterized the early pioneers, he set to work and soon had a good double log-cabin erected on his land, also negro cabins and a horse cotton-gin, the latter being the first erected within a radius of twenty miles. After a few years he put up a steam cotton-gin and grist-mill, at a cost of about $3,500, and hauled his machinery from Des Arc, a distance of thirty-five miles. In 1867, he, in partnership with his son Caleb P., engaged in the mercantile business in El Paso, and the latter is now one of the wealthiest merchants of the State. Mr. and Mrs. Warren are now seventy-five and seventy-four years old, respectively, and the latter has been a member of the Missionary Baptist Church for nearly seventy years. Mr. Warren has belonged to the same church for about forty years, all their children being members of the same, and those who are deceased died in full communion with the church, and with the hope and belief of immortality. Mrs. Warren is an active member of the Ladies' Aid Society, and she and her husband are ever ready with open purse to aid the needy and afflicted, and when their Master calls will be found ready and waiting to pass "over the river." The paternal ancestors of Mr. Warren came to the United States prior to the Revolutionary War,

and took sides with the Colonists in that struggle. Of his maternal ancestors he has no knowledge.

Col. Thomas Watkins, known as a prominent early settler of White County, is a Virginian by birth, and a son of Joel and Fannie (White) Watkins, whose birthplace is found in the Old Dominion. Mr. Joel Watkins was born March 4, 1784, and was married in Virginia, removing in 1830 to Tennessee. He served in the War of 1812, was a justice of the peace in Tennessee for several years, and a member of the Missionary Baptist Church, as was also his wife. He died in 1863. He was a son of Thomas Watkins, of English descent, and an old time Virginian, who was an officer in the Revolutionary War; the latter was with Gen. Washington at the surrender at Yorktown, and represented his county in the State legislature a number of times. Fannie White, the mother of our subject, was a daughter of Thomas White, also originally from Virginia, and a captain of a company in the American troops during the Revolutionary War. To Mr. and Mrs. Watkins nine children were born, three of whom are still living: Thomas, Catharine (wife of William H. Watts) and Fannie (now Mrs. Crossett). Thomas Watkins first saw the light of day in Halifax County, Va., in January, 1820. When fourteen years of age he went to Lebanon, Tenn., where he was employed as clerk in a store, remaining there until twenty-two years old, at which time he bought a farm in De-Soto County, Miss. In 1853, coming to Arkansas, he located in White County, on the farm which he still occupies, consisting of 218 acres, with 150 acres under cultivation. In 1838 he was married to Miss Moore, of Tennessee, who died in 1843, leaving three daughters, all deceased. In 1848 Miss Amanda Dowdle, a native of South Carolina became his wife, surviving until her death, in 1854; she bore two children: William M. (a merchant of Searcy) and Allen D. (a farmer of White County). Mr. Watkins' third wife was formerly Mary Walker, to whom he was united in 1856. A native of White County, she was a daughter of James Walker, and departed this life in 1857, leaving one daughter, who died when an infant. In 1863 Mr. Watkins married his fourth and present com-

WHITE COUNTY.

panion, Mrs. Margaret E. Stone (*nee* Core), a widow, whose birth occurred in Haywood County, Tenn., July 25, 1834. They are the parents of two children, living, and two now deceased. Those surviving are: Mary Kate and Maggie C., both at home. Mr. Watkins is a member of the Masonic order, in which he has taken the Royal Arch degree, and belongs to the Methodist Episcopal Church, South, as does his wife. He is an enterprising and highly respected man, enjoying universal esteem.

Hon. T. W. Wells, Searcy, Ark. Every community is bound to have among her citizens a few men of recognized influence and ability, who, by their systematic and careful, thorough manner of work, attain to success which is justly deserved. Among this class is Mr. Wells, a man esteemed as a prominent and substantial, as well as one of the pioneer citizens of the county. He was born in Haywood County, Tenn., May 18, 1834, and was the second of eight children, the result of the union of William Stokes and Penelope (Standley) Wells, natives of Kentucky and Tennessee, respectively, who were married February 15, 1832. When a boy William S. Wells occupied the claim where Brownsville is now located, and later traded it for a suit of clothes. He was married in Tennessee, and followed farming all his life near the city of Brownsville, Tenn. His death occurred July 20, 1867 (he was born August 2, 1807), and his wife previous to this, on April 9, 1866. Her birth was February 28, 1811. The grandfather, John Wells, was a native of Kentucky, and a pioneer of that State in the time of Daniel Boone. Grandfather William Standley was a native of Tennessee, and among the pioneers of that State. T. W. Wells was reared to farm life, and educated in the district schools of Tennessee, although the main part of his education was obtained by personal application. He left home at eighteen years of age without money, attended school at Cageville, Tenn., worked his way through by labor, but was under the tutelage of Prof. William A. Allen. After leaving college Mr. Wells engaged in teaching, and followed this profession from 1852 to 1854. On October 25 of the last-mentioned year he was

united in marriage to Miss Jeannette Edwards, a native of Tennessee, and the daughter of William and Lavinia Edwards, natives of Edgecombe County, N. C. Mr. and Mrs. Edwards settled in Tennessee in an early day, or in 1835, and here both died the same year. After marriage Mr. Wells settled in Tennessee, and was engaged in teaching and farming on the shares. During 1857 and 1858 he was engaged in the book business, but in the last-named year he moved to Avoyelles Parish, La., where he was occupied in overseeing. In May of 1859, he moved back to Tennessee, followed teaching for three months, and in the fall of that year came to Arkansas, landing at Des Arc with 15 cents and a sick wife. From there he went to El Paso, White County, Ark., and taught school for about ten months, when he and wife regained their health. After this Mr. Wells engaged in the mill business at El Paso, and in partnership with James M. Wright erected the first steam mill in that place, being connected with it until 1861, when Mr. Wells was left to conduct it alone. In 1862 he engaged in milling in Van Buren County, and in July of the following year he purchased the McCauley mill, at Prospect Bluff, and had the only fine flouring mill in White County. This he continued until 1867, when he moved to Clay Township, White County, and bought a timber tract of eighty acres. This he opened up, and has now 360 acres, with 165 under cultivation. He owns a good steam-mill and gin. He moved to Searcy in 1868, but still continued the milling and farming business. He lost his wife in 1875, and his second marriage was in 1877, December 5, in Woodruff County, to Mrs. Delilah J. Bosley, a native of Tennessee. Three children were the fruits of this union, only one now living, Thomas W., who was born on January 1, 1886. The other two were named Thomas Clarence and Felix Grundy (both of whom died with measles, April 25, 1885, at the age of two and five years, respectively). Mr. Wells takes a prominent part in politics, and is a stanch Democrat. He represented White County in the legislature in 1874, and was re-elected two years later, serving until 1878. In 1882 he represented the Twenty-seventh senatorial district, com-

HISTORY OF ARKANSAS.

posed of White and Faulkner Counties, and served until 1884. He is in very comfortable circumstances, and this is all the fruits of his own exertion. He is one of the honored pioneers of White County, and during the many years he has resided here, he has not only become well known, but the respect and esteem shown him is as wide as his acquaintance.

Dr. M. C. Wells, has been for years successfully engaged in the practice of medicine, but also pursues the occupation of farming. He was born in Haywood County, Tenn., in 1848, and was the youngest in a family of eight children born to W. S. and Penelope (Standley) Wells, natives, respectively, of Kentucky and Tennessee. The father was a farmer by occupation, and after settling in Tennessee, which was at an early day, he opened up a farm on which he died in 1868, his wife having died a year earlier. Dr. M. C. Wells was reared to a farm life and was educated in the schools of Haywood County, in that county also receiving his first medical knowledge. In 1869–70, and the winter of 1870–71, he attended lectures in the Washington University of Baltimore, Md. (now known as the College of Physicians and Surgeons), and later took an intermediate course at Louisville, Ky. He first settled in White County, in the year 1871, and began his practice in Des Arc Township, but since November of the same year he has been a resident of Marion Township. During his medical career of nineteen years he has won the reputation, and deservedly, of being a skillful physician, and his practice lies among the best people of the county. He keeps his own medicines and is ready to answer calls at any time. He is giving his attention to farming also, and owns a good farm of 150 acres on Big Creek Township, of which seventy are under cultivation, and all is well adapted to the raising of stock. Dr. Wells owns a handsome home in Searcy, his residence being situated near Galloway College, in a very pleasant part of the town. He has always been public spirited, and in his political preferences is a Democrat, and as he has always taken a deep interest in school matters he has served a number of years as a member of the school board. He

was married in 1872 to Miss Mary Cheney Knowlton, a native of Tennessee, and a daughter of Hon. H. C. and Mary Agnes (Stone) Knowlton, the former born in Vermont and the latter in Tennessee. In 1870 they settled in White County, Ark., and here are now residing. The Doctor and his wife are the parents of four children: Beulah S., William H., Grace Garland and Lois Lina.

George G. Wells is in every respect worthy of being classed among the successful farmers of White County, for by his own industry and good management he has become the owner of 160 acres of land, sixty of which he now has under cultivation. He assisted in tilling his father's farm in Haywood County, Tenn., there also receiving his education, and when Civil War broke out, he joined Company G, Fifteenth Tennessee Cavalry (being regimental flag bearer for that regiment for two years), under Gen. Forrest, and was at the battles of Fort Pillow, Harrisburg, Yazoo City, Corinth, Pulaski, Columbus, Mount Pleasant, Spring Hill, Franklin, Nashville and others. He was taken prisoner at Columbus and Nashville, but both times was soon retaken. He surrendered at Jonesboro, N. C., in June, 1865, and returned to his home in Tennessee, where he resumed farming. He was married in his native State in November, 1867, to Callie B. Hooks, of Kentucky, a daughter of Henry Clinton and Rebecca (Somersault) Hooks, also Kentuckians, who moved to Tennessee at an early day. The father died in April, 1865, and the mother in 1885. Mr. Wells and his wife continued to reside in Tennessee until 1872, when they sold their farm and came to White County, purchasing, in 1880, their present farm. They now have sixty-five acres under cultivation. They first bought an improved farm of 100 acres near El Paso, paying $12 per acre, but owing to defective title, they afterward lost it, and were compelled to commence anew, but owing to their frugal habits and shrewd management, they are now in good circumstances. Mr. Wells is a believer in temperance, is a Democrat, and he and wife are believers in the Christian religion. He has three children by his first wife, who died in April, 1883. Mr. Wells subsequently married M. V. Choat,

WHITE COUNTY.

widow of Stephen Choat. By her first husband she has two children: Lee and Willie. Mr. Wells is a brother of Dr. M. C. Wells, whose biography appears elsewhere in this work.

William C. West is justly conceded to be among White County's most extensive merchants, and his career as such is one which redounds to his own personal credit. A native of Alabama, he is a son of William and Mary (Howard) West, natives of North Carolina, who moved to Alabama shortly after their marriage, and in 1837 to Marshall County, Miss. After the death of his wife, in 1844, Mr. West went to Arkansas and located in White County, where his death occurred, in 1859, at the age of eighty-four years. He was a Baptist minister, in which work he had been engaged for forty years. He was the father of eleven children, two of whom only are living: R. R. West (who is a chancery clerk in De Soto County) and William C. (our subject). The latter was born in Perry County, Ala., March 14, 1828. At the age of nineteen he was employed as a clerk in a store; but, on coming to White County, started into the mercantile business for himself on a small scale, a short time after, however, entering the employ of a firm in West Point. In 1858 he resumed general merchandising, with a capital of $400 or $500. Just before the Missouri campaign he enlisted in the Confederate army and served as adjutant for Gen. Mitchell, remaining in service throughout the Missouri raid. During the war he lost all of his property, and had to start from the beginning after returning home; but by hard work, energy and perseverance he has built up an extensive patronage, and his yearly sales will now average $25,000. He also owns 1,200 acres of land, with 300 acres cleared, and a good portion under cultivation. May 27, 1856, Mr. West was married to Miss Frances Adams, a daughter of Hardin S. Adams, of Mississippi. She died in 1886, leaving four children: Charles E. (who is in business with his father), Lavenia H., Fannie H. and Mary E. Mr. West is a member of the Missionary Baptist Church, as was also his wife. He is a Democrat in politics and a member of the Masonic order. He was postmaster of this place in 1877–78.

Judge N. H. West, Searcy, Ark. This much-esteemed and representative man of the county was elected to his present responsible position in September, 1888, and has effectively conducted the affairs of the same since. He was originally from Madison County, Tenn., where his birth occurred in 1836, and was the oldest in a family of five children born to the union of Philip T. and Hurelia (Harris) West, natives of Tennessee. The father was a farmer, a local minister, and in November, 1851, he moved to White County, locating in Marion Township, where he entered land. He died there in 1853, and his excellent wife survived him until 1886. Their family consisted of these children: N. H., H. T. (married and resides in White County), Thomas N. (died in 1870), Mary A. (was the wife of R. G. Thomas, died in the county in 1888) and Martha J. (was born in White County; married W. A. Patterson and resides in Marion Township). Judge N. H. West came to White County when fifteen years of age, was early taught the duties on the farm, and received his education by his own exertions and by the aid of the pine knot, by the light of which he spent many hours poring over the pages of his books. He stood between the handles of the plow at the age of seven years, and has continued agricultural pursuits ever since. He learned the blacksmith trade and followed that pursuit for some years, but later purchased a timber tract of eighty acres, which he has since added to until he now has 191 acres, with 125 acres under cultivation. He is pleasantly situated two miles from Searcy. During the Civil War he enlisted under Capt. Critz's Company, Eighth Arkansas Infantry, Tennessee Army, and was in the battles of Corinth, Chattanooga, Murfreesboro, Chickamauga, and participated also in Bragg's invasion of Kentucky. He was paroled at Atlanta, Ga., on May 6, 1865, and returned to White County where he engaged in farming. He is active in politics, was justice of the peace for some time, and votes with the Union Labor party. He is a member of the Agricultural Wheel No. 145, and was president of the County Wheel at the time he was elected to his present office. He is a member of the Mount Pisgah Lodge No. 242, A. F. &

HISTORY OF ARKANSAS.

A. M., and was secretary of the same for about eight years. Mr. West was married in White County in 1856 to Miss Martha J. Stayton, a native of Georgia, and the fruits of this union were two children: William F. (married and resides in Clay Township, White County) and Nancy Jane (now Mrs. Mayo, resides in Marion Township). The mother of these children died in 1868. Judge West selected his second wife in the person of Miss Ellen Robinson, a native of Pope County, Ill., and was married to her in 1870. She was left an orphan at the age of two years, and she came to Arkansas with an uncle in 1853, where she grew to womanhood. By that union nine children were born, six now living: Harriet E., James T., David N., Henry Clay (died in 1887), Sarah Malvina, Lillie (died in 1888, at the age of six years), Viola, Martha Ellen (died at the age of two years) and Anna Elizabeth. Judge West has seen a great many changes in the country since his residence here. Searcy was then a small hamlet, there were no railroad facilities, and game was plentiful. He has been active in everything pertaining to the good of the county, and is one of the foremost men of the same.

A. J. West is one of the most successful of White County's farmers and stockmen, and deserves much credit for the way in which he has battled with fate and conquered, for he not only possesses large landed estates, but is extensively engaged in stock raising. He is now the owner of 2,462 acres of some of the best land in the county, 600 acres in cultivation, and his residence in West Point is surpassed by none. He was born in Mississippi in 1850, being the youngest of seven children of Adam and Mary (Jarvis) West, both Tennesseeans. The former was a son of John West. He was educated in Cannon County, Tenn., and when a young man moved to Alabama, near Tuscaloosa, where he followed farming. After his marriage, in 1833, he moved to Mississippi and settled on a farm, being the owner of a one-half section of land. His wife was one of a large family of children born to Levi Jarvis. Adam West served with distinction in the Mexican War. He and his wife were both members of the Missionary Baptist Church,

and were honored and respected wherever they made their home. They both died on the old plantation in Mississippi. Their son, William, was for many years a prosperous and influential citizen of Memphis, where he acquired considerable property, and was beloved by all. He was a Mason, belonging to St. Elmo Commandery. He died in 1885. Emily, a daughter was married to Thomas Bice. Rachel married W. C. Wooten: they are both deceased, also Caroline, who died in 1867. Mary married Patrick Smith, and in 1887 she and her son moved to White County, Ark., with A. J. West, where they now reside. A. J. spent his early life on the plantation in Mississippi, and received his schooling at Oxford University, and afterward at Murfreesboro, Tenn. After leaving college he farmed and taught school; his father and brother-in-law being dead, he devoted the best years of his life in caring for his widowed mother and sisters and their families. He was married January 15, 1888, to Miss Jessie Bramlitt, of Corinth, Miss., who was a daughter of Jessie L. and Mary (Anderson) Bramlitt. Her father was for many years a successful merchant of Jackson, Miss. He moved from there to Prentiss County, Miss., and purchased one of the most desirable farms in the county. Her mother was the only daughter of Samuel Anderson, of Pulaski, Tenn.

Samuel A. Westbrook, of Beebe, White County, Ark., was born in Maury County, Tenn., April 29, 1833. Being left a poor boy, after arriving at the age of eighteen, he followed overseeing for several years, and came to Arkansas in December, 1858, where he engaged in the mill business and farming. The former he has discontinued, and now gives his attention to farming and stock raising. He has become noted for the fine stock he raises, and especially for his Short-horn cattle and Clydesdale and Morgan horses. In addition to his land being well adapted to stock raising, it is exceedingly fertile, and all kinds of fruit and grain can be raised in abundance. Mr. Westbrook is one of the pushing men of the county, and from his mill lumber was procured with which to build nearly every church and school-house in the county. He served three months in the army, but as he was

WHITE COUNTY.

exempt, and on account of his services being required at home to operate his mill, he returned to Arkansas. He was a Whig in former times, but is now Independent in his political views. On March 30, 1865, he was married to Miss Susan A. Walker, a daughter of Rev. C. B. Walker, of Mississippi, who removed to Arkansas in 1857. Of eight children born to Mr. and Mrs. Westbrook five are living: Charles B., S. A. and W. H. (twins), Jennie, Robert T., Willie and Walker Lipsey.

Daniel W. Wheaton, son of James and Betsey A. Wheaton, was born in Pomfret, Conn., October 3, 1833, on the old Wheaton homestead, which had been in the family since the Revolutionary War, being the youngest of a family of thirteen children. His father, James Wheaton, a native of Connecticut, was born in 1790, and his mother, Betsey (Angell) Wheaton, was born in Rhode Island, in 1795. They were married about 1815, and the following are the names of their children: Marshal (who died in Rhode Island. in 1840, at the age of twenty-four years), Mason N., Angell, Seth T., Gurdon N., Monroe, Nancy L., Horatio, Henry W. and D. W. James Wheaton was a farmer all his life, and died on his old homestead in Connecticut, in 1876. He was twice married, his first wife dying in 1814, left him with two children: Warren L. and Jessie C. His second wife, the mother of our subject, died in 1857, on the old farm in Connecticut. James Wheaton, the grandfather, reared a family of five children. D. W. Wheaton, our biographical subject, remained on the home farm in his native State until he was twenty-five years of age, then came West and spent twelve years in the State of Illinois, Du Page County, and was there married to Priscilla P. Beith, a daughter of William and Mary (Allen) Beith, her birth having occurred in Illinois. Her parents were Scotch and settled in Illinois about 1844, where they became the parents of three children. Mr. Wheaton and his wife have become the parents of four children: Mary E. (wife of A. P. Moody), Julia, Clara and William. Since the year 1871, Mr. Wheaton has resided in White County, Ark., his farm, comprising 275 acres, being situated one and one-half miles from Judsonia. At the time of his purchase, the

land was heavily covered with timber, but he has cleared about seventy-five acres and devoted it to the raising of fruit, for which he finds a ready sale. He and his wife are members of the Methodist Episcopal Church, he being one of its stewards, and in his political views he is a Republican. He has two brothers who are large land holders at Wheaton, Ill., the town taking its name from them.

James K. Whitney has risen to a position as one of White County's leading citizens through his own merits. A native of Tennessee, he received his education in this county, and graduated from the Bryant & Stratton Commercial College, after which he went into the mercantile business in company with C. P. Douthar, at West Point, there remaining until 1874. He then wound up his father's business, and engaged in farming and stock raising, and in 1884 commenced the breeding of Holstein cattle, the only herd of which breed he now has in White County. Mr. Whitney was born in Fayette County, Tenn., January 27, 1846, being a son of Elijah and Mary (Anderson) Whitney, of Kentucky and Tennessee nativity, respectively. Mr. Whitney, Sr., learned the machinist's trade when a young man, and was engaged for a number of years in selling cotton-spinning machinery, through Kentucky and Tennessee. After his marriage, February 22, 1842, he removed to Fayette County, Tenn., and carried on farming, in 1859 removing to Arkansas, and locating in White County, where he lived until his death, in January, 1873. He was a son of Hiram Whitney, a soldier in the War of 1812, and was with Gen. Hull on his disastrous campaign. His wife was a niece of Gen. William H. Harrison. The Whitney family are of English descent, and the Anderson family of Scotch origin. Mr. and Mrs. Whitney had a family of five children, two of whom only are living: a daughter (now Mrs. Douthar, whose husband is a merchant of White County) and James K. (our subject). In 1876 James K. Whitney was married to Miss Ella T. Black, daughter of W. D. Black. She was born in White County in 1858, and has borne six children, four of whom are still living: Leslie E.,

HISTORY OF ARKANSAS.

Floyd W., Bessie and Mary E. Mr. and Mrs. Whitney are members of the Missionary Baptist Church, in which the former is clerk and treasurer. He is one of the leading Democrats of the county, and as a citizen and neighbor enjoys wide respect.

I. J. Whitsitt is also numbered among the well-to-do farmers of Dogwood Township. He was born in Alabama in 1848, as the son of Wilson and Elizabeth (Price) Whitsitt, Kentuckians by birth. Wilson Whitsitt was born in 1808, and moved to Alabama when a boy with his father, being married in 1828 to the mother of our subject. Her birth occurred in 1812. Mr. and Mrs. Whitsitt were the parents of ten children, seven of whom are still living: Jane, Camily, Sallie, Harriett, I. J. (our subject), Katie and William. The father was a prosperous farmer and a member of the Methodist Episcopal Church, South, as was also his wife. He died in 1878, having survived his worthy companion eight years. I. J. Whitsitt passed his school days in Alabama, and commenced his occupation of a farmer in that State in 1864. In 1873 he chose for his life associate, Elizabeth Sherwood, a daughter of Thomas and Ruth (Jinkins) Sherwood, natives of Tennessee. They have a family of two children: Benjamin and Hughes. In 1876 Mr. Whitsitt moved to Texas with his family, and was engaged in farming until 1881, then coming to White County, Ark., where he bought his present farm, consisting of 160 acres of land, with fifty acres under cultivation at the present time. He is a stanch Democrat and a member of the Missionary Baptist Church, as is his wife. Mr. Whitsitt is indeed a good citizen of White County, taking an interest in all work for the benefit of the community in which he lives.

William M. Williams, a native of Randolph County, N. C., and a son of John and Ellen (Craven) Williams, also originally from the old North State, was born in 1842. John Williams was a son of James and Frances Williams, and was married between 1825 and 1830, rearing a family of seven children: Evaline, Sauliman, Robert, Susan, William M., Alexander and John. Mr. Williams died in 1846. William M. started in life for him-

self, in 1868, at farming, and, in 1871, came to Arkansas, settling on a farm in White County, which he rented. A short time afterward he bought 320 acres of land, and now has eighty acres under cultivation. During the war he enlisted in the Confederate army, in the Forty-sixth North Carolina Infantry, and was engaged in the battles of Seven Pines, Oak Grove, Sharpsburg, Fredericksburg and the battle of Plank Road and others, serving until the close of the war, and being present when Lee surrendered under the famous old apple tree at Appomattox. Mr. Williams was married in 1872 to Miss Frances Tote, a daughter of Andrew and Mary (Tees) Tote, natives of North Carolina. Himself and wife are members of the Methodist Episcopal Church, South. Mr. Williams says the soil of Arkansas will raise anything that can be grown elsewhere. He has been very prosperous in the nineteen years of his residence here and counts his friends by the score.

Dr. F. M. Winborn, one of the most prominent physicians of White County, is a native of Alabama, and was born in Florence, February 27, 1835, being one of nine children in the family of William and Mary (May) Winborn. The former's birth occurred in North Carolina, July 5, 1800. He was educated in the schools of Alabama, and immigrated from the latter State in 1816 to Tennessee, whence, after a residence of two years in Tennessee, he returned to Alabama and was married, there passing the rest of his life. His wife, Mary May, was a daughter of John and Elizabeth May, of Alabama. Mr. Winborn's demise occurred in December, 1875, his wife having been called to her final home some years before. The grandfather, William Winborn, was of North Carolina nativity and a soldier in the War of the Revolution. He died in Alabama in 1832. The maternal grandfather, John May, was originally from Georgia, and served in the War of 1812. His death occurred in 1854. His father was born in England, his mother being a native of Ireland. F. M. Winborn was educated at the Diasburg Academy, Tennessee, and received his medical education at the University of Mississippi, graduating with honors from that institution. He was married in November, 1858, to Miss Amorett

WHITE COUNTY.

Doyle, a daughter of Sarah and David Doyle. Dr. and Mrs. Winborn are the parents of nine children, four boys and five girls: William G., Robert L., Lemuel H., John B., Ida, Edgar V., Dock, Louella and Olla A. Dr. Winborn moved from Mississippi to Arkansas in 1878, and settled in Lonoke, where he practiced his profession successfully for three years. Thinking, however, that White County offered better inducements as a place of residence he came here, and has established an enviable reputation as a careful, able practitioner. He is almost constantly at the bedside of the sick, and is invariably given the most hearty welcome, for his coming means the alleviation of their suffering. But though his attention is so taken up in the pursuance of his chosen profession, he aids and supports all enterprises of a worthy character. He is a member of the Masonic order, and has held the office of magistrate for two years. He served in the late war, and enlisted in 1861 under Gen. Polk, Preston Smith's Brigade, Forty-seventh Tennessee Regiment, being wounded at the battle of Shiloh by a ball passing through the calf of his left leg. The Doctor also held the office of first lieutenant in the Kentucky campaign, a position which he filled with honor. The company was known as the Miller Guards of Richmond, Ky.

Robert J. Winn is a Buckeye by birth, and during the period of the Civil War served in the Federal army, enlisting in the Second Ohio Infantry, August 16, 1861. He was in the battles of Stone River, Chickamauga, Missionary Ridge, Mill Creek Gap, Buzzard's Roost, Peach Tree Creek, Atlanta and a number of others, and was captured at Pulaski, Tenn., May 30, 1862, by Morgan, but was exchanged and received his discharge, October 11, 1864. March 7, 1866, Miss Alma Wymer became his wife, a daughter of John and Rebecca (Gormer) Wymer, originally from Pennsylvania. Robert J. Winn was born in Muskingum County, Ohio, in 1837, and was a son of Adolphus and Rebecca (Jordon) Winn. Adolphus Winn was a Virginian by birth, his existence dating from 1810, and he was one of a family of twelve children born to William and Rebecca (Russel) Winn, also of the Old Dominion. He

was married in 1836 and moved to Ohio, where he bought a farm of 500 acres, there residing until his death in 1885. Mrs. Winn, the mother of Robert J., was a daughter of Cabot and Rachel Jordon, natives of Maryland, and who went to Ohio in 1825, where Rebecca was born. Her parents lived to an advanced age, her father dying when seventy-six years old, and her mother at the age of seventy-eight. Mr. and Mrs. Adolphus Winn were the parents of thirteen children: Robert J., Martha R., Nancy J. (deceased), Caleb J. (deceased), Elizabeth and Margaret (twins), Fennan S., John A., Albert J., Mariah, Hattie, Harmon S. and Simeon S. Mrs. Winn is still living. To the subject of this sketch, and wife, six children have been given: Lillie C., Herbert H., Edith R., Louis A., Mable O. and Clarence A. Mr. Winn moved to this State in 1875 and settled in Judsonia, White County, where he bought a farm of eighty acres, and is engaged principally in raising fruit and vegetables for market. He also owns considerable town property and an interest in the Judsonia Canning Company, of which he is president, being also president of the board of trustees of the Judsonia University, and is a member of the board of trustees of the Building Association. Besides he is secretary of the Arkansas Fruit Growers' and Shippers' Union. Mr. Winn is a member of Judsonia Lodge No. 54, I. O. O. F., and of the Grand Lodge of the State. He and his wife and eldest daughter belong to the Baptist Church, and take an active part in all religious work. The former has been engaged in teaching school for a number of years.

John W. Womack is the son of Jacob and Nancy (Bates) Womack, and was born in Meigs County, Tenn., February 16, 1833. Jacob Womack was a Virginian by birth, his natal day being in 1797. His youth was passed in the Old Dominion and in 1822 he was united in marriage with Miss Bates, also a native of Virginia. One year after this event Mr. Womack moved to East Tennessee and died there in 1863, his wife surviving until 1865. He was a successful farmer and a quiet, law-abiding citizen. In his political views he sided with the Democrats, and was a Primitive

HISTORY OF ARKANSAS.

Baptist in his religious belief. Mr. and Mrs. Womack became the parents of eight children, three of whom are now living: John W., Martha J. (Mrs. J. N. Brown, of East Tennessee), and Elizabeth (widow of James Masner, of Independence County, Ark.). Those deceased are: David, Sarah (Mrs. Heard), Daniel, Mary A. (Mrs. W. C. Grubbs) and Susana (wife of Thomas Bonner). John W. Womack was reared in Meigs County, Tenn., and received such advantages for an education as the schools of the period afforded. Remaining on the farm with his parents until thirty years of age, at the expiration of that time he branched out for himself, engaging in farming and stock raising, which is his present occupation. In 1867 he removed to Arkansas and settled on his farm where he now resides. The farm consists of 240 acres of valuable land, highly cultivated and his stock is of various kinds, all of the finest breeds. Mr. Womack was married in 1867, in Meigs County, Tenn., to Miss Ellen B., daughter of Uriah and Mary Denton, of Virginia, and to them a family of five children have been born, four living: Daniel U., Mary A., John and Sabinus. Mr. Womack served in the Confederate army, in Col. McKenzie's Third East Tennessee Cavalry during the war, and was mostly on scout duty in various skirmishes and fights, but in no regular battles of any prominence. He was captured while ill, in 1865, being released just before the final surrender. Mr. Womack is an influential member of the school board, a stanch Democrat in politics, and has been a Master Mason for over twenty years.

Alfonsus A. Wood might well be called a self-made man. His father, Joseph P. Wood, a native of Weakley County, Tenn., was a farmer by profession, and very successful in that calling. He was united in marriage, in 1836, in Weakley County, Tenn., to Mary E. Freeman, of Virginia. In 1870 they moved to Arkansas, and settled in Jackson County, where Mr. Wood was residing at the date of his death, in 1872, though he was in Tennessee when he died, having been called there on business. His belief was with the Methodist Episcopal Church, South. Mr. and Mrs. Wood were the parents of eleven children, five of whom are now living: Fannie (wife of T. M. Thompkins, of Carroll County, Tenn.), Mary F. (Mrs. W. B. Gamble, of White County, Ark.), Emma B. (Mrs. H. S. McKnight, residing in White County, Ark.), Alfonsus A. and Portia S. (wife of B. F. Whitley). Mrs. Wood makes her home at this time with her son in White County, and notwithstanding that she has reached the age of three-score years and ten, is still active in all church and charity work, and a liberal contributor to these enterprises. Alfonsus A. began for himself at the age of eighteen, choosing his father's occupation, which he has successfully conducted ever since. He owns eighty acres of excellent land in White County, and a half interest in a large steam grist-mill and cotton-gin, at Russell, Ark., where he is now residing. Mr. Wood was married in White County, on December 16, 1875, to Miss Lucinda F. Plant, a daughter of William and Emily Plant, old settlers of White County. By this marriage one child was born, who died in infancy. Mrs. Wood died November 18, 1876, and in 1881 Mr. Wood was united in marriage to Margaret L. Drenan, whose parents, A. R. and Mary Drenan, natives of Tennessee, are now residing in Russell. Mrs. Wood died in February, 1884, leaving two children: Tennie and Alvis A. Mr. Wood is a Democrat in his political views, though not an enthusiast. He is an earnest worker and a member of many years' standing in the Methodist Episcopal Church, also belonging to the Triple Alliance, a secret mutual benefit association. He is a man of quiet habits, charitable, and very popular in the society of his little town, being respected by all.

Daniel T. Woodson was the eldest son of James M. and Pauline L. (Gregory) Woodson; the former was a native of Virginia and went to Western Tennessee in 1845, removing in 1858 to Arkansas, and settling in White County. Daniel T. Woodson first saw the light in Virginia, on October 19, 1839. He accompanied his parents to Arkansas at the age of nineteen, where he was married at the age of twenty-one years to a Miss Park, of Tennessee nativity, and who came to White County four years previous to the Woodsons. Daniel T. en-

WHITE COUNTY.

listed during the war, in May, 1862, in the Confederate army, first in the cavalry and afterward in the infantry service, being a member of a foraging force throughout the war. Foraging was a dangerous occupation at that time, and he had many narrow escapes from capture. After the cessation of hostilities Mr. Woodson bought a place of 160 acres in White County, on which he resided until 1877, when he sold his farm and purchased another of 211 acres in the same township, near Centre Hill. In 1882 he bought a mill and cotton-gin, in which business he has been very successful. Mr. Woodson's wife died in 1870, leaving two sons, James M. and Joseph Y. He was married the second time in November of that year to N. L. Dollar, by which marriage five children have been born: Phillip C., Mary L., Bula L., Zula B. and Bertha D. Mr. Woodson is a member of the Masonic order, to which he has belonged since 1862; his membership is now in Centre Hill Lodge No. 114, where he has held an office for the last fifteen years. He is a decided Democrat, politically, and held the office of justice of the peace in his township in 1887–88. Mr. and Mrs. Woodson belong to the Missionary Baptist Church, of which they have been members nearly all their lives. In the organization where they worship, Mr. Woodson is leader in the choir and also superintendent in the Sunday-school.

James R. Woodson. There is generally more or less similarity in the sketches of those who have for the most part been engaged in agricultural pursuits from boyhood, but Mr. Woodson's career has been sufficiently diversified as to render him well posted with different affairs, people, etc. The State of his nativity is West Virginia, where he was born in 1841, being the second of a family of ten children born to James M. and Paulina (Gregory) Woodson, both of whom were Virginians, the former's birth occurring in 1813. They were married in 1838, and their union resulted in the birth of the following children: Daniel T., James R., Elizah, John L., William J., Martha J., George W. D., Clements and Bettie. James R. Woodson removed to Tennessee with his father in 1843, and after residing there twelve years came with him to

White County, Ark., but the latter's death occurred in Memphis, Tenn., in 1862. James R. Woodson gave his attention to farm work until the outbreak of the war, then enlisted in Company A, Seventh Battalion, under Col. D. Shay, and took part in the following engagements: Perryville, Dalton, Spring Hill, Franklin, Nashville (Tenn.) and Atlanta, and in the last-named engagement received a gunshot wound in the thigh, and thirty-six bullet holes in his clothes. At the time of the surrender he was filling the position of teamster. He came to Arkansas, and in 1866 was married to Amanda Goad, a daughter of Henry and Mary (Sowell) Goad, natives of Tennessee. He now owns a farm of 120 acres, and has fifty acres under cultivation, all his property being acquired by hard and persistent labor. The children of this marriage are: Mary L. (the wife of Monroe Henderson and the mother of one child, Julia E), Docia A. (the wife of William Elded and the mother of one child, Martha J.), Emma G. (was married to Thomas Baker, by whom she has one child, Elmer J.), Martha F., James H., Alice M., William E., George E., Lula E., John S. and Joel F. Mrs. Woodson died February 2, 1889, her infant son, Aaron, also dying. Mr. and Mrs. Woodson held memberships in the Methodist Episcopal Church, South, and he has always been an active worker for schools as well as churches. He is a member of Mount Pisgah Lodge No. 242 of the A. F. & A. M., and has been an officer of the same.

James Maury Wright ranks among the most prosperous of White County's agriculturists, and enjoys the reputation of being not only a substantial and progressive farmer, but an intelligent and thoroughly posted man on all public affairs. He first saw the light of day August 12, 1834, in Madison County, Tenn., and through his paternal ancestor, James Wright, has inherited Irish blood, his grandfather having come from Ireland to America about the year 1780, and took up his abode in Franklin County, N. C., where he engaged in farming and died at an advanced age. James Wright was married in North Carolina in the year 1818 to Miss Patsey Stigall, and after they had become the parents of five children they

HISTORY OF ARKANSAS.

removed to Gibson County, Tenn., where their family was increased to eleven children. James Maury Wright was born in the latter State, and was the tenth of the family in order of birth. His early education was confined to the subscription schools, and he was reared to the duties of farm life on his father's plantation. September 11, 1856, his nuptials with Miss Martha R. Vann were celebrated, she being also a native of Tennessee. Their children were as follows: Elizabeth (born June 14, 1857, was married to William G. Ross in 1878, and has five children), Mary (born in January, 1858, died February of the same year), Martha (born May 15, 1859, was married to Thomas Burns in 1878, and bore one child. Both she and her husband are now dead, the former dying in 1884, and the latter in 1879), James Henry (was born on January 31, 1860), William N. (born Janury 31, 1863, and is now a salesman in the mercantile house of Messrs. Warren & Phelps of El Paso, Ark.), Charles T. (born May 19, 1867), John R. (born August 27, 1869), Nettie (born in July, 1871), and Hattie (born in June, 1874). The mother of these children died in July, 1880, an earnest member of the Missionary Baptist Church, and two years later Mr. Wright wedded Miss Minerva Hendricks. In 1857 the family came to Arkansas, and Mr Wright began to make improvements on a tract of railroad land, but one year later moved to El Paso, where he began working at the carpenter's trade having served an apprenticeship under his father, but also continued his farming operations on a tract of land containing forty acres adjoining the town. In 1860, in company with T. W. Wells, now of Searcy, he erected the first grist-mill in the vicinity of El Paso, a need which had been long felt by the people of the community. Peach Orchard (now El Paso) at time of Mr. Wright's location only consisted of a double log-house, but in the fall of 1859 and the winter of 1860, there were three business houses erected. Wild game was plentiful in the surrounding woods, and many a deer was brought low by the unerring aim of Mr. Wright's rifle. In 1861 he sold his land and purchased two acres in the town upon which he erected a dwelling house and other buildings, oc-

casionally working at his trade in connection with his milling operations. After purchasing a farm of 160 acres in Conway County, in 1862, he settled his family there, and June 20 of the same year he enlisted in Company A, Col. Glenn's regiment, and was on detached duty in Arkansas for about a month as teamster, and was afterward promoted to the position of wagon master, in which capacity he served until January, 1864. While at home on furlough the Federal troops got possession of the State of Arkansas, and Mr. Wright was cut off from his command, and did not again enter service. In 1864 he bought an interest in a large flouring mill, which was known as the Peach Orchard Tap Mill, but sold out two years later, and. in 1869 purchased the farm where he is now residing, and since 1870 has also operated the Warren & Davis flour, grist and cotton-gin mill, following the latter occupation in El Paso from 1872 to 1886. He has been very successful and at one time owned 240 acres of land, but at the present time has in his possession 160 acres with about 100 acres under cultivation. Mr. Wright and his wife belong to the Missionary Baptist Church, and in his political views he is a Democrat. He belongs to El Paso Lodge No. 65 of the A. F. & A. M., and has attained the Chapter degree. He has taken an active interest in the advancement of education in his county, and was one of the few who voted for the special school tax. He has also contributed liberally to schools.

James A. Wright, postmaster and express agent at Higgins, grew to manhood in Alabama, and in Independence County, Ark., receiving a good education. In 1861 he joined the Confederate army, in the Eighth Arkansas Infantry, and served the first year east of the Mississippi, afterward being transferred to the Trans-Mississppi Department, and undergoing capture as a prisoner of war, at Little Rock, though he was only retained only six weeks. He was in Price's raid through Missouri, and participated in the battles of Prairie Grove, Helena, Pilot Knob and a number of skirmishes, and was accidentally wounded, losing his right leg. After being discharged in the latter part of 1864, he went to Searcy and engaged in farming

WHITE COUNTY.

and the mercantile business, and in August, 1874, moved to his present location where he has since been selling goods with flattering success. Mr. Wright was born in Jackson County, Ala., February 21, 1842, to the union of N. A. and Martha (Byranny) Wright, natives of Alabama. The former was a Methodist minister, and upon his removal from Alabama to Arkansas, located in Independence County in 1858, ten years later coming to Searcy. After one year here he went to Red River County, Tex., and died there October 2, 1877, at the age of sixty-two years, his wife preceding him two months; she was a member of the Methodist Episcopal Church. They were the parents of nine children, six of whom are living: James A. (our subject), Lovenia (wife Mr. Gideon, of Alabama), Malinda (now Mrs. Malden, of Texas), Amanda (also Mrs. Malden, residing in Texas), Mary (Mrs. Taylor, of St. Francis County), and Ellen (widow of a Mr. Malden). In connection with his other business Mr. Wright held the position of agent of the Iron Mountain Railroad at Higgins, from 1875 until July, 1889, also being appointed postmaster of Higgins, in March, 1875, which office he still occupies. May 15, 1864 he was married to Mary A. Ellis, who was born in Carroll County, Tenn., in 1846. They have a family of nine children: Mattie (wife of W. H. Chrisp), W. H., Maud L., Tommie, P. H., George D., Ollie and Willie. Mrs. Wright is a member of the Methodist Episcopal Church, South. Mr. Wright belongs to the I. O. O. F., is a decided Democrat and is one of the founders of the village of Higgins. As an esteemed citizen he is widely known.

158

ALBINA, 33
L.D., 32
MARGARET (PRICE), 33
THOMAS, 33
BOYD
WILLIAM, 19
BOYER
FLORA, 29
HANNAH, 29
JOHN, 29
BRADEN
ELIZA, 14
BRADLEY
AMELIA (NOW MRS.
MOSIER), 21
B.B., 5, 6
BURTON, 21
J.W., 5(2)
JACKSON, 20, 21
MADELIA (NOW MRS.
THOMAS), 21
MARTHA (FERGUSON),
20
MAUD E., 21
R.S., 21
RICHARD S., 21
SUSAN (NOW MRS.
BAILEY), 21
W.F., 21
WILLIAM F., 20,
21(2)
BRADLEY & CORADINE, 21
BRADLEY, CORADINE & CO.,

21
BRADY
MIRAH (CORDAL), 91
NANCY, 91
WILLIAM, 91
BRAGG
GEN., 83
[GEN.], 33, 106, 147
BRAMLITT
JESSIE, 148
JESSIE L., 148
MARY (ANDERSON), 148
BRAY
BOLDON, 89
CHARITY E., 89
HENRY R., 88
IRADEL, 89
KATIE, 89
MARTHA, 89
MARY E., 89
MARY E. (FOLLIS), 88
REV., 89
SARAH A., 89
WILLIAM R., 89
BREWER
ANDREW T., 22
ARA ANNA, 22
BARRETT, 21
BENJAMIN, 21
BENJAMIN A., 22
HENRY W., 22
HOWELL C., 22
JAMES M., 22
JAMES R., 22
JOHN B., 22
JOHN POLLARD, 21, 22
JOHN WILLIAM, 22
KARILLA W., 22
LELA LEWIS, 22
MARTHA (NOW MRS.
SANDERS), 21
MARTHA M., 22
MARY E., 22

MINNIE LEE, 22
POLLARD J., 22
R.E., MRS., 86
RICHARD J., 22
ROBERT B., 22
SARAH (NOW MRS.
SCOTT), 21
SARAH W., 22
SUSAN E., 22
WILLIAM SACKVILLE,
21, 22(2)
BRICKELL
WILLIAM P., 118
BRIGADE
CARROLL'S, TN VOLS,
34
DOBBINS', 83
McCULLOUGH'S, 86
BRIGGS
B.W., 72
BERTON W., 8
CHARLES, 67
BRIMM
H.M., 19
BRITT
DAVIS, 99
MARY (BARKLEY), 99
T.T., 6
BROADWAY
AVEY, 107
BROMSON
LEAMIA E., 142
BROWN
ALGERION R., 22(2)
BERNARD, 22
BERNARD O., 22
BEZAKEL, 22
BEZALEEL T., 22
CHARLES E., 23
CHARLES T., 22
CHARLES, M.D., 22
ELDER, 12
ELIZABETH (DANCY),
22
ELIZABETH D. (NOW
MRS. JONES), 22
ELIZABETH M., 71
ELVIRA, 22
EMELINE, 104
EZRA M., 22
ISAAC, 104
J.N., 152
JAMES A., 11
MARTHA E., 23
MARY, 22
MARY (THOMPSON), 22
MARY W., 23
MILLIE (DUNN), 104
SAMUEL H., 23
SARAH P., 71
SUSAN, 46
SUSAN W., 23
WALTER L., 23
WILLIAM R., COL., 71
BROWNING
CARROLL ELLIS, 23
FRANCIS J., 74(2)
HARRY R., 23
J.H., 23
MAGGIE (NOW MRS.
MARSH), 23
R.C., 23
R.L., 23
R.L., DR., 23(2)
VIOLA (NOW MRS.
DRAKE), 23
W.C., 23

BRUCE
DANIEL, 109
DR., 55, 56
SALLIE (PRENCT), 109
BRUNDIDGE
S., JR., 6
BRYANT
ALBERT M., 15
JOHN THOMAS, 15
LINDSAY E., 15
MARY ELLA, 15
OLIVER, 15
BUCHANAN
ASIA, MRS., 66
BUCKNER
GEN., 60
BUDRELL
ELIZABETH, 20
BUMPASS
A.W., 24
AUGUSTINE W., 23, 24
E.L., DR., 23
EDWARD K., 24
EDWARD W., 24
GABRIEL, DR., 24
HERBERT R., 24
LUCINDA E. (YOUNG),
23, 24
MARY E., 24
MARY MOYNER, 24
PRENTICE, 24
ROBERT H., 24
ROBERT W., 24
ROMELIA C., 24
ROSS H., 24
SAMUEL J., 24
BUNDY
MARY E., 25
SARAH (COBBELL), 25
WILLIAM, 25
BURKET
J.F., MRS., 81
MARY J., 132
RACHEL, 18
RACHEL (HUGHS), 18,
133
WILLIAM, 18, 133
BURNETT
ISAIAH, 128
JANE (HERNDON), 128
BURNS
KATIE (LARNER), 25
MARY, 55
PATRICK, 24
THOMAS, 25(2), 154
BURRIS
PATON, 46
BURTON
A.M., 21
BENJAMIN H., 25
CATHERINE, 25
ELI, 25
ELI N., 25
ETHEL B., 25
GEORGE T., 25(3)
ISOM, 25
JOHN P., 25
JOHN W., 25
MAHALA (CONLEY), 25
MARY, 25
MILTON P., 25
MORTON, 25
MR., 21
NANCY E. (NEAL), 31
REBECCA, 25
SIMPSON, 25
WILEY G., 25

WILLIAM H., 25
BUTLER
J.M., 81, 111
L.R., 111
BYRAM
MARGARET (WILLIAMS),
93
MATTIE, 93
WILLIAM W., 93
BYRD
L., MRS., 46
R.C., 6

-C-

CALKINS
CALEB, 29
DANIEL, 138
JOSHUA, 138
SARAH J., 29
CALLAWAY
MARY A., 112
CAMP
CHASE, OH, 40, 54,141
DENNISON (OH), 97
MORTON
(INDIANAPOLIS),
60
TURNBULL, 83
CAMPBELL
DANIEL, MRS., 56
L. (& CO.), 142
CANADA
ALMEDA, 26
ALPHA C., 25
CATHERINE, 25
HUGH, 25
J.A., 89
JAMES R., 25
JOHN F., 25
JOSEPH, 143
JOSEPH B., 26
JOSEPH V., 25
MAMIE, 107
MARTHA, 46
MARTHA A., 26
MARTHA J., 143
MARY E., 25
MARY M., 26
MELISSA R.
(DUCKWORTH), 25
MILES C., 25
ONTARIO, 87
PRINCE EDWARD
ISLAND, 86
ROBERT W., 25(3)
SONORA E., 26
THOMAS, 143
THOMAS J., 107
WILLIAM J., 25, 143
WILLIAM R., 26
CANFIELD
L.C., 5
CANTRELL
J.D., 32
CARNES
ALICE (NOW MRS.
MAGNESS), 26
ANNA BELLE, 27
BARBARA A., 26
JOHN D., 26, 27
NEELY, 27
R.W., 5, 26(3)
SALLY MATTIE, 27
SARAH (DUNN), 26
CARODINE
JONES D., 27

174

JOHN T., 130
JOHN W., 130(2)
M.F. (NOW MRS. RISSELL), 130
MARTHA A. (NOW MRS. WEEKS), 130
N.B. (NOW MRS. TROXELL), 130
NANCY (WEAVER), 130
NANCY JANE, 130
OLLIE B., 130
R.C., 130
ROBERT BRUCE, 130
WILLIAM BEDFORD, 130
STAYTON
MARTHA J., 148
STEELE
J.P., 6
PRES., 6
STEPHEN
CAPT., 62
STEPHENS
JOHN, 11
REUBEN, 4, 5
STEVENS
EUGENIE, 37
GREEN, 37
MARGARETTE (McRAE), 37
STEVENSON
ALEXANDER, 77
ANN (ROBINSON), 132
HENRY, 132
MARY A., 132
NANNIE, 77
STEWART
ADALINE, 131
BETTIE, 131
CATHERINE (WALKER), 130
CORA, 131
D.M., 131
DORA, 131
J.G., 131
JOSEPH, 131
LEE THOMAS, 130, 131(2)
MOLLIE, 131
R.M., 130
RENA, 131
ROBERT G., 131
ROBERT M., 130
SUSAN, 131
W.C., 131
STIGALL
PATSEY, 153
STONE
B.P. (JOHNSON), 73
MARGARET E. (CORE), 145
MARY AGNES, 73
WILLIAM H., 73
STORY
ANNIE (MOORE), 95
HENRY, 95
M.J., 95
STOWBUCK
JAMES, 43
STOWELL
A.L., 131
AMANDA (HARRINGTON), 132
JOSHUA, 132
STRANGE
BEVERLY, 132
FLORENCE, 132
H.B., 51

HENRY BEVERLY, 132
HENRY C., 67
HUBERT, 132
SUSANNA (MARTIN), 132
VIDA, 132
STRANGE & WARD, 84
STRAYHORN
ALEXANDER, 133
BENJAMIN, 133
ELIZABETH, 133
ELVIRA, 133
GILBERT, 132
J.K., 132
JOHN D., 132(2), 133
JOSIAH, 133
MARGARET, 132
MARY A., 133
PONEY, 133
RACHEL E., 133
REBECCA, 132
SAMUEL W., 133
WILLIAM H., 132(3), 133
WILLIAM JAMES, 132
SUMMONS
EVALINE, 111
SUTHERLAND
SARAH, 40
THOMAS, 40
SUTTON
ALFRED, 133
ALFRED B., 133
HENRY, 133
JESSE, 133
JESSE L., 133
MRS., 17
NORA L., 133
SWICK
GEORGE, 52

-T-

TALIAFERRO
DR., 56
TALKINGTON
ANDREW JACKSON, 134
CORA ANN, 134
ELIZABETH, 134
HENRY F., 134
J.M., 11, 133, 134(2)
JAMES M., 134
JANE, 134
JOHN, 134
JOHN WESLEY, 134
JULIA (NOW MRS. SHERROD), 134
MARGARET, 134
MARY ANN (ISBELL), 134
MARY ANN (NOW MRS. ARNOLD), 134
MARY S., 134
PEARL JOSEPHINE, 134
VINCENT, 134
VIRGINIA, 134
WILLIAM PIERCE, 134
WILLIAM T., 134
TAPSCOTT
A. BYRON, 135
A. BYRON, M.D., 135
BYRON, 135
CHARLES V., 135
EMMA J., 135
IRA, 135
IRA BYRON, 135

MARY (JONES), 135
MARY G., 135
SAMUEL F., 135
TATE
AGNES J., 134
ANDREW B., 134(3)
ANNA B., 134
CAROLINE, 134
HETTIE B., 134
JAMES L., 134
LAVENIA G., 134
MARY J. (COLLINS), 134
ROBERT J., 134
SAMUEL, 134(3)
SARAH M., 134
TIRZAH A., 134
WILLIAM V., 134
TATUM
JAMES, 118
MERCY, 108
TAYLOR
ALBIE, 135
ALEXANDER, 110
COL., 96
DICK, GEN., 53
E.A. (MOORE), 135
ELLEN (HICKMAN), 135
EMMETT, 135
HIRAM A., 135(2)
IRMA, 135
JAMES, 135
JAMES M., 110
L.F., 11
MAGGIE, 135
MAGGIE J. (BARKER), 110
MARGARET (DAVIS), 110
NEWTON, 135
NEWTON W., 135(2)
PEARL, 135
PETER, 135
RUTH J. (CHRISMAN), 109
SUSAN, 110
SUSAN M., 110
THOMAS P., 135(2)
W.H., 109
W.J.H., 135(2)
WESLEY, 135
TEATROFF
JOHN, 123
TEDFORD
WILLIAM, 43
TEER
FRANCIS E., 136
HAYWOOD S., 136
LUDWICK, 136
MANUEL, 136(3)
MARY (SHEPPARD), 136
SUSAN J., 136
TERRY
ENOCH, 43
JESSE, 5
THARP
KATHLEEN, 137
SUSAN PAYNE (WHITMORE), 136
W.H., 10(2), 136(4)
W.H., DR., 136
WILLIAM J., 137
THOMAS
CARLYLE, 137
CLIFTON B., 137
ELIZABETH, 48
GROVER C., 137

J.C.C., 137
JAMES, 138
JANE (POST), 117
JOHN FRANKLIN, 51
MAJOR, 37
MARY ELEANOR, 51
NANCY, 51
R.G., 147
SARAH A., 137
SARAH A. (WILLIAMS), 137
SUSAN I., 117
W.A., 117
WILLIAM C., 137
THOME
ALICE, 137
DAVID C., 137
EVIA I., 138
ISABELLA (HAYHURST), 137
JACOB, 137
JOHN A., 137
JOHN A., M.D., 137
NAOMI, 138
NATHALLIA, 137
VERA B., 138
THOMPKINS
T.M., 152
THOMPSON
CAPT., 18
HENRY, 50
J.W., 12, 121
JAMES, 115
JOHANNA, 50
MARGARET, 115
MARTHA, 115
SARAH, 66
THORN
D.H., 106
MR., 106
THORNTON
D.A., 127
THURMAN
JOHN, 128
TIDWELL
WILLIAM, 103
TIMMS
JAMES E., 111
TOMPKINS
JAMES, 71
TOTE
ANDREW, 150
FRANCES, 150
MARY (TEES), 150
TOWN OF
ADRIAN, MI, 73
ALAMO, TN, 55
ALEXANDRIA, 73
ALTON, 65
ALTON, IL, 102
ANDERSON, IN, 73
ANNAPOLIS, MD, 73
ANTIOCH, 105
APPOMATTOX, 150
ARGENTA, 125
ARKADELPHIA, 10, 74, 75, 76, 143
ATHENS, AL, 89
ATLANTA, GA, 40, 147
AUGUSTA, 61, 65, 105
AUSTIN, 51, 129
AUVERGNE, 88, 89
BAINBRIDGE, IN, 27
BALD KNOB, 4, 7, 8, 33, 37, 44, 102, 128
BALDWYN, MS, 69

www.ingramcontent.com/pod-product-compliance
Lightning Source LLC
Chambersburg PA
CBHW080240270326
41926CB00020B/4315